PRO FOOTBALL BROADSIDE

PRO FOOTBALL BROADSIDE

Elinor Kaine

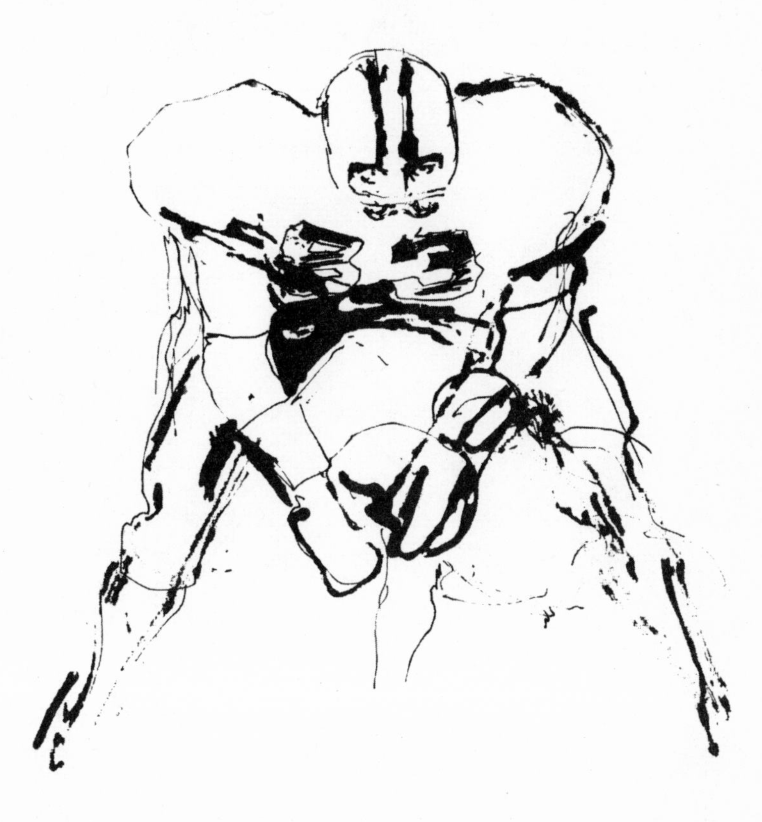

The Macmillan Company
Collier-Macmillan Ltd., London

Library of Congress Catalog Card Number: 68-31603
First Printing
The Macmillan Company
Collier-Macmillan Canada Ltd., Toronto, Ontario
Printed in the United States of America

To
GAGA

Contents

PRO FOOTBALL BROADSIDE

PART I

1 The Locker Room

"It's something to be a pro football player," said a young boy who was standing just inside the door of the New York Jets' locker room. "You can't even get dressed without a bunch of people watching you."

It shouldn't come as much of a surprise to anyone, that most of the time when they are in the locker room football players don't wear many clothes, but the stages of undress vary considerably. Some dress early, some wait until the last minute before donning such uncomfortable equipment as shoulder pads, and some, the Jets' Johnny Sample for one, just seem to prefer to sit around naked.

Sample's pregame scene is unique in football. He has this strange ritual he goes through, psyching himself up for a game. Johnny sits by his locker, his head nodding "No, no" in spasms, fists clenched, cheeks clutching, eyes screwed up tight. Sample, whose habit is to make the Sign of the Cross before a play when he is on the field and who wears a wooden cross carved (by Sample at age 8) from a broomstick around his neck, always waits until the very last minute before he dresses for practice or a game. Before Super Bowl III he was, naturally, the last man dressed and spent the final five minutes by himself, praying on his knees in the washroom.

There are as many different superstitions and locker room customs as there are teams and players. Pregame locker rooms can be quiet like churches, full of uptight players, or noisy, loose and relaxed like the Jets' locker room before they won the Super Bowl. Jet Coach Weeb Ewbank sometimes uses dirty jokes to relax his players before games and after the Super Win Weeb said, "We left the locker room laughing."

Jet Cornerback Johnny Sample being taped before a game. "His face looks like a jazz musician's," says the artist, LeRoy Neiman.

Ballplayers almost always get extra emotional before big games. Before Super Bowl II Green Bay's retired Guard Jerry Kramer, who has had so many operations they call him Zipper Head, was supercharged.

"It was so bad that I put my undershorts on backward," said Kramer. "When I realized what I had done I got so confused I forgot our team meeting before the game. You should have seen the look Coach gave me." ("Coach" was that legendary iron-handed ruler Vincent Lombardi.)

The veterans, like Kramer, are the worst offenders. The Oakland Raiders, after waiting seven years to play their snotty National Football League neighbors the San Francisco 49ers, were expectedly sky-high. "Was I emotional?" Jim Otto, Oakland's center, answered a silly question. "Well, I'll tell you, when I was dressing for the game I laced my cleats on first. Have you ever tried to pull on a pair of football pants with your shoes on?"

What Jim Otto is intimating is that everybody pulls their pants on before putting on cleats—that, as the grand cliché goes, everybody puts their pants on one leg at a time just like everybody else. (The coach of an underdog team always tells his skinny weaklings, before they go out to play David to some powerhouse Goliath, "Boys, they put their pants on just like we do.") But Jim Otto didn't know about Baltimore's big Bubba Smith. Bubba has this superstition, that when he gets into uniform the first thing he puts on is his left shoe. Then his pants. If Bubba were a she he would put on high heels *before* pulling on his panty girdle.

"Do you know how tough it is to pull your pants on over a size 14½ shoe?" asked Billy Ray Smith, Baltimore's *other* Smith who plays alongside Bubba in the Baltimore defensive line. "You never heard such groaning and grunting."

Before a game Billy Ray Smith is usually the first Colt to arrive at the stadium. Many players like to arrive several hours early (an old Giant linebacker Cliff Livingston used to come before 11 A.M. to get himself "up" for a two o'clock kickoff) but at Minnesota there isn't time to establish any pregame traditions. The Vikings' Coach Bud Grant believes in a late arrival, which of course is better than never arriving at all, but by football standards the Vikings are living dangerously. The Minnesota team bus arrives at the stadium no sooner than an hour before kickoff. Once in Detroit the customers were being entertained by a pre-game Peewee League game on one half of the field while the Vikings were still running plays on the other half; another time the Vikings were warming up when the pre-game show began and Fred Cox was practicing place-kicking right into the middle of the marching band.

A friend of mine described his first post-game locker room visit, after the 1959 College All-Star game in Chicago, with great glee: "Vice-President Nixon came down to congratulate the All-Stars," he said, "and he had evidently gone to some trouble to learn something personal about each boy—his school, his college coach, the name of the president of his college, something like that. The All-Stars lined up and Nixon met each one, and I want to tell you it was some weird sight—fifty naked All-Stars shaking hands and chatting with the nattily attired Nixon. I mean, the scene just hit me. Here was the Vice-President of the United States standing chatting with all those naked players who of course were so oblivious to the contrast." It was pretty hip of Nixon to recognize five All-Stars without their numbers on, let alone fifty.

Later that same year Nixon, who once confessed that there was nothing he would rather be than a sportswriter, was one of the first laymen to make the Colts' dressing room scene after the championship game in 1959 when Baltimore beat the New York Giants 31–16. When the madding crowd of football writers was at last let in Nixon was already on the scene talking to the late "Big Daddy" Lipscomb. Big Daddy was wearing his birthday suit.

In the Jet dressing room at Shea Stadium each player's little cubicle is separated from the next by metal mesh screening. Each locker has a stool in front, a rod with wire hangers for clothes hanging (although most Jets skip the hangers and throw their clothes over the rod) and a shelf at the top which is used for shoes, odd bits of equipment and a wide assortment of personal belongings—from Jet Quarterback Joe Namath's package of chewing tobacco and can of hair spray, to the watermelon Boston Defensive Back Leroy Mitchell brought to the Patriots' training camp locker room when he was a rookie.

At summer training camp, before the regular season begins, the newcomers—mostly first-year players (rookies) along with a few unaffiliated veterans hoping to make a comeback—are kept apart with rather austere accommodations, until the successful ones who make the team are assigned permanent jersey numbers and lockers alongside the veterans. Next to an injury the saddest scene in football is a player, after being chopped off the team, gathering up his few belongings at his locker, keeping up a brave front, and shaking hands goodbye and good luck.

The locker room is very like a football player's office, but it's only one part of his team's training headquarters. The practice field should be adjacent. The Jets are lucky because their setup is conveniently in the bowels of Shea Stadium where they both practice and play. There are various rooms for meetings, movies, therapy and exercising, and offices for Head Coach Weeb Ewbank and his assistants, but it's doubtful if all Weeb's assistants can fit in their tiny office at the same time.

Even in the off-season when the baseball Mets are at Shea Stadium the Jet dressing room is busy with players getting an early start on their physical conditioning and with coaches getting a head start, literally, planning strategies for the approaching season. There are movie projectors all over the floor, which is carpeted in bright Jet-green wall-to-wall Astro-Turf, and a giant closet is crammed full of trays of film cans. Movies are shown in slow motion, forward and backward, and coaching has evolved into such a science that the films are broken down into parts—offense only, defense only, kicking game, etc.—for each game and on each opponent.

Coaches described as "real students of the game" claim to watch 40–60 hours of game movies each week. (When a football talent scout studies films of college players he will watch each play eleven times, watching a different player each time in order to grade his performance.)

Locker room plumbing is elaborate, with huge floor-to-ceiling washing machines and dryers for all the underwear (uniforms are sent to the cleaners, which costs the Jets $115/week). The Jets switched laundries a year ago because of a shrinkage problem.

"We went to a new company," said Jet equipment man Billy Hampton, "the one the Giants use, but they weren't good enough. Then we found out the shrinkage was caused by bad fabric, so we got new uniforms and went back to our old cleaner."

For laundering the Jets themselves there is a very large community shower room and a couple of whirlpool baths. The whirlpool baths are very high, narrow steel tubs, so narrow that the player has to fold up to fit. The Boston Patriots named their whirlpool bath the U.S.S. Graham in honor of their fastest receiver Art Graham who is All-Infirmary almost every season.

Whirlpool baths make fantastic bubble baths in only a few seconds with just a tiny drop of detergent, which was ably demonstrated by

Bear Trainer Ed Rozy. Like Rozy most trainers seem to enjoy showing off their complex inner sanctum.

"There is no other sport that takes so much preparation in such a severe atmosphere," said LeRoy Neiman, an artist who has spent most of his career drawing the sports scene. "It's like spending an hour in an infirmary. The bandages and tape lying around, the smell of alcohol and liniment, and the taping room with the exercise and therapy machines —the mood is really like a hospital's."

"Locker rooms after games are filthy," said a pal of several Jets, Harry Stevens. "Piles of dirty tape, bloody bandages and sweaty underwear are thrown all over the floor."

Outside the Houston Oiler training room there is a big table with nothing on it but different jars of pills—huge bottles with handwritten labels for different kinds of salt pills, vitamin pills, and pills for special problems—all different colors like an old fashioned apothecary's window.

Gary Cartwright wrote an article about his adventures as a sportswriter. "No one talks about it," he wrote, "but training rooms are portable pharmacies. It is the trainer's job to have his forty men ready. If a player is injured they shoot him full of cortisone. If his pain threshold is low they give him morphine or another opium derivative. If his metabolism is skimpy they give him amphetamine. When Commissioner Rozelle outlawed the free use of amphetamines a few years ago several players and maybe a few sportswriters were ruined. Rozelle got pep pills out of the aisle and under the tables. It was explained to me by an NFL player that every man lets the trainer know his requirements. When you get to the stadium there is a paper cup of whatever you need waiting in your locker." Gary himself was in the habit of dropping by the Dallas locker room before a game for a shot of B-12.

On a normal day during the season, even if no one was seriously hurt in the last game, the first two hours each morning are hospital hours when the trainers attend to sprains, bruises, stitches, and assorted muscle pulls and pains. Monday is, of course, the busiest morning. The Los Angeles Rams won their division title in 1967 and were unbelievably lucky; after their big Defensive Tackle Rosy Grier severed his Achilles' tendon a week before the regular season opened, the Rams didn't lose another player from serious injury for the rest of the season. However, they considered more than two hundred other injuries serious enough to report to their insurance company. The sweetest sight in football is to see a team's trainers snoozing on the plane trip home from a game away, which means no one was hurt.

Trainers come to know the players better than anyone. They know which players are fakers and which ones are playing hurt.

"We have to know each guy," said Jet Trainer Jeff Snedecker, who has a master's degree in athletic training. "In pro football it takes eleven days to recover from a game. If they can't do it in seven they can't play."

Actually the training room is the team's open house where the trainer may play the role of disciplinarian, clown, confidant, analyst, father, or even mother—either alone or in combination. With a few notable exceptions pro football trainers are a discreet bunch.

"I guess a lot of the ballplayers come in here to relax," said Snedecker. "It's informal and sometimes they tell you their troubles." It's obvious that a trainer's unique vantage point puts him in a key position, one from which he may make an important contribution to his team's success whether he's attending to a psyche or taping an ankle.

No players are allowed to practice without having their ankles taped. "We spend at least six thousand dollars each season on tape alone," said John Robel, who manages the equipment for the Philadelphia Eagles. "Of course it's an investment, preventive spending." It takes anywhere from twelve to twenty yards of tape for two ankles and the trainers are so expert they take no more than a minute for each ankle. Toward the end of the season more tape is needed.

"In December I use thirteen yards of tape on each leg," said Rams' Trainer George Menefee. "I start out in July with ten yards, but after a season's beating if I sent them out with only ten yards we'd have twenty-five guys on crutches tomorrow."

The owner-coach of the Chicago Bears, George Halas, fines a player half a week's salary if he shows up for practice untaped, and when blue-chip rookie Joe Don Looney refused to be taped at the New York Giants he was traded forthwith.

Every team has a "taping legend," but tape is an inexpensive neurosis. Jim Colvin, a tackle who played for several teams before winding up with the Giants, came four hours ahead of game time and taped his ankles, knees, hands, forearms, you name it.

"When Ed Henke was here," said St. Louis Trainer Jack Rockwell, "he started taping at his armpits and went all the way down to his fingertips. He didn't stop until he reached his toes." The Pittsburgh Steeler taping title goes back to Elmer Hackney in 1943.

"I tape my hands to protect them from people stepping on them," says Oakland's Defensive End Ben Davidson. "A cleat under two hundred fifty pounds of player doesn't feel good. And I tape my forearm to keep it from getting all cut up. When you tackle a guy high, if you hit the bar of his face mask with your forearm it gets cut and bruised." No player on the Raiders uses more tape than Ben.

Tape supports as many superstitions as it does ankles and forearms. Larry Wilson (St. Louis Cardinal defensive back) and Charlie Bradshaw (Detroit Lion offensive tackle) tape their big toes for luck. They used to call Baltimore's Halfback Lenny Moore "Mr. Spats" because he taped over his shoes and socks. (The usual way is to tape one's naked ankle.) At Houston, Chicago and the Giants every player has his left ankle taped first, and Houston Oiler tradition holds that the team leader is taped last. After veteran Quarterback George Blanda left Houston there was no one to tape last, and the Oilers' record has reflected their plight accordingly.

Daily taping brings up the evil necessity of leg shaving.

"These guys shave their legs to about eight inches above the ankle," said Boston Patriot Trainer Bill Bates. "Hell, no, they don't use a regular razor. They'd probably cut their legs all up. I have a special 'small animal clipper,' and it's better than an electric razor. They have to shave twice a week because it really hurts, pulling the tape off, if the hair gets any longer."

Sometimes ankles are taped over gauze but knees are not. "You've got to shave eight inches below the knee and a foot above, to be safe," said Bates.

At the Jets, Joe Namath would take a plain old safety razor and just sit and shave, dry.

Trainers are as proud of their methods and innovations as they are of their equipment. Two of the most delightful and industrious imaginations in pro football belong to Boston's Bates and Houston's Bobby Brown. Brown laughed disdainfully when he heard about Bill Bates's small animal clipper.

Before a game Joe Namath sits and shaves, dry.

"Bates's clippers are for shearing sheep," said Brown. "I use a surgical depilatory cream, which is what they use before operations in hospitals, sort of like Nair. It doesn't leave a stub." Imagine a player catching hell from his wife for borrowing her favorite depilatory.

Brown once went to a lingerie store for a girdle with a strong front tummy-remover panel, for one of Houston's defensive backs who was suffering from a torn stomach muscle. He described the shopping and successful treatment with evident glee.

At Cleveland, Gary Collins wears a corset-like garment when he needs to put padding over his back, or ribs, to protect bruises. At San Diego, Lance Alworth uses a girdle to try and keep a pinched nerve from causing muscle spasms in his lower back. "I'm all right as long as I keep my girdle on," said Lance, a fast flanker (pass receiver), as is Gary Collins.

One wonders if Alworth and Collins emerge from their girdles with a ladylike sigh of freedom and relief.

The Jets have a beautiful big sauna, also carpeted with AstroTurf. Up to twenty Jets can fit in at once, to sauna together, and there is a big picture window in one side in case Weeb wants to watch what's going on. Houston and St. Louis have beautiful big saunas too, which are very popular with the players. The head coach of the St. Louis Cardinals is Weeb's son-in-law, pupil and ex-assistant, Charley Winner. Charley was expected to be a conservative chip off Weeb's round, conservative block.

"Weeb was so surprised when he found out Charley allowed smoking in the locker room," said Cardinal Trainer Jack Rockwell, indicating that pro football players' attitudes reflect the changing times. In the old days before Weeb players used to smoke at halftime, play a hand of poker between elevators, drink between trains, and swear on Sunday. During most of Weeb's era players have been treated rather like children. The coach told his players when to get up, when to go to bed, how to have their hair cut, what to wear and what they would be paid. The idea of players organizing and going on strike, or turning overnight into suave $50,000-a-year executive types, would have struck the players of the early '50s, and before, as some sort of huge joke/fantasy. Would you believe that ten years ago the Giants fired Don Maynard, a skinny young Texan, for wearing sideburns and cowboy boots?

Today's hip players sauna and smoke and even wear girdles. Every locker room has a cosmetics counter and the players chip in for grooming products that are not necessarily manufactured by Mennen. The Patriots prefer Estée Lauder Aramis and the Giant trainer allowed as how his players were using "lots more cologne lately."

It's to Weeb Ewbank's great credit that he has been able to swing with the changing times and adapt to this new breed of contemporary ballplayer. From all appearances the Jets, if they discovered a barber in their locker room, would lynch him before they would let him ply his trade. When the Jets won their division title in 1968 there was a sign on their locker room bulletin board which quoted some doctor as saying that spending the night before the game with a girl friend wasn't any more harmful than a full week of abstinence. Ten years ago Weeb would have fined the perpetrator who pasted such a public notice.

As the times change no specific area of football has progressed more erratically than the field of medical treatment and injury prevention. Knees can cost pro football teams $500,000 a year or more. The Jets' team physician, Dr. James Nicholas, estimates that each year for every eight men on a team there is one knee operation. When you consider that each team pays over a million dollars each year in player salaries, you would expect that every employee would be given the very best, most modern medical care, but this isn't the case. Some teams have doctors-in-residence who have been in residence for years, and are still doing things—treating delicate knees worth thousands of dollars for example—the same way they did twenty or thirty years ago; one longtime team doctor is nicknamed "Knife" by the other doctors in his hospital. A subject of serious concern, the medical side of pro football has recently made definite progress. In the last year or two several of the old-fashioned teams finally put in a thorough preseason physical examination that didn't leave a sideburn unturned.

Trainers today are knowledgeable and are given serious responsibilities, but it wasn't always so. The Bears have had only two trainers in fifty years and Ed Rozy, now in his 21st season, is one of them. Rozy started the first course for athletic trainers ever presented in the new school of training. The old school was aspirin, mercurochrome and a strip of adhesive.

Rozy surely deserves ranking on any list of pro football's Top Ten Characters. He gets away with murder. The old war horse who founded the Chicago Bears, George Halas, allows no players or coaches to go without shirts on the practice field, but on hot days guess who wears no shirt? No one except Halas rides around in Halas's chic white fringed-top golf cart, except guess who—who sits in it, shaded, cooly enjoying Bear practice drills and watching Bears exercising. Rozy must have the goods on Papa Bear Halas. Guess who kneels at the sideline during Bear games, resting himself on Halas's 74-year-old shoulder? Guess who accompanied Halas on a summer vacation in Italy which included an audience with Pope Paul VI.

"I tell these players to keep their fingernails short, and no rings," said Rozy, hardly a shrinking violet. "Of course they can't wear a ring in a game anyway, not only to protect the other guys but themselves too. If they hurt a knuckle in a practice or a game, then I'm the one who has to cut the ring off, and I don't have time for filing off any rings."

Rozy is the mentor of the Bear lair. He takes it upon himself, when players arrive with goatees or long hippie hair, to tease them and needle them until the hirsute adornment is removed. He's batting near 1.000. Rozy had never failed until a Bear guard, George Seals, reached such pre-eminence in the Bears' offensive line that he kept his Fu Manchu intact for a whole season under Rozy's withering eye.

With the possible exception of Buffalo's ancient War Memorial Stadium, Chicago's Wrigley Field, where the Bears play, has the most old-fashioned dressing room and the smallest showers. (Buffalo players can bathe without taking a shower; their dressing room has a leaking roof, part of which fell down upon the players several seasons ago.) The same Bears always make the last shift into their crowded shower room.

"All Bears sing in the shower and I have to yell at 'em to get out," said Rozy. "They can get a combo goin', a quartet, and I swear they'd be in there all night."

Jack Rockwell has a theory about the long, hot post-game showers that many of his Cardinal players find so much fun.

"No good," says Jack. "Especially in cold weather, long hot showers are no good. I tell these guys to cut them short. If they go out in the cold with their pores open they're liable to catch all kinds of ailments, or a cold."

No trainer—Rockwell, Rozy or the rest—can recall a single tough, vicious warrior of the gridiron stoic enough to turn on the cold faucet at shower's end. Jack Rockwell is always worrying about colds.

A person with any sense might not want to shower with the Cardinals anyhow. One typical Tuesday in St. Louis the Cardinals gathered for practice at Busch Stadium. One of the first to arrive was Right Guard Ken Gray. Gray came carrying a large wooden box, an apple for the teacher. Ken had spent the previous day driving from his hometown, Llano, Texas, to St. Louis.

Gray's Coach Charley Winner is something of a gourmet. Both he and his wife Nancy enjoy adventures of the palate. For example, when Charley first saw in the 1968 schedule that the Cards played a game in Baltimore he immediately thought "crab cakes." Images of breakneck Colts came through second. (The Colts won the game 37–0.)

Ken Gray knew about his coach's epicurean tastes and had overheard Winner wishing he might taste some rattlesnake which, in case you didn't know, is a delicacy. Gray's ranch in Texas hill country is loaded with delicacies and so Ken caught a big one, put it in the big wooden box and drove it to St. Louis. The rattlesnake, of course, immediately escaped and began rattling into the Cardinals' shower room. The locker room area became full of loose ends, and players at other positions as well.

The excitement ended calmly enough. Gray held the rattler with a plunger while Winner sent him to snake heaven. Winner dressed it up,

Texas rancher Ken Gray who also guards for the St. Louis Cardinals. (Herb Weitman)

cooked it on an outdoor grill, and ate every bite except for one tempting morsel he saved for Nancy.

"It was delicious," said Charley. "Almost like chicken, but much better."

Charley's father-in-law, Weeb Ewbank, divides the Jet dressing room systematically into four parts so that players at like positions have lockers close together, the offense to one side, the defense to the other. (The Jets are also supposed to sit in order, by position, on the bench during games, so they can be found quickly.) Weeb's system makes it possible for each of the assistant coaches, at halftime, to go to one section of lockers and talk to his particular group (e.g., the defensive backfield coach would talk with his six or seven backs) about their first-half progress and about possible changes or adjustments which might help in the second half.

"It's interesting," said LeRoy Neiman, "the way the ends are way off in one corner, by themselves, just the way they are on the field. They are like young Air Force majors among infantrymen. They are almost outside the violence, almost immune to it, and they're even separate in the locker room."

After the smallest groups are finished, all the defensive players meet together (and the whole offense) for more general discussion, and finally, just before returning to the field, Weeb addresses the whole team with instructions and encouraging words. If the Jets perform sensationally in the second half, the Monday newspapers laud Weeb's "halftime adjustments."

The greatest halftime adjustment of all time could end up winning a national presidential election for the Republican Party if on election eve a television movie were *Spirit of Notre Dame,* the epic film about Notre Dame's famous Coach Knute Rockne (played by Pat O'Brien) and his star Halfback George Gipp (played by Ronald Reagan). Comfortable in the living room, America would watch Ronnie beating Army, Ronnie riding noisy cross country trains, Ronnie running wild for 80-yard touchdowns, Ronnie beating Indiana despite broken bones, and Ronnie dying (". . . sometime, Rock, when the team's up against it—tell 'em to win one for the Gipper"). Rockne told 'em. That was a halftime speech. When Reagan's Democratic opponent demands "equal time," it hasn't been invented yet.

Before every game and during the half, players will lie around helter-skelter on the floor or anywhere, legs high, trying to save energy and store up rest. Most teams say a prayer together before a game; the Jets say the Lord's Prayer both before and after the game and neither newsmen nor TV cameras are allowed to intrude.

Sometimes the amount of praying that goes on in pro football rings phony. Religious trimmings seem as appropriate before a professional football game as before a Broadway musical. Both football games and Broadway shows are materialistic enterprises and entertainment, pure and simple. Young actors and actresses are just as dedicated as athletes, perhaps more so because they don't plan to retire at thirty. Yet whoever heard of a cast prayer before a performance of *Hair?*

"I don't think praying is something that should be publicized," said Detroit Lion Coach Joe Schmidt. "A lot of people get the impression that we're a bunch of holy rollers and some people try to use us to get ahead by making this impression, that we're a bunch of knights in shining armor. I don't think that's what praying should be used for. It's personal and I think it should be solemn, and private.

"At Detroit we've never had a locker room prayer except when Bill Glass was here, and he led one. But then last year we started a silent prayer both before and after the game. Basically, I think the thing you should ask for in a pregame prayer is that everyone play to the best of his ability and that no one is injured," said Joe. "But whatever the ballplayers want to do is fine with me."

Baltimore Quarterback John Unitas tells a story about a pregame prayer when he happened to look up, and down the hall Halfback Joe Don Looney was getting "up" for the game swaying away to a rock 'n' roll record.

"I'm very proud of the fact that we were the first club to start a chapel service," said Baltimore's Coach Don Shula. "We have some pretty good citizens here." Luckily, the Colts have some of the other kind too, to balance things.

The Colts' spiritual needs are periodically attended to by the self-proclaimed "Sports World Chaplain," Dr. Ira Lee Eshleman. Dr. Eshleman wears a red blazer and white turtleneck "game uniform" to sidelines he can wiggle onto and says things like, "My clothing as well as my message must be free from ecclesiastical trappings."

Dr. Eshleman toots through a dozen training camps every summer playing Gantry of the Gridiron. He gives the players spiritual pep talks, and most coaches grant him permission to conduct one team meeting. Attendance is optional.

"The most complete ballplayer is the fellow who gives attention to the needs of body, soul and spirit," Dr. Eshleman told the Colts. He also told them he was a retired playing-card addict—sort of a one man Poker Anonymous.

The Colts' blithest spirit was Alex Hawkins. One of Hawkins' better-known escapades was a scandalous arrest at 4:00 A.M. on Halloween, 1967. The Hawk had been picked up at a poker party in the back of a Baltimore barber shop, and his picture made the newspapers in fifty states. Hawkins opted to attend Dr. Eshleman's meeting.

"Just thought I might get him into a game afterward," said Alex.

Dr. Eshleman, the former pastor of the New York World's Fair and founder of Bibletown, is self supporting on his mission, which costs around $15,000 annually. "God blessed me and my blue chips," he says succinctly. His son spends full time working with jockos in the Big Ten but Dr. Eshleman devotes full time to the pros.

"Even the taxi squad," says Dr. Eshleman. "God is interested in every one of those boys." Even losers. "There are no won-lost records kept up there."

There is no doubt that Dr. Eshleman reaches some of the players. He will frequently mention that so-and-so "trusts now" and announced as he left Baltimore's training camp that several Colts had accepted Christ at the meeting the night before.

"If *he's* on it," said one Colt, referring to one of the meanest, most ill-reputed Packers. "Eshleman must do good work."

"But twenty minutes isn't long enough," Dr. Eshleman told Tom Matte. "Perhaps you could tell Shula that I need more time to do the boys some good."

Dr. Eshleman, a balding, fiftyish groovy dresser, has become a vintage football fan in the course of his endeavors. During one Baltimore practice session, the always sartorially splendid doctor, a vision in burnt orange, was standing in one end zone observing kicking practice. Suddenly he broke into a sprint and charged downfield toward the equipment manager, Freddy Schubach.

"Quick," he said breathlessly, "the punter needs his shoe. David Lee wants his shoe."

A contemporary sort of traveling salesman, Dr. Eshleman believes in the value of publicity. When he meets a reporter he smiles happily and whips a recent press clipping or two from his billfold, "in the fashion of old prize fighters, always alert to turn the last taste of publicity into another," according to Myron Cope.

Dr. Eshleman seems destined to loom ever larger on the football scene. He has been regularly giving an invocation before Miami Dolphin games and is anxious to do likewise on national television before important games, like Super Bowls. Compared to Dr. Eshleman's product the little locker room pregame prayer is like timidly whispering "Now I lay me down to sleep. . . ."

There are many times when the locker room is the setting for emotional postgame letdowns, even tears, and it isn't unusual for a coach to keep the doors closed to newspapermen for ten minutes of after-game togetherness . . . giving everyone time to collect himself after a loss or to calm down after a win.

A losing locker room empties quickly, but the winner tend to linger, enjoying the limelight. After a win Johnny Sample and Lamar Lundy, a defensive end at Los Angeles, never leave until the last newspaperman from the littlest newspaper has asked his last question about the victory.

Between the newsmen, relatives and friends, a locker room can get very crowded with a sardine-can atmosphere. Late in the season it isn't at all unusual for fifty or so nonplayers to be wearing overcoats in the steamy environs while fifty or so players aren't wearing anything at all.

During postseason championship games, television cameras invading locker rooms have made for many memorable moments, as unrehearsed as when big, mustachioed Ben Davidson of Oakland loomed into the camera rasping, "Hello, Mom," while a naked fanny disappeared into the shower in the background. After Green Bay won the national championship the violent Packer Middle Linebacker Ray Nitschke was hugging his teammates up and down the aisle when called for a word for the television audience. Before he could voice the usual platitudes on television Nitschke had to excuse himself and insert one of his front teeth, which remains in the dressing room while he is playing. (Players leave a wild variety of valuables—money, teeth, jewelry—in one mad tumble with the equipment manager, who locks it up for safe-keeping during the game.) Most players don't look their best for postgame television because they don't have their teeth, or because they have black glare

New York 23–San Diego 20; Joe Namath's postgame scene.

grease sweating down their cheeks, or because they haven't shaved. Football players shave after games, on their way out.

LeRoy Neiman in his role as the Jets' resident artist has become a familiar figure to Jet fans. His beret and handlebar mustache poke into the locker room or peep into a huddle and during games Neiman tweedily stalks the sidelines with pen and sketch pad in hand searching for subjects.

"There is no sight on earth quite like that locker room shaving scene," said LeRoy. "All the players shave after they shower and there are only a few sinks, with mirrors above them. Naturally they are all trying to shave at once. "To see all those naked figures, all leaning forward trying to see into the mirror—all the different-colored skins, all different shapes and sizes—all pushing and crowding together around the sinks and mirrors—it's crazy. In fact, that bare-assed shaving scene, three deep, is the wildest sight in the world."

2 Equipment

Pro teams play an equal number of games at home and away. Because they pack for everyone, the equipment managers prefer playing at home. With Ed Rozy supervising packing, the Bears travel in style; they stow their gear in specially-made Oshkosh trunks ordered by Rozy ("exactly like the ones made for King Farouk"). Papa Bear George Halas has this thing about white shoelaces, so the Bears *always* play in white shoelaces. The Eagles change shoelaces before every game just in case a broken lace might cost a time-out.

Not counting shoelaces each player needs about twenty different items of equipment and most teams travel with about 2500 pounds of baggage. The homeward-bound tonnage is always greater if for no other reason than that a used uniform gains two pounds of sweat during a game. If Hannibal had been moving a football team across the Alps he might never have made it.

When the weather turns cold, teams need about 500 additional pounds of thermal underwear tops and bottoms, gloves and parkas. The Jets have pockets sewn in the jerseys of the receivers and defensive backs to keep their hands warm, and sometimes the Jets wear plastic bags over their socks to keep their feet warm and dry. Philadelphia Trainer Moose Detty goes one step further with the Eagles, who wrap themselves up in cellophane plastic wrap next to the skin like mummies before they put on underwear.

The muddy games are the worst. After a game in the mud against Houston the Jets said they felt like they were carrying 20 pounds of mud on their backs. The mud sticks. It cakes and begins to dry. After the 1968 Thanksgiving Day disaster between the Eagles and Lions, which was on national television and enough of a mud bowl to spoil the tastiest turkey, the players looked like pre-historic mudbeasts with hardly the white of their eyes still in evidence.

"After one Buffalo game we came home carrying thirty pounds of mud per man," said Chuck Ziober who used to manage Miami's equipment. "On Monday morning we took all the shoes into the shower and hit them against the floor to try and crack some of the mud off. We let the showers run on all those shoes for an hour, and then we let them sit in the sun to dry before we oiled them good."

Isn't that hard on the plumbing?

"Well, there's always a bit of a drain problem," said Ziober.

The player's size presents a big problem. Equipment manufacturers haven't quite caught on that kids are coming in bigger sizes, even big football kids.

"I had to order special shoulder pads for Bob Brown," said John Robel at the Eagles. "I got size 56 extra-extra-large, which is the biggest size, and we still had to adjust them a little."

Like trainers, equipment managers have to deal with players' superstitions.

"Every one of them wants to wear exactly what he wore the year before," said John Robel. "You can't ever throw anything away, even an old chin strap. It might be lucky or have some special significance attached to it."

"When Johnny Sample played here I used to have to put his jersey on for him, for luck," said Kelly Miller at the Redskins. "Now I have to do the same thing for Bobby Mitchell. Thank God they don't all have that superstition."

Kelly Miller, a mischievous midget of a man, has a superstition of his own, being first off the plane. Plenty of players *hate* to fly. Lamar McHan, an eccentric quarterback of several years ago, hated flying so much he threatened to quit before far away games. Once in the air McHan stood up front near the pilot holding whatever was handy in a death grip, dripping with sweat. His post-game procedure was to juice up in the airport bar so as to be less conscious on the trip home. Once when he was playing for Baltimore, the Colts were about to fly to San Francisco. McHan got as far as the ramp before he retired, this time for good. (Flight insurance costs teams roughly $50,000 per year. Each flight is covered for at least $10,000,000. In the future, with flights to Mexico and Hawaii, insurance will be higher.)

Kelly Miller estimates the cost of outfitting a Redskin player at around $300; traveling outfits (team blazer and slacks) are extra. Helmets plus suspension lining can cost up to $70, stretch pants are $25, shoes $25, jerseys $20, shoulder pads $40, and other pads $15. A player wears out two or three pairs of shoes each season and an offensive lineman who does a lot of butting with his head can go through more than one helmet a season. Rookies sometimes arrive not knowing what size shoes they wear. One boy came to the Bears wearing size 12½ D and suffering with painful foot problems. He went home for Christmas wearing 10 EEEEE.

Football pants have interior pockets for protective hip, thigh, and knee pads. Padding accounts for that popular gridiron pastime, fanny patting. If one player wants to spur another player on, or congratulate him, he can't poke or pat the other fellow any place where he's padded because he wouldn't feel it. So he pats where only nature pads.

With all the tape and padding, "contact" in football is different from the skin-to-skin contact of other sports like basketball or wrestling. Contact between football players is almost no-contact.

"Fighting's tougher than being a football player," said Jet Fullback Matt Snell who, when he was young and worrying about how to get ahead, thought of becoming a professional boxer. "When you're in the ring there's nobody between you and the other fellow but God. You're alone. Man, it's frightening and there's no substitution like in football. Fighters have got better condition than anybody else in sports, and they don't know how great they are."

The contact of blocking and tackling is rather like a collision of padded high-speed tractors but even with protection, injuries are a dime a dozen. Fascinating statistics emerge—like number of original teeth remaining in player's mouth . . . or number of times player's nose broken—which really should be used to jazz up game programs. Instead, programs list dull information like player's home town and alma mater. When 43-year-old George Blanda is announced as "George Blanda from University of Kentucky" it's really ridiculous. Blanda was graduated from Kentucky twenty years ago.

Programs also list the players' height and weight estimates, but no player who lists himself at 5′ 11″ is as tall as 5′ 10″ and weights are often the product of wishful thinking; no one ever heard of a 227-pound or 229-pound linebacker, for example, but dozens weigh exactly 228—or so they say. Weighing 228 must be the size 10 dress of linebacking.

If you want to find out the weight of an Oakland Raider you have to bring your own scale and weigh him yourself. Ask Oakland Boss Al Davis about 280-pound Ben Davidson and he'll estimate "about 235," but if you stare at him long enough and hard enough Davis will finally have to grin. Davis always talks about how great other teams are, how the draft of college players is greatly overrated, and always picks the Raiders to finish sixth in the AFL's Western Division, which has five teams.

An Al Davis con job leaves one conclusion—if Oakland wins with players like Davis describes, the Oakland boss must indeed be a genius.

When face masks were first introduced players refused to wear them. They feared the masks would hurt their images—the virile, devil-may-care, hell-for-leather image that's in just a little trouble right now. There were two kinds of face masks in the early days—one consisting of a bar or two across the face for ends and backs, and one for linemen, known as the bird cage, which produced the effect of putting one's face in a sieve.

Note different facemasks worn by backs (Quarterback Karl Sweetan, 14, wears single protective bar) and linemen (Defensive Tackle Chuck Walker, 79, wears the birdcage style).

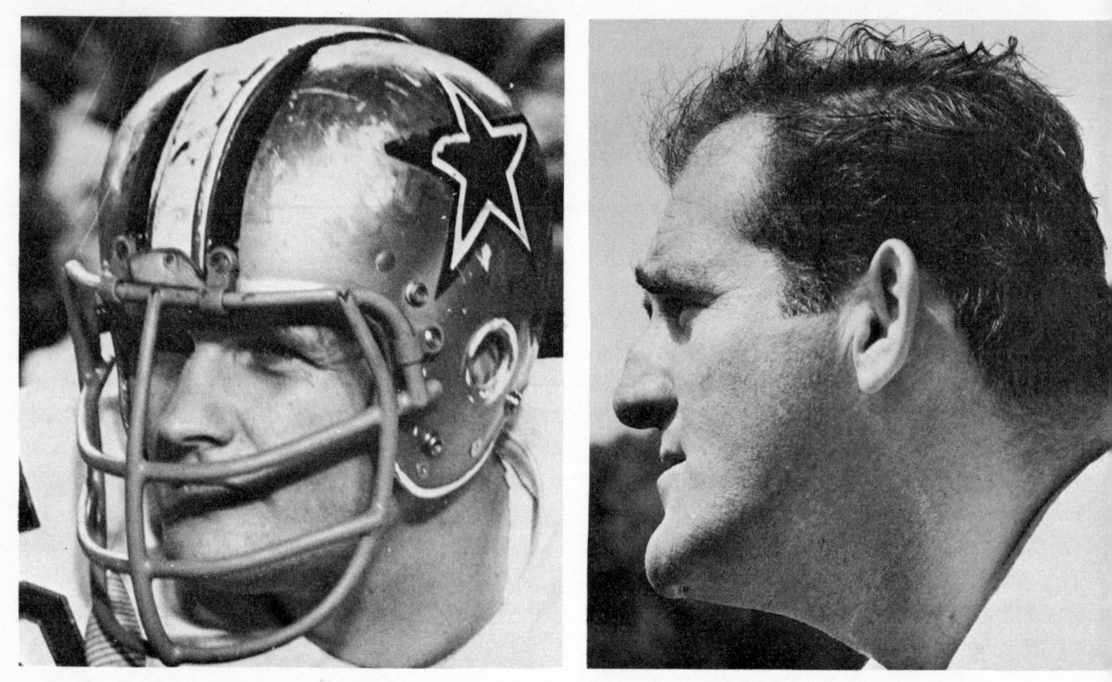

Dallas Cowboy Tackle Ralph Neely wearing typical lineman's "birdcage" facemask.

Jesse Richardson, the hardest nose of all —retired.

One of the severest penalties (15 yards) is meted out for grabbing a face mask, theoretically because a delicate but deliberate twist can break even a football player's neck.

It was gutsy of Bobby Layne to refuse to wear a face mask for 15 years, but he played quarterback, a position that's supposed to be safest for profiles, and Layne retired with a nose that wasn't as large, east and west, as it was north and south. Jesse Richardson didn't.

"I could see better without it. The first masks were big, cumbersome things," said Richardson, who played defensive tackle for eleven years and now coaches that position. "I didn't wear tape either, and no pads." Jesse looks like anything but the last of the great hardnoses, but he had that reputation. Even now Richardson has his defensive linemen wearing thin hockey type, instead of football type, pads for more mobility.

Jesse got around enough himself to get his nose broken nine times. "That was only five times in the pros," he said, surprised that anyone would be any more interested in nose breaks than mosquito bites. "The rest of the times were in high school and college."

Jesse never made any bones about it and just set his nose himself, when he had time after the game.

"When I was taking a shower," he said, "I'd just take a glob of Vaseline and put it on my nose and rub up and down, up and down, till I felt everything get back in place."

My favorite sore subject is teeth.

"The new generations coming up won't ever lose any teeth," predicts the Jets' team dentist Dr. Ben Koplik. "But the older players, they're so stubborn. They refuse to wear a mouth guard."

The early mouth guards were just as heavy and uncomfortable as the first face masks. "Like old fighters used to wear," said Dr. Koplik. "But the new types are light and come in different sizes. We make a wax impression, just like for braces, and one of the new guards fits perfectly. Joe Namath says it's hard to talk and breathe wearing a guard, but a quarterback is unique. He has to talk in the huddle and isn't knocked down often, or he isn't supposed to be anyway. Don Maynard wears an old guard from when he played in high school but it's all chewed up and doesn't do him any good at all."

Out at flanker, Maynard doesn't have much contact either, but he probably only wears a mouth guard for superstitious reasons. Maynard *is* a superstition whom his Coach Weeb Ewbank describes rather unimaginatively as a "fun guy . . . a country boy, but you don't take the country out of him."

Maynard is the team nut and the Jets love to tell stories about his eccentricities, like leaving for road trips with two suitcases, one empty, which he fills up with soap, towels and anything else the hotel didn't happen to nail down, except Bibles. Maynard's frugality became a cause célèbre a week before Super Bowl III when he complained loudly about who was going to pay for a pair of new shoes he had bought. Weeb said Maynard had a lockerful of shoes; it's a good bet that Maynard still has the first pair of shoes he ever owned. After all, he's still wearing his high school mouth guard.

Dr. Koplik is a great fan and roots from the Jet bench where he listens to games through a tiny transistor radio in his sunglasses. It is from Dr. Koplik that the Jet substitutes warming the end of the bench hear about what's happening in the game, because no one at field level ever knows what's going on. They can't see anything.

Dr. Koplik has a temporary office in one corner of the training room for immediate repairs and is often busy with split lips, broken teeth or jaw injuries. He has a good record for almost never losing an injured tooth. When Defensive Back Dainard Paulson had two front teeth knocked almost 180 degrees backward into the roof of his mouth, Dr. Koplik swung into action.

"I've never seen a bloodier mess. It was a miracle we could save the teeth. Paulson came in the next day, to have my temporary work repaired permanently," said Dr. Koplik. "Do you know, I was so busy that Monday that I never thought about getting a photographer. Paulson's case would have caused a sensation in the dental journal."

Dr. Koplik is frustrated that the old Jets won't pay attention to him, but the young ones have been wearing the new-fangled guards in school and don't have to be converted upon arrival at the pros. "Rarely does a man wearing a mouth guard have a concussion, besides not losing any teeth," he says, "because the guard cushions so much of the shock." What mouth guard supporters need is Ralph Nader working for them.

Between newfangled mouth guards, face masks and chin straps, the number of mouth injuries is diminishing. A chin strap not only keeps a player's hat on, it also keeps his mouth shut, reducing the chance of damage to his rear teeth from kicks in the chin. If Dr. Koplik's prediction comes true players will be able to be interviewed for television as they come off the field. They won't have to fetch their teeth from the locker room first.

Losing teeth is not the worst thing that can happen. One day Ben Hawkins, the cool Eagle, is going to lose his whole head. In the middle of a game Hawkins is often hatless—too often. At first he refused to fasten his chin strap because it was uncomfortable, Ben said, but now it's become a symbol, his trademark, flanking strapless. Everybody's got a gimmick. Sally Rand had her fans, Ben Hawkins lets his chin strap dangle.

Hawkins is a super flanker, fast and shifty, but he looks like a skinny kid with peaceful granny glasses and absolutely nothing on his mind. The truth is that Ben has a chic pad in Philly's Society Hill Towers with a pool table and closetfuls of clothes. He digs those inverted pleats ("the European look") and Indian-style threads. He collects progressive jazz records, drives a gray Aston Martin, and vacations in Sweden. What is so odd, Ben *always* wears a silly tennis-type hat, even in swimming, but last season in the heat of a game he lost his helmet at least ten times.

Ben wouldn't last long at Minnesota where Viking Coach Bud Grant plays "Captain Queeg" and runs a tight ship. Grant believes mental discipline eliminates mistakes. To that end he begins with little things, like chin straps; if one is unfastened in practice, practice st[illegible]

"If a fellow forgets little details off the field I have to think he is likely to forget them in a game," says Grant.

Viking chin straps don't dangle.

In the Eagle highlight film Ben Hawkins is shown catching a pass. As Cardinal Safety Larry Wilson moves to slug him Ben's helmet pops off. Wilson pulls back. Very unusual.

"I had a chance to get him real good, with my elbow," said Larry. "But there's no reason to hurt each other. We're all in the same game. Hell, with that chin strap bit, I think Hawkins is a hot dog."

Dallas Safety Mike Gaechter calls Ben a showboat. One naturally assumes that when next they meet Hawkins will lash Wilson and Gaechter with his chin strap.

"No, no," said Ben, who oozes natural ability and can leap and dodge better than most. "I won't do anything. I don't want 'em to tattoo their name all over me. There is a lot of heat in our games. You get on edge and little things get to you. But I want to show 'em I'm not a showboat."

In the past the National League has sometimes legislated on equipment changes. They passed a rule in 1945 making it mandatory that players wear socks in games. Eight years later Commissioner Bert Bell put through the edict requiring players to wear face masks. Chin straps and mouth guards may be next.

Even if they aren't used for anything else, at least they make good souvenirs. Collecting souvenirs is an old gridiron pastime. It begins with autographs and chin straps and ends with the ultimate, bringing home a ball. Fans go to all lengths, risking death from trampling throngs, to collect a ball. Balls, which are made of cowhide not pigskin, cost $25 and each home team must provide twelve per game. (Almost ten centuries ago football of a sort was played in England, between neighboring towns, and an inflated pig bladder was used as a ball . . . at least that's one theory as to why the ball is called a "pigskin.")

Each of the two leagues, National and American, uses a different ball—"The Duke" (NFL) and the "J5V" (AFL). When teams from each league play each other each team uses its own league ball on offense. The fact that such trivia occupies the football braintrust for as long as ten seconds is just another example of how the rugged romance of the game is deteriorating and the "guts" image fading. Ye olde Steeler Johnny Blood wouldn't give a damn which ball he carried. As one of the least-computerized quarterbacks of today, the Vikings' Joe Kapp, says: "I don't care if the wind is blowing at thirty miles an hour and who the hell needs to get the ball with the laces just so anyway. My job is to hand the ball off and kick a lot of ass."

"The NFL ball is larger, a little more rounded," says one of the new breed voices from The Establishment, Mark Duncan. "The AFL is definitely more pointed. And the lacing is a little different."

"The AFL ball looks like a needle," said Vince Lombardi whose habit is having the last word, "like a Long Island frankfurter. I would guess its easier to throw."

Lombardi's comments are suspect. The greatest allowable difference between two legal league balls is ¼″ in length (11–11¼″) and circumference (21¼–21½″). Cleveland Quarterback Frank Ryan who has a Ph.D. in mathematics was sure he could tell the league balls apart blindfolded. He couldn't. Lombardi hasn't a Ph.D.

Teams spend about $5000 on footballs in a season. In a high-scoring game greedy fans can easily clutch $300 worth of footballs to their battered, stomped bosoms, but such thefts reveal a strange inequity. The one-point-after-touchdown placekick automatically costs a $25 ball, as does a three-point field goal, but a six-point touchdown costs nothing unless the ball carrier is carried away with exuberance and flings the ball into the crowd. At Florida A&M the after-touchdown custom is to burst the ball, or bounce it hard in the end zone which might send it up into the crowd. A&M grads like Bullet Bob Hayes and Hewritt Dixon continue their custom in the pros, although players are urged not to throw balls into the stands as a safety measure, hopefully avoiding scuffles and injuries among the fans. On cold days, especially in the fourth quarter, many fans have been warming themselves with nips of brandy or inexpensive facsimiles for much of the afternoon and are far from sober. A scuffle over a ball could easily end up a knockdown-dragout brawl sending dozens out of the ballpark on stretchers.

Dangling chin straps and "bursting" the ball A&M style are crowd-pleasing gimmicks. So, too, were Alvin Haymond's Eagle-green shoes, Lenny Moore's "spats," and this thing Joe Namath has for white shoes. He orders them specially made in white leather, but the whiteness is immaterial because Joe always tapes over his shoes anyway.

Defensive Back Leroy Mitchell played end in college at Texas Southern, where he and the other receivers wore white shoes so that their quarterback could spot them easier and quicker. When Leroy brought his college shoes to the Patriots the smart-aleck veterans gave him a hard time. Leroy hadn't known that pro teams usually furnish shoes for their players.

When Baltimore played at Cleveland in the 1968 Championship game the Colts' equipment man, Freddy Schubach, packed various types of footwear anticipating Cleveland's peculiar winters. The Colts came prepared, with conventional cleats, ripple soles, tennis shoes and soccer shoes. Packing and unpacking are such dreary tasks at best, imagine packing for San Diego's kicker Dennis Partee who owns and uses fourteen different pairs of shoes.

The trend in football has been toward low-cut shoes* because they are lighter weight, but many players still prefer the old-fashioned hightops for extra ankle protection against sprains and strains. Quarterback John Stofa used high shoes instead of his old low-cuts while making a comeback from a broken leg at Miami, but at the end of the season the Dolphins traded Stofa to the brand new team at Cincinnati. On Stofa's last pay check the chintzy Miami management deducted $24 for the new high shoes.

*Playing in the Astrodome requires an $8000 investment by the Oilers for shoes for visiting teams. Players can't wear the usual cleats on the indoor turf. The Oilers ordered 235 pairs of hard-rubber soled mountain climbing shoes for visitors. When the City of Miami fathers began planning to pave their Orange Bowl with synthetic turf they complained loudly about the additional cost for special shoes.

PART

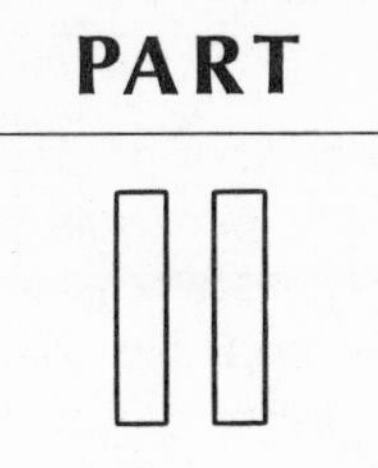

3 About the Game: Especially for Beginners

The Kickoff

When you go to a Broadway musical the show begins when the curtain goes up. A football game begins with the kickoff. Which team will kick is the first question, and neither team wants to. Both teams would prefer instead to *receive* the ball, to begin the game on offense, for a team can't score if it doesn't have possession of the ball.

To resolve this standoff and to avoid a free-for-all, a coin is tossed about twenty minutes before kickoff, during the "overture," while the teams are on the field warming up. The team captains and the referee meet in the middle of the field, the referee flips the coin, and the visiting captain calls heads or tails. Pro football is so escalated that the coin the referee flips is a silver dollar.

"Each official has a silver dollar," said Mark Duncan when he was head of NFL officials. "They've had 'em for years, but I suppose if a referee forgot he could always borrow from one of the rich players. Now don't you say *that*. I'm only teasing." Officials always remember to bring a coin. "If they forget they don't work," said Duncan.

The team that wins the toss gets to choose between receiving and kicking, or between goals. The captain who wins the toss almost always chooses to receive; the losing captain then chooses which goal will be behind him, the one his team will be defending. (This situation is reversed at the beginning of the second half.) Teams switch goals after the first and third quarters.

On a windy day the team that wins the toss may decide to choose between goals, instead of to receive, in order to get the wind at its back during the first quarter. The wind is desirable for two reasons: the kickoff will go farther and the other team will have a harder time moving back, passing particularly, and then perhaps having to punt. In this case the choice between kicking or receiving goes to the team which lost the toss. (If a team has an excellent defense and a weak offense it might occasionally prefer to kick off and begin the game on defense, hoping to stop the other team cold and take over the ball near mid-field, instead of backed up to its own goal.)

Twenty minutes later the players have been introduced and *The Star-Spangled Banner* has been played and the captains and the referee meet at the middle of the field to pretend to toss the coin again, for the benefit of those who missed it the first time, which includes the TV audience. The referee indicates which team will receive by pointing in the direction the offense will go. Everyone shakes hands with everyone else and in these days of three co-captains the handshaking takes ever so much longer than when each team had only one captain.

The ball is stood on its point in a rubber cradle (a "tee") on the kicking team's 40-yard line, and players, except the kicker, line up across the field. No member of the receiving team is allowed to come closer than ten yards to the line of scrimmage (40-yard line) until the ball is kicked off. The kicker is poised, eight steps away, waiting for the whistle. The referee, whistle in mouth, is waiting for the signal. The man in the red hat from the television network is listening, at the sideline. When the commercial is over permission to begin will travel down the chain to the kicker. Finally, action. Explosion. The little rubber cradle is empty.

Football isn't like other games. Baseball, for example, is very watchable. A pitcher and a batter stand sixty feet, six inches apart and the game starts in an orderly fashion with the first pitch. Football is different; there are so many players on the field that they can hide themselves behind other players and their mistakes behind wasted motions. Not until Monday's game films can the coaches find out who was hiding what. Especially when some are hidden, watching twenty-two players at once is impossible, but what looks like a mass of confused action is actually a planned sum of one-against-one situations—each man with a specific assignment, to beat his particular opponent.

If it is taken two-at-a-time, football can be broken down for spectating purposes into eleven individual duels. Watching one duel at a time is absorbing. Superb athletes, football players use finesse, quickness, and cunning as much as size and strength. The mini-wars are violently sophisticated and highly unpredictable.

The team that wins the most duels should, after 60 minutes, win the game. You may not dig the war but the battles scream for attention. Marshall McLuhan, the television-oriented philosopher, argues that the complex miniduels are what make football so perfect via video. Like boxing. Whether you are a fan or hate the sport, you can't watch a fight

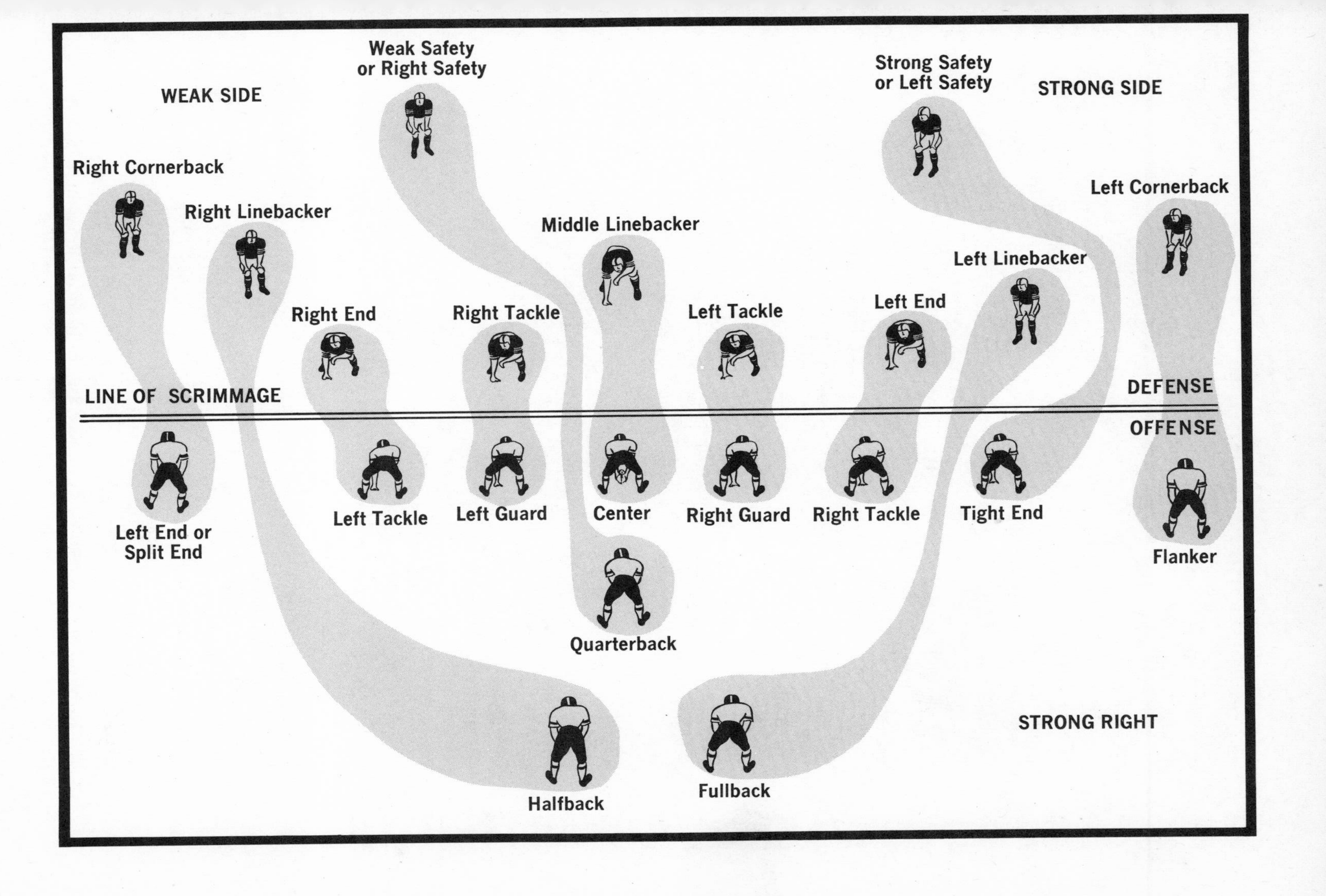
WEAK SIDE
Weak Safety
or Right Safety
Strong Safety
or Left Safety
STRONG SIDE
Right Cornerback
Right Linebacker
Middle Linebacker
Left Cornerback
Left Linebacker
Right End
Right Tackle
Left Tackle
Left End
LINE OF SCRIMMAGE
DEFENSE
OFFENSE
Left End or
Split End
Left Tackle
Left Guard
Center
Right Guard
Right Tackle
Tight End
Flanker
Quarterback
STRONG RIGHT
Halfback
Fullback

without somehow becoming involved. "Somehow" varies with the viewer. Football spectators come in the widest and wildest assortment:

"I always watch the center and the guard," said Green Bay's Defensive Tackle Henry Jordan. Jordan always duels with an offensive guard who occasionally gets help from the center. "I just never seem to get over that. Even in front of television you can't just sit down and enjoy a game, like an average fan."

"America has lots of icing. Football is icing—and violence," said Londoner Donald McCullin, the first newsman to reach the Wailing Wall in the 1967 Israel crisis. "America is a violent country. People are always fighting their way to the top. This is violence. So is football."

"Football, like courtship, is a game of desire," said an American newsman.

"They look like dandelions," said a newsman's wife, looking at the deadly Steelers. "The field is green, chalk marks yellow, and the Robbers . . ."

"Steelers, luv."

"The Steelers have yellow hats."

"The blue capes they wear, they're absolutely marvelous," raved designer Warren Lawrence, watching the Giants' bench.

"That Yankee Stadium," said Quarterback Sonny Jurgensen, "is not on the level. It goes up and down and somehow I always seem to be going uphill. No wonder Mickey Mantle's legs are bad."

"All the while it was fascinating to watch how Mr. Brodie (Quarterback) and his supporting cast enriched the warp and woof of their 'filmscape' by the prudent application of Jungian symbolism," said the film critic.

"Never be late for the kickoff," said her mother. "It's better to be late for the altar."

"You use more of your body when you kick off," soccer-style kicker Charlie Gogolak said, explaining his brother Pete's backache. "You take only three steps on a place-kick but on a kickoff you run eight steps and the jolt is really much greater."

The kickoff teams are a special bunch of extra-tough players who play hardest of all, either because they enjoy the crunching or to show their stuff to the coach if they're second-stringers. Dr. John Perry, the Los Angeles Rams' team physician, says that at least four times a game there will be a collision on the field of concussion dimensions.

"The body stops suddenly when advancing full speed but the brain keeps going, that's the problem," said Dr. Perry. "The force exerted is hundreds or even thousands of Gs. By contrast, an ascending astronaut is asked to withstand only six or eight Gs. But players expect this. It's momentarily uncomfortable, but there are no harmful long-range effects."

On every kickoff there are at least ten and sometimes eleven collisions, each of the hundred-G variety. The first play of the game may be the most violent one; later on some players will be tired.

Game Plan

"Acting is just like playing fullback," said Jimmy Brown, fullback turned movie star, in a *Playboy* interview. "I had to get the first play under my belt before I'd stop trembling. I still get keyed up but I keep it under control, and go in front of the cameras like I used to do before a game. I just cut off my emotions and go act out whatever the script calls for."

A football team uses a script, called a *game plan*. Game plans keep coaches busy during the week before a game. They study scouting reports and watch movies to see what the other team does, how often they do it, and how they react in different game situations. Then the coaches come up with a loose plan based on the opposing team's strengths and weaknesses. They send their quarterback into a game with a so-called "ready list" of plays which have been culled from the team's overall playbook and practiced during the week before the game. The plays on the ready list are expected to work best against the opponent's particular defenses.

Some coaches, particularly Allie Sherman and Vince Lombardi, prefer to attack the other team's strength, hoping to neutralize its power; then later on in the game they go toward the opponent's weaknesses. Other coaches go instead immediately to the Achilles' heel, trying to overpower the other team and keep momentum for themselves. All coaches share the same problem—the talent they go after the other team with.

The game plan is always written for the same cast, the some forty players, week after week. You know, yourself, that no matter what occasion you're planning for, there's only so much you can do with your basic black dress. You can add something here, subtract something there, change your jewelry, but it's still the same black dress. And it's still the same team with the same forty players. A passing team can't, all of a sudden, try to run, and a running team can't take to the air and become a passing sensation overnight.

"Basically Oakland did what we expected, and I'm sure we did what they expected," said Vince Lombardi after the second Super Bowl. "This is our twenty-third game this season and it would be pretty foolish to make some kind of change, just for the sake of change."

Most game plans are vastly overrated and function as semi-security blankets for coaches. Game plans give coaches something to talk to reporters about ("Sorry, but I can't disclose anything like that"), something to talk to their quarterbacks about, and provide an alternative to nail-biting. Game plans are invented by coaches for coaches. They are based on the only factor in the coach's control during pre-game week, the game films of the opponent. In the middle of a game ther are dozens of factors which must be taken into account—field conditions,* weather, injuries, field position, the score, time remaining, and what has already transpired in the game. Has the enemy shown anything new? How often? In what situation?

But when the game plan is invented, these crucial factors are unknowns. Coaches can base their game plans only on films, old injuries, films, scouting reports, films, and team habits (called *frequencies*) which are in chart form for each player to study.

"The game plan is nothing more than what we think we're going to do, based on what we anticipate from the defense," says Sonny Jurgensen, quarterback of the Washington Redskins. "But the key word is anticipate. They're spending all week trying to figure out ways to surprise us, too, so once you get in the game it's basically a question of outguessing them."

"The only difference between acting and playing football is that in football we didn't have a specific script," said Jimmy Brown. "Of course the other side wouldn't have followed it anyway, even if we did have one."

The Oakland game at New York in 1967 provides a perfect example of an outguessing game. Several hours before the game Oakland's Defensive End Big Ben Davidson showed me eleven mimeographed pages of the Raider game plan which charted how frequently the Jets do what and when, and what the Raiders expected after watching movies of all the Jet games.

"They never use the draw play on first down," said Ben. "See here, they like to use it on second down and seven yards to go."

Later that night Joe Namath called four or five draw plays on first down, for good gains. Oakland lost, the Raiders' only loss that season.

So much for creatures of habit and their frequency charts.

Game plans are superb, but often for only the first few minutes of a game. They are always conceived as an attack with a balance between running and passing, but when panic sets in the running is forgotten. When a team falls a few points behind (some low-scoring teams clutch when they get three points behind, all teams clutch when they're losing by ten points or more), more often than not the game plan goes out the window and the team begins to play catch-up, as they say on television.

*A muddy field eliminates most outside (wide) running. Inside running behind straight-ahead blocking works best. Suppose the game plan were based on running outside, before the rain started.

Playing catch-up only means pass, because successful passing makes more yards more quickly than by running. (A passing game is extremely risky, however; nothing loses yards quicker than an intercepted pass.)

"Sure, we start with a game plan," says Baltimore Coach Don Shula, "but we may leave it in the first five minutes. Football is a game of game-day adjustments. Things never go the way you expect. Something always goes wrong."

In Super Bowl III it was most shocking the way panic betrayed the Colts. In the third quarter with the Jets leading 10–0, Earl Morrall began heaving long passes on first down. The Jets later reported that the Colts began to punch and curse as their frustrations mounted.

Shula's game plan was to take away the Jets' running game by stopping Matt Snell and Emerson Boozer early. Baltimore then planned to clamp down on Joe Namath when he was throwing as his only hope. The trouble was the Colts couldn't stop Snell, who established a beautiful running game. Snell ran and ran and ran. Baltimore couldn't establish the right time.

"The Colts panicked," said John Sample afterward. "They went away from their game plan. Their quarterback panicked."

Don Shula advocates immediate adjustments if the game plan turns out wrong. Shula can't stand to see a team pound away on the ground without getting anywhere, or keep throwing passes that don't work. He would prefer to try an alternative.

Vince Lombardi is exactly the opposite. Lombardi always advocates sticking with the plan.

"If you start changing things it will only get worse," says Lombardi. "You have to keep trying to do the things you do best."

The Green Bay game plan didn't have to change as much as other teams' game plans because the Packers were so strong. They rarely had to discard their plan or to adjust it at halftime because they usually controlled the game.

In the second Super Bowl game the Packers started out like a geiger counter, poking around an unknown island for uranium they were sure was there. One unversed in the intricacies of the game would have wondered why Green Bay's Quarterback Bart Starr seemed so unimaginative—shooting Donny Anderson straight over guard, sweeping Ben Wilson around Ben Davidson, wasting a down here and there—but sophisticated fans were smiling smugly, knowing the Packers' patience, knowing Starr was testing, probing, wanting to see what the Raiders would do in a certain situation, how they would react to a specific formation, whether or not a linebacker would come up if so-and-so went left. Green Bay was picking and probing strictly according to game plan.

"A typical Packer game," said Vince Lombardi after Super Bowl II. "We went ahead by thirteen points and went on vacation for a while."

Super Bowl III was an especially delightful victory for ex-Colts, now-Jets Coach Weeb Ewbank and Cornerback Johnny Sample. (Nathan Benn)

The vacation lasted until the next season, 1968, when a funny thing happened to Vincent's Packers. They found themselves muddling through games they couldn't control, games full of atypical situations. QB Bart Starr would find himself in the huddle on third down with 18 yards-to-go.

"We have plays for third-and-five," said Starr, "but not for third-and-eighteen. We hardly have any plays in our playbook for third-and-long."

Times change.

The Game

In any game there is no such thing as an isolated play. The quarterback is like an architect with his blueprint (game plan) for building a victory. He starts out trying to build a foundation (establishing a solid ground game) for the full flower of his attack later on (balance between run and pass). The quarterback is always thinking about what play is coming next or what play is coming after five more downs. The quarterback's play selection always anticipates, tries to set up a "coup" for later the way a fighter does, or a hog casino player.

"I had thrown a short out (short pass toward outside) to Bernie Casey on the previous play," said Los Angeles Quarterback Roman Gabriel, explaining how he threw a touchdown pass. "We noticed that the defensive back came up very fast, so on the next play I faked the same short out to Bernie by pumping my arm once. The cornerback took the fake and came up fast, again expecting the short out, but this time Bernie went downfield and boom! A touchdown."

"Most quarterbacks call a play at a time," said Gabriel's former teammate Irv Cross, now an Eagle, "but Baltimore's John Unitas is thinking in terms of a whole series. He is always setting you up for something else. He'll fool around for a few plays and then come back with a pass that looks like a pattern he had tried previously. Only, it's different."

Cross, like other defensive backs, usually uses John Unitas as the hero of his dissertations on quarterbacking technique. Or Bart Starr. Or, for AFL backs, Joe Namath. In the second Super Bowl Bart Starr won his second Most Valuable Super Bowler trophy and his second car. Joe Namath won the car in Super Bowl III, which explains why quarterbacks are paid more.

Starr called one of the smartest games of his career in Super Bowl II and a spectator, Miami's rookie Quarterback Bob Griese, was properly impressed.

"Starr set up that 62-yard TD pass to Dowler perfectly," said the rookie. "About three or four situations before, I noticed the Oakland safety playing about twelve yards deep. Every time Starr came up in the same formation I noticed he would look over the defense to see what a deep safety was doing. Then he went ahead and ran a simple off-tackle play."

In a nutshell, Starr is a star because the next time the Packers came up in that same formation, Starr saw that deep safety come in tight, expecting the simple off-tackle play to be repeated. The safety was only four yards deep instead of twelve. Bart didn't jump for joy. Instead, he checked off [changed the play] and threw deep, a touchdown pass to Boyd Dowler right over the spot where the safety should have been. Dowler was all alone. Oakland's safety had learned the hard way.

There have been whole books written on such things as offensive strategy, or blocking techniques, but Vince Lombardi was kind enough to boil the game down to several basic points, which follow:

THE RUNNING GAME

THE RUSH: "Rush" is a sophisticated term for "run," and redundant. Any runner who doesn't hurry is automatically in serious trouble.

1. *Inside Rush* Quarterback hands ball to a running back who runs up the middle.

2. *Outside Rush* Quarterback hands or pitches ball out to a running back who runs toward the sideline and tries to make it around the edge of the pack. Since everyone on the team, even the QB, might be called upon to help clear the way for the runner, an outside rush is a "power play." (It is also called an end sweep.)

THE TRAP*: Play begins with offense trying to make it look like an outside rush, but QB only fakes to the outside. Instead he gives the ball to another runner who goes up the middle. Fakes are the red herrings of football.

THE DRAW: A fake pass. The QB takes ball and drops back as if he intends to pass it. The running backs join the offensive linemen, who form a semi-circular protective wall (a "pocket") to protect the "passer." But, as the rushing linemen try to get past "the wall" to get to the QB, he hands the ball off to a running back

---

*"Trap" came from "mousetrap." A defensive tackle (the mouse) is lured over the line of scrimmage by the cheese, the QB. The tackle is allowed to think he has a clear path to the QB, but half-way there he is knocked sideways (trapped) by an offensive lineman, leaving an empty hole in the middle for the ball carrier.

who then runs wherever he sees the most room ("running to daylight"). "Draw" here means to draw in the defensive linemen. Hopefully they will rush the QB hardest at the same moment that the ball carrier is able to slip by them.

THE PASSING GAME

Inside: Typically called a "look-in." The wide end runs a short distance downfield, then cuts toward the middle. An "inside" pass puts the receiver in mortal danger because there are more defensive players toward the middle and the receiver is almost sure to be clobbered immediately after he catches the ball, perhaps by more than one man.

Outside: The wide end runs straight down and breaks to the outside. Just before he reaches the sideline, he looks back over his outside shoulder. The timing should be so perfect that the quarterback has the ball there and waiting when the end looks around. Because the end and the defender are usually "one-on-one" and rather far downfield by the sideline, this play is very risky. A pass completion can easily mean a touchdown. Or the cornerback might intercept. Coaches prefer cornerbacks to forget about making interceptions; conservatively, coaches would prefer their cornerbacks to prevent a catch, to knock the ball to the ground. But some cornerbacks take chances; they miss the interception, the end catches the pass, the team scores a TD, and the cornerback's coach gets gray.

The Bomb: A long pass outside or down the middle. Outside bombs are called corner passes, flag patterns, down-and-outs. A bomb straight down the middle is called a "fly"; other bombs down the middle are known as zig-ins, down-and-ins, V-ins, and turn-ins.

Screen Pass: The offense acts exactly like it does when executing a bomb. The QB acts as if he's trying to pass, but can't find a receiver in the clear—and so he retreats farther back, which forces the linebackers to come after him too, hoping to rack him up. At the last second, the QB passes a short blooper over the rushers' heads to a running back who was pretending to protect the passer. If the defense has been fooled, the running back is already past a good part of them when he gets the ball.

"We took the ball and did what we should," said Matt Snell after the Jets won the Super Bowl. "We held onto the ball and kept it for ourselves. And the Colts will tell you that you can't score without the ball."

Snell and the Jets sound like a speech from Vince Lombardi's notebook. Vince Lombardi's own thing is *defense first*. His Green Bay offense played "ball control"—a simple running game—which is actually defensive football, because it keeps the ball away from the other team.

When the other coaches saw Lombardi was winning, and winning, and winning some more, they tried to copy him, but it didn't work, any more than it did when, in the '50s they tried to copy Jim Lee Howell and Allie Sherman's iron defense. They learned what the fat lady in a miniskirt has already learned, to her dismay, that everything depends on the equipment. Other teams didn't have the runners and the blocking for the "simple" Packer ground game, which wasn't anywhere near as simple as it looked.

"I've always been a believer in establishing a running game," said Houston's coach, Wally Lemm. "If all you do is throw the ball, all you get is a pass rush." And more interceptions.

Imagine if an offense took over the ball on its own 20-yard line and the quarterback called only running plays. If the ball carrier ran for 3⅓ yards on each down, he'd make a first down after every three plays; after eight first downs he would score a touchdown. The only trouble is that nobody in the stands would be awake to notice.

The defenses of today are really too complicated for a team to win by simply running; teams are forced to mix it up. They all want a balanced attack.

"I kept on telling Charley [Johnson] to use his runners," said Bobby Layne, who was once hired to coach Johnson and the other St. Louis quarterbacks for a season. "You can't go over 60–40 in passing to running. You do and you are in a hell of a mess."

Layne was a great quarterback in his day without being a classic passer, and echoes Lemm's fear of the pass rushers.

"If you don't get your SOBs running, the other team will rush your fanny off. Look at Johnny Unitas. People said he was washed up in 1960, when Alan Ameche, his fullback, retired and Baltimore didn't have much rushing. But Unitas was the same. It was just that much harder without a great ground game. Look at Bart Starr. He always had a solid running game, and look how it helped! The defense could rush Unitas, but against Starr they have to delay an instant, to see if one of his runners is coming out for a pass."

Building a balanced attack requires both running and passing talent. Versatile players who both run and pass well come in especially handy for coaches, not just for their athletic ability, but because players add to the element of surprise when they can do more than one thing well. Coaches, of course, are always trying to come up with something new. In 1968, for example, the Bears said they'd unveil a "new," "total" offense, and at Green Bay Lombardi's successor, Phil Bengtson, said he would try three runners instead of the usual two. Neither "new look" was new. The Bears and Packers were only saying that they wanted all five potential pass receivers to be strong runners too. But so does every other team. So what else is new?

Actually, there isn't anything really new in football. Lombardi's list of basic plays has been good for years, and will be good for many more. When they talk about football "styles" they don't mean a new style; they mean a new emphasis. Offense was emphasized in the early fifties. Then, with Howell and his pupils, Sherman and Lombardi, dominating the game, defense came to be the major factor through the '60s. By 1970 offenses will be catching up again.

"There's nothing really new in football," reiterated John Rauch, Buffalo's coach, then with Oakland. For example, we put in what I thought was a new play this morning, but George Blanda informed me he did the same thing his rookie year with the Bears." That was eighteen years ago.

Blanda was the oldest player in the second Super Bowl game. "Hell. I was the oldest Bear on Chicago's divisional champions in 1956," said George, a handsome and graying 42. But there was one big difference. Losing in 1956, Bear Blanda collected $2,485.16; losing in 1967, Raider Blanda collected $13,000.

A coach's worst fear is that his offense (or defense) will be stereotyped. A versatile attack is a partial solution. So is a player who can line up as flanker or end on one play and at running back on the next. Coaches must always try to surprise the other guy.

"If we have a third-and-eight situation we must make the opponents worry about ten different things we might use," says Lenny Dawson, Kansas City quarterback. "Nothing becomes automatic. We have more than a hundred plays in our playbook, with variations. Besides plays, we can vary our ball handling, certain blocks, fakes—all changing our attack."

Len Dawson is a master of the play-action pass. A play-action pass is just a fake run, much as a draw play is a fake pass. A draw play is a running play that looks like a pass; play-action is a passing play that looks like a run.

With play-action the quarterback takes the ball and pretends to hand off to a runner, while the quarterback's blockers pretend to be blocking as if a run is forthcoming. As the defense reacts to the run—the linebackers freeze in their tracks, the front four hesitate an instant, and the cornerbacks leave their ends loose and come up for tackling—the quarterback throws a pass. Surprise!

"A quarterback shows a run to the defensive line (front four), faking the ball to a back," says Ben Davidson, Oakland's mustachioed defensive end, "but when he comes through the line, the runner is empty-handed." The surprise is greatest when the run is expected most, as on third-and-one situations.

Downs

If you'd never been to a football game in your life, you could fool all of the people all of the time if, on each third down play (the down and the yardage remaining are always indicated on the scoreboard in bright yellow letters) you shuddered and, as the team left the huddle, muttered: "you know, I think football is a game of third downs."

No one can argue against that. Winning teams are successful on third-downs; losers aren't. Winning quarterbacks win on third downs.

Downs aren't complicated. They are like pieces of pie. Just the way a pie is cut into slices a touchdown can be cut up into so many *downs*—actually so many *first downs.* (A first down is at least one tenth of a touchdown. There's no way ten straight first downs on the field don't mean six points, at least.)

When the offensive team first gets the ball the quarterback has four chances (downs) to move forward at least ten yards. If successful, the offense makes a first down, and gets four more downs—and so on until the team either scores, fails, or loses the ball to the other team through a fumble, interception, or kick. A failure is a double tragedy because a team not only loses its own scoring opportunity, it also gives the ball and the scoring threat to the enemy. The enemy team then takes its turn trying to gain at least ten yards in, at most, four plays.

Downs are such a basic ingredient of a football game that they are the favorite topic of the hardnoses. When a hardnose talks about downs he always talks about *situations;* situations and downs are like Sonny and Cher or bread and butter. In offensive situations it is offensive not to use the word situation when you talk about downs.

FIRST DOWN

The first down is the most fun for the quarterback because he is under the least pressure. He knows he has at least two more chances to make his 10-yard minimum, so he can be as creative and experimental as he wants.

On first down and ten yards to go—or "first and 10"—the defense knows least what to expect. There is nothing a team likes better than running for a big gain on the first play in a game. A big opening burst can give enough momentum to last for the whole game. Experts tell you how important it is for the quarterback to complete the first pass he throws, to set a precedent.

Coach Don Shula has a special first down drill at Baltimore. The object is to gain five or more yards on the first play of a series so that the second down can be a shocker for the defense. Shula's drill should be named Wishful Thinking; if he could devise a 5-yard play, he would use it on *every* down.

When the Colts are on defense they have a theory about first down plays. The Colts like to use a variety of crazy complex alignments on first down, hoping to put an offense in the limiting situation of second down and eight or nine yards to go. Then, figuring the quarterback has to pass, the Colts play a tough zone defense or blitz hard. The result is that it is difficult to put together long drives against Baltimore.

SECOND DOWN

Second-down strategy depends a lot on what happened on the first down. The obvious plan is to run on second down with less than five yards to go and to pass if more than five, understanding that at different stages of the game, situations vary. For example, if a team is far behind in the fourth quarter, the QB wouldn't think and plan the same way as he would with a good lead in the second quarter.

Early in a game there is a greater chance of running on second down. Harland Svare, who coaches Washington's defense, has the idea that intimidation is the best way to win. First, you show the opponent who is boss, physically. The idea is to batter him, weaken him, and discourage him with lots of running early. Then, later on, when you've gained control, you can come up with the fancy stuff, the passing.

Suppose it's second down and one, a running situation, with Johnny Unitas as QB. John thinks he'll try a long pass, because he still has the third down to get the necessary yard. The middle linebacker, meanwhile, is plotting and, knowing how unorthodox Unitas is, he might just guess *pass*. But John Unitas is worrying that the middle linebacker will guess, correctly, that he plans to pass, so Unitas changes his mind and decides on a pitch-out. The middle linebacker, of course, is still plotting. He thinks that Unitas thinks that he thinks . . . , which is why it's just as well to forget about second downs and leave them to the players and coaches to worry about. Second down situations are the most difficult to anticipate; they are hardnosed.

THIRD DOWN

Third downs are softnosed, dramatic, and feminine. As on second downs, the quarterback tends to run for fewer yards and pass for more yards—but third downs are the "last chance" downs. It's then or never, and so the quarterback and his coach usually decide to take the risk and pass.

If the offense fails to make the necessary ten yards on their first three tries, they cannot take the chance that they might fail on the fourth and so will punt, to give the opponents the ball as far as possible away from their own goal line. Good kickers (punters) can kick up to 60 yards, and sixty yards can mean six series of downs worth of work for the opposition, just moving the ball back to where it started from. Punting is a very conservative approach to the oval world—the better-safe-than-sorry school.

No team wants to punt, naturally, which is why football keeps coming back to the crisis of the third-down situation. On third down the pressure is unbearable. Because it is a last-gasp situation, the defense can afford to be very aggressive, which can be most disconcerting to the quarterback, especially when he needs many yards and time to throw.

Before the first Super Bowl, Kansas City Safety Johnny Robinson was talking about Green Bay's power. "Their running game sets up so many third-and-three situations. Third-and-three is a tough defensive situation, because you never know what play they'll throw at you. On third-and-five, you know teams will pass most of the time; on third-and-three you have to guess, because it's a fifty-fifty proposition. As a result, the defensive backs have to play the receivers a lot closer, and your line can't rush the passer right away. They have to hesitate—it's just a horrible situation."

What's horrible to Johnny Robinson is beautiful to us fans. The third is the do-or-die down—the nitty gritty.

You can liken the gridiron to a kitchen. Creating a complicated soufflé is a situation full of surprises. If you experiment with the new recipe, planning it for a family supper, it's like a first down. But if your Grand Marnier soufflé falls when company comes for a black tie buffet, it's like a third down failure. So you punt.

Scoring

A frustration deeply rooted in men of football is the urge to rename their game.

"The name of the game is hitting," says the coach.

"The name of the game is defense," say the linebacker.

"The name of the game is quarterbacking," says the quarterback.

All the hitting and defense in the world can't beat winning, and you do that by scoring more points than the other guy.

A touchdown (TD) = 6 points. A touchdown is scored when a runner carries the ball across the goal line or a pass is completed to a man in the end zone. If the ball as much as *touches* the vertical plane of the goal line it is a score, even if the ball carrier ends up pushed down at the two or three yard line.

Many ballplayers have a habit of expressing their glee by throwing the ball into the stands from the end zone. Some go the other way and casually let the ball dribble groundward, almost as a part of the goal-crossing motion, but such nonchalance is phony and meant either to show off or to provoke the opponents. Washington Defensive Half-back Brig Owens made careful plans for when he scored his first touch-down as a pro. Brig had planned to spring across the goal, turn a cartwheel, and throw the ball into the stands, but Linebacker Sam Huff discouraged him and said a cartwheel wasn't very professional. As it happened, Brig's first touchdown crossed the goal line at the open end of the stadium.

After scoring a TD, a team is allowed to try for an extra bonus, a point-after-touchdown (PAT) by placekicking through the goal posts, or, though this option is not used once in ten years, passing or running the ball across the goal line. These plays are run from the 2-yard line.

A successful attempt at a PAT is almost automatic, and it is a rare and soon-fired placekicker who will miss more than two PATs a *season*. Considering the small amount of effort put into making the kick good, the one-point reward is way out of proportion.

Field goals are placekicked exactly like extra points, but from farther out on the field, and they may be attempted any time the team has the ball. In practice, though, they are usually only attempted on fourth down, when a team has the ball in the opponents' territory. The ball is snapped back to the holder, seven yards behind the line of scrimmage, the kicker runs up, and BOOM, followed by, the kicker hopes, cheers. The record distance for field goals is 56 yards, by Bert Rechichar.

When the first scoring system was begun in 1883, field goals counted three points, extra points counted *two* points and touchdowns counted four points. The points by kicking, therefore, out-totaled touchdown points five to four. Today, kicking (PAT and FG) totals four points, a touchdown six—*foot*ball is now foot*ball.*

When the American Football League was organized in 1960, the AFL founders decided to allow two points for a PAT scored via a run or pass, hoping to add excitement to the new league's game. Unluckily, the AFL coaches stuck mostly to kicking the extra point. AFL coaches were brought up in the NFL, and you can't teach a conservative old dog anything new.

One group besides placekickers loves the single extra PAT—the concessionaires. When the two-point option was introduced in the AFL, people sat in their seats to see what would happen and the food and drink business fell way off.

The new look in football may be footless football, if the almost automatic point is abolished, an option which is being considered. The kickers are aghast. At St. Louis, Kicker Jim Bakken thinks that his scoring title is directly reflected in his salary negotiations and that it is most unfair for the league to consider abolishing the extra point. To Bakken, extra points mean bread.

At the end of a season, when all the statistics are added up, there's something bizarre, when eight of the top ten scorers in the NFL in 1967 (nine in 1968) are kickers who spend fifty-nine minutes of each battle on the bench. At least kickers could be separated into a special category—like quarantined sailors—or given a Roger Maris-type asterisk: No grimy third-down-and-inches fullback I know wants to share any scoring spotlight with some clean prima-donna's kicking foot.

Clean or dirty, kicking or running, the scorers are the envy of the rest, the offensive linemen and the defenders. Giant Baltimore Tackle Jim Parker blocked in the salt mines of the line for a dozen years, usually at the bottom of a ton of sweaty muscle. He roomed with that glamorous runner, "Mr. Spats," alias Lenny Moore.

"I always tell Lenny when he gets out in the open to pitch it back to me and I'll take it in," said Jim, Lenny's convoy to the end zone.

In college at Ohio State Parker did score once, running a fumble 45 yards for six points. There weren't very many Colts who became ex-Colts without having heard the story of Parker's TD.

Buffalo's Jim Dunaway, a 300-lb defensive tackle, had scored a 92-yard TD in high school. Ten years later, Dunaway ran back a blocked kick against the Jets 72 yards for his second score.

"On every stride I thought that somebody was going to get me from behind," he said afterward. "'That ball will be autographed by our whole team and I'm going to have it preserved and mounted."

The Los Angeles Rams' defensive line is famous for its fast, aggressive style. Giant-sized Lamar Lundy holds the all-time record for defensive ends—eighteen points—by running for TDs three times with intercepted passes. On one of the scores a defensive back was clinging to Lundy's head as he crashed into the end zone.

Down the line from Lundy looms Merlin Olsen who, like all defensive tackles, has forgotten everything else twice except the day he made a touchdown on a pass interception. "Against Green Bay," he will remind you, proudly.

Before he retired, Rosy Grier used to play tackle next to Olsen. Rosy once scored a safety, which is not to be confused with the defensive player with the same name. Rosy tackled scramblin' Giant Quarterback Fran Tarkenton in Fran's own end zone, which scored two points for the Rams—a *safety*.

(A safety is a rare bird, usually happening when a team, deep in its own territory, gets caught trying to move the ball out of its own end zone. Caution: it is a *touchback*, not a safety, when a man with the ball is *pushed back* into his own end zone. In order to qualify for the two points, the man with the ball must be willfully trying to advance, and must be tackled by the defense *behind* his goal line.)

When Rosy Grier tackled Tarkenton for a skimpy pair of points, he was jubilant: "I've been in the league thirteen years, and I played four years in college. This is the first time I ever scored, and I'll never forget it."

Norman Mailer explains it all in *Advertisements for Myself*. "Anyone who has ever put on a uniform knows how much attention is given to football. The offensive line feels at its best in the moment it is waiting for the center to pass the ball . . . and when the ball goes . . . they are back to being peons, a working class mining out holes for the upper-class heroes of the backfield."

When the peons get the ball, they know what to do with it. Tackles love to make touchdowns.

And quarterbacks love to make tackles. Bill Munson's most singular accomplishment while playing quarterback for the Rams was a block, when he knocked a Packer defensive back flat. "I really got a kick out of seeing him fall over," said Munson, now quarterbacking the Detroit Lions.

A quarterback loves to run, too, and the greatest passers—Unitas and Namath—are quick to discuss their rushing averages. Cleveland Fullback Jimmy Brown always complained, "I don't like to be typed," and the greatest runner of all time would happily point out his passing statistics. In nine years Brown completed four passes for 117 yards. Even on a dirty gridiron, the grass is always greener.

PART

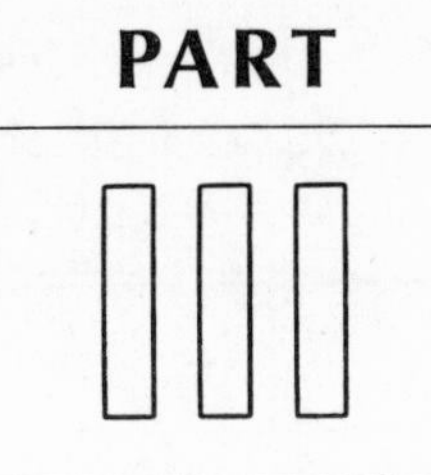

4 The Quarterback

A guard on the St. Louis Cardinals, Dave O'Brien, told me about this girl he knew.

"She thought all football players started playing quarterback," he said, "and then, when they improved they played halfback, and when they were really good they played fullback."

This girl was wrong twice. Really good isn't good enough. "If you don't have a quarterback," said Washington Redskin Coach Vincent Lombardi, "you don't have a team."

Like the symphony or movie director, the quarterback runs the show. He is always in the limelight, the star. If he is any good, he is aggressive. He gets the most publicity, makes the most money, helps lay the plans, calls the plays, and gets blamed in defeat. He needs brains, intuition, poise, imagination, guts, nimble hands and feet, and a flair for dramatics.

The best old quarterback is John Unitas (age 36) at Baltimore. The title of best young quarterback belongs to Joe Namath (26) at the New York Jets. Both John and Joe have terrible posture, with very round shoulders; on the street you would mistake them for basketball players.

A young college quarterback looking for a job in pro football should have:

bad posture
strong arm
quick release
intelligence
coolness
and the taller he is, the better.

If you had to choose just one item on the list, you would choose the strong arm. Much of the rest can be acquired. Even when it isn't, a strong arm and experience can take a team a long way.

"There are no bad quarterbacks in professional football," says one of the oldest, Babe Parilli, who backed up Joe Namath in 1968. "Everyone is a stick-out at his job. Sometimes he's hot, sometimes cold, but he's never bad."

Parilli makes an important point. After all the years and dollars are counted, only twenty-six quarterbacks have leading roles on any Sunday afternoon. It's highly unlikely that any is a bad quarterback. When one is called a "bum" it's only relative—the worst the bum can be is twenty-sixth, and that's out of a whole country of quarterbacks, if you judge from the sounds emanating from the stands.

Before every play the quarterback gives instructions in the huddle. The offensive team gathers *in order* about the center, the backs to the rear of the huddle with the quarterback. The quarterback faces the defense, so he can look them over. He uses shorthand language to tell each player his assignment on the upcoming play. One or two words or numbers is enough to tell each group—the wide receivers, the running backs, and the blocking linemen—what to do next. The spaces between the linemen are numbered—usually even numbers to the left of center and odd numbers to the right—and often the runners are numbered too. Thus the quarterback, by calling out "23" can tell his "No. 2" back to run through the "3" hole.

Often in the huddle the players will tip the QB off about their man. A receiver might tell his QB that he can get open for a pass with an "outside move" toward the sideline.

"No one talks in the huddle but me," said QB Fran Tarkenton when he was with the Minnesota Vikings. "I don't believe in suggestions once we're in the huddle. We've only got twenty-five seconds and the quarterback has to be master."

After five years at Minnesota, Tarkenton was traded to New York and he is much happier with the Giants. Apparently Fran has changed his huddle theories a little, because after he had been with the Giants awhile Tarkenton became more receptive to last-second information.

"Here we all understand the defensive structure and my receivers will feed me information," said Fran. "Joe Morrison might tell me in the huddle 'I can beat him on a zig-out.' He'll be right. I like cooperation of this sort because it makes them feel more a part of the team."

Tarkenton has changed his mind about any number of things any number of times. He is a "today quarterback," a rather wordy new breed. After an article by Tarkenton appeared in *Sports Illustrated*, Vince Lombardi became a literary critic and said it is too bad they print things like that.

"What does he mean?" asked Lombardi. "That's mumbo jumbo. That's not football, that's sandlot."

At the beginning of a play, the quarterback does one of three things after he receives the ball from the center. He hands the ball to a runner, throws a pass, or keeps the ball and runs himself. A quarterback runs the ball himself only in desperation, usually after something goes wrong and all else has failed; this disaster play is called a *quarterback keeper*, which sounds like a well-to-do female with a penchant for young ball tossers, but isn't. Most of the time when a quarterback ends up keeping the ball, he will run like hell for the sideline to get safely out of bounds, except for that tough competitor who quarterbacks for Minnesota, Joe Kapp. Kapp doesn't believe in running out of bounds. "I can run with authority," says Kapp, who does.

In the game the quarterback calls each play based on:

what yard line his team is on
which down it is
how much time is on the clock
what the score is
the overall game plan.

These five items contribute to the pressure the quarterback is under on each play.

Pressure builds up:

near the goal lines
the later the down
toward the end of each half
as a team begins to fall behind.

The only way to come from far behind is the long pass, the quick-striking big bomb. On bombs the risk of interception is much the greatest.

The eyes of the quarterback are in the spotters' booth, somewhere by the stadium's roof, where an assistant coach or two watches the whole game with high-powered binoculars. These spotters are in constant contact with the sidelines, describing in detail exactly what the opposing defense is doing. The worst seat in a stadium, of course, is at field level, which is why coaches can't answer any newsmen's questions after a game. ("I can't say until I've seen the films.") From the sidelines the coach hasn't seen much of anything; he has been *told* about the game by his spotters and has relayed the information to his quarterback. The newsmen have seen the game perfectly, from the pressbox right alongside the spotters.

There are all kinds of quarterbacks and each has his own style. If he can score points and win games a quarterback has great style. If he loses, he hasn't. Cleopatra, famous for her infinite variety, would have made an excellent quarterback, though it isn't recorded that she had to throw many passes. Good quarterbacks are full of surprises and veiled purposes, and they never wither. They get better and better with age, and should be best at thirty, or later.

The Rams' Bernie Casey, a flanker, had played for several teams and in several Pro Bowl games, and is well qualified to compare passing styles.

"John Brodie [San Francisco] throws a softer pass than Roman Gabriel [Los Angeles]," says Casey. "Gabriel whips it in, but it's not uncatchable, just tougher to defend against. Sonny Jurgensen [Washington] really zips the ball, like Gabriel, and he's the best I've seen at getting it away fast."

For many a moon Sonny Jurgensen has been asking, "Why run when you can throw?" and throws accordingly, leading the league every year in most passes thrown. "What's more, Jurgensen throws any time he feels like it," says Casey.

The fact that Jurgensen is such a good passer must have made the Redskins' offer to Vince Lombardi that much more tempting. Taking over a team with Jurgensen is like being brought in to direct a movie starring Paul Newman. Sonny is spectacular.

"Sonny is different," says Eagle Cornerback Coach Irv Cross. "On a short yardage situation he figures that there's no reason to run for two yards when he can pass for ten. Sonny is so confident, and he's a gambler."

Even though he throws so much, Sonny is never dull or stale because his custom is to throw home runs, the big TD bombs. Jurgensen began learning "Pass!" at the Philadelphia Eagles in 1958 under the Eagles' quarterback, Norman Van Brocklin, the Dutchman who now coaches at Atlanta. Van Brocklin used to warm up by knocking a ten-gallon hat off a groundskeeper's head, according to Philadelphia legend, and he did it without ever hurting the guy's head. A man with a golden arm, Van Brocklin said, "A quarterback should only run from sheer fright," so often it became his anthem.

The old-fashioned method of passing was for the quarterback to take the "snap" of the ball from center and retreat quickly for seven yards; at this point a protective human wall would be formed by the offensive linemen, who would hold off the defensive rushers for three or four seconds—time enough, supposedly, for the quarterback to complete his pass. The semi-circle of protecting linemen formed a pocket; leaving it was supposed to be almost instant death.

The seven-yard dropback is supposed to be the safest for the quarterback, making the best angle for the blockers and the most difficult angle for the pass rushers. In his first year at Detroit, Bill Munson enjoyed little success. Opposing coaches said that Munson wasn't dropping back far enough and so was unable to avoid even a moderate rush. Munson was also dropping back too slowly, using short, choppy steps, and couldn't get set up (get his weight balanced) in time.

The quarterback hopes to drop back out of the rusher's range and then, as the blocking pocket materializes, he steps forward behind his blockers and scans his receivers. Waiting takes courage. After a few seconds it's as dangerous in the pocket as it is outside. John Unitas and Jurgensen have plenty of courage; for the last few years they have been playing while hurt and wait in the pocket with painful tennis elbows and a variety of other arm, shoulder, and rib injuries.

"You can depend on John Unitas to stay in the pocket," says Merlin Olsen. But Cowboy Tackle Jethro Pugh is trying to "pick the pocket"! (Robert Hume Photography)

"You can depend on John Unitas to stay in the pocket," says Merlin Olsen, the Ram defensive tackle, "and you still can't hurry his throw. He waits until the last second and just when you think you've got him he lets go, right on the button."

Quarterbacks famous for passing are usually not very mobile, and so become famous as targets of the pass-rushers. The only weapons the sitting-duck quarterback has are his quick arm and faking talents. Like Jurgensen and Unitas, Joe Namath has a quick arm which must be all the quicker because Joe sets up extra deep, sometimes as far back as twelve yards behind the line of scrimmage. On bad knees Namath can move back five yards farther than most quarterbacks and still get the ball away faster. Amazing. People are always surprised by Namath's fantastic natural athletic ability.

"He can really wing that ball in there," said Cincinnati Coach Paul Brown in admiration. "He has strength and accuracy and you'd better get to him or he'll pass you out of the park."

The Baltimore Colts thought *the blitz* (linebackers rushing Namath too, along with the linemen) was the best way to run Namath out of the Super Bowl, but Joe picked it up almost every time. "Not many quarterbacks can do that to us," said Colt Coach Don Shula.

"People have learned that it's not such a good idea to blitz against us," said Weeb Ewbank. "Joe has such quick wrists—bing! It's there. We like a blitz."

"Nobody can read defenses like Joe," said Don Maynard after the Super Bowl. "We'd get in the huddle and he'd call 'play at the line.' That meant that we didn't have a set play, that he'd call it when we got up to the line. I'd say he did that almost half the time."

Joe's one great hang-up has always been interceptions, from passing even when he hasn't a receiver in the open. The Jet coaches constantly harangue him either to throw out of bounds or to "eat" the ball. In 1966 Namath threw 27 interceptions, in 1967, 28. In 1968 he continued apace for one-third of the season but then he shaped himself up, throwing only six interceptions in the last nine games. Nothing could have made Weeb Ewbank happier.

"Eating" the ball only means keeping it, when your receivers aren't open. In such situations tons of defensive linemen usually crash down on the quarterback. Which hurts. It takes a long time for young quarterbacks to learn to be safe (eating the ball), not sorry (getting intercepted).

A couple of years ago after a big game against Boston, Ewbank was ecstatic. The pupil (Namath) had finally followed the teacher's (Ewbank's) advice and eaten the ball. When the Patriots landed on Joe en masse, you would have thought Namath had pulled out a knife, fork, and bottle of catsup.

When Coach Weeb Ewbank and Joe Namath confer at the sideline during Jet games, one sees the Generation Gap in dialogue.

"That was great," said Weeb. "I've been telling him you can't throw the ball into a pile."

"I'd like to put the coach in my position and see what he does," said Namath.

The alternative to eating the ball, when receivers are covered, is to *throw it away*. There is a rule which says the quarterback mustn't pass without an intended receiver, which turns the art of throwing the ball away into a delicate art—the pass must look like it's intended for a certain receiver, but mustn't go near a potential intercepter. Namath is a master at throwing the ball away.

"Joe is fantastic," says University of Texas Coach Darrell Royal. "The way he avoids the rush and the way he seems to know where every receiver is. He won't seem to be watching a man but he'll whirl and throw to a spot and the man will be there."

John Unitas also throws to spots. Such timing requires great receivers and long hours of practice. Unitas has had more of both and has less of an interception problem. Maxie Baughan, one of the great linebackers, says the reason John can spot problems better than any other passer is his great peripheral vision; Unitas can pick up alternate receivers in a split second.

"If he has to pass in three seconds, it has to take at least one and a half to set up," says Baughan, a Los Angeles Ram. "That doesn't leave much time for looking around to see who's open."

Against the great Ram defensive line, John often tries a quick count, unloading his passes in a hurry. Sometimes it works. "No lineman in the world can get to Unitas or any quarterback when he is throwing in one or two seconds," says Deacon Jones, the left end of the Ram front four. "But if they fall behind, then Unitas has to throw deeper, and that's when we get him." The Deacon licked his chops. "That extra split second John needs to get rid of the ball long is just what we need too."

So much depends on the receivers. They can't always get in the clear quick enough.

On each play the defensive backs have a plan to cover the receivers as they run out in predetermined patterns. Each commitment—a move, fake, or change of direction—by a defensive back is a "key." The quarterback should be able to react to each key either by throwing or by looking for an alternate receiver. If the quarterback is reading the keys correctly he unravels the defensive scheme, and should complete a pass. On some plays, when there is one primary receiver and are as many as four alternates, it is only the very best quarterback who can check out the alternates and get rid of the ball within the few seconds' limit. Quickness counts most. A strong, accurate arm counts little for a quarterback if he can't get the ball away fast.

"You've got to teach a quarterback how to take his key per pattern," says Norm Van Brocklin, whose young pupils at Atlanta have the advantage of learning from the master passer. "You have your pass patterns set up for each receiver, and you teach your quarterback which key to look for and how to react accordingly. If he reads the key it's automatic and he goes to an alternate, reads the key and goes to another alternate, and so on until a key tells him that a man is open. It's different each time and it's hard work."

Chicago Bear Coach Jim Dooley, who played end in the pros, comes to the task of quarterback-coaching with more empathy for the receivers than the quarterbacks. At the end of his first season as head coach he was most impressed with the youngest, greenest QB of them all, Virgil Carter, a rookie.

"He doesn't have the experience or the physical equipment of the others," said Dooley, "but the kid has the discipline of a veteran. Carter could pick up his keys—boom, boom, boom—and he was as calm and cool as a cucumber."

Carter was most unusual. Experience is the big factor in reading keys, and keys are the reason it takes young quarterbacks years to become good quarterbacks.

"Coach Landry told me it takes five years to become a good quarterback," said young Cowboy Craig Morton. "I didn't believe it then, but I had no idea of the complexity of reading defenses. Now, after four years I feel more prepared, the keys are easier, and I have a lot of confidence."

Joe Namath was unusually quick at learning to read defenses. Namath has all the speed required of a quarterback—quick mind, quick hands, quick wrists, quick feet—but with crippled knees, no choice but to be as immobile in the pocket as Sonny Jurgensen or Norm Van Brocklin. An immobile quarterback's favorite way of keeping a defense honest is borrowing from the theater of improvisation and calling a screen pass or a draw play. Both require excellent faking.

Screen passes usually go to a back who follows a wall of blockers (the screen). The success of a screen pass depends on the anguish conveyed by the QB's theatrics. Y. A. Tittle was the master, the Barrymore of the screen pass. If he ever blew one, Tittle's theatrics turned to reality and he was likely to rip his helmet off and throw it to the ground in a temper tantrum, stripping his bald head to the slick. It was a grand sight.

When the QB receives the snap on a screen pass, he puts the ball into his waist, the better to hide it and the safer to keep it. He pretends to hand the ball off to a running back, always using two hands, but just as the faking back runs by, the QB pulls the ball back. One reason sophisticated fans claim they never watch the ball is that they can't find it. Faking by the quarterback is too adept. Quarterbacks fake runs to help their passing and vice versa.

Tittle advocated throwing to the outside, to avoid trouble up the middle. "A passer throwing over the center has to be able to see two directions at once, since there are defenders on both sides of the receivers," said Tittle. "When you throw to the outside you only have to look in one direction, and trouble can only come from the inside, so you can see it easily and quickly." "Trouble" in this case is linebackers.

John Unitas is a good pocket passer, but he isn't like Jurgensen or Van Brocklin. Unitas will run if he has to, but it is fair to note that he enjoyed running in his 20s more than in his 30s.

Fran Tarkenton is still in his twenties and enjoys running. When a classic pocket passer like Van Brocklin is forced from his pocket, his heavy feet produce rather a lumbering gait, which is not to be confused with running. When Tarkenton's protection breaks down, or his receivers aren't free, Fran quits the pocket and runs, which is called scrambling.

(Tarkenton likes to run so much that when he was traded to the Giants after their dismal year of 1966, it was noted that he had gained more yards running the year before than any of the Giants' running backs.)

The twain met in 1961, when Van Brocklin went to the brand-new

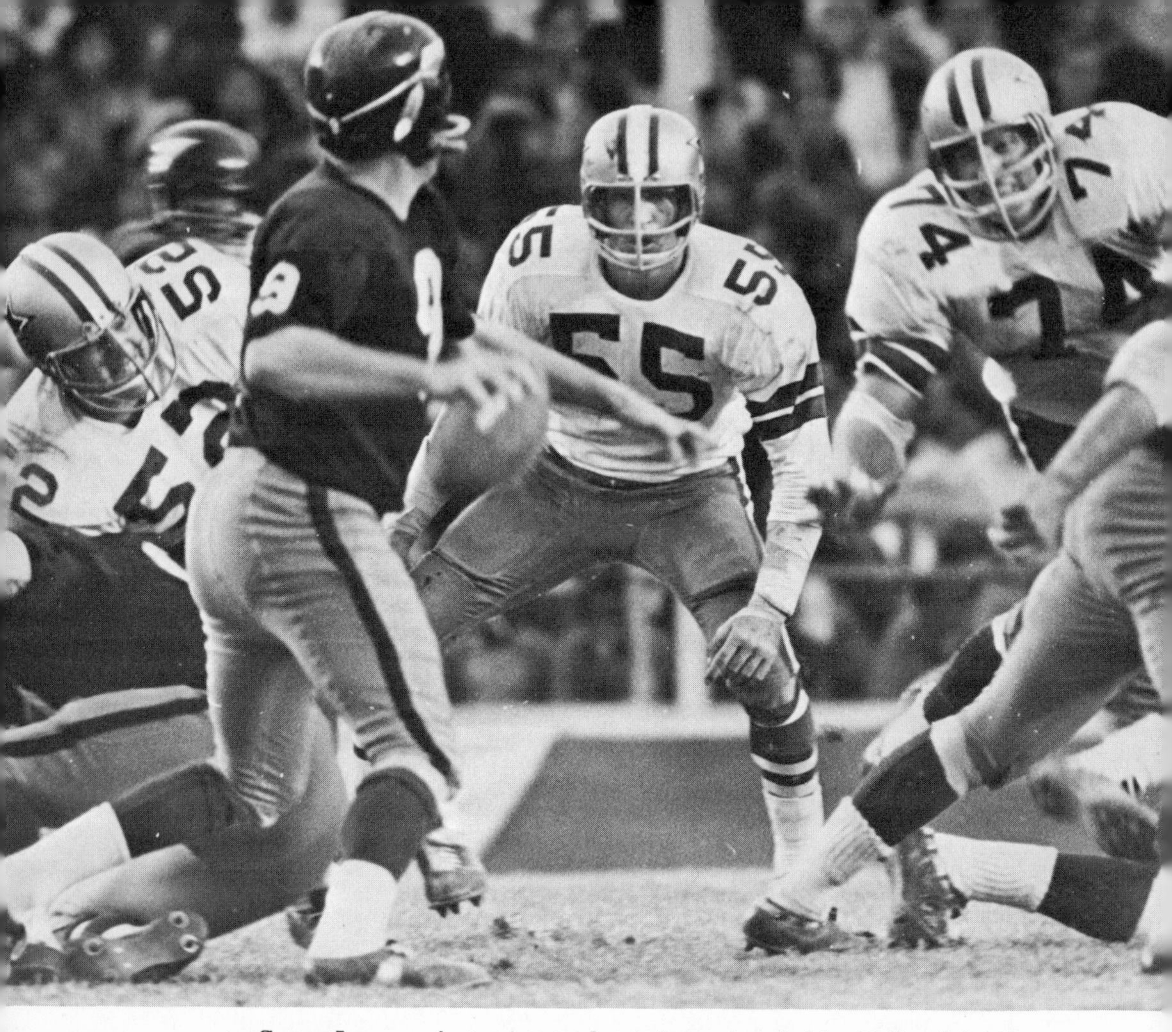

Sonny Jurgensen's passing pocket is being invaded by Dallas defenders.
(Russ Russell Photography)

Minnesota Vikings as their head coach. Van Brocklin had retired after winning the championship with Philadelphia the year before. At Minnesota Van Brocklin, the quarterback who only ran from sheer fright, found a rookie passer, Tarkenton, running quarterback.

"There is a place for a running quarterback in pro football today," Van Brocklin said immediately, the tone of his voice sounding like spikes were being driven under his nails. "More teams today seem to be taking advantage of a running quarterback."

"Norm is a fine football mind," replied Tarkenton. "He didn't have the physical ability to run, but he recognizes that every quarterback has his own style and personality. He has never tried to change my style as such."

Tarkenton always said the game was changing, that the running quarterback was on his way into fashion. Van Brocklin shuddered.

"Norm judges things by the number of points a quarterback helps get up on the scoreboard. My concept of the game is to get points however I can. I like to run."

The Dutchman and Tarkenton made quite a combustible combination at the young Vikings and after five frustrating years and not many wins, both Norm and Fran resigned within a few days of each other.

The Fran-and-Van act of the Vikings is now Fran-and-Allie at the Giants where Tarkenton's coach is Allie Sherman. Tarkenton is still leaving the pocket, and the jury is still out on the subject of scrambling, though most are against it.

Lamar Lundy, the Ram defensive end who once played a man-eating tree in a science fiction movie, can argue either way, though he rarely gets into arguments. Too big. Lundy was once described by John Brodie, San Francisco quarterback, as so tall that "when it rains, he has snow on him."

"Tarkenton is tough because he's so unpredictable," says the man-mountain. "Neither he nor you knows what he is going to do from second to second. However, neither do his offensive linemen or his blocking backs, which makes it more difficult to help him with blocking."

The anti-scrambling school believes that a quarterback who stays in the pocket helps his blockers because they know exactly what they have to do and exactly where he is, which makes it tougher for the rushers to get at him.

Pass rushers like Lundy have an uncomplicated job, really—to get the quarterback before he throws the ball—but a scrambling quarterback complicates things. A moving target, a scrambler is even more of a problem for the pass rushers late in a game when the big defensive linemen are tired—especially if they are old and it is hot. The mature, sophisticated Packers always have trouble with scramblers like Tarkenton and San Francisco's George Mira.

Kansas City Coach Hank Stram invented a pocket vs. scrambling QB "compromise," a *movable pocket*. The quarterback doesn't drop back and throw from behind a circle of linemen, and he doesn't roll out by himself and scramble around in the open. Instead, everybody, quarterback *and* protectors, moves out together in Stram's rollout passing pocket. It's a mass scramble.

Ex-master Y. A. Tittle says no scrambling quarterback ever won a championship, hinting broadly that he thinks one never will. Allie Sherman admits that he thinks Tarkenton leaves the pocket too soon on occasion. Fran himself says the label "scrambler" is a misnomer, that he doesn't scramble more than three or four times a game. In his series of magazine articles Tarkenton continually contradicted himself on the subject. The question seems to be: how many times does Fran have to scramble before he will concede he's a scrambler.

Tarkenton's most common knock has become a cliché—that he wins some he ought to lose and loses some he ought to win. In the 1968 Pro Bowl Tarkenton almost did both. He came off the bench and looked like a hero, putting his East team ahead. Tarkenton then turned into a goat, threw two interceptions, and gave the West the game. But Tarkenton's scrambling tactics win as many games as they lose, and the result balances at .500. He and other scramblers seem to be far away from winning a championship; so are their coaches, and coaches are fired more quickly than quarterbacks. When a quarterback takes a chance and fails, his coach is the one who pays the penalty. The most secure coaches are the ones with a good passing quarterback. They sleep more soundly than the coaches who try a scrambler in a desperation move.

Tarkenton's assets are mostly theatrical. Scramblers win or lose spectacularly. Given a chance, Pearl White would have been history's first scrambler, confidently devastating the best passing pockets with only seconds to go. In lieu of Pearl, the Giants traded for Tarkenton, because they were losing, which is bad enough, but losing dully; while on the other side of town the Jets and Joe Namath, while also losing, were losing with thrills. In Tarkenton's second year in New York the Jets won big; Tarkenton's scrambling shenanigans paled in comparison.

New York can beautifully illustrate the "Cleopatra QB" tradition, with quarterbacks-in-residence Tarkenton—married, square—and Namath—single, hip. Fran and Joe aren't entirely opposite. Both are male and intelligent. Neither smokes (Namath gave up smoking on a $5000 bet in 1967). Both have southern accents, though Fran's is native and Joe acquired his in college in Alabama.

Otherwise, to put it mildly, they differ. Tarkenton believes "when in doubt, RUN." When in doubt, Namath would throw a bomb. Namath lives in the city, drinks, swings, loses his temper, and has a good sense of humor. Tarkenton says he likes to go home, skip the night life, and look at TV.

Fran and Joe were guests on the Johnny Carson show one night, and their appearance was filled with surprises. Namath was dressed conservatively, while Tarkenton wore a wild, hand-painted tie. The audience never suspected that Namath is so much bigger than Tarkenton. Most people don't realize how powerful Namath is, or how strong.

In Minnesota Fran Tarkenton was just another immature quarterback, but in New York, where he has the same agent as Arnold Palmer, Fran's every word is hung upon. Long chronicles are written about his real estate investments and stock portfolio, his commuting (with briefcase filled with the Giant's playbook and the Wall Street Journal) from a typical suburb, his vacation ("We take June off. I don't care what offer I get for even one day, for no matter how much money. June is my month off"), and his refusal to endorse too many different products.

"I don't want to become associated with just anything," says Fran, who seems to be associated with just about everything except a mink coat. He turned that one down—a one-photo, you keep the $5000 coat deal—because Joe Namath had done it already. The Tarkenton promotion has run into Namath more and more often.

Tarkenton doesn't smoke or drink but doesn't mind if others do. He is patient and religious, a member of the Fellowship of Christian Athletes. He is chatty and relaxed on his half-hour television show, tries unsuccessfully to be a little controversial and always ends up sounding like the minister's son he is. It's odd, the combination of minister's son and mercenary, but that's Fran. He's the best bounty hunter to come down the pike since Marco Polo.

Off television, Tarkenton likes, "talkin' to people from different walks of life to gain understanding and a total outlook." In an interview last year Fran allowed as how he had recently met and talked with a man who had never in his life said grace before a meal. That jump from the Vikings to the Giants is giving Fran a broader view all the time.

Tarkenton practices what he preaches on the field as well as off. If someone suggests a play that doesn't work he shoulders the blame.

"It's entirely mine, my burden," says Fran. "If I called it I had to have a conviction on the play too." Tarkenton often answers people who ask why he wastes time playing football by saying that he feels that he can do God's work on the gridiron as well as in an office or wherever. His checkbook proves how well God's work is working out.

One man who is definitely not a Tarkenton fan is Vince Lombardi. Lombardi wants a meticulous quarterback. To Vince, the good head is more important than the good arm. The feet, he forgets. When Lombardi was at Green Bay, the Packers referred to him not as "the coach" but as "coach" as in "coach says a quarterback shouldn't have to run very often." Like Ewbank's at the Jets, the Packers' quarterback almost never has to. Vince finding stationary Sonny Jurgensen at Washington was a match made in heaven. To make the Redskins a champion Lombardi has to build up Packer-like blocking for Jurgensen as he did at Green Bay for Bart Starr.

During Lombardi's regime, Bart Starr had everything going for him. He was rarely behind in a game, and was rarely forced to take chances or improvise. By superior execution and few weak spots, the Packers just played to their plans. And won. "My number one rule," said ruler Vincent, "is to get on the scoreboard every time we're inside the thirty. I'll take a field goal (three points) every time rather than gamble all or nothing when I'm not forced to." (Coaches carry such conservative thinking to all lengths. Twice, to avoid shutouts, Minnesota Coach Bud Grant went for three points when his Vikings were losing 39–0 and 31–0.)

Under Lombardi, Bart Starr was the only quarterback who worked under the "take a field goal inside the thirty" rule for sixty minutes per game, game after game, season after season. In many ways Starr was a robot, competent but uninspired. If you consider that the quarterback's eyes are on the roof with his spotters, his brains are at the sideline in the heads of the coaching staff. The coach and the quarterback work together, plotting and planning for long hours, and if they see eye to eye after a number of years the coach's theories become the quarterback's. Proof of the pudding was Green Bay, where Bart Starr, QB, and Vince Lombardi, coach, even though they have dissimilar personalities, blended into a combination of near-perfect leadership. When Vince used to send Bart into a tense third-down situation it was hardly different from Henry Higgins sending Eliza Doolittle out to the races at Ascot. Vince worked on Bart from 1959 to 1968.

"I'm standing on the sidelines and thinking now's the time for 47-zone, or 36-X slant, and do you know, Starr calls it," said Vince. "He's always right."

The chemistry between Lombardi and Sonny Jurgensen is fascinating. When Vincent arrived at the Redskins both he and Jurgensen drank Scotch. End of similarity. But Vincent and Bart Starr weren't always thick. When Vince went to Green Bay, he gave Starr a brain-washing that took a couple of years.

"Starr has changed, but I've changed too," said Lombardi. "The longer we know each other the shorter the learning sessions."

In the beginning the sessions were livened up by Lombardi's Italian ancestry. Vince periodically exploded like Vesuvius.

"I don't like to get chewed out," Starr says. "It hurts your pride. It hurts you a little inside and I guess it's human nature when anyone gets on you, no matter how right he is, to rebel a little." (The new Packer general manager and coach Phil Bengtson is less gruff and more informal than Vince: "My approach to getting things across is a little different.")

Starr and Lombardi shared Lombardi's theories so thoroughly that people call Starr Mr. Milquetoast. He isn't. Starr drinks, has parties, swears. But in a game where everyone swears all the time—coaches possibly swear more than the players—Starr, who's rather reserved and quiet, probably swears less than most.

"I'm not necessarily trying to live any of that down," says Bart, "but none of it is true. I'm not that nice-guy stuff, nice on the football field or at home. Ask the players. Ask my wife. If people regard me as a push-button quarterback I regard it as a compliment because it means that I've absorbed and am able to apply the things Mr. Lombardi has taught me over the years."

Starr is extremely polite, perhaps partly a result of being raised in a military family. He may be quiet because, coached by a loud, indomitable legend, he was never able to get a word in edgewise. Of all the Packers, the least intimidated by Lombardi were Henry Jordan, Willie Wood, Jerry Kramer and Fuzzy Thurston; when Lombardi left Green Bay, Starr belonged to the group.

"When we heard he was coming to coach," says Starr, "we heard he was a very devout Catholic. After he was here a week we knew he went to daily Mass because he HAD to."

Football players never knock their own teammates—another unwritten law. Once Starr lost his temper and let one of his blockers have it, chewing him out with gusto. "I ripped him up and down," said Starr to a reporter, "but I wish, sir, that you wouldn't mention Wright's name in a derogatory sense because I'm not given to that sort of thing. I don't think it's necessary." (Wright was promising Tackle Steve Wright who became a celebrity without ever starting. Lombardi's "own story" in *Look* confided, sensationally, to sell magazines, that a good player had to *hate* his opponent, and that once he himself, Vincent, had become so enraged at a Packer for not being mean enough that he had hit the player. Rumors named Wright as the "too nice" Packer and soon afterward Lombardi traded Wright to the New York Giants.)

"People are different," says Starr, who by recognizing this truth is already way ahead of 90% of the employed coaches. "You've got to treat them in different ways to get them to respond. Coach knows how to handle men, and I think it's the big reason he's so successful."

One of the big reasons behind Lombardi's success is Starr. Starr is cucumber-cool under pressure. Before the Packers could play in either of the first two Super Bowls they had to win the NFL championship, which they did, both times against Dallas in cliffhangers. Both wins boiled down to single key plays in the final seconds. In 1967 an offside penalty prevented a Dallas touchdown and in 1968 Starr kept the ball himself and followed his guard, Jerry Kramer, into the end zone to win Green Bay's second last-minute title.

"My language in that huddle was stronger than most people would imagine," said Starr. "There were words you don't use in polite company."

Because the Packers play in so many really big games they have to be masters at psyching themselves up for all-out efforts.

Before the second Super Bowl the Packers and Raiders indulged in some psychological gambits, warfare in reverse. The previous year, 1967, before Super Bowl I, the Kansas City Chiefs shot their mouths off about what they were going to do against the Packers. The next year Oakland tried the opposite tack and praised the Packers to the sky.

Even Lombardi pulled a reverse. After the game against Kansas City, Vince said that the Chiefs didn't belong on the same field with the top teams in the NFL. Twelve months later he was saying what a fine football team Oakland had. The Packers kept praising Oakland's talent, balance, and linebackers. The Raiders kept saying how afraid they were of the Packers and their experience ("What great linebackers you have"); it was hard to believe they'd show up for the game.

"It'll be just like playing our fathers," said Raider Linebacker Billy Budness.

Afterward Oakland's young QB Daryle Lamonica said it was a day of learning—a game to file away and learn from.

"We learned something all right," said Oakland LB Dan Conners. "How to lose $7500. In two hours."

"After the game Starr came over to me and shook my hand," said Lamonica. "He said, 'Don't let it get you. It took me seven years to learn this game.' I'm still learning. I've got two more years to go to reach seven."

As Lamonica was being interviewed in the Raider dressing room, he had a book lying on the bench beside him—*Quarterbacking* by Bart Starr. Such a black comedy put-on shows Lamonica has a bit of the devil in him and makes one hope that Daryle turns into a top quarterback.

Before the Raiders' first game against San Francisco—the bitter across-the-Bay rivalry had been building for years and the game was a quick sellout—Daryle showed great potential as a pregame psychology professor. Reams had been written in the local newspapers, but none of the pregame slings and arrows came close to the needle delivered by the young newcomer Lamonica.

"I've always had the greatest respect for Mr. Brodie," said Daryle, 26, about San Francisco's Quarterback John Brodie, 33. "When I was a boy in high school he was my idol. I listened to all his college games on the radio and used to keep records of his passes. I even tried to get pictures of him, to copy his style." Here is a master touch.

Lamonica, a bachelor, is an outdoorsman. He fishes and hunts deer and rabbits, sometimes switching to a bow and arrow, left-handed, for a change of pace.

Lamonica is a handsome Italian, a good athlete with a strong, quick arm and plenty of potential at quarterback. Much of the Raider future depends on him. (Lamonica is in the tradition of Notre Dame QBs, who wear low jersey numbers, under 10. Daryle wears No. 3.)

The best young quarterback on the other side of the country hunts chicks on Sunday night instead of rabbits on Monday morning. Joe Namath did the unheard of before Super Bowl III. He broke every rule. A week before the game Namath went out on Sunday night, ran into Baltimore Kicker Lou Michaels, and told Lou the Jets would kick the hell out of the Colts. Namath got in at six the next morning and missed the Jets' only picture and interview session. He was sleeping.

When queried about the Colts during that week, Namath said Daryle Lamonica is a better quarterback than the Colts' Earl Morrall. Namath, in fact, said there are four quarterbacks better than Morrall in the American League. As the NFL Establishment was turning purple, Joe added a new dimension to pre-game psychology. He personally guaranteed that the Jets would win the Super Bowl. More than once. As nothing is more infuriating than a cocky braggart delivering the goods, the subsequent Jet victory left Namath-haters with exploding blood pressure.

Namath has Achilles' knees. He has played in pain more often than not, suffering several ailments in each knee. After three operations Namath seems much more mobile and looks, for him, almost frisky. Yet after games his knees would look puffy and discolored, the original shape almost unrecognizable, and it can take three to six days of therapy before they would get back into playing condition, or what approximates playing condition.

"It's step two and knit one," he'd say. "The only days I feel I can play are Saturday and Sunday."

It's a shame that any attempt at rating passers meets with one problem after another. No one knows how good a Namath with knees might be. No one knows how good a passer Philadelphia's Norm Snead would be with better protection. Houston's Pete Beathard has all the physical equipment one could want in a quarterback—size, arm, legs, strength, and a good football mind. Beathard on paper looks much better qualified than Daryle Lamonica, who has thus far been more successful. Beathard seems to lack *chutzpah,* but his only obvious drawback is that he never threw from a pocket in college.

Raps stemming back to college tend to stereotype the non-stars throughout their quarterbacking careers. Don Trull, a good leader, has been blasted as a roll-out passer for years, like Beathard, like Jerry Rhome, now at Cleveland, like George Mira at San Francisco, like countless others. For years critics have been tritely complaining that when Jack Concannon and George Mira run with the ball "they hold it like a lunch pail" (making it easy for a defensive player to steal the ball). The label "sidearm" preceded Notre Dame's John Huarte to the pros, and if you had a dollar for every time someone has blasted Huarte for his sidearm style you'd be a millionaire. Quarterbacks are more accurate and have fewer interceptions when they throw "over the top," releasing the ball high and away from the body. Critics of Cleveland's Frank Ryan say that his semi-sidearm style has prevented him from ranking at the top.

When you add the personality factor the picture gets even more complicated. At Chicago, where three quarterbacks are vying for the starting role, Jack Concannon has all the physical requirements, though he's often hurt, and is a cocky enough leader. After losing a summer exhibition in his first season with the Bears, Concannon turned on veteran Center Mike Pyle, who had long been an articulate team leader, and let him have it for an uninspired performance in the game. Concannon had quickly demonstrated to the Bears he had the spunk for quarterbacking, but as a play-caller Jack lacks discipline. Young Virgil Carter has the play-calling ability, though he's inexperienced; and the third Bear quarterback, Larry Rakestraw, hadn't much charisma as a field leader but he had a better winning percentage than the other two. What is a coach to do?

If only brains counted, Frank Ryan would be number one by a mile.

"The ideal quarterback must have serendipity," says Frank, explaining the mental qualifications. (One can only imagine Lombardi's reaction to such a statement.) "The times I have felt best on a football field, my mind was following no logical conscious-thinking pattern. There was no effort to analyze, evaluate, to review, to study the defense. Something just came to me in a flash and it worked—not just once or twice, not occasionally, but almost every time." If Ryan sounds ethereal, like a professor, he is. He has written his doctoral thesis on "A Characterization of the Set of Asymptotic Values of a Function Holomorphic in the Unit Disc." Dr. Ryan teaches math at Case Tech in the off-season. He is witty, humorous, brave, and his choice of jersey number, 13, is symbolic of Ryan's defiance of the "sweat school" establishment. There is a little of George Plimpton under Ryan's gray crew cut and, sad to say, a little of Plimpton's arm in Ryan's too. He can be good, and he can't.

Roman Gabriel, at the Rams, is the opposite type from Ryan. A non-scrambler, Gabriel is the biggest, strongest quarterback in captivity. His strength allows him to shrug off a 280-pound rushing lineman, set up again, pick out a receiver, and throw—probably a bomb by that time. Gabriel is not a pocket passer in the same sense that a smaller quarterback is, or a quarterback like Joe Namath. Namath, who has sometimes played with his oft-operated knee protected by a cage contraption, dares not leave the pocket. Gabriel dares; in fact he stands there while all hell breaks loose around him and waits . . . and waits. If a receiver doesn't get open, Roman finally converts himself into a fullback, puts his head down, and runs, straight ahead—which is to say he doesn't scramble around, like a Tarkenton. Gabriel weighs 40 pounds more than Tarkenton and is 4" taller, which makes him a bulkier, more powerful runner.

Gabriel is an unorthodox field general. TV announcer Pat Summerall was stunned by a series of plays Gabriel called late in a 1968 game against the 49ers. So were the fans, who couldn't believe their eyes.

"I was shocked," said Summerall, "but it's not my place to criticize the quarterback. If I can't justify his call I'll just shut up."

Gabriel may or may not be a total illusion. Opposing coaches dismiss the Ram offense, believing that if they can score seventeen points they have a good chance of winning, but the strong Ram defense makes seventeen points hard to come by. The Rams actually do most of their winning defensively; a large percent of their touchdowns are set up by the defense, not Gabriel, although the Rams really haven't ever given Roman much to run with.

The Rams don't seem to play well in cold weather. Los Angeles lost a 1967 title game in below-zero weather at Milwaukee, and much of the abuse fell upon Gabriel—the warm weather quarterback.

When Gabriel came to the Rams from North Carolina State in 1962 he was shy, introverted and farsighted. He and his wife even named their son Ram. One might have thought Roman was brought up by a wolf near the Tiber, but he is part Filipino.

Roman got off to a slow start with the Rams because he threw the ball too slowly and because he lacked confidence. He was an easy-going, gregarious sort until a drunken driving incident, which Gabriel says made him grow up. He got serious, went on the wagon, and his quarterbacking improved.

For several seasons early in Gabriel's career, the Ram quarterback situation was complicated by the presence of a second young quarterback, Bill Munson. Both Munson and Gabriel were looking good and the coaching staff and players were divided over who should start. A coach is miserable without a starting quarterback; it's as if his hands are tied. Before the Gabriel/Munson situation was settled, one coach, Harland Svare, was fired for making the alleged wrong choice (Munson), and when new Coach George Allen chose Gabriel as his starter, Munson went on strike, played out his contract option, and demanded to be traded. He was, at last, to the Detroit Lions.

A quarterback who thinks he is good enough to start sits on the bench in agony. What makes the situation even worse, a coach can't count on his number two quarterback improving while observing from the bench. When No. 2 gets into a game, the problems of moving the ball multiply because his style is strange to the rest of the team. The rest of the team is equally strange to the No. 2 quarterback, who has been working in practice with, and getting used to, the second-string runners, blockers, and, especially, receivers. If a backup quarterback is used to the "moves" of backup receivers and is thrown into a game throwing to the unfamiliar first-stringer, he will be even less comfortable and confident. 'Tis a rare coach who uses his second-stringers to make his No. 2 quarterback feel more "at home."

"If you have two fullbacks you can use them both," says George Allen. "If you have five good receivers, you can use them all. If you have two good quarterbacks there is no good way to use more than one."

Oakland's Boss Al Davis explained the situation in typical fashion.

"I think it goes deeper than that," Davis said. "This involves a theme in our whole society. No one will tolerate being held back anymore. The number two quarterback wants to be number one, the Negro wants his rights, the Red Guard wants to change China. But for an organization to operate effectively there must be control. There must be a sort of dictatorship, but a dictatorship with reason."

There are two schools of thought on the bringing up of a rookie—sending him to a minor league team so he can learn under fire, playing in real games, or keep him on the bench or taxi squad. (The taxi squad is a group of inexperienced young players who aren't good enough to make the team but are considered worth keeping around for the future. They work out with the team and are paid around $200 per week while they try to gain poise and polish.)

Sending a young player to a badly run farm team doesn't help anyone. When the Redskins farmed Harry Theofiledes out to the minors, his experience was an unhappy one. Harry said he was wasting precious time, that the coaching was inferior and that he wasn't learning anything. He wanted to stay with the Redskin taxi squad where he could watch the Sunday games from up in the booth with the assistant coaches, charting plays and watching opposing defenses in action.

"I was always checking to see what would have happened to the play I would have called if I were playing," said Harry. "In practice Jurgensen helped me a lot, especially with faking and learning to hide the ball."

Generally speaking, the quarterbacks on a team are pretty good friends. The regular tries to be helpful to the substitutes, which makes it harder and harder for them to wish disaster befall No. 1. With each ill wish a No. 2 feels more guilty. But there is a big difference between No. 1's relationship with a young taxi-squad quarterback compared to one with a hustling eager beaver who is on the regular team and experienced enough to be pushing for the starting job. It's much easier for No. 1 to practice charity and patience with a know-nothing rookie.

Several years ago Cleveland had three quarterbacks on the regular team roster: Frank Ryan was number one and Dick Shiner and Gary Lane fought for the number two spot.

"When I was playing behind Ryan he would never volunteer any information," said Gary Lane who was traded to the Giants in his third season. "It was a selfish thing for him to do. I was looking great in practice and he was getting old. I guess he figured I was going to take his job if he got hurt.

"Every time Frank gets hit you wonder whether he will get up," said Dick Shiner, who wouldn't be human if he hadn't hoped Ryan stayed down, at least once in a while. It wouldn't have been good quarterback thinking. Shiner was traded to Pittsburgh in 1968. Now he is number two for the Steelers.

"You don't get the chance to look at game films of the opponent very much," said Shiner. "Frank usually took them home to study, or the coaches were using them."

Substitutes work under a tremendous psychological disadvantage. They must go through the practice routines, working all week on game plans and movies preparing for a game which they probably won't get to play in. It is difficult for any player to be at an emotional peak for twenty-two weeks of football and fourteen no-second-chance Sunday games (baseball has 162 games, where one loss is less than one tenth as important). It is most difficult for the starting quarterback, but for No. 2 it's impossible.

"Really tough," said Gary Lane. "You can't have a lackadaisical attitude. You've got to go through the process of getting ready each week knowing the chance to play probably won't come, but just might."

Daryle Lamonica was a basket case when he was No. 2 at Buffalo. "I'm not a phone guy," he said. "I can't sit on the sidelines and keep the charts and get stuck on the phones. I'm a pacer. I like to get right up close and see what the defense is doing."

Lamonica's system for getting "up" was to lie to himself and keep hoping he'd get a chance. "In my mind, I had to go into every game thinking I was number one," he said. "It's tough to prepare for a game mentally. I'd try different gimmicks and gadgets to psych myself up. I'd make up my own game plan and call plays and see how they'd compare. The only good thing about it, if I made a mistake it was only a mental mistake!"

A reserve quarterback should have a unique temperament. Perhaps it's a coincidence but three Super Bowl teams—the Jets, Green Bay and Oakland—had super backup quarterbacks who were old enough to like it like that. The Jets' Babe Parilli was 38, Green Bay's now-retired Zeke Bratkowski was 35 and 36, and Oakland's George Blanda was 41. These three are special. Other reserve quarterbacks aren't mentally and emotionally suited for the job and they don't have the experience. Angry young men like Munson and Lamonica bench-sat as quantities very much unknown compared to the "Brat," now a Packer coach, Parilli, who coaches at spring practice at University of Washington, and Blanda, a well-to-do citizen about Chicago. The two-quarterback situation in Oakland now with Blanda backing up Lamonica is ideal.

"We have the perfect relationship," says Blanda. "He wants to play and I don't."

Some of the wackiest stories have to do with No. 2 quarterbacks whose deeply rooted frustrations turn them into eccentrics. So many of them are treated callously, shunted from team to team to team, and rarely emerge as regulars.

Once, during a game against St. Louis, George Izo, a Washington reserve quarterback, sat on the bench and wrote a letter home. Izo, Earl Morrall and Dich Shiner are all examples of journeymen quarterbacks but the all-time champion at not playing quarterback, career-wise, was one Terry Nofsinger, a journeyman quarterback's journeyman quarterback.

At Pittsburgh once, in the twelfth game of the season, volatile Steeler Coach Buddy Parker told Nofsinger, "Go in."

"Can't," said Nofsinger.

"What's wrong?"

"Pulled muscle. I can't run." He hadn't bothered to tell the coach about the muscle before the game.

Nofsinger's was not the guts approach to bench-sitting. About the quarterback job, he wanted it less, or seemed to. Anyhow, Terry left the Steelers subsequently. He went to St. Louis and then to Atlanta. Nofsinger was not a starting quarterback in high school, nor in college and he was never a regular in the pros.

"The hardest thing about learning quarterback is defense," said Harry Theofiledes. "We see the movies of the other teams. I watch the different defenses, but recognizing them on the field—that's the hardest thing of all."

Of course after he recognizes them Harry is supposed to decide instantly if he thinks the play he called in the huddle will still work. If the defense has guessed the QB's play correctly he must call an "audible"—he cancels the old instructions and yells new signals at the line of scrimmage, loud enough for all his team to hear. It's important that the two wide ends, who are fifteen yards out to either side, hear the new instructions.

"Suppose I see the linebackers real close, taking little steps like they're moving up to blitz," explained Harry. "I might call an audible and throw a little bloop over the linemen and blitzers." Learning about the little bloops is what takes up to five years. After that you're either a QB or back home with a real job.

Many coaches, like Paul Brown and Harland Svare and Tom Landry, aren't crazy about their quarterbacks calling their own signals at the last minute. There are grounds for thinking they weren't always too crazy about their quarterbacks either, but that's another story.

Harland Svare had an idea that audibles were overrated, as did Paul Brown when Milt Plum and Otto Graham were his quarterbacks at Cleveland. Svare felt his game plan should be followed because it was devised calmly, away from all the excitement of the game.

"Then, in the game itself, the game plan is discarded," said Harland, "just because the quarterback sees a linebacker take two steps. Does it really make sense to change all your plans just because a linebacker takes two steps? If we think that, by studying game films, we've spotted a flaw in somebody's defense, that weakness is going to be there whether the linebacker takes two steps or not." Svare is a Washington assistant now, but is sure to be a head coach again one of these Januarys (hiring/firing is done in January). It will be something to look for, whether he still feels that sticking with the game plan is the best bet. Svare's game plans were probably ten times longer and more complicated than most because of all the coaches he is one of the most serious students of game films. Svare deserves an Oscar for watching, in some weeks, the equivalent of thirty feature-length movies.

Paul Brown thought his brain was better equipped for running the team than his quarterback's and sent in each play by alternating "messenger" guards. On the side of this argument is the fact that the quarterback is able to make full use of his spotters, who have the best view of the defense and can continually telephone fresh information and instructions down to the field.

However, when a quarterback can't call his own signals he gets an inferiority complex, rebels against the coach, loses his leadership, and the road starts downhill. A winning team must have a quarterback who takes charge. Bobby Layne took charge at the Steelers and the Lions and later as a quarterback coach at St. Louis. Layne was known as the drinking man's quarterback and claimed he played better with a hangover. When he retired several years ago Bobby was the last quarterback who refused to wear a face mask. He was a tough Texan, blond and beautiful, and the best take-charge quarterback of them all. Even the mature addition of a pot belly didn't detract from Layne's intimidating style.

Unlike Harland Svare, Layne loved audibles. "That's the whole quarterback business today, recognize the defense or you're dead," said Layne. "Defenses, crazy damned defenses are catching up! The only answer is audibles, changing a play at the line."

It may be that Layne's theories are a little old-fashioned in today's era of complicated defenses. Checking off the planned play at the line of scrimmage isn't as necessary as it once was.

"When the defenses keep moving audibles aren't as important," said Baltimore's retired Center Dick Szymanski. "Unitas used to know the defense was anticipating what we were going to do and call another play, but now that they're moving he can't tell what the defense is trying to do to him until he has already pivoted, or is in the pocket. That's when his reactions are just fantastic. So quick."

If audibles go out of style no one will be happier than the young quarterbacks who can't recognize defenses anyway, either at the line before the snap, or later in the pocket. When an inexperienced young quarterback used to go to the line and look over the defense, it was a battle of wits, his against the linebacker calling defensive signals—a guessing game that went on, and on, until the whistle blew and the offense was penalized for taking too much time.

Don Meredith, the Dallas Cowboys' quarterback, tells a story about calling a play, but finding Washington Middle Linebacker Sam Huff calling the perfect defense to stop it. So Meredith called an audible, but so did Sam, guessing perfectly. And so a frustrated Meredith called another audible, and so did Sam—and finally, Meredith called a time-out.

Don Meredith is a one-of-a-kind quarterback who is nicknamed Dandy. He sings in the huddle, wears foam-rubber “falsies” stuffed in his pants legs to make the skinniest legs in football look fatter, and was married, divorced, remarried and redivorced from his college sweetheart. “She was Miss Everything and I was Mr. Everybody.” Meredith is a complex nut, but he plays with courage and bravado through multiple painful injuries. His teammates think Dandy is the greatest and respect him accordingly. If they want Meredith to lead them, so be it, as they are in the best position to judge, but even with everything going for him Dandy has certainly pulled some dandies—the kind that make quarterbacks unemployed.

Meredith has a blind spot which prevents him from seeing that the yard touchdown pass isn’t the greatest invention since the wheel. In the last minute of the Cowboys’ first title game against Green Bay Dandy called a pass on second down from the one, but his tackle, Jim Boeke, jumped offside, and the penalty blew a possible overtime victory. “I threw against the Packers because you have to put a little intrigue into it,” Meredith “explained.” Say this much for Dandy; he doesn’t learn from his mistakes. He’s still throwing passes near the goal line. He’s unpredictable, entertaining and seemingly happy-go-lucky, but underneath there’s a streak of pure common sense. Shucks, Dandy still knows what happened to that first drop of “awl” he got when he signed up in 1960, and no matter what plaintive country ditty he’s singin’, or what corny color combination he’s wearin’, or how horribly he’s playin’ football, Meredith still presents the exterior of a fellow going straight. He’s the boss, full of confidence.

Once, so beside himself with anger after being dumped with the ball, Don called one of his blockers “a yellow dog” for having missed a defensive end, and ordered him off the field. “You didn’t try to hit him,” Meredith screamed. Subsequently Meredith went to Landry and offered to pay the man’s salary for the year just to be rid of him; he’d use some “awl” money.

“It’s true,” said Al Ward of the Cowboys’ front office. “The player, whose name I won’t mention, had a no-cut contract, but he’s not with us any more. Don’s a hip guy. He kids around a lot, but on the field he’s all business. He’d had a tough time. He was getting beat up by pass-rushers regularly. He had a right to scream.”

The Washington Redskins seem to have a hex on the Cowboys and beat them up regularly, which is curious because Dallas is usually favored over the Redskins. Meredith is like the little girl with the curl, and he was horrid against Washington on the same afternoon that the daughter of Cowboy President Tex Schramm was married. Meredith saw Schramm the next morning and asked how the wedding was. "Fine," said Schramm. "I'll bet you're glad she didn't marry me," said Meredith.

From the beginning with the Cowboys, Dandy was overconfident, lazy, and spoiled—anything but dandy. Meredith didn't dig his coach, Tom Landry, or Landry's system. For five years they did subtle battle until, finally, Meredith gave in. With their opposite personalities it was possible that Landry and Meredith might meld into a team like Lombardi and Starr, complementing each other—it's still possible, not probable.

"I came into pro ball a highly touted college quarterback," Meredith said. "I was a bonus baby. I wanted to fall back and rely on things I'd done well in college. But I couldn't do them in pro ball. That first year I didn't play much. Instead of trying to learn, I fought it. I became lax in things. I cut off my nose to spite my face."

His features are intact, although there was a time when people doubted Meredith would ever live long enough to learn Tom Landry's complex offense. The Dallas blocking was as awful as Meredith's quarterbacking.

Meredith was a leading candidate to take over the crown of Bobby Layne, who long reigned as the game's blithe spirit. We'll miss him.

"Meredith has this charisma about him," said Ram Tackle Merlin Olsen. "He's like Layne . . . a great player and leader and an exciting person to be around. A quarterback should be like that."

There are few quarterbacks with the potential to grow up into Bobby Laynes. Several seasons back when quarterback tutors were the In thing, the funniest combination was at St. Louis where Layne worked on incumbent Charley Johnson. Bobby was trying to develop Johnson, one of those serious students of the game, into a hell-for-leather chip off the old block. At the time Johnson was using his 140 IQ to write his Ph.D. thesis on some liquid aspects of chemical engineering. In his heyday Layne and his pals could have served as a portable laboratory for Charley's experiments. Layne always led a rat pack. Johnson is a dreamer. "In dreams the play always works," says Charley, "but never in postgame dreams."

"Charley's a leader in his quiet way. He has their respect," said Layne. "I want him to drop back quicker. The quicker you get back the more time you have to throw. Sometimes I wish I could take him out for a few belts."

"He's a pusher," said Charley. "He'd con guys into something they might not normally do. But that's his personality. It's not mine."—which is too bad.

Discounting Meredith there are only three candidates able to take over Layne's honors as drinking man's quarterback—Karl Sweetan at Los Angeles, Joe Namath, and Vikings' Joe Kapp.

Sweetan qualifies with three off-the-field misadventures—two in bars and one knocking down a girlfriend's door. On the field he is a battler, yelling and emotional.

Sweetan spent several years being seasoned in the "minor" minors, the school of hard knocks, where because the blocking isn't the best the quarterback learns to throw fast.

"He throws the ball quicker than anyone," says Deacon Jones, the Rams' great defensive end. "We hit him once and he had no right to even get up, but he did and then he stuck his tongue out at me." Sweetan's problem is helmsmanship, not a lack of courage.

So far Sweetan hasn't shown the class of Bobby Layne, who could really hold his liquor. Layne was once arrested for drunken driving in Detroit and was arraigned. He might have been behind bars (not the ones on his helmet, nor the ones he'd been leaning on) for the next game because the arresting officer said Layne was drunk and his speech incomprehensible. "That's because I'm from Texas, your honor," drawled Layne. He got off. If Sweetan ever expected to become another Bobby Layne, he would have to be a better drinker besides a better passer. The trouble with Karl and that other potential, Joe Namath, is they have thimble bellies. They haven't the capacity to grow up into drinking man's quarterbacks. All the ruckus over Joe Namath's retirement, when he was told that his Bachelors III bar was full of bad apples. could have been avoided if Joe had made his decision to retire on a day when he wasn't going to so many parties.

Namath and Layne had so much in common—loving night life and good times. Both can throw quickly and take a beating. They are tough, good-humored, and smart, though Namath won't ever be as extroverted as Bobby. Layne couldn't throw half as well as Namath but he was mentally the tougher, always uncompromising. He inspired winning. Namath didn't always, until 1968, but perhaps before then he was too young. Still, a little old-fashioned "Layne" influence wouldn't have hurt Namath and might have helped shape up Broadway Joe and some of the modder Jets into tougher specimens. Bobby Layne would have made an admirable helpmate for Joe not only on the field but on Broadway besides.

Sometimes Namath sounds like Layne talking. "No fault of mine?" Joe shouted after a loss. "I'm the quarterback. You kiddin' me? We didn't get enough points on the board. That's my job, man. I'm the quarterback."

Cut from less colorful, but sturdier, cloth than Namath is Viking Quarterback Joe Kapp, a fugitive from Canadian football at the ripe age of thirty. "I play aggressively and hope it becomes contagious," says Kapp, a formidable competitor reminiscent of Bobby Layne's no-facemask school. Kapp is the eternal pragmatist. He can't be bothered how the ball is snapped from center and couldn't care less where the laces are.

"All quarterbacks want to get the ball the same way, with the laces up," says Oakland Center Jim Otto, who obviously never snapped the ball to Joe Kapp. "I have to put the ball down so that when I snap it the ball comes up to the quarterback with the laces up, so he doesn't have to turn the ball to pass it."

Kapp also pays little attention to the elements. Once after a game on a very gusty afternoon, Kapp dismissed the wind factor: "Wind or not, my job is throwing." And he just plain throws—flutterballs, spirals, lobs —like Layne, whose passes used to do a frug on their way to the receiver. It was in a Yukon brawl in a typical Bobby Layne home-away-from-home that a broken beer bottle decorated Kapp's complexion with a long scar, which cuts down his right cheek and meanders dangerously under his chin. Kapp's face looks lived-in.

Kapp, who drives a '39 LaSalle, is an exceptional leader. "Tarkenton talked you into playing," said one Viking. "Kapp says he is going to do something and then he goes ahead and does it." Joe expects the same from his teammates and has been seen grabbing a blocker by the face mask and cussing him out at the sideline.

After one loss, Kapp and Linebacker Lonnie Warwick, a mad cut-up, got into a fight at the post-game party. Kapp said the loss was his fault, Warwick said he was to blame, and both went outside into the snow. It took them twenty minutes to come to no-contest and Kapp came inside with a black eye, hardly his first. Black eyes and broken bones are everyday happenings in the world of Kapp. In a title game at Baltimore, Kapp took a terrific beating and on one play was practically planted in the muddy going. A Colt offered his hand, which Kapp ignored.

"Why should I have taken his hand?" asked Kapp. "The Colts are not nice people. Hey, neither are we for that matter. That's the game."

The Clock

Late in a game against Kansas City, Buffalo moved into the lead. "Now all we have to do is eat up the clock," said Joanne Kemp, who is married to the Buffalo quarterback, and who was watching the game on television. Her daughter Jennifer, age three, couldn't believe her ears. "Mommy," she said, "we can't eat up our clock."

The single reason Vince Lombardi loved having his Packers play ball control is simply this—when the Packer offense was on the field, the opponent's offense wasn't, and so could not score.

The Packer theory was based on horsepower—simple running plays and short passes—which tired out the opposing defenses. Lombardi drove the

Packers to such training heights that they didn't tire out as quickly as their foes. Green Bay steadily ground out the yardage until they ran out of field and scored. Grind-it-out football eats up the clock; the key to Lombardi's ball control was *using time*.

In football, no one cares what time it is, but everyone cares how much time is left. There are three things which make up a QB's mind what play to call—the score, where the ball is, and the time. How the quarterback uses the clock (or how the defense prevents him from using it) separates the winners from the rest of the pack, especially in close games.

There are sixty minutes of playing time in a game, two independent thirty minute halfs. Each half is divided into fifteen-minute quarters, with two minutes between each quarter to give the teams time to switch goals. Goals are switched to equalize the conditions for the teams. Possible variations between the halves of the field are puddles, and wind. The clock is stopped for fifteen minutes between halves, when the ball goes out of bounds, after incomplete forward passes and when a team or an official calls a time out.

Each team is allowed to call three timeouts (one and a half minutes each) during each half. The officials call timeouts for measurements and for meting out penalties—and if all these don't add up to enough time for TV commercials, the officials call timeout for these.

Games usually take a little more than 2½ hours. Passing games take much longer to complete than running games because the clock is stopped after incomplete passes. A passing down takes from five to ten seconds; the average running play takes less than five seconds, but the clock keeps running between downs and from one center snap to the next takes about half a minute. Outlandish as it might seem, a football game in which both quarterbacks threw passes on every play could take ten or twelve hours to complete.

By playing ball control, a team gives its defense a chance to rest. Imagine a game between Green Bay and Dallas where the Packers use seven minutes to grind out a TD every time they got the ball and the Cowboys score a bomb to their speedball End Bob Hayes on first down every time they get the ball. The first half, which usually takes an hour, would arrive thirty minutes after the opening kickoff, the halftime score would be 28–28, but the Packer offense and the Dallas defense would have to be carried off the field on twenty-two stretchers.

Arizona once played a third quarter which lasted almost an hour and included 150 yards of penalties. One late season a friend of mine, a neophyte fan, heard the two-minute warning (two minutes left to play) at a Giant game and twenty-five minutes later she was still in her seat, still freezing to death. It isn't at all unusual for the last two minutes to last fifteen minutes; actually, in a close game, it is de rigueur.

In the last two minutes, NFL rules change a little and say the clock does not start until the ball is touched (on a kickoff), and stops when the ball changes hands (after an interception or fumble). It's therefore possible for the ball to be kicked off, received, fumbled, recovered, and for the kicking team to score a touchdown in less than ten seconds.

If both team's time-outs were used in the last two minutes, they would take care of nine minutes without a minute of actual playing time. In the famous Jets-at-Oakland game in 1968 an NBC special, "Heidi," interrupted the game broadcast after three hours and the last ninety seconds lasted twelve minutes longer. With ninety seconds to go Oakland was leading, but the Jets scored and won the game. The outburst from fans caused the NBC switchboard in New York City to explode. Any uninitiated chef who begins cooking minute steaks before the end of a game had best prefer beef very well done. The closer the score, the more well done the steak.

If you break the game down, live action takes only twelve to fifteen minutes out of the sixty, and these few minutes are divided among offense, defense, and special teams. It's hard to understand why players are so worn out after a game when they've only been in action for five or ten minutes.

An official timekeeper keeps time in the NFL, but the scoreboard clock is official in the AFL. NFL scoreboard clocks are rarely exact, which causes confusion for fans, coaches, players, TV announcers, and officials too. Especially confused are the fans, who can't be sure when it's time to rush out and tear down the goalposts.

The most contemporary contribution of the clock is the "two-minute offense." Such an offense is a bombing attack, a series of quick, prearranged plays designed to beat the clock at the end of a half. The defense knows the offense is going to throw on every play, and it's usually a matter of who runs out first, the clock or the quarterback.

The most tempestuous stars of the silver screen never got as flustered as pro quarterbacks in the last minute of a game with no time-outs remaining. With no time for huddling, the quarterback begins yelling plays as his team pulls into formation. He plans to throw incomplete and out of bounds to gain free time, but instead haste makes waste and he often gets called for illegal procedure, or offside. When the official takes his own sweet time to blow the timeout whistle, he wastes five or ten seconds of the quarterback's time.

During a two-minute blitzkrieg, a smart two-minute quarterback naturally throws short out passes, and to save time the receiver jumps out of bounds after he makes the catch. When this happens the receiver isn't chicken, as fans are wont to observe. He is following orders. Ends must be as clock-conscious as quarterbacks. By remaining in bounds when only seconds remain, a receiver can waste a down and lose a close game, regardless of his quarterback's best-laid plans.

"I had six seconds to run a helluva long pass pattern," said Jackie Smith, the Cardinal tight end, after losing a close one. "We had nine seconds left, and I should have headed out of bounds after the catch, but I didn't think there was any time left. When I looked up and saw three seconds left—well, it hurt, I tell you."

When one play might mean the difference between a win or a loss, the outcome of a game can depend on a single timeout—one last chance. San Diego's Linebacker Chuck Allen once showed the sterner stuff that football players should be made of when he broke his ankle playing against the Jets. Chuck managed to hop off the field on one leg, under his own power and in great pain, to save the Chargers a timeout.

Time-outs can take too long for television. When Buffalo played the Jets in Shea Stadium in 1967, Fullback Jack Spikes was trying to block a punt and ended up lying unconscious in convulsions, having swallowed his tongue. As Spikes was saved from strangulation by the team doctors (they have a special instrument which can force the clenched teeth apart and free the player's tongue, but which also often costs a tooth or two in the jaw-unclenching process), and then removed from the field on a special mattressed stretcher which is used only for the severest cases, writers in the press box could hear the NBC production unit urging their man on the field to "hurry things up." Spikes recovered in several days, and couldn't remember anything about the disastrous play.

Dramatically speaking, much of what's enacted on and off Broadway can't compare with some of the methods used to fake injuries when a team has run out of time-outs. The Cowboys have a defensive tackle called Willie "Babycakes" Townes who once was "injured" on what would have been the last play of a game against the Eagles. Willie lay writhing on the field and the Cowboy Trainer Larry Gardner ran out.

"Larry told me, 'Just keep your eyes closed and don't get up,' so I didn't move a muscle."

Finally Willie was helped off the field by Gardner and they watched the last play of the game. And Willie ran off to the locker room.

5 Offensive Line

Several years ago two young ladies were escorted to a party in New York by two professional football players-about-town. The girls heard the two players discussing the success of their "lines," and, knowing a little about football the girls assumed they played for teams with good offensive lines . . . which shows a little knowledge can be a dangerous thing. There are all kinds of lines.

At least seven offensive players must stand on the line of scrimmage; that is the legal minimum. The seven are named by their location—two

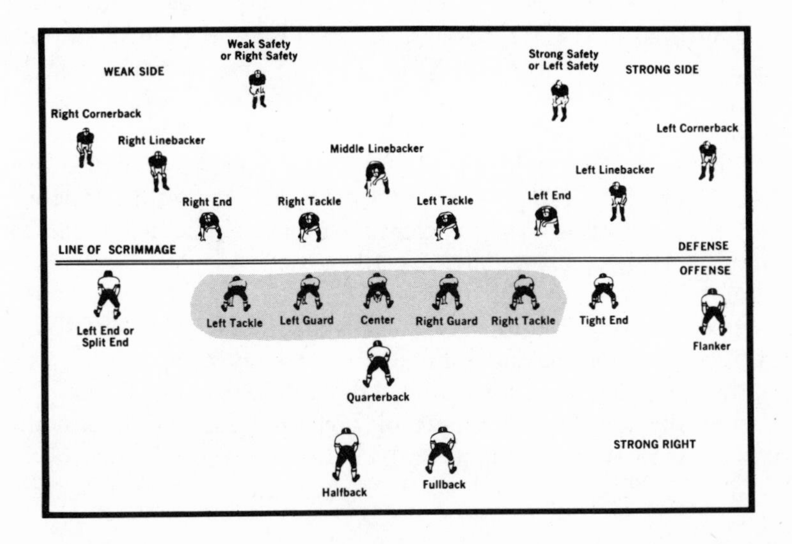

The line of scrimmage—Giants vs. *Cardinals.*

ends and five interior linemen. The interior linemen—one center, two guards and two offensive tackles—are called collectively the *offensive line.* If you ever see a quarterback throw a pass to a lineman—linemen wear jerseys numbered in the 50s, 60s and 70s—you'll know he made a mistake. Linemen are ineligible receivers. Only the two ends may catch passes.

No team is ever better than its line. A quarterback looks at his line as a wall of guardian angels fending off the defensive devils until he has time to throw. A flashy halfback like Chicago's Gale Sayers depends upon his line to act like a catapult into the open, and a possible touchdown. A big fullback like Boston's Jim Nance expects his linemen to act like a motorcycle escort in heavy defensive traffic.

Without blocking by the offensive linemen there wouldn't be any running. You wouldn't hear very much about famous runners like Gale Sayers, Emerson Boozer, and John Roland. Jimmy Brown wouldn't be a movie star and Paul Hornung, Green Bay's "Golden Boy," would probably be in the insurance business in Louisville instead of announcing sports on TV in such chic spots as New Orleans and Miami.

Because the running and passing depends on them, and because scoring depends on running and passing, it is unfair that the most unsung and unheralded players on any team are the offensive linemen. They are like five Cinderellas who do the dirty work, while the ends and back are like Cinderella's sisters. The sisters get to have the ball, go out, score points, and get the glory.

It's especially unfair that all the other positions have come into style, at least for a season or two, while the offensive linemen have thus far been mostly undiscovered—disputing the adage that every dog has its day; the dogs in the line haven't yet. Football fandom has occasionally divided its attention to the extent that *defensive* linemen have made infrequent forays into the limelight, but the fact that the defensive line became celebrated before the offensive line is loathsome. All linemen have brawn; offensive linemen need brains.

The Minnesota Viking All-NFL Center Mick Tingelhoff insists that blocking is a science. "The way the game is played now, there isn't any place for stupid linemen." And at Denver, the Broncos have a young lineman from Notre Dame, Pete Duranko. When someone asked him which position he would like to play he said, "Defensive line. On offense you've got to be good."

A good offensive line performs with supersubtlety and uses plenty of finesse. While a defensive line acts like a combination of ape and elephant, the offensive linemen are more the tempting type, like the cat family.

"It's not all strength any more," says Baltimore's Dick Szymanski. "If it was, your strongest guys would be playing. It's part strength, sure, but it's also quickness, finesse and intelligence. It's like chess."

After victories, Vince Lombardi usually shrugs, "Football is a game of execution—blocking and tackling." The offensive linemen do three quarters of their team's blocking.

Blocking is tackling without using hands. Offensive players are not allowed to use their hands because of football's underlying premise: offense *acts*, defense *reacts*. In the guard's duel with the defensive tackle, for example, the guard knows where his initial charge will take him, knows that he will try to push the defensive tackle in one direction or another. The defensive tackle knows nothing. He tries to be prepared for every possible move the guard might make—then he reacts.

To make up for the offense's advantage of knowing the upcoming play ahead of time the defensive players are given extra freedom—unlimited use of their hands and arms. The defense goes about its job with almost a free rein while an offensive player toils under the hands-off restriction, required to keep his hands in close to his body. A football offense disputes an old saying—to be forewarned is to be *unarmed*.

A blocker sets his feet wide apart to make a broad base and, basically, he pushes. Straight ahead blocking for a running back requires the blocker to stay low, for better balance. He moves forward, always trying to keep himself between the defender and the runner with the ball. He pushes the defender (probably a tackle) away from the path he already knows the running back plans to take, trying to keep the defender from slipping off the block. The blocker always aims for the defensive man's middle, his chest. You can fake a move with your eyes, head, and knees, but you can't fake with your chest. Whither it goest, thou goest.

A blocker uses his head in two ways. Suppose an offensive tackle blocks with the ball-carrier planning to run to the tackle's left. The tackle keeps his head to the left of his defensive man's head so that even if the defender slipped away he would have to go the long way around the tackle—and by that time the runner would be gone.

Blocking wide, as on a sweep, the guards must pull out of position and get going even before the running back gets the ball. They lead the ball carrier around the traffic.

"Ideally you have your man picked out," says Viking Guard Larry Bowie. "But you can't forget a basic rule in any football play—never pass up a different-colored jersey." (Ideally the second lineman picks up any defender who filters through the blocking line; the lineman, probably a guard, who pulls out first usually takes his primary target.)

Pass blocking is a different story, negative and passive. Pass blockers drop back a few steps at the snap and form a "screen" trying to prevent any defensive linemen from getting around or through them to the passer. Everyone knows what stands behind every great man but it's just the opposite with every great quarterback—his line stands in front.

A quarterback needs *time* to throw—time to go back seven yards, set up and look for his receivers, and his receivers need time to get down the field. Sonny Jurgensen is supposed to throw as fast as any quarterback and his arm has the power to throw for distance, but even if Jurgensen's ready in two seconds his receivers might not be. So he waits. If his linemen don't give him enough protection he ends up waiting flat on his back.

Pass blockers can't just slow down the charging defensive linemen; they have to stop them, and absorbing the rush of a charging line can be a painful proposition. The defenders have tricky moves and fakes—they use an elbow, pull at jerseys, yank at heads, and slam at helmets. The pass rusher charges forward, freely, naturally on the attack. The offensive lineman *unnaturally* has to run backward, trying to maintain good balance, and is further frustrated by the rule against using hands. Through it all, the guards and tackles take the abuse, wish they were bigger, and swear to themselves about their quarterback, and is he ever going to throw the damn ball.

On third down with ten yards to go, the classic idea of the protecting pocket doesn't happen. The rushers know *pass* and they charge without the tiniest hesitation. "When the defense knows you are going to pass it's impossible to block," says Jon Morris, Boston's center, "because there's just no time to set up." Which can often be harder on the quarterback than his linemen, unless they're very good.

The Baltimore line, which has been charged with protecting John Unitas for lo these many seasons, is very good. When Baltimore began running more and passing less, in 1968, Colt offensive linemen were most jubilant.

"When the defense knows you're going to drop back to protect the passer all the time things get turned around," said Tackle Sam Ball. "We become the defense and the pass rusher gets to make the first move. But with more running we could go aggressive, the way an offensive lineman should go. We could step forward, or back, or both. We could really play football."

The Center

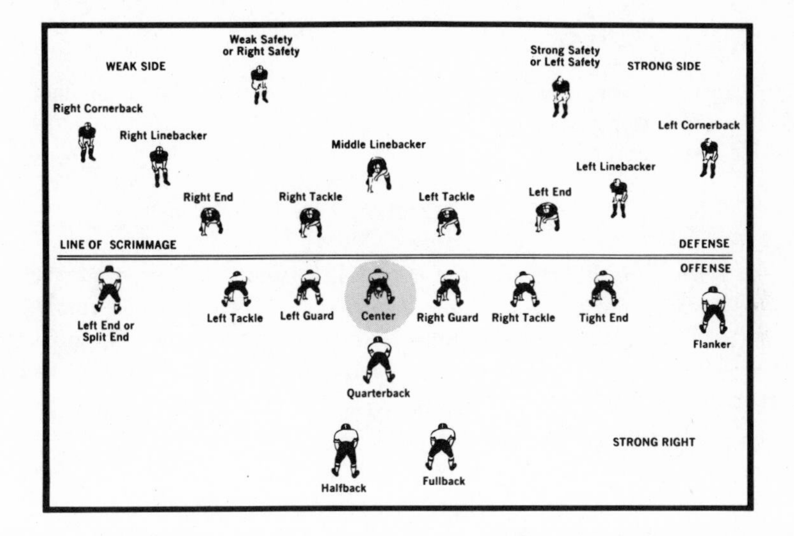

Two zoologists were at their wits' end trying to describe how an African mongoose prepares its favorite dinner of hard-shelled bugs (millipedes), by hurling one backward between its legs against a hard surface with such force that the bug is smashed. The only way the scientists could finally explain mongoose behavior was by comparing the mongoose and the football center. Imagine! No other natural phenomenon could compare.

Each offensive team has two ends, two guards, two tackles, and four backs. There is only one center. Because he starts every play, by snapping the ball, there is some basis for arguing that the center is the most important player on the offensive team. If he doesn't get the ball to the quarterback it doesn't matter a whit what the other ten players do.

The center is like a silent butler. You have to look a long time to find someone who ever knew one personally and only some kind of a nut would dig his scene. But centers are fascinating creatures who suffer almost constant traumas of inadequacy; after all, you can only recognize one by his fanny.

On a normal snap the center's spinal curve makes him look like a swaybacked camel. He keeps his head up (to look ahead to see where he's going next) and his seat up (to make it easiest for the quarterback to get the ball). Imagine a grown man making his living by handing a ball between his legs to another chap leaning over his backside. He really is the funniest fellow in football. Why must he be forced into the awkward situation of having to get the ball back to the quarterback and in the same instant fire quickly up and out like a lineman? Why can't one of the officials who is just standing around hand the ball to the quarterback? Why can't the quarterback just hold it himself while he calls the signals? The center proved an irresistible topic to one formidable football fan, Norman Mailer.

> There is no bad taste equal to commenting on the sexual themes of a national sport but psychology is granted its medical dispensations, and so I will dare the attempt.
>
> —Norman Mailer,
> *Advertisements for Myself*

Mailer wrote an advertisement for the T formation. The *single wing* is an old-fashioned formation where the quarterback stands several yards behind the line and the center snaps the ball the way he does now only for punts. In the T formation, the quarterback's right hand is pressed into the center's rump and his left hand is below, forming a basket to catch the ball safely. Norman says:

> In the Single Wing the ball is passed from the center to the backfield . . . it travels in open air from three to ten feet. In the T, the quarterback crept up behind the center, indeed he moved directly behind him.
>
> The ball instead of being passed was handed back between the legs . . . one's argument must remain that the T formation is more Hip than the Single Wing because it is closer to the sexual needs of a team.

"Well, that's an interesting idea," said Mike Pyle, center for the Chicago Bears. Mike was graduated from Yale in 1961, which makes him immediately unusual; you can count the Ivy Leaguers playing pro football on two hands and have fingers left over. Mike is an ex-president of the NFL Players' Association, has his own radio show, golfs in the summer and

The silent butler, Giant Center Greg Larson, about to serve the ball to Quarterback Fran Tarkenton.

ny
10

skis in the winter. Before he was married, Mike always made the Most Eligible Bachelor lists in the Chicago newspapers. The fact that a center could make a list of most eligible anything, anywhere, shows how far offensive linemen have progressed up the peck order.

"I'm going to have to buy that book of Norman Mailer's," said Mike. "I want to read it."

The center's job begins in the huddle where the players encircle him *in particular order*. The center and the two wide ends leave the huddle first—the wide ends because they need more time to reach their stations and the center because the rest of the team uses him as a pivot point to line up around. "Now, of course football was always oriented around the ass," says Norman Mailer.

As the center goes to the ball he will often look over the defense and yell a signal to the other linemen, to tell them whether their blocks have been set up correctly or if there should be a switch, almost like a quarterback calling an audible.

"That's why we like a long count," said Los Angeles Offensive Tackle Charlie Cowan. "We have signals between the linemen, and between the linemen and backs, too."

The center, crouched there in the middle of the line, is hard to find—until you find his towel. Most centers wear a dirty towel (the Jet Center John Schmitt wears a green towel) stuck in the back of his pants for the quarterback to wipe his hands on, which the quarterback does—especially in hot weather or when the quarterback is high-strung and nervous. The better the line blocking, the dryer the towel. The towel makes the center a kind of team maid, besides his being a silent butler.

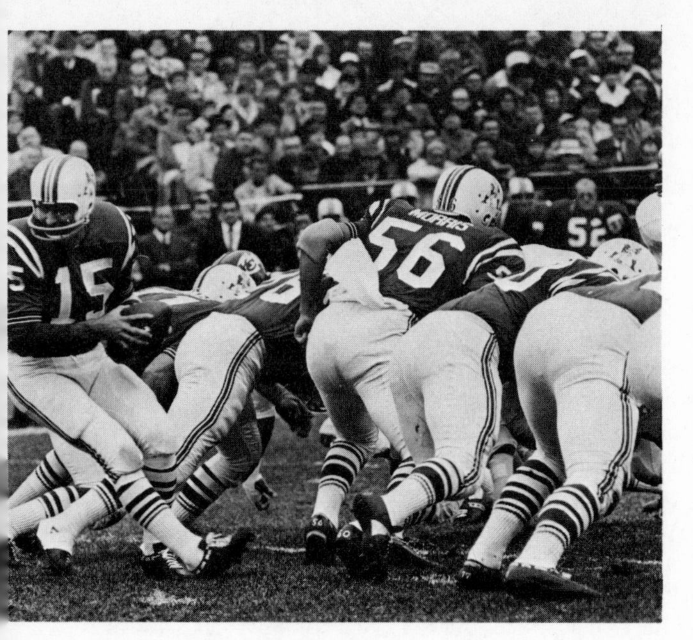

"No one wants to be bothered wearing the towel," says Boston Center Jon Morris.
(Dick Raphael)

If you watch the center's towel, you can't help but see the ball put into play. The towel is a bib effect and flaps there in the turmoil like the American flag at the attack on Fort McHenry. Miraculously it never seems to fall out of place. It's incredible that out of eleven players the center is the one who wears the towel. His most urgent responsibility is to hand the ball back to the quarterback with the least chance of fumble; to put the towel in the way is the most logic-defying credibility gap.

"It does seem crazy," says Boston's Center Jon Morris. "I ask one of our guards, Charley Long or Lenny St. Jean, to wear it, but they usually refuse. No one wants to be bothered. I don't know why centers have to wear the damn towel myself. Why can't the quarterback wear his own towel?"

Jon Morris is named after his father and grandfather, both Johns. "My grandfather worked all his life on a dictionary of phonetic spelling," said Jon, the oldest of nine children whose father is a Washington correspondent for *The New York Times*. "When I was born my parents decided to name me Jon, because of my grandfather—to kind of put him on."

Like Jon, other centers are trying to pass the towel to a guard to wear—a bad move for the fan who uses the towel as a landmark.

While the quarterback is calling signals, the center is busy watching for things, little tip-offs by the defense. All the offensive linemen are busy watching and waiting. A center might see a defensive tackle's knuckles all of a sudden turn white and he would know the tackle was leaning forward, getting ready to charge. The defense is also observing the offense. When Baltimore Center Bill Curry switched temporarily from center to linebacker (which isn't unusual and explains why so many linebackers wear numbers in the 50s, like centers) he found himself playing opposite a rookie center in an exhibition game.

"I knew what they were going to do by the way he put his hands on the ball," explained Bill, now back playing center. "When he had his weight on the ball his hands were forward and I knew they were going to run. When he had his weight back, on his feet, his hands were up and back on the ball, so I knew he was going to move back—which meant a pass." The rookie center was chopped from the team a few days later.

Normal snaps from scrimmage begin with the laces of the ball facing to the left, so that the ball winds up snapped into the quarterbacks hands ready for throwing, with the laces against his right palm and fingers. (Some game officials "spot" the ball on the line of scrimmage with the laces facing to the left to save the center the trouble of rotating the ball.) Quarterbacks throw with their fingers against the laces to achieve a spiral effect, for better aim. The ball is never served with an olive. It's always served with a twist.

A quarterback's height and hands have a lot to do with how he stands over the center. All quarterbacks are different sizes, but for that matter so are centers. Boston had a center once, Joe Avezzano, who had such long fingernails he gashed the quarterback's palm when he snapped the ball. Ah, well, every game has its hazards.

"Quarterbacks are all different," says Bill Curry who centered for two years at Green Bay before Baltimore. "You've got to figure out where the laces are, how hard to hand the ball off, and where the ball hits his hand. It's very exact."

Can centers tell the difference between quarterbacks if they (the centers) are blindfolded?

"Of course I can tell. Absolutely," says Bill. "At Green Bay Bart Starr and Zeke Bratkowski were the quarterbacks, and they were easy to tell apart. Every quarterback has a different way of putting his hands under the center."

"All quarterbacks have a different personality," says Mike Pyle, rating Bear passers he has known. "Billy Wade had the tender touch. Wade was so gentle you hardly knew his hands were there. Rudy Bukich was firm. He's a slapper, and so strong he almost knocks me forward on my nose. And then we used to have a nervous one—Dick Norman I think it was—who was fluttery. His hands twitched." That's the type that's a towel user.

Good centers must be very *quick*. They have, after all, two jobs on each play. The rest have only one. After he gets rid of the ball the center turns into a lineman and blocks, usually trying to knock a big tackle to the outside. Centers can be smaller than guards and tackles because their blocking angles are more favorable; it's easier to block from the middle out.

"Mike is a good blocker on running plays," says Chicago's ex-QB Billy Wade. "Timing is the key to playing center. It's easy to center the ball in practice without any opposition, but it's a different matter when you have to center it and then make a block. The more experienced a center becomes, the more the passing of the ball becomes natural and the more he can concentrate on blocking."

"Many centers can't snap the ball and move at the same time," says Oakland's Jim Otto, who can. "Snapping and moving makes me look quicker off the ball. I think the fast start helps me to move faster laterally (sideways) to block on running plays or to move backward to block for the passer."

On passing plays the center protects the middle area from the charge of the middle linebacker, picks up any stray blitzers who are after the quarterback, or helps out when somebody breaks down. The center's job is getting more and more complicated in this era of shifting, blitzing linebackers.

"That's the toughest assignment," says Jon, "getting the Mike Man (middle linebacker)." At the New York Giants they nickname the linebackers after girls—Sarah, Wanda, and in the middle, Meg, instead of Mike.

"He's like a vacuum cleaner," says Charley Long about Jon Morris, continuing the team maid analogy. "If I let someone past I know Jon will pick him up."

"You've got to be strong to be able to pick up red-dogging linebackers," says Jim Otto, living proof of an interesting axiom—that once a lineman, especially a center, is voted All-Pro he keeps repeating and repeating, receiving the honor year after year. Why? Because none of the sports writers who vote know what a center is supposed to be doing, and so can't possibly know if he's doing it right or not. Otto was All-AFL in his first season, and except for one season when Jon Morris had a spectacular year, Otto has been the All-AFL center. Who's to argue? The only all-star teams that count are the ones where the players themselves do the voting, but even then many of the results are based on hearsay.

The word "snap" does not come from the pigskin-against-palm snapping noise; it comes from the snap of the wrist. A strong wrist action is required to snap the ball to the holder on a placekick (7 yards) or to the punter (15 yards). Especially on punts, centers need fantastic reflexes for snapping the ball on the exact signal count. Talk about split-second timing—John Schmitt of the Jets estimates the snap to the quarterback takes one half of a second normally and .7 seconds on a punt. Centers also need strong legs.

"Snapping on punts puts a big strain on your knees," says Schmitt. Remember, the center's weight is on his legs; his hands aren't supporting him, they're holding the ball.

The snap to the punter begins differently. The center puts the laces of the ball facing *to his right* with the palm of his own right hand over them. He needs much greater accuracy and speed for passing the ball all the way back to the punter, whose safety of life and limb so depends on getting the kick up, up and away, and so the center takes advantage of the more secure grip afforded by grasping the laces.

"Accuracy on snapping the ball on punts and field goals is one of the most important things," says Jim Otto. "Sometimes you can get in a slump where your snaps are off line. You don't have your confidence, and you worry. I've been lucky. I've never lost a game on a bad snap, even though there was a time when I had to make the old-fashioned long snaps because we ran from a shotgun formation." Shotgun formations are like punting formations, and require a long snap just like the single wing.

Some centers aren't always able to look ahead while snapping the ball. Mike Pyle looks backward on long snaps so he can see the punter, which means that he can't see the defensive tackles or linebackers who are getting ready to hit him.

"Of course it would be better to look ahead, but I just can't do it," said Mike. "I've tried but I just have to see, or I'm inaccurate. Snapping on punts puts you in a very awkward position, and it's not all safe. If you're looking back there's no way to defend yourself. They can just bang into you and there you are—with your head down between your legs, your whole neck unprotected. It's very dangerous."

Jon Morris had a string of bad snaps in 1967. The year before was his best season. Boston's veteran quarterback was Babe Parilli. Now at the Jets, Parilli has played for so many pro teams that he is an encyclopedia on the subject of centers, and said that Jon's snaps were as quick and accurate as any. No one could explain the slump, mostly on punt snaps, which may have cost the Patriots a game or two. In pro football two games is one seventh of the whole year.

"If you see him, tell him I sympathize," said Bill Curry, who still snapped on Baltimore's punts when he was playing linebacker, which isn't unusual. Several teams who happen to have a real good punt snapper (most likely a No. 2 center or a player who has played center at one time or other) substitute for their regular center on punts.

Bill Curry had only been playing defense for two months when he played against Jon Morris. "Morris is the best I've played against," said Bill, and at that time he was making a brave statement because Boston and the AFL were hardly recognized by the Baltimore/NFL in-crowd. "He's so good because he's so quick. But don't you *quote* me, because the others would really be out to show me how good they are the next time we play them. They'd be coming at me with something extra." Bill moved back to center at Baltimore a year ago when the incumbent, Dick Szymanski, began to talk of retirement.

"There is nothing worse than a bad snap," says Curry. "Everyone in the place is looking. When I was at Green Bay, in one game against Minnesota, I had a bad snap on a punt and it went off to the right. Don Chandler (kicker) had to run with it and he went thirty-three yards for a first down. We scored several plays later. I was *lucky*."

Jon Morris's slump continued, like a streak of shanking five-iron shots to a golfer on the pro tour. He tried everything—shifting his weight, gripping the ball differently—but nothing helped.

In one game Jon centered the ball a couple of feet over Kicker Gino Cappelletti's head, twice. "I don't know what it was. It scares me," said Jon. "I thought both of them were perfect snaps, and when I looked back there was the ball rolling around. It looked like I was trying to set a record for longest snap from center."

"Looked like? You did," said Charley Long, the pink-cheeked angel who plays guard next to Jon. Charley is Boston's Dennis the Menace, though with an Alabama accent, and ever alert for a good time. He's a college pal of Joe Namath and when Namath appeared at a Boston sports exposition for one week Charley showed him around the town.

"When Joe left, poor Charley was so worn out he went to bed for a week," said Jon. "We all did. Namath sets a fast pace."

When Namath isn't around Charley seeks amusement with Jon Morris. They look hardest after a game against the Kansas City Chiefs. Kansas City has this defensive tackle, Ernie Ladd, who leaves Jon and Charley sorely in need of rest and relaxation. Many times the center can help out a guard against a particularly tough tackle and let the other guard take his tackle alone. Kansas City has such big tackles that both guards need help, and sometimes the Chiefs will shift their defensive line so that a giant tackle like Ladd (6′ 9″, 290) stands right in front of the center.

"It was dark," said Jon Morris after a game vs. Ladd. "I couldn't see the linebackers. I couldn't see the goal posts. It was just like being locked into a closet. He comes out there, and you can't get your eyes off his arms. He has those long arms and all over them he has these pads and bandages. He keeps hitting you with the right forearm over and over and over again."

Once against Boston, Ernie was wearing a 50-pound cast on an injured wrist.

"After each play Ladd cracked either me or Jon," said Charley, "He hit us on the helmet with that cast so hard I didn't know if I was conscious. The noise was terrible, bells were ringing—I thought my head would explode."

"Your head aches so bad I suppose your body reacts and you start to flinch," said Jon. "You try hard not to flinch, so he won't know he's got the edge, but after a while you can't help it. What could we do? I knew what I could do. I told him how great he was—just praying he wouldn't get mad and hit any harder."

"The Big Cat," Ernie Ladd, doing his thing, to Joe Namath.

LeRoy Neiman

This is nine of football's Ten Commandments. Compliment thy opponent. Love thine enemy out loud.

"Everyone tells how good the other team is," says Jon. "One time I missed a block against Linebacker Sherrill Headrick and he said, 'That was a good try.' He hoped I'd miss again. Ernie Ladd doesn't say too much. Oh, if they get a big lead he gets rambunctious and noisy but usually nothing is said. If I talk it's strictly 'How's the wife?' or 'Nice day.' Don't believe all that name-calling stuff you hear about. No one wants to get the other guy mad, or any madder than he can help."

"The worst thing we ever say about an opponent," says former Packer Guard Jerry Kramer, "is that he's a fine football player."

Guards

Georgia Tech's offensive line coach, Dick Bestwick, describes his material to his material: "Let's face it. The reason that you're playing offense is because you aren't good enough to play defense. When you play guard it's because you aren't smart enough to be a quarterback, not fast enough to be a halfback, not rugged enough to be a fullback, not big enough to be a tackle, and don't have the hands to be an end."

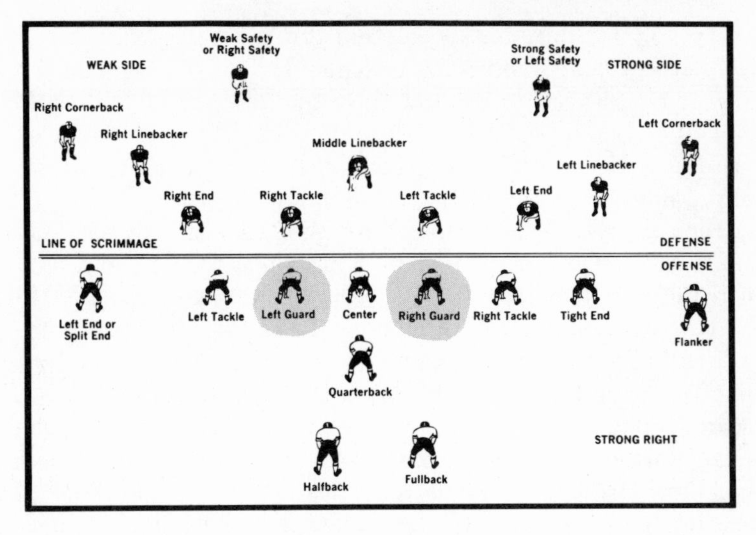

Nevertheless, the guard is the connoisseur's favorite player. The touchdown play is not for the true fan. Watching the guard is. Since long before the invention of the forward pass, old fans have been giving new fans free advice—watch the guards.

"Watch the guards pull," they say, pointing at the field. It's a kind thought, but watching the guards gives you less than a 50% chance of seeing the ball. Unless they are relatives or friends, one only wishes to watch the guards on a running play.

You might ask what are guards? or where are they? Usually they wear numbers in the 60s but still, when linemen are crouched over at the line their jersey numbers are hard, even impossible to read.

Never ask what guards pull. They never actually pull anything. What they do, on a running play, is pull out of the lineup and run ahead, leading the way for the running backs by blocking defensive players out of the way. The guards throw themselves at the would-be defensive tacklers to trip them. This is called running interference.

The technique of blocking is very similar to supermarket shopping. When a shopper in a supermarket uses her shopping cart to get a better place in the checkout line, she is blocking. The cart "paves the way" just as a guard paves the way for the ball carrier on a running play.

When a lineman acts like a shopping cart he is *pulling*. What makes the job so difficult, of course, is the no-hands rule. Guards aren't allowed to *grab*—their hands are tied. Then, too, the requirements for the position—size and speed—hardly go together like ham and eggs. When a guard wants to open a hole at the line he must be big, to have the strength and power to lead the initial charge against defensive linemen who weigh 40 or 50 pounds more. But if a guard is too big he will be too slow, especially for duty on an end run, for example, when the running back will try to sweep wide. On this play the guard might have to run sideways ten to fifteen yards, and then turn downfield leading the way for the ball carrier behind him. It wouldn't do if the ball carrier overtook the guard and ran into him from behind. It wouldn't do at all—which is why the pulling guard must be very fast for his size.

The Packers under Vince Lombardi were always famous for their blocking. They had to be because of power plays like their famous end sweep which requires perfect teamwork, coordination, and blocking by linemen and running backs alike. Line blocking is the key to any offense; the whole thing on running plays is the timing between the two running backs in coordination with the guards. Without good guards running backs are like Mary Poppins in a hurricane . . . without an anchor to windward.

A guard takes a three-point stance about one yard to the left or right of the center. His feet are about as far apart as his shoulders for the best balance, his back is parallel to the ground, and he is looking ahead. He must have his head up to be able to see his man. Instinct says duck your head and shoulders, to cushion the blow of the defensive lineman. All a guard has to do is duck his head and he's dead—the defensive lineman will be around him in a flash and well on his way to get the quarterback. If a guard keeps his head up both he and his quarterback remain on their feet.

The distance between the center's outside foot and each guard's inside foot should be about two and a half feet. When a lineman talks about "splits" in the line he is talking about the distance between lineman—two and one-half to three feet is average.

On a passing down the linemen are spilt wider apart; they are closer together on a running play. The offensive linemen position themselves first and then the defensive linemen line up accordingly. By changing their spacing the offensive linemen can create gaps in the defense, hopefully weakening it or catching it off-guard. Blocking should follow football's underlying strategy—the offense wants to force the defense to the outside (where there's more room) keeping the middle clear for the quarterback, and the defense wants to contain the offense to the inside. Splitting the linemen only one foot wider apart can give the passer more time and the receiver more room. Closer spacing makes blocking for the runner easier, with everyone closer together.

If a guard is supposed to take care of the defensive tackle on a running play, he will drive right at his middle with all the strength he can muster from his toes on up, perhaps wheeling the tackle around to the outside. The guard tries to straighten the tackle up, uses his head—called spearing—to help push the tackle off-balance and hopes to keep him as far away from the ball carrier as he can, leaving the ball carrier with the biggest possible hole for running room.

Guards keep up a steady churning of short, choppy steps to maintain power. Legs pumping, like two pistons, the guard has to keep the bigger defensive tackle occupied for roughly four seconds. If the blocker can lodge his head in the mid-section of the defensive man, he stops his charge and controls him.

"My head is my number-one weapon," says the Jets' Tackle Dave Herman. "That's where my strength is." Herman, who played guard in Super Bowl III, was only sensational at his new position, playing against a giant, Bubba Smith. Before the game Joe Namath said, "Bubba's going to find out that Herman is a machine gun in his chest." Bubba found out.

Herman's No. 1 weapon comes in size 7⅞, biggest on the Jets; his neck measures 18½ inches. Speaking from the point of view of the artist, LeRoy Neiman once described Herman:

Green Bay's famous "sweep" with Guards Jerry Kramer (64) and Gale Gillingham (68) leading the ball carrier Jim Grabowski (33) with blocking help from halfback Elijah Pitts (22).

Houston Fullback Hoyle Granger (32) blasts through a "hole" made by Bobby Maples (50) and Walt Suggs (76). Both linemen are driving their opponents to the outside, away from the ball carrier.

"The spaces between his front teeth are something," said Neiman. "He's got a beautiful head, magnificent. He's a good guy, really good-mannered, fantastic smile but those spaces between the teeth just knock me out . . . He's marvelous looking, and a strange thing happens with his uniform, hiking up in the back with an odd line across his shoulders and a strange way of standing. I really like Herman."

Herman breaks up a lot of helmets drilling such stalwarts as Bubba Smith (6′ 7″, 295) and Kansas City's Buck Buchanan (6′ 7″, 290) in the belly. Such sport has left him with a calcium ridge smack in the middle of his forehead. You can come to an interesting conclusion about the headwork of offensive and defensive linemen by comparing Dave Herman, who runs through two or three helmets each season, and Boston's retired defensive end, Bob Dee, who wore the same helmet for fourteen years.

Oddly, Dave Herman (6′ 1″, 255) has his best games against the biggest tackles like Bubba, Buck and Ernie Ladd. What can a midget 250-pound guard do to ward off a 300-pound giant?

"There's only one advantage," says Fuzzy Thurston. Green Bay under Vince Lombardi always had super guards. The littlest one was Fuzzy Thurston, the funniest Packer, recently retired. "We know the snap count and he doesn't. If I can get the jump on some giant like Roger Brown, I can handle him." Roger Brown is a defensive tackle who was traded from Detroit to Los Angeles in 1967. He has football's biggest thighs, almost a yard around.

"Brown's so good I enjoy playing against him," said Thurston, shooting the bull with more love-thine-enemy nonsense. Brown's good, but not *that* good. "He never shows you the same move twice. He comes like a bull one time, the next time he spins you like a top, or he pounds you on the head like a sledgehammer."

Roger Brown is famous for pounding guards with brute force. When the Los Angeles Rams' promising young Guard Tom Mack played against non-jolly Roger as a rookie, he was worried beforehand. Mack was the only rookie playing for the Ram offense at the time and so opposing defenses were naturally laying for him every Sunday.

Tom Mack is blond, calm, 6′ 3″, 245. Roger Brown is 6′ 6″, 300-plus, and so tough they say he drinks milk out of dirty glasses. Tom's baptism under Roger as he fired at him the first time is still a vivid memory.

"I hit him too high and it was just like hitting a brick wall," Tom reminisced fondly. "I didn't budge him an inch. He was quick as a cat and slapped my helmet so hard it almost took off my head. He must have slapped my helmet at least twenty times during the game and each slap felt like I'd been kicked in the head by a mule."

Young linemen are always surprised when they find out that strength isn't enough for playing pro. "I'd always considered myself pretty strong," remembered Mack. "At Michigan I went into every game confident I could move any man. But I couldn't budge Roger Brown. I was finally able to stop him by using cut blocking—cutting his legs from under him. I'm tall enough to do it, and fortunately Roman Gabriel was throwing mostly short passes and I didn't have to hold the block so long. If I could keep Brown tied up three or four seconds I had him beat. Thank goodness that's all over." (It was the next fall that Roger was traded to the Rams. Now he and Tom are buddies and practice on each other all week.)

There is hope for offensive linemen. One of the brethren, Green Bay's retired Jerry Kramer, has arrived—as an author. His diary of the Packers' second Super Bowl season, 1967, *Instant Replay*, went through a dozen printings and Kramer's offensive lineman image underwent a severe transformation as the success of his book grew and grew. From a burly, crew-cut guard—No. 64, wearing green and gold—Kramer emerged as an articulate, sincere, side-burned fashion plate, a sophisticated man of the world whose opinions on a wide range of non-gridiron topics were sought and quoted. If ever a man could put the offensive line on the map, it was Kramer.

Jerry's past was as exciting as his present, though it's like comparing a local Grange war with the supercharged machinations of Madison Avenue. In 1963–64 Kramer missed a year and a half of football with a mysterious bellyache. No doctors could come up with any answers, and Kramer underwent a series of exploratory operations.

Kramer spent the 1964 season at the Mayo Clinic. "I felt very sorry for myself. I'd say, 'poor kid, you've just got it made and everything's nice and now you're gonna go—you're gonna die.' "

Kramer's experiences with the Children's Ward kept him from too much self-sympathy. Someone sent him a picture of himself and Jim Taylor. "I thought, look at that big dummy, wearing an NFL championship ring and expensive clothes. He's the toast of the town—had a great life. He's been there and he's really got no complaints, no bitches. These little kids are going to die and they've never had an opportunity, never known life. At that time I made a little arrangement—a little peace—with myself."

Offensive Tackles

Oakland's Gene Upshaw is one of the best young guards in football. A late blossomer, Gene was too small for pro football until, in his sophmore year in college he, all of a sudden, started growing and added three

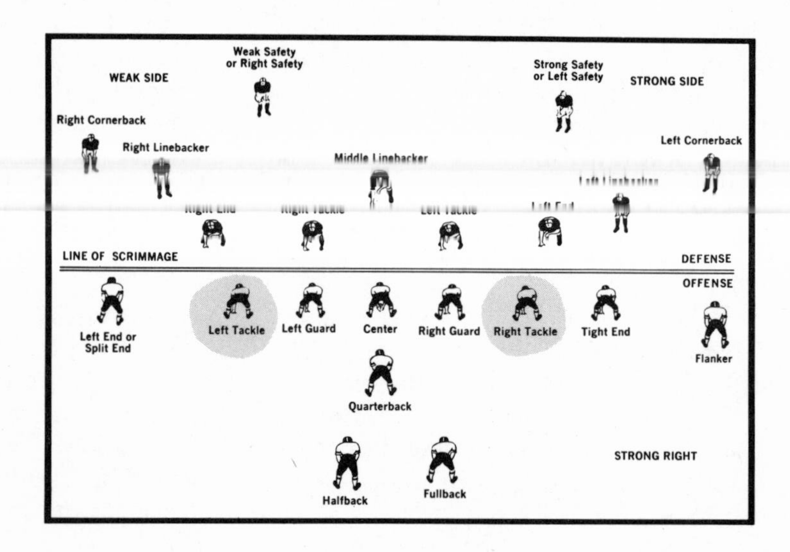

inches and thirty-five pounds. Now 24, 6′ 5″, and 255 pounds, Gene is giant-sized for an offensive lineman and he says he's still growing.

Gene's description of his rookie year is beautiful: "You meet one guy and you say this guy is tough. Then the next Sunday you meet one even tougher, and the next week another one tougher than the others. You start wondering when this madness is going to end."

Upshaw's rookie season was a much madder whirl because of two major events—Oakland was playing for the AFL championship on New Year's Eve in Oakland, and Gene was planning to get married the day before—in Texas.

Oakland did everything that Boss Al Davis could think of except move Texas to get Upshaw to postpone his nuptials, but it was no soap. Then Davis tried to talk him into getting married by phone. He had checked the details. ("The marriage would have been just as legal" said unsentimental Al.) Finally the Raiders let him go, but Davis bought three different sets of tickets back and sent an Oakland bodyguard along with Upshaw, just in case.

Upshaw's mad whirl ended in Super Bowl II against Green Bay, 14–33. After the game, Gene visited the Packer dressing room to pay a call on his adversary of the afternoon, Henry Jordan.

"He asked me to tell him what he did wrong," said Jordan. "He was real nice. I wouldn't have thought it the way he was knocking me around."

Upshaw had played against the Packers once before, five months earlier in the College All-Star game. But in that game Gene played at tackle instead of guard, against Willie Davis instead of Henry Jordan. Like Jordan, Davis was most complimentary and said Upshaw's footwork was unusually proficient for a college kid. Gene played tackle only with the All-Stars. At Oakland he immediately went back to playing guard, which he prefers, though he says it's more difficult than tackle.

"On running plays, pulling out, I've never had much trouble," said Gene. "I ran a forty yard sprint in the All-Star camp in 4.8 seconds. But on pass protection, the work of a guard is more demanding than a tackle. As a guard I have to take my man at the line of scrimmage. As a tackle I can invite the guy outside and take him *around* the pocket."

The tackles line up about a yard outside the guards and are usually numbered in the 70s. Often you find a guard who extends his playing days for two or three years by moving over to tackle. As a guard grows old, the first thing that starts to go is his legs. He loses mobility and quickness, and 40-yard sprints in five seconds slow towards six or seven seconds. Because the tackles don't range as far afield, operating in a smaller area with less running (pulling), legs and speed aren't quite as important, but guards converting to tackle had better be big and still strong, because tackles face the biggest, fastest defensive linemen; petite guards who grow old and try tackle just fade away.

Offensive tackles are taught to keep their eyes on their targets. The key to successful blocking is the same as with tennis, bowling, or golf. You must *follow through*. The offensive lineman hits, lifts (with his shoulders and head), and then tries to stick with his man with his full weight concentrated through the defensive man's middle.

The Vikings' Line Coach John Michels is an authority. Of course, any coach who isn't is probably unemployed. "The best block and the most effective is to aim for a spot about a yard behind the defensive man and run right through him, to aid in sustaining the power of the drive after making the first pop."

Another expert, Giant Coach Allie Sherman, teaches the same thing a little differently: "Pretend there's another defender behind the real one and go after him too."

Tackles know that defensive linemen will be charging the quarterback on every play. The tackle's job is to slow them down. If they can keep their man away from the quarterback for a count of four, they can figure they've done their jobs and the pass is thrown.

"I'm in a four-second business," says Ram Tackle Charley Cowan pithily. "The only time that makes any difference to me is the first four seconds after the center snaps the ball."

Even though it only lasts four seconds, it's a pretty tiring job. Holding a defender off for three seconds is hard enough; for five seconds it's almost impossible. On a long drive of perhaps fifteen or twenty plays, blockers get plenty of exercise. The backs and ends may only be faking, acting as decoys, but the linemen are always toiling away.

"It's a fight between me and the man opposite on every single play," said Alex Sandusky, who toiled at tackle for Baltimore for years. "And not just on a dozen plays a game. We're under terrible pressure every play. Now you take a guy playing end, like Jimmy Orr. Orr can get under a pass out in the clear, with every eye in the stadium watching him, and making the catch can win or lose a game. But Jimmy may catch only five balls a game. On all the other plays he never gets touched." Sandusky is hinting broadly that no one ever bothers to watch drones like him. "We can't ever root. On a play when you decide to root maybe they break through and get Unitas for the play that costs a game." No one ever thinks about a tackle losing a game on his own.

"That's what you worry about when you're an offensive lineman," Alex continued. "You worry about Unitas, not yourself. After every play you ask yourself, 'Did I keep this guy off Unitas?' And you know you'd better, because those coaches will be watching every play on film, over and over again."

The offensive tackles assume greater importance on teams with great quarterbacks, like the Colts and the Jets. The Jets had a jolly green giant named Sherman Plunkett protecting Joe Namath for several years. Plun-

Sherman Plunkett, world's largest tackle.

kett sometimes admitted to 335 pounds, and when he retired he admitted to thirty-four years.

"If I get beat only twice a game I'm doing all right," was Plunkett's philosophy as a senior citizen in a hostile environment. "Football is big business. Everybody's got a family to support and nobody's going to break a guy's leg on purpose. Especially Joe's. I've seen guys that coulda killed him, but after a while you get older and smarter, you get to know everybody, and you just don't want to hurt anybody if you can help it."

Many defensive players scoffed at Sherman's reported weight of 300, because that's as high as Weeb Ewbank's scale used to go. Defensive players said that running into Plunkett was like butting your head against a wall.

Sherman Plunkett was the closest thing to a mobile skin farm on two legs. His neck was 3″ bigger than Scarlett O'Hara's waist.

"Sherm knows the scale now," explained Ewbank after one weighing in session. "He knows how to step on it and how to play the corners. He studied that scale like a playbook, and now we can't rely on it much any more."

Weeb liked Plunkett because Weeb likes experience and consistency. No tackle was as consistent as Sherman. He did the same thing on every play. He took a semi-stance, pushed forward, straightened up, and dared a defensive lineman to get by. The very best pass rushers said Plunkett was so big and wide it was impossible to get around him.

"Plunkett is more power than fat," says LeRoy Neiman.

Plunkett made little or no pretense at blocking on running plays. His own move on a run was to lie down on the line of scrimmage to force the pass rushers to run over him . . . but Weeb Ewbank loved him anyway. Trying to get past Plunkett to Namath was like trying to run around the world.

"In the locker room I can't keep my eyes off Plunkett," says LeRoy Neiman. "He isn't fat, he's hard. Sherman used to be a fat, amusing guy to me, but not any more. His stomach doesn't mean a thing to me any longer.

"He is more power than fat. He lets you look at him. There's a tribal proudness about him and he's very dignified."

Pass blocking by younger, more mobile tackles than Plunkett should be non-aggressive and relaxed. The offensive tackle arranges himself in position and plays the waiting game, careful not to commit himself too soon. When the defender charges, the offensive tackle stands his ground, hovering . . .

At all costs the blocking tackle must keep *in between* his quarterback and the rushers. If worse comes to worst he may give ground, because there are at least five yards leeway between the tackle and his quarterback. Giving ground, what Gene Upshaw called "inviting his man outside and around," is allowed, but letting the charging lineman get by is grounds for divorce.

A pass-blocker needs exceptional balance because he has to move sideways to keep the rushers from getting around him, and backward to form the pocket—and, like the ripples on a pond, he must be able to come back, over and over, after the initial contact or "pop." Good blockers recover to hit again.

The Baltimore Colts' left tackle, Bob Vogel, depends on technique rather than strength. "Blocking is a thinking man's game," says Bob. "It's not simple at all. I think the most important thing is to vary your tactics, do something different each time."

Bob Vogel hasn't much choice. His approach to playing tackle takes a cerebral turn because he weighs only 245. A midget.

"It's very difficult controlling your man—maintaining your block—when you can't keep your hands out. We are warned about holding, to keep our hands in. We're allowed to push or jab *for a moment,* by putting clenched fists against the defensive lineman's shoulders, but we're not allowed to keep them out.

"After all, he's charging. We're blocking. He has the advantage from the start. We have to jab, quickly—and if it's not quick enough the official will call offensive holding. Anything the official takes away from me makes my job just that much harder. And I'm just a little guy. Those defensive ends weigh 280 and are tough to keep off."

Bob is polite and patient, unlike the usual forbidding football image. He is conscientious and intelligent, and in training camp he spends extra time helping the rookies, almost like an assistant coach. Bob is too talented to have to fear any young upstart stealing his job away. The only way he can lose his job is feet first—from an injury or old age.

Bob was graduated from the only university in the country that has a credit course in pass blocking—at least it seems that way when the draft choices are made—Ohio State. When the class of 1969 was picked over by the pro teams, Ohio State's two offensive tackles, Rufus Mayes and Dave Foley, were snapped up as first choices by the Bears and Jets, both in need of some blue-chip blocking. When Vogel attended, Ohio State had a running reputation and was using a tight T formation.

"When I was there we never did any pass blocking at all," remembers Bob. "If we had to pass, like third-and-long, it was always play action, which meant our blocking was like for a running play. All our blocking was double-team; I always worked in tandem with the tight end next to me."

(The tight end next to Vogel at Ohio State was Matt Snell, the Jets' fullback. The quarterback was Tom Matte, the Colt halfback. Such is football.)

"I couldn't believe Ohio State in the Rose Bowl," added Vogel. "Whoever heard of them passing thirty times. They have an offense these days that's very much along pro lines. Foley and Mayes won't have as tough a time in the pros as I had, trying to learn pass blocking when I came to the Colts. It's the most difficult thing to learn. You have to back up, which is hard to do, still maintaining maximum balance, which is that much harder, and very unnatural besides. Downfield blocking on a run is so much easier, because it's straight ahead and natural."

What seems so amazing is that a tackle like Vogel can run downfield as fast as a running back, at least for ten or twenty yards. But if Vogel is amazing, Bob Brown boggles the imagination. Bob Brown is 6′ 5″, like Vogel, but Brown weighs 300. He is the world's largest offensive tackle, yet he is still fast enough to lead a runner downfield. When Bob was a senior at Nebraska, every professional scout was drooling over him. He was the first choice of the Philadelphia Eagles in 1964, and he demanded a bonus of four on the floor, which he drove away after signing his contract. He was traded to Los Angeles.

Bob played basketball and went out for track in high school. He was a top student at Nebraska, a senior when Olympic sprinter Charlie Greene was a freshman. Greene weighs exactly half of Brown, 150 pounds, and is nine inches shorter. Before Bob reported to the Eagles in 1964, he and Charlie worked out together. Greene wears dark glasses and a watch when he runs, hates to practice, and is the World's Fastest Hippie. The sight of one-and-a-half athletes running starts next to three-quarters of an athelete on the Nebraska track must have been flabbergasting. Bob marveled at Charlie's acceleration ("He gets off faster than anything walking") and Charlie complimented Bob: "He's very quick for his size. For the first ten yards Bob stays very close." When an Olympic sprinter compliments a 300-pound tackle's speed, it's strong praise.

Bob's idea of fun off the track and off the football field is to spend the day in a gym seeing how much steel he can lift. There were those among the Eagle flock who think this isn't necessarily a beneficial pastime. They wonder about ankles and knees, football's tender trouble spots, and how Bob's can last under the duress of lifting hundreds of pounds of weights in daily workouts. Imagine two knees carrying 300 pounds sixteen hours a day, through six months of workouts, practice, and twenty fierce games, plus six other months of lifting thousands of pounds of iron and steel for fun in a gym.

Brown is usually All-NFL and plays in the Pro Bowl game in Los Angeles every January. Bob flew back to Philadelphia after one Pro Bowl, picked up his wife and brand new baby at the hospital, dropped them and his suitcase off at home, and left for the gym, to begin working out all over again for the next season. It was only the middle of January, with six months still to go until training camp, and Brown was already training. Such intense dedication explains why Bob is the premier offensive tackle. Besides all the physical qualifications, he has the proper sentiments for the job.

"I dislike every man I play against," he says. "I may not know his name, but I hate him all the same. I think of him as standing between me and my paycheck."

Bob sounds cold-blooded and mean. He is.

"I must have violence. I have to punish somebody, run over people, lay on them. I'm a professional. I have this need inside, to have sixty thousand people screaming around me on Sunday. Violence fills my need."

Bob sounds like he loves his job. But other tackles and linemen secretly wish they could play a more glamorous position. Not all of them wish this all the time, but most of them wish for a chance to carry the ball. Norman Mailer wrote how the backfield and the line live in an unhappy class relationship, and that the problem can't be solved. Football players play the same position for the duration. It's impossible for players to play in the line for a while and then move to the backfield, or vice versa.

Bob Vogel had to learn to love his job. At first, he worried about the lack of recognition given to offensive linemen. So did his mother. His wife would ask him, after a game, whether or not he had played. Now Vogel has come to grips with the situation and says that one of the very few things an offensive lineman gets out of a game is satisfaction from doing his job well.

The Tackle That Failed

"My wife and my mother don't want me to be a football player," says Alphonse Dotson, who doesn't seem to want to be one either, although he's been irregularly employed as an offensive tackle.

Alphonse inherited his mother's artistic nature. When he was graduated from high school (*cum laude*) she wanted him to paint and study. Instead he went to Grambling, where every college talent scout had him picked out as a future superstar.* In 1965 Green Bay and Kansas City fought over him, but so far Alphonse has been a classic bust. That as a non-player he is still around, proves Dotson's potential was head and shoulders above the masses. Alphonse himself is head and shoulders higher than the masses at 6′ 4″.

In his first year with the Kansas City Chiefs, he painted a self-portrait which tells of the hot and cold moments—the conflict in a football player between an artistic, peaceful soul and the raw passion to destroy.

*Alphonse is one half of all the Grambling grads to make any major All-America teams, although Grambling's league sends more players to the pros than any other—which gives ground for continuing to be suspicious of all All-Anything teams which aren't voted by the players themselves.

"It's me," says Alphonse, whose vicious side is missing. "It's an autobiographical portrait, showing a football player with a three-in-one split personality. I call it 'The Angry Football Player.' One part shows a player off the field—in the locker room—carefree and happy. The middle part shows him on the sideline, looking on, wanting to get into action. In the third part the player is playing—in a mean mood, angry, wanting to destroy."

It's the third part that has been Waterloo for Alphonse, who is jolly and good-humored, and who says, "Football is my best shot to avoid working year around."

Any vocational guide would send Alphonse to a peace march, or a love-in, instead of to the violent football stadium scene. About football, he thinks things like "Mankind is fortunate the giants are generally peaceful." Alphonse should know. Two of the most monstrous giants of all, two other Grambling grads who play defensive tackle at Kansas City, Ernie Ladd and Buck Buchanan, are his good friends. Alphonse happens to have sold paintings to each of them.

"We're lucky the little fellows are the hot-tempered ones," he says, "because they can be kept under control." Alphonse weighs 260. He eats a half-gallon of ice cream and a couple of chickens in one sitting. "He's only mean or angry when he's hungry," says his wife. Not to take any chances, or rush things, Alphonse arrived at one Miami Dolphins' training camp with a sweet potato pie, ribs, and a barbecued chicken. And a mustache.

"I've had a mustache since the seventh grade," said Alphonse. There was some talk about shaving—Coach George Wilson's orders—but Wilson meant goatees.

"I couldn't do that, man," said Alphonse. "It's part of me. It would be like cutting off my ear or nose." Very Van Gogh—and like Van Gogh, Alphonse works in oils. "I hope to get into commercial art," he said. "Teaching art would be my second choice—after football," he added, optimistically for one who hasn't gotten into many games. At his latest stop, Oakland, he's been switched to defensive tackle.

The Dotson household moved from Houston to New Orleans last year, and Alphonse began painting the jazz scene. His wife is starting to paint too.

"I lean toward Kandinsky," Alphonse explained, "and like him I try to use color to express emotion and feeling. My style is really very natural; I only *lean* towards the abstract."

When Bear Halfback Roosevelt Taylor moved into a new home in New Orleans, he commissioned Alphonse to do all the paintings.

There is no end to the madness named Dotson. He is a culinary artist as well, and a gourmet. During the football season he gives his wife Monday, Tuesday, and Wednesday off, and he does the cooking. With this schedule he is the perfect husband (at least three days a week), a skilled chef, and talented with a paintbrush.

His only failure is in football, where he wasn't mean enough to make it. About the only thing that Alphonse has successfully tackled is himself, on canvas.

The Artist Colony

Alphonse isn't the only aesthetic athlete in football. Bob Kilcullen retired straight from the Bears into his paintbox. Mike Reid will be coming to the pros from Penn State in 1970. At State he was a mild-mannered music major during the week, and a fiercely fighting defensive tackle on Saturday. When Mike was a child he wanted a piano, not a football, and he began taking lessons when he was five. Now he writes music and hopes someday to compose a symphony about football. "Something that would combine the different elements—peace, turbulence, the clearing after the storm—like Beethoven's Pastoral Symphony," Mike explains.

John Love, Redskin flanker, studied art in college at North Texas State, and his instructor told him he could have earned his living painting if he hadn't gone instead into football. Love paints mostly abstractions. So does Willis Crenshaw, a fullback with the St. Louis Cardinals.

Willis (don't call him Willie) is a sensitive man, a bit shy, who is interested in the martial arts ("I want to become an authority on all hand weapons—guns, knives, sticks"), has a black belt in judo, a brown belt in karate, fences, plays the guitar, does welded metal sculpture and paints, only in oils. Willis is the Rennaisance running back, talking with sensitivity about judo and karate ("When you realize you can maim a guy for life you walk away during the spurt, the blur of anger.") and in the next breath castigating the fashion industry's "system."

"I like *Vogue* and *Harper's Bazaar*," says Crenshaw. "I buy them a lot, and read them, but I don't like Twiggy. It's as if they decided they were going to take her and make her number one . . . or take another girl . . . or another . . . It didn't matter who the girl was or what she was like underneath. They just took any girl at all and made her Twiggy, just like that."

Willis studied yoga. He may not be the only yogi of the gridiron, but if there's another it's a big secret.

"I got started on yoga through a friend," said Willis. "He would say, 'foot go to sleep . . . leg go to sleep . . . knee go to sleep . . .' and it worked." But Willis is selective. "I don't practice all of the things, but I use some. I can't get into the lotus position because my thighs are too big. I do stand on my head a lot, but I can't go for the one where you swallow a whole length of gauze, and then you pull it out. That's supposed to clean everything out, but I'm just not going to try it."

Yoga has one definite advantage for Willis, the fullback, who likes to take naps during the day. Yoga taught him to go to sleep in a second, any time he likes. Fullback is a vigorous job for such an aesthetic soul, and Willis's arms attest to the fact that he has been as welded and scraped as his sculptures. Willis explained that black skin is different from white skin, that it marks up easier and raised little scars remain—keloid tissue—from the rigors of grid wars. "Every single cleat mark shows on my arms and legs," said Willis, holding out a pockmarked forearm which looked like a long-time junkie's. Even his upper arms were dotted with lightish lumps. "I'm going to wait till I'm through playing, and then I'll have 'em all taken off at once."

Willis first tackled the art world rather pragmatically. "I went down to the Thieves' Market to buy some paintings and saw some I liked, by a first-year student. I asked this cat how much he wanted for 'em and he said 'two bills apiece.'" At the time Willis was studying art himself. "I figured that would be OK if the guy had spent a lot of money studying, but two bills for paintings by a first-year man? Like me? So I decided to paint my own." Willis took theory of color—and design. "People think abstract paintings happen by accident. But that's not true. You have to have a good idea of what you're doing."

"I guess I'd have to say my artistic career is in abeyance right now," said Joe Auer, a halfback whose football career is also in abeyance. "I only paint when I feel like it."

Joe hasn't felt like it for four years. "It was a challenge, to see if I could sell any, to tell you the truth. Getting ready for the art show, I painted for two or three weeks straight—nothing but painting. I sold all but one. They went for around twenty-five dollars apiece. But then, like, I'd done it, that was it, you know?"

Joe was attempting to reach the mass market by selling his op art works in Miami's "arty" suburb, Coconut Grove. Critics say he had good perspective. "Op art is objective—the lines create an optical illusion. Maybe it was my engineering background, but I had all these lines and concentric circles that really weren't concentric, and definitely not abstract. People asked me how I made them. I've never told anyone. But movement, form—it was so unusual then. I guess I was psychedelic before anyone else."

His best painting, Joe said, was a nude—made by stopping lines at points so they made a silhouette. The background was about fifty concentric circles.

"And then I did a seascape, except wherever you'd expect blue I did it in red. It was wild—like a bomb had just gone off, like doomsday.

"The guy who exhibited his painting next to me in the Grove show had a big canvas, and when he painted he always used to wipe the paint off his brushes onto the canvas. Well, for the show he framed it and sold it! And you know, I liked it. I'm not abstract myself—not at all—but his painting, it was nice."

Joe hopes to begin another marathon session at his easel soon, because he has a new outlet.

"A friend of mine, Gene Roffler, owns sixteen barber shops around Miami, and he wants me to do some paintings for him. Isn't that a groovy idea, to sell art out of barber shops? When you go to a barber you have to sit there for a half an hour with nothing to do but just look around anyway."

Auer qualifies as the Dr. Doolittle of the gridiron. From the time he was eight, Joe rode in horse shows. He has been the master of a lion named Clifford, an alligator named Dammit, a goat, a possum, and a raccoon. At the Dolphins, of course, Joe was with Flipper.

"Stories get all out of proportion," said Joe. "Dammit was a little caman, only seven inches long, not an alligator, and we kept him in an aquarium in our living room. But it's true about Clifford."

Joe bought Clifford for $130 and no good reason, when Joe was at Georgia Tech and Clifford was just a babe. After several years, Joe finally had to send Clifford to a circus, where he learned to jump through a flaming hoop and do all the things that are expected of lions. Clifford hadn't always known what a lion's life was all about.

"Clifford didn't know he was supposed to roar," reminisced Joe. "In fact, living in my living room, he didn't really know he was a lion. I finally started roaring at him and pretty soon he learned and started roaring right back. He had never seen another lion until I took him to the circus in Miami, and he was absolutely scared silly. He tried to jump in my arms, but he scratched me—the first and only time. Clifford thought I was his mother.

"Clifford used to work out with the Rambling Wrecks, fetching punts and running wind sprints. He always won the sprints and when he brought the ball back it was always a little worse for wear. I'd even play hide-and-seek with him. I'd walk by a bush and shout 'Where's Clifford?' and he'd spring out of the bush and flatten me."

It's Auer who should go back to the bush, to learn hostility. Joe has been less than a roaring success at Kansas City, Buffalo, Los Angeles, Miami, and Atlanta. His coaches say he continues the do-little motif—refusing to practice and unable to adjust to benchwarming—always with a glib demeanor. Joe's swan song at Miami came about one night during a training camp when Joe was hurrying back to camp in his little dune buggy and missed a turn. The Dolphins wouldn't have cared particularly much, except that Joe had a passenger, the Dolphins' heralded and expensive rookie fullback, Larry Csonka. It was goodbye, Dr. Doolittle.

Of all the gridiron artists, recently-retired Flanker Bernie Casey has probably progressed the furthest. Three offseasons ago, while Bernie had progressed all the way to Europe, he was traded to the Atlanta Falcons from the San Francisco 49ers. Carefree, beat, and bearded, Bernie was absorbing culture and blowing about the south of France aboard a motorcycle. When he came back and found he was a Falcon, Bernie refused to play in Atlanta, was traded back to the Coast, even nearer his Los Angeles gallery, and became a Ram. "He is young but talented," said his gallery owner, "an unusually sensitive and lyrical painter."

"I'm a stark realist," says Casey, who kept the football in his life separate but almost equal to the art. "Football is my hobby and painting is my profession."

Bernie, who is 6′ 4″ and weighs 210, was offered many scholarships but chose Bowling Green State University because of its strong art department.

"I decided," said Casey in his freshman year, "that this is me, my bag, man, sink or swim. It was a new romance, a love affair I knew would never stop."

Bernie has had five one-man shows. Some of his paintings have sold for as much as $500. He has run the gamut from realism to abstract and is now settling down about half a gamut back.

"I'm doing fantasy landscapes, miracles, a nice groove for Bernie Casey. My involvement is in shapes and images—somewhat unreal but not as severe as surrealism." As an artist, Bernie doesn't like labels.

"It's a mistake to pigeonhole things and people. Nothing fits in a pigeonhole but a pigeon." Nevertheless, critics call Casey's work abstract and regard him as a romantic expressionist.

Bernie can't help but be labeled in his chosen hobby, where labels last forever. He was a flanker with medium-fast speed and "great hands," or so read the tag.

"There are no set ways to look at football," says the non-pigeon. "You can act and think many ways and still be an outstanding athlete. I don't have to hate, get into a frenzy. I tried the cold, efficient, smooth approach. We all march to our own drummer.

"Football isn't life and death. There are more important issues. I like the game; it's tremendously thrilling, and I liked the money because it gave me independence as a man and an artist, but it's a game."

In the midst of a game, Penn State's musical tackle Mike Reid will read a quarterback's vibrations. Mike believes that from his study of music he has developed a way to anticipate the enemy quarterback's rhythm. Bernie Casey says he frequently got ideas for a painting in a game.

Bernie Casey.

"I've been in the huddle and seen a section of light before me—a part of the grandstand or a collection of cigarette butts—and the whole scene freezes and comes out in one of my paintings," says Bernie, who never paints any football scenes even though he often painted in his room at the Ram training camp.

Bernie has recently been inscribing some of his paintings with poetry, which isn't the first noble wedding between sport and the Bard. In *The Odyssey*, Homer mentioned the crafty Odysseus' skill at putting the shot while more recently Simon and Garfunkle recorded the picture of a broken-down fighter in "The Boxer." Casey's poetry sounds very like some poems by the Beatles:

I saw a man today
I said
Hi Man
He looked at me
With Curious Eyes
And he wondered why
I was here
Why are you here
His eyes asked
But all I could say is
Hi man.

His teammates think Bernie was a little strange. Perhaps because he is so quiet and introspective and moody—a daydreamer who says, "I think I have a gap with everybody." But even though he doesn't sound like one, Bernie was a good football player and he liked his job. He liked the feeling when he caught the bomb and shared the same dream with every other ballplayer—a championship.

"Being All-Universe isn't the thing. But a championship would be a nice thing to have in your lifetime. It's one of the reasons you play. It would be a memory tucked away in the secret places of your soul that you can look back on reflectively some day and say, 'a Super Bowl. A good experience. A nice year.' "

6 Receivers

Each offense uses three players for most of the pass catching—the two ends, left and right, and the flankerback. In the beginning there were only two main receivers. They were called ends because, logically enough, they stood at each end of the line of scrimmage, outside the two offensive tackles.

Then along came the T formation, and the emphasis switched from running to passing, and the football brain trust decreed that each team needed more than two receivers—which posed something of a geometry problem. How could a line have three ends?

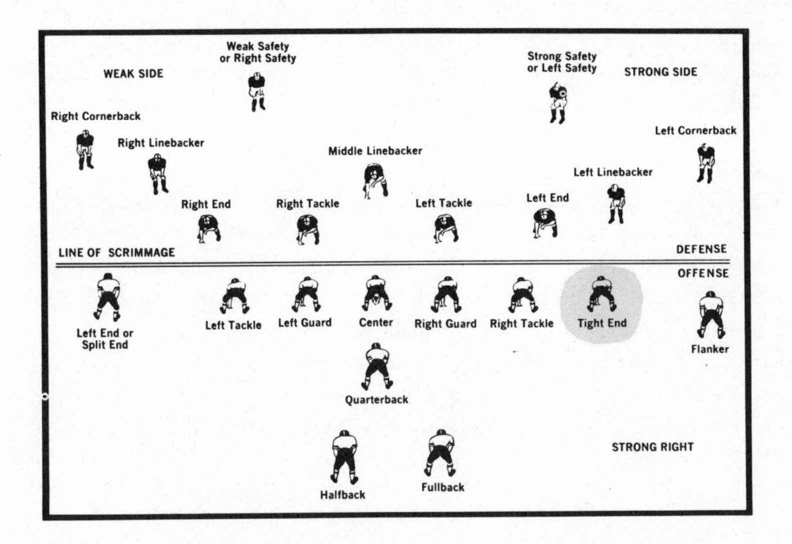

Today, after considerable experimenting, only the right end still stands in the same place. The left end was moved way out wide to the left and the right halfback was moved up near the line, out wide to the right, and named a *flanker*. The original right end was renamed, to rhyme, the *tight* end, because he is the only one left in close (or "tight") next to the tackle.

From his position the tight end plays a dual role—blocking like a tackle and catching passes like an end. "Tight end is a tough spot," says Cleveland's 6′ 4″, 245-lb. Milt Morin. "It's like being two different players at once, without a dull moment. You're expected to run patterns like a flanker and block like a tackle, so there's not time to pace yourself." Somehow Milt makes time, and along with Gary Collins and Paul Warfield makes up what is probably his league's best trio of passcatchers. Morin played seven sports in school (basketball, baseball, track, wrestling, swimming, lacrosse, and football) and had his own family baseball team with four brothers and four sisters, all sportsminded.

As a "blocking end" a tight end has to be bigger and stronger than a wide end, or flanker, but much faster than a tackle. At the St. Louis Cardinals, Tight End Jackie Smith is rangy and lean for a blocker. Jackie weighs 225 and the men he blocks weigh at least 240 and are constructed like lighthouses; he's more of an Eiffel Tower.

You frequently find similar conflicts between size and speed. Tight end is only one. The guard wants to be fast enough for pulling out on an end run, but strong enough for dropping back on pass protection. A defensive back should be all speed and quickness, but he has to be tough and strong too, or his tackles would feel like mosquito bites instead of bee stings.

Size and strength are on one side of the coin, agility and speed on the other side. Each player tries to find a weight where all four factors are at a maximum, and the ones who fail are described thus: "He's not big, but he's slow." (A rule of thumb: Offensive players generally play against defensive players who are about the same size—200-pound defensive backs against 200-pound ends and flankers, 225-pound linebackers against 225-pound running backs, and 250-pound defensive linemen go up against equally huge offensive linemen.)

A tight end must be physically strong, not only for blocking but for catching balls in the heavy traffic area just beyond the scrimmage line where a receiver takes the most punishment. He must also be quick and flanker-wily enough to maneuver himself free in this crowd of defenders, and he needs good hands to be able to catch the ball.

Tight ends block the defensive end, or left linebacker, at the beginning of a play. The tight end is at a weight disadvantage in either case. If he is still on his feet when he gets by this quarter-ton of impediment, there is still a defensive back lying in wait. One such back, Cleveland's Erich

Miami Tight End Jim Cox.
(Don Robins)

Barnes, professes to love tight ends. "They're nice people," says "E," "because the defensive end bumps 'em a little, the linebacker bumps 'em a little, and when they get to me they're all calmed down," and E gave a gleeful high-C giggle.

"I take a physical beating in our games," says John Mackey, Baltimore's tight end. Mackey is exceptionally dangerous after he has caught a pass because at various stages of his career he has played fullback and can run like the devil. If he gets a few steps in the clear he's gone, like a runaway steamroller. "When I catch it I'm going for six," he says. "I don't know who's grabbing me. I try to beat them off my legs if I can, with my forearm. If I can do that I'm hard to bring down."

About that forearm, John? "The word 'brush off' connotes I do it lightly," said Mackey. "That's wrong. I use my forearm to *knock* them off me."

Another fullback, John David Crow, was converted into a tight end with the 49ers for a year before he retired. Crow's first trial at the new position was in a game against the Ram left End Deacon Jones. Crow said after that first experience he expected everything else would be downhill. "As a running back," said Crow, "I thought I'd had everything done to me that could be done. I've been hit every way you can be, but as a tight end I don't know where it's coming from. I guess I've made more mistakes in the six games I've been there than I made in the last two years. There's something new all the time."

After the play has begun, and bumping chores are out of the way, blocking is forgotten and tight ends turn chameleon-like into potential receivers and run out on pass patterns. Because they're big, tight ends make good targets for passers, but their job is hardly a cinch.

"Take a simple square-out pattern," explains Jackie Smith. "You have to go at controlled speed, plant your left foot and push out on it; you must cut at a 90° angle. The problem is to do this without tipping off the defender. If you lean even slightly before you cut, he'll know. If your timing isn't perfect he'll know too. And every time you line up, you have a head full of different defenses you're trying to recognize. This is my sixth year and I'm still learning.

"Don't forget, you're always trying to get away from a man who doesn't want you to get away," complained Jackie referring to the defensive back who's waiting, and watching.

Sometimes the tight end doesn't even have to bother with a blocking assignment. He only fakes a block, turning immediately into a primary receiver. When a tight end releases from blocking and goes into a pass pattern, someone must pick up his block against the linebacker or defensive end.

"Usually it's a running back, like either Curtis McClinton or Mike Garrett," says Kansas City Tight End Fred Arbanas, "but sometimes I have no one to block anyway and go straight out for the pass."

As tight ends go, Arbanas is extremely strong. "If I see a roughhouse coming," says Mike Garrett who, though smallish, has been known to pick a fight or three, "what I do is look for Fred Arbanas and get behind him. He's so strong. I just love that man."

Pass-catching should be hardest for Arbanas, especially when he lines up at the right side of the field, because he is legally blind in his left (inside) eye. Five years ago he was attacked in the street by a couple of thugs with brass knuckles, and was cut up pretty bad about the eyes. After the accident, Fred had to learn to move his head and catch the ball all over again. Now, if he is cutting in for a hook pass over the middle he has to turn his head—jerk it all the way around to the left—so that he can see to make the catch with his right eye. (On a down-and-out pattern he would have little trouble, making the catch over his right shoulder.) Seventy-five per cent of the time Arbanas's bad eye is to the inside; Kansas City likes to switch its tight end over to the left side for about 25 per cent of its plays.

(During one training camp the Jets' split end, George Sauer Jr., found he had 20/20 vision in his left eye and 20/200 vision in his right eye. Lining up on the left side, Sauer, as he turned to look for the pass, would pick up the ball's flight with his bad eye first. Now he wears a contact lens in his right eye. "I realized after I started wearing the lens," said George, "that my depth perception hadn't been accurate on long passes." Roy Jefferson solved a similar problem at Pittsburgh.)

In the last two or three years, coaches have been experimenting more often with lining their tight ends up on the left, outside the left tackle, or with using two tight ends. Coaches welcome extra blocking on short yardage plays or near the goal line; in these situations the additional tight end replaces one of the wide receivers, sacrificing speed for blocking strength. Speed isn't as necessary near the goal where there isn't much room. Most of the time, however, the tight end is in his usual spot at the right of the tackle.

There have been attempts at ambidextrous formations. The double wing has two wide receivers to each side, and three years ago the Detroit Lions and Dallas Cowboys each had two good tight ends and everyone was waiting for both teams to capitalize on their assets and come out with a new two-tight-end offense, which never happened. Dallas tried half-heartedly, Detroit didn't even bother. The coaches decided the extra blocking wasn't worth the sacrifice in speed. The emphasis is still, and always, on speed—the more the merrier.

Offensive formations are usually "strong right" because most players, particularly the quarterbacks, are right-handed and so most plays go to the right. It's more natural. (Only one left-handed passer became a star —Frankie Albert who played for the 49ers from 1946–52. The Bears have reservations about young Bobby Douglass because he is a southpaw passer.) Football is a right-handed game. A quarterback can naturally see the right side of the field easier (his left side is called the *blind side*) and would therefore prefer passing in that direction. The best defensive ends are usually left ends, perhaps because more plays go to their side.

"That's not true. It's just a coincidence," said Oakland's defensive right end, "The Mustache," who also answers to Big Ben Davidson. "It's true that more plays are run to the other side and that they get more exercise than I do, but most of the time players start playing wherever there's an opening. Coaches don't put their best man to the left. If a coach drafts a defensive end on the first round he doesn't move the man who has been playing left end for four years over to the right side just because he thinks the rookie has more potential and may someday be a better player. I think it depends upon what position is open when the player comes along."

Nevertheless, the premier defensive ends seem to be left ends. Willie Davis has been crashing over offenses for years and Willie's television performances on behalf of the Packers have made his 87 a household number. Beside Willie Davis, such crashers as Jerry Mays, Deacon Jones, and Gerry Philbin just happen to be left ends.

"Left defensive end is easier and more natural for a right-hander to play," says Ben Mustache. "The left end has the best aim to the inside, because his best arm is inside and closer to where most of the action is." It is just the opposite for Ben, playing at the right. His best aim is to the outside, the better to stop sweeps with.

"Given a choice you would put your best man at the left," said Detroit Lion assistant coach, John North. "Look at Paul Brown, starting a new team at Cincinnati. I'll bet he put his best end prospect at the left. But as Ben says, lots of time there isn't any choice and when a player is used to playing one side you hate to move him. And there are extremes. Two years ago we had a quarterback who threw to the right ninety-nine times out of a hundred. The defenses had such a tremendous advantage, knowing we were always going right. The perfect defense would be about 60–40–60 per cent of plays to the right, 40 per cent to the left."

Football players hardly use "right" and "left" at all, which you must admit does eliminate a lot of ambiguity—right? Instead, because there are two receivers (and two linemen) to the right of the center, and only one receiver (and two linemen) to the left, the right side of the offense is called THE STRONG SIDE, and the left side becomes THE WEAK SIDE. Almost always, the tight end's position determines which is the strong side. Whither he goest is named strong. When the Giants named their outside linebackers Wanda and Sarah, Wanda stood for weak side and Sarah for strong.

It's always important to think of offense vs. defense as each side looking in a mirror—"RIGHT" to the offense is "LEFT" to the defense. By substituting "STRONG" and "WEAK," all forty members of the team can communicate with each other, thus avoiding a situation where a quarterback tells the left end, "You're right!" and starts pandemonium, when all the quarterback was doing was politely agreeing with his teammate.

The right-handed rule of football has exceptions. Baltimore's Kicker Lou Michaels is a left-footed, left defensive end. Donny Anderson at Green Bay punts lefty, and when the Bears use Gale Sayers on the option play (Gale is given the ball and it's his choice to run or pass), he throws left-handed. So does Donny Anderson. Sayers runs left-footed as do most natural southpaws and makes a large part of his yardage running to the weak side, to the left, which as Ben Davidson says is most unusual. In an archery tournament, Daryle Lamonica, a right-handed quarterback but left-handed archer, discovered he established a sight line with his left eye. Daryle may be the only left-eyed, right-handed quarterback extant. "I should really be pulling the bow right-handed, too," he said.

Even the trenchmen, the linemen, come left-handed. The St. Louis Cardinals have three left-handed offensive linemen—Ken Gray, Ernie McMillan, and Dave O'Brien. "I use a right stance," said Dave. "I didn't use to, but I finally changed and put my right hand down. If I took a natural stance, and put my left hand down on the ground, it would be right next to the next guy's right hand, and we both might be off-balance. It's better to conform. I play golf right-handed, but I guess everyone does things differently." Little things like this are the things that show up when teams study game films over and over.

Kansas City Fullback Curtis McClinton is left-handed, and movies showed he rarely ran right. "I feel more natural running to the left," he said, "and in college I only ran sweeps to the left, to the weak side. I've had to work in the off-season on running to the right. In the spring I would start jogging, at six-thirty in the morning, and run in circles to the right, pivoting off my right foot."

McClinton thus developed "strong-side feet." Someone once asked Ron Mix, a San Diego tackle, what ambidextrous meant. "It means I can run with both feet," said Mix, who moonlights as a Wheaties champion and an occasional writer, and plans to run for public office in 1970, when he retires. Mix is very ambitious for a glamourless tackle.

Tight ends are sometimes called "closed" ends or "strong side" ends, but as a group they really don't overwhelm. They seem to have less stamina and more ailments per pound than players at any other position. In the National League Mike Ditka, Marlin McKeever, Milt Morin, and Jim Gibbons have been bothered with assorted injuries for the past couple of seasons. No player has had more misfortunes than Marlin McKeever, whose twin brother Mike died after several years in a coma, following an automobile accident. Mike had also suffered head injuries playing football at Southern California, where the McKeevers were the toast of the Coast. While Mike was in the coma, Marlin lost the ring finger from his right hand in another auto accident and was later traded to the colds of the Minnesota Vikings, where he was unhappy and unsigned during 1967 and had less than a banner season. "The main thing that bothers me now," said Marlin," is that when I get change out of my pocket the coins keep falling through the hole where my finger was. I really think I can hold onto the ball better now than before the accident. I'm concentrating harder and have to give something extra because I don't have the finger." McKeever is now a Washington Redskin. It's up to Vince Lombardi to see what can be salvaged of his unlucky amputee.

When Mike Holovak coached at Boston, he believed that the tight ends in the American League were not high quality, and that as a result the defensive safeties who played opposite them didn't need to be top quality either, and weren't. It sounds like another which-came-first-the-chicken-or-the-egg dilemma, but Holovak's theory was pretty accurate. (The same argument holds in the National League; top tight ends are scarce there too.) No one knows for sure who will be starting permanently at tight end for Cincinnati, or Miami. Denver's is named Beer, Kansas

City's is half blind, Oakland's is too old, Boston's too little, and San Diego has two, both of whom seem to have been born injured—Willie Frazier and Jacque MacKinnon.

MacKinnon is the type of tight end, like Mike Ditka and Marlin McKeever, who is 75 per cent tackle and 25 per cent end. Jacque (pronounced Jack) is a two-time loser on TV's "Dating Game." "The last time I was on it the program was what they called an alumni game," said Jacque. "They brought back all the losers. There was a guy who had lost twice (he got the girl), a guy who had lost five times (an all-time record), and myself."

MacKinnon is a free-living bachelor-about-San Diego who spends the off-season sunning himself, storing up strength, and attending to promotional details, like escorting the finalists in the Miss San Diego contest around the Chargers' new stadium. Jacque is blond, good-looking, tremendously unsophisticated, and a health nut, swilling vitamin pills with abandon. He once sold an old icebox to his coach, Sid Gillman, when he needed a bigger one with more room for keeping special health supplements, vitamin pills, and nutrition formulas. San Diego's other tight end, Willie Frazier, competed for and won the job away from Jacque. "I think I can hold it," Jacque keeps saying. "I've always had a high opinion of myself."

Jacque only plays when Willie Frazier is hurt, but for several seasons he's been the regular tight end for San Diego. Willie is always hurt. After every Charger game there is a note in the following Tuesday sports section that reads something like: "Monday was a day off for the Chargers, but Jacque MacKinnon and Willie Frazier were among players reporting for treatment of a bruised this or a pulled that." San Diego's tight end department suffers from acute hypochondria.

Willie Frazier came to San Diego from Houston, in a deal for Ernie Ladd, and he still corresponds with Houston's Trainer Bobby Brown, relating his latest ailments in installments. While he was at Houston, Willie immortalized the Oiler whirlpool which Brown officially refers to as the "Willie Frazier Memorial Swimming Pool."

Bobby Brown has a vivid imagination, but the legend of Billy Cannon, a tight end of course, doesn't need any coloring by Brown.

"Billy was the best there ever was," says Brown. "He had injuries that haven't been invented yet. Next to him Willie Frazier was hardnosed."

Billy Cannon is now at Oakland. Cannon was the most coveted player to come from the colleges in 1959, was the winner of college football's biggest award, the Heisman Trophy, and was the prize in the first major battle between leagues. Billy acted generously and signed contracts with teams in both leagues—with the brand new Houston Oilers and the Los Angeles Rams—and was finally awarded to the Oilers by a judge who condemned the Rams' signing tactics. The judge said the Rams, whose

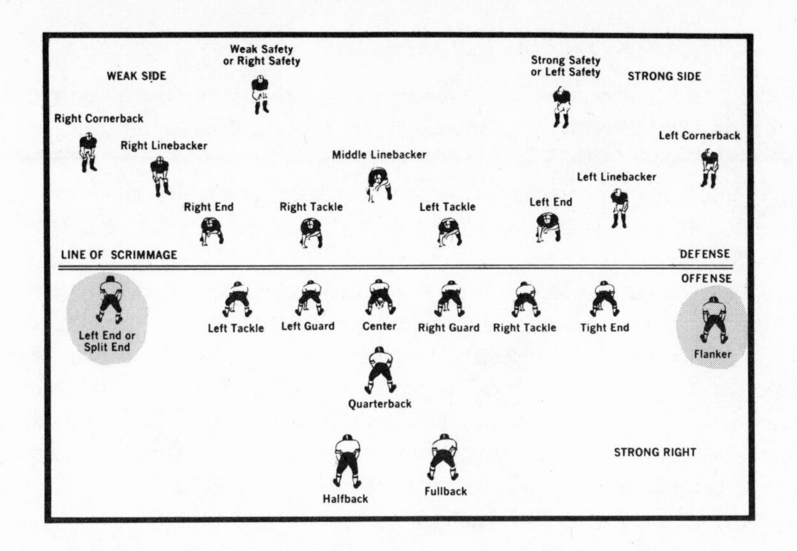

general manager at the time was none other than Commissioner Pete Rozelle, had taken advantage of "a poor country boy."

The poor country boy came a long way. For signing with Houston he got a huge Heisman-sized bonus, a couple of gas stations, and some other Texas-sized valuables. Cannon began his pro career at halfback, was moved to wide end, and slowed to tight end. Though Cannon has lost his speed he's gained some sophisticated "moves," and so he's still around and very often wide open. For a rich kid he did all right.

TV broadcasters are trying to take the fun out of football by making it sound so complicated and themselves so smart. They take a simple little word like s-p-r-e-a-d. To a normal person "spread" conjures up images of middle age, corsets, peanut butter and jelly, loan payments made easy, Thanksgiving dinner for eighteen, what you cover a bed with, what Paul Revere did with his alarm, what you phone a bookie for, and what John Wayne wants to finally settle down on—a little one of his own. But in football "spread" means wide, or split. All three are interchangeable terms.

The left end lines up wide to the left, split out away from the traffic. For all practical purposes the flanker should be considered a split end wide to the right, several yards outside the tight end. Originally the flanker was one of two running halfbacks, but when modern football wanted a third pass receiver there was no one available except a halfback —who was borrowed, and moved wide to the right where he now catches passes.

"Temperamentally," says Bernie Casey, who always sounds like he's twenty days through *30 Days to a More Powerful Vocabulary*, "flankers are never really happy unless the ball is being thrown to them." Split ends feel the same way.

College football tends to be conservative, flankerless, and it emphasizes the running game with close-together formations. Flanker formations are more sophisticated. By spreading the receivers out wide, an offense has greater freedom for expression—more running room to divide up into more creative pass patterns. In the old days everyone was cluttered up in the middle.

According to the rules, at least seven players must line up on the line of scrimmage, and only the two widest are eligible to catch passes. (Note that if ten players, all except the quarterback, stood on the line of scrimmage there would be only two potential receivers; with seven on the line there are five potential receivers.) Which explains why the flanker is technically a back and must stand a yard behind the line of scrimmage. If the flanker stood right *on* the line he would automatically make the tight end into a tackle (ineligible receiver).

The best wide receivers have speed, good moves and fakes to throw defender off-balance, and sensitive hands. Butterfingers don't do. Ends catch with their fingers, not with their hands cupped as children are taught in fourth-grade gym classes. There is an old adage: If you get close enough to touch it, you should catch it. And after you catch it, "all you think about out there is 'don't get caught from behind.' That's most embarrassing," says Bernie Casey, the artist with the violent hobby.

Wide ends get a quick dismissal from LeRoy Neiman, the artist who is a football fan. Neiman discovered at the end of last season that his Jet portfolio didn't contain a single drawing of a receiver. "I can't get excited about them," says Neiman. "They're almost outside the violence. They may be shot down from time to time, but they aren't in the muck where it's at on every play."

One of the Jet receivers not in the muck is a skinny eccentric who likes it like that, George Sauer Jr., who carried Albert Camus' *The Myth of Sisyphus* around in his pocket during the week before Super Bowl III. Sauer Sr. was a football father to end all football fathers. He sent George Jr. out for football as a kid in Waco.

"I really didn't like football that much," said George, "especially at the University of Texas. I began reading a lot. I didn't like to block and tackle and all that crap. I just like to catch the football." Sauer majored in mathematics, wears horn-rimmed glasses and has plenty of hippie hair, blond. "I still like to catch the football, but there's more to life than catching footballs."

Art Powell, who played on as many teams as needed his quick feet and could stand his quicker temper, thought he should never have to do any blocking, but not all wide ends are such prima donnas. Others, and that includes such miniflankers as 5′ 8″ Tommy McDonald (Ret.), 180-pound Lance Alworth and Cleveland's Paul Warfield, do block, and

"Bambi."

their occasional descents into the muck make them more complete players. Sometimes they even enjoy themselves.

Tommy described his blocking duties with becoming modesty. "When I try to block the big boys high it's like a fly spatting against a tree trunk. I have to go for the shoelaces."

Lance Alworth is slender, not too tall, baby-faced, and vulnerable to injury. Lance looks like anything but a jocko, yet he has everything for flankering—grace, moves, sure hands, speed, reflexes, smarts. He has such style and runs with perfect control, so relaxed he looks like he's skating. With tremendous spring in his muscular legs he has great leaping ability, the better for outjumping taller defensive backs, and an appropriate nickname "Bambi" which he detests, believing he has outgrown such unsophisticated nonsense. Lance also has that grandest of prerequisites: desire; he'd probably quit a Las Vegas crap table after twenty straight passes if someone invited him outside for a game of touch. About the only thing Lance doesn't have going for him is something he can't do anything about—the Chargers have never had a super quarterback throwing to their super receiver.

"I rate every flanker I ever play against," said the Jets' Johnny Sample. "I use five categories to rate a man—speed, patterns, blocking, how he goes after the ball once it's in the air and his ability not to be intimidated. On a zero-to-five scale Alworth is the only one who gets fives all the way."

It's not quite the Life of Riley he's living out there by his lonesome. Flankers get their lumps too. Most of the time when he goes out for a pass, a receiver knows he's going to get a good going over—first they check him at the line, they bump him as he starts his pattern and then he gets hit hard as the pass arrives, sometimes by two or three defenders at once.

"That Oakland game was one of the few times in my life when football wasn't fun," said Lance when he was getting over a painful back injury two years ago. "I was lined up, in tight, and those linebackers just kept grabbing me, grabbing my clothing, anything they could get away with. I've played against a lot of football teams, but they held me more than anyone. I just couldn't get away." (The defensive players are allowed to bump and jostle as much as they like until the quarterback throws the ball; after that it's hands off.)

Alworth had a bad leg a little later that season. With his hand he could feel a hole in his torn calf muscle. Even so, Lance wanted to play in the final game against New York. New York was less keen about Lance playing. "Why is he going and risking his whole career for this one game?" asked Jet Coach Weeb Ewbank hopefully. "Allsworth [Weeb's own translation of Lance's name] is nuts." Weeb would love a few nuts like Lance in Jetville.

In the National League, Cornerback Irv Cross says the Saints' Dave Parks is probably the toughest end, both mentally and physically, that he has to defend against.

"I love to play against Parks because he slugs it out toe-to-toe and that's the way I like it," says Cross. "I don't think receivers should be treated like prima donnas. It's a contact sport and that's the way it should be played. When you play against Parks you go up for the ball, and may the best man win. He's also a good blocking end, and this gives their offense a great deal of confidence." Dave Parks is 6′ 2″, 210. Spread ends come in all sizes. So do cornerbacks. In one game you might have Cleveland's big Flanker Gary Collins (6′ 4″, 215) matched up against Washington's Pat Fischer (5′ 9″, 170). The disadvantage is definitely Fischer's, but Pat has been known to come up with some miraculous, last-minute saves.

When a midget like Tommy McDonald (5′ 8″, 175) is matched against a tall cornerback like the Giants' Scott Eaton (6' 3", 195), the midget's disadvantage is obvious. Eaton can just reach over and flick the ball away. Simple. Therefore the smaller flankers (Houston's Jerry Levias is a perfect example) must use a "heady" approach, hoping to deceive and receive. They stay up late at night thinking up David-type tricks to outmaneuver the Goliaths, who try guile too, but who really needn't bother their heads. "When Fischer tries to pull my arms apart," explains Gary Collins, "to make me drop the ball, I meet force with force," and he has seven inches and forty-five pounds more force than Fischer. It's really very simple.

Collins is one of the super flankers, but with cornerbacks using a more positive, aggressive approach and studying game films under a microscope even the superstars can't rest on their reputations—they must keep varying their routes, changing their moves, trying new fakes, keeping defenders guessing. "Collins changed his move off his post pattern in our last game. He usually comes down strong outside, keeps faking, and cuts inside. Last week he came down inside, faked out, and then cut back in," explained Dallas Cornerback Cornell Green, who didn't go to Cornell but gets greenish with envy when he talks about Green Bay. "Them Packers never change. They don't go for new plays and new formations. They depend on execution to beat you. Their blockers give Carroll Dale (flanker) all sorts of time to get loose, and no one can keep a receiver covered forever. Give a quarterback enough time and he'll hit his man."

Carroll Dale and Bernie Casey are both tall, and fast enough. "They have a nice fluid motion," says Irv Cross. "They present a problem because they can make their catch while in full stride." Cross is, of course, in full stride too, which shouldn't be a problem. The Ram doctor, John Perry, says Cross is a perfect physical specimen—strong, every muscle rippling, in perfect condition. "People sometimes don't realize what good condition these boys are in," says Dr. Perry.

The hardest part for a receiver is to keep balanced even though the defender, at the very least, is breathing down his back. Balance is one reason for the success of Dave Parks at New Orleans. Parks runs with a shambling, flat-footed gait and can't easily be knocked off his feet. If the two best quarterbacks, John Unitas and Joe Namath, both have terrible slope-shouldered posture, can someone be telling us something when two of the best wide ends, Dave Parks and Homer Jones at the Giants, both have the flattest of feet?

One of the greatest ends of all time, Tom Fears, now coaches at New Orleans. Fears teaches his Saints two basic rules of receiving:

1. Keep hands and arms down by your sides until a moment before the the catch, to gain a little speed and to prevent the defender from knowing exactly where you plan to catch the ball.

2. Don't wait too long. Catch the ball at its highest point, because there's less chance of losing it to a defender.

Coaches take every precaution to prevent a fumble. To make sure each receiver watches the ball all the way into his hands, the Chicago Bears devised a special passing drill. A number was painted on the end of each ball. As passes were thrown, the receivers had to call out the number before making the catch. At Pittsburgh's training camp, the receivers and running backs do some of the conditioning exercises and drills while *holding a ball,* to get them used to it.

There is always the risk of dropping the ball, fumbling it away. Baltimore's great end, Raymond Berry, had a trade secret: "Once I get the ball I pull it into my body, so I won't lose it if I fall. If you fall with your arms extended, it's trouble."

Defenders vary as much as receivers. Some keep crowding their man, picking him up right at the line of scrimmage. Others, like Green Bay's, play back 8 or 10 yards and wait for the receiver to come to them.

"I prefer a cornerback playing me back like that," said Bill Miller when he played end at Oakland. "The theory is that the pass rush (defensive linemen) will be getting our quarterback at about the time I've gone out eight or ten yards, where the cornerback is waiting. So it's a calculated risk."

"Of course Green Bay's cornerbacks are fast," said Miller, who wasn't very. Some schools of thought hold that Miller would have trouble beating a defensive tackle across the street. "You'd be surprised, but a lot of slower receivers would rather work against a real fast cornerback. Some fast receivers would too. Art Powell used to feel that way. "It's like a defensive lineman with a tremendous charge. You get a real fast man going one way and it's tough for him to change his direction—control his speed."

Bill Miller wasn't as slow as his reputation. "Let'em think we've got no speed," says Al Davis, Oakland's boss. "I love everybody thinking that way."

One fast reason why a jury would decide Miller was slow was the end across the field, Art Powell. Compared to Powell, anyone runs up a tortoise. When Powell was running deep, Miller wasn't, so people guessed he couldn't. No one can look like a "burner" running short pass patterns. For this reason many receivers who work across the field from a speedball get labeled slow when they aren't so slow. Lance Rentzel, across from Bullet Bob Hayes at Dallas, is another example of a bum rap, but Rentzel escaped from Hayes' shadow by showing up frequently in the end zone for touchdowns, and by showing Hayes up with publicity. A fast worker off the field, Rentzel was a busy swinger, gave concerts on the organ, started a Dallas discoteque, and married Joey Heatherton, cementing his show biz ties.

"Well, I read in the papers that I'm not fast," said Bill Miller, now a coach at Buffalo, "so I'm not fast." And so the verdict—fine hands and good moves.

"Our receivers are sneaky-quick," said Al Davis, who probably started the rumors about Oakland's slow receivers.

"Size and speed aren't everything," Howard Twilley is fond of saying, and it's no wonder. Howard is 5′ 9½″ and slow. "Maybe there are fellows who can outrun me for a hundred yards, but they don't play this game at a hundred yards. For thirty yards I can run with anyone." Most plays don't even cover thirty yards.

Twilley, a flanker for Miami, is a wit, an electrical engineering whiz on his way toward a master's degree. He wears the expression of an inquisitive bulldog. "I majored in engineering," said Howard, who caught more passes than any other college end when he was at Tulsa, "and I know there is more to catching passes than just following the lines they put down on paper. That's why I think I can make it in the pros." Which gives him an immediate headstart. He thinks.

Two other sneaky-slow, quick-witted ends are Atlanta's Paul Flatley and Baltimore's Jimmy Orr. Some of the speedballs talk about shifting speeds but Flatley doesn't. He has one speed. Flatley studies the defensive backs, how they respond to moves and fakes, and their particular running style. "I'm not that slow," he says, "but the only way I can get open is to catch my man with his weight on the wrong foot, and then cut."

Norm Van Brocklin, who is attempting to resurrect Flatley for Atlanta, has his usual last word: "You throw to Flatley when you want to run out the clock." Flatley played for Van Brocklin at the Vikings for four years but was dismissed a year after Van Brocklin left. The Viking computer told Coach Bud Grant that Flatley was failing to stay in his pass patterns.

The Colts' Jimmy Orr has played amazingly well for a dozen years considering he is small (5′ 11″, 185), slow, and works amazingly hard at enjoying himself.

"I don't have speed," admits Orr. "But I can go deep. Going deep and having speed don't necessarily go together. It's a matter of moves, of making people play you short. I didn't know a thing about moves when I was a rookie but I watched others, made adjustments, and found out the things that work for me."

Orr owns a profitable restaurant in his hometown, Atlanta, has fun with a post-game radio show direct from the Colt locker room that is amazingly free from the trite public relations pap so synonymous with broadcasting jocko-style, sharpens his wit spinning yarns about some of the more garrulous Colts like Lou Michaels, avoids over-training like the plague, and doesn't set too much store with studying game films.

"I've studied them at times until my eyes were about to fall out, and then the defensive back would do something totally different,' says Jimmy.

"The only way I can operate is to feel out the guy for five or ten minutes and then make up my mind what to do."

Orr says he will play as long as he can ("I don't have anything better to do"). He's the end I'd most like to be shipwrecked with . . . although the idea of a desert island would be appalling to Jimmy ("Man, you know I hate to stay in one place very long, whether I'm sitting or standing").

The man who played across the field from Orr at Baltimore was Raymond Berry. Berry was probably the most serious student of pass-catching that football has ever known. Berry watched game films the way the rest of the world used to watch "Peyton Place." Although they had pretty much opposite personalities Orr and Berry shared a sense of humor and several theories on the proper way to catch a pass. Neither was a burner. Both took a mind-over-matter approach to the receiving business, out of necessity.

"It's concentration," said Orr, "one hundred per cent keeping your eye on the ball and not worrying about getting hit. You're gonna get hit anyway, so there's no sense thinking about it. Grab the ball first and worry later."

Many gaggles of receivers have gotten into trouble and never become stars only because they lacked concentration. The good ones never fail to run out their patterns, even during practice drills; it's good discipline and an obvious way of getting into good habits. A quarterback wants to anticipate his receivers and is more confident when he knows they always complete their patterns; he needs to know where they are and when—all of them. Even if a quarterback sends out five potential receivers and one is designated fifth-least-likely, it wouldn't do for number five to lazily fail to run out a pattern or to run it carelessly, without precision. Just as a quarterback calls an isolated play a receiver should never run an isolated pattern. He should always be thinking ahead, trying to learn a little something extra about his defensive man's reactions or weaknesses. He will never discover a weakness (or strong point) if his mind is absent.

The Jet receivers are in sharp contrast. George Sauer Jr. pays strict attention. Don Maynard doesn't always. It took Maynard several years to decide to concentrate at the Jets. Weeb Ewbank had to bench Maynard on several occasions for blowing his patterns. Then, en route to Super Bowl III, Maynard shaped up. In the championship game against Oakland, Maynard caught a pass for the winning touchdown when he was the fourth on Joe Namath's list of receivers. The other three had been covered and Maynard had been paying attention.

In Super Bowl III Maynard didn't catch a pass, but he proved an exceptional decoy by running his patterns precisely. He was often double-covered, which eased the pressure on the rest of the Jet receivers, particularly George Sauer, who caught eight passes for 133 yards.

"On most of the passes I was the prime receiver," said George. "On five of the passes I caught I was No. 1, and the other three were passes which could go to anyone. You know, like back in grade school—everybody out for the pass and someone gets open." Joe Namath was quick to admit that his Super Bowl performance wasn't one of his best games. Sauer's performance was super.

"I would describe George as a fast Ray Berry," said Weeb Ewbank. "Berry was not fast but he ran great patterns. George is fast and he's also a master of patterns."

No one worked harder than Raymond at perfecting his basic skills. Not a natural-born receiver, it was a tremendous task that Berry performed, turning himself into a master at the art of deception. He beat his man with technique. Berry could move his head one way, his shoulder another, and wiggle his hips—all the while running at his top speed—and finally the chances were good that he would elude his defender.

The Berrys hadn't been married a week when Raymond had his wife Sally helping him get ready for the next season.

"He starts with hiking, up to five miles, and then running," said Sally. "Sometimes I run with him, and we play catch. I can't throw far, but Raymond needed someone to throw to him, and I was the best he had."

"Sally is afraid people will think she's not very feminine," says Berry, "but they just wish their wives could throw."

Sally was lucky, married to an end. Jim Martin, now a coach at Detroit, was a kicker whose wife was his holder when Jim kept in shape in the off-season. Before too long Mrs. Martin was minus her long fingernails. Heaven help Mrs. Martin if her husband played tackle.

Females are much more important to the flanker of the species. They have more opportunity to become actively involved in their husband's profession, though just playing catch can be hazardous on the helpmate.

The case of Mr. and Mrs. Fred Biletnikoff proves just that.

Fred Biletnikoff is Oakland's flanker. After the 1966 season Mr. and Mrs. Biletnikoff had planned to take their two children home to Florida, but their son Freddie needed a kidney operation, and they decided to stay in California during the off-season, to be near the boy's doctor.

"I had always wanted a ski lodge, so we just had one built, near Lake Tahoe, high in the California mountains," said Fred, who could afford it. Fred had played for Florida State in the 1964 Gator Bowl and after the game two events took place on the field—he and Jerri were married under the goal posts and Fred signed a $200,000 bonus contract with the Oakland Raiders.

The goal post wedding didn't cut much ice with the elder generation of Biletnikoffs. They are strict members of the Russian Orthodox Church, though Fred and his brother Bob (Bob is trying to make it in major league baseball) are two generations removed from Russia. The grandparents had set up American housekeeping in a little Russian community in Erie, Pennsylvania.

After college Fred and Jerri went west to Oakland, where he served at flanker for the Raiders with a worried lack of distinction and a couple of injuries. After a postseason operation, his leg in a cast, Fred found himself snowbound in Lake Tahoe trying to work out in the basement of his ski lodge ("the tallest igloo this side of Nome"). Florida State had not prepared the Biletnikoff family for the big freeze.

"It turned out to be the worst winter in Lake Tahoe history," said Fred. "The county plow was supposed to come by once a day but so much snow fell that we got snowed in for two or three days at a time—for maybe a dozen times. It stayed around ten degrees, sometimes went below zero, and it was worse than Erie."

Even though he was still wearing a cast, Biletnikoff had planned to get in good shape that winter. After the snow plow came through Fred would go out and run in the ruts and Jerri would throw him passes. With Jerri throwing, Fred's fly pattern improved, but it's not easy to run a buttonhook in a rut. The cast came off, and Fred went to training camp, sure he was going to be cut. He'd always had a case of jitters, but by September he was a nervous wreck and dropping every ball he couldn't get his hands on.

Finally, after the last cut was made, Biletnikoff felt more secure and began to gain confidence. He started making catches and was starting by the fifth game of the season. By Super Bowl II he was one third of Oakland's slow-but-sneaky-quick trio of ends. Biletnikoff has continued to hold onto the ball and has broken out of the vicious circle—more worrying means more dropped passes means more worrying. He may even be getting over his ulcers. Before Super Bowl III he was asserting himself against a tough foe, loudmouth Johnny Sample. Biletnikoff ran Sample ragged in Oakland (the "Heidi" game) and in the championship game in New York, Biletnikoff caught seven passes, [illegible] performance.

Sample tried hard to get Fred's goat. He gave him the best of his big mouth and belted him around. He leaped on him illegally, out of bounds; luckily for Sample it was also out of official sight.

"I was out of bounds," yelled Biletnikoff furiously.

"I'm going to hit you all day," said Sample.

After the game Biletnikoff testified to the villain's behavior: "Sample's a bum. He stinks. Anybody who can't beat him ought to hang it up."

Oakland is finally getting its $200,000 worth. The power of thinking positive has turned the nervous Biletnikoff into Mister Bold.

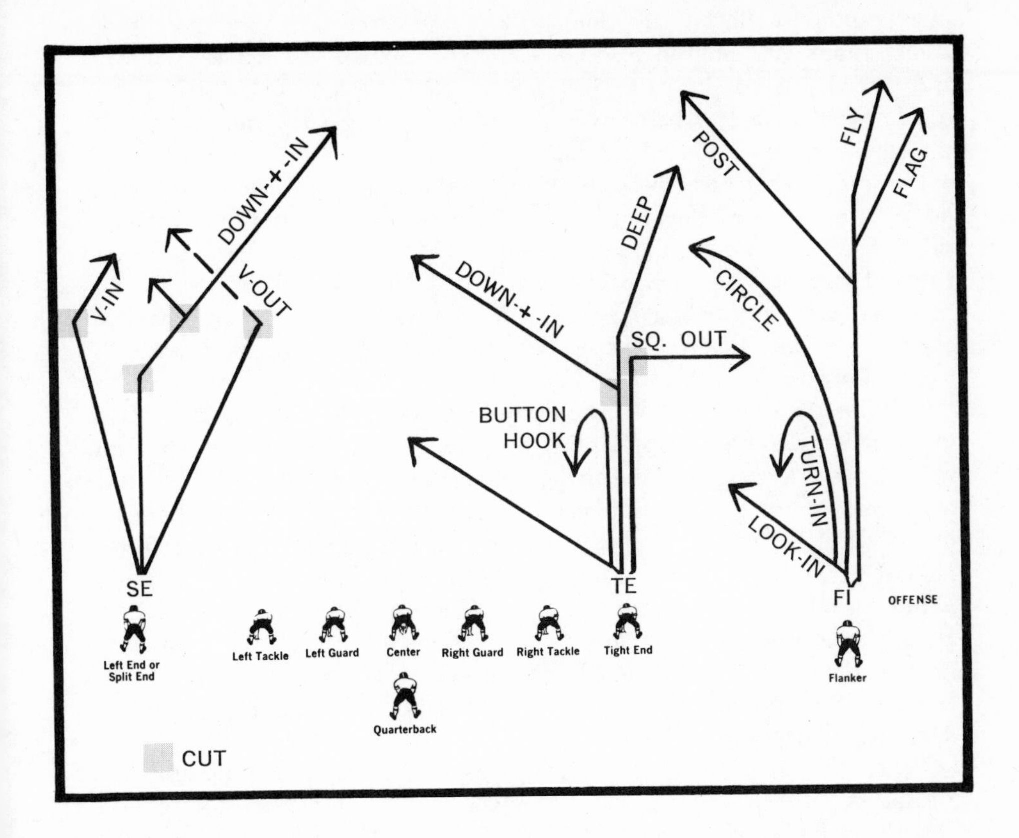

Cuts, fakes, moves, wiggles—all put together—make up the *pass pattern.* It figures that the more complicated the pattern, the more practice and rapport are necessary between quarterback and receiver. Raymond Berry and John Unitas worked together for thirteen years.

Many fans, though they'd spent many thousand words discussing them, had never seen a pass pattern develop until the television replay showed them one. Nothing is more exciting than to pick out an end, in an obvious passing situation (third down and many yards to go) and to watch him race downfield, shake loose with a wink and a shuffle, and catch a long bomb "for six"—a touchdown.

Patterns aren't at all as obscure and complicated as they've been advertised—or named. One hears the buttonhook, z-out, zip-in, square-out or in, slant, flare, go, pop. And some are named for their inventor—like the New York Giants' Pete Provot Special, which was named for a locker room assistant. A non-expert shouldn't be intimidated by language. It's only those TV announcers, trying to complicate things so they'll appear more expert to the fan at home. In one game the TV color man kept raving about Washington Redskin End Jerry Smith, and his great moves and patterns. After the game Jerry explained his game: "All three of my touchdowns were flag patterns," he said. "I just ran toward the flag at the corner of the field and the ball was there."

For simplicity's sake, pass routes are named *for their shapes*—square, hook, flare—*for their directions*—in, out—or *for the location*—post, corner, sideline. What sounds complicated isn't. A "post pattern" simply means the end runs toward the goal post and that the quarterback will try to have the ball there when he arrives. When the goalposts were changed a year ago from H- to Y-shaped, exactly one half of the post patterns were eliminated in one fell swoop.

Sideline patterns were Raymond Berry's specialty and required absolutely perfect timing. John Unitas threw so that Berry caught the ball with his feet legally touching in bounds, inside the sideline, but the rest of Raymond was practically parallel to the ground, falling safely outside in the clear. Now John Unitas is working on timing with Berry's replacement Ray Perkins. Perkins certainly doesn't sound like Raymond Berry ("I'm on my way out to hit the little white one around," says Perkins, about to play golf), but the opportunity Perkins had—to learn by watching Berry from up close in his rookie season—must have been a great advantage. After Berry left Baltimore, Perkins said he planned to be more dedicated. That sounds "very Berry."

When time is running out, sideline passes can ruin a defense and win a game because the clock stops as the receiver (and the ball) goes *out-of-bounds*. Whether the receiver had possession of the ball *before* he went out-of-bounds is a question which has occasioned many, many rhubarbs between officials and receiver, and rhubarbs which occur at such a delicate time as the final two minutes of a game are the most emotional rhubarbs of all. Because the Rams' Coach George Allen is so meticulous and thorough, the Rams have daily sideline-pass practice—catching the ball, taking two quick steps which the rules require to establish possession, and then stepping or falling out-of-bounds. When Raymond Berry retired he immediately became end coach at the Dallas Cowboys and was given one specific assignment: teach Bob Hayes all you know. If Berry is successful, Hayes will be the greatest end football ever saw, because Berry had almost perfect technique and Hayes was almost perfect raw material.

Hayes was nicknamed the World's Fastest Human for winning the 100-meter sprint in the 1964 Olympics. When you talk about football "speed you are talking about players who can run 100 yards in less than 10 seconds; Bob Hayes could run the 100 in 9.1 seconds. That is super speed. (The ones who can't break 10 seconds learn to block.)

A half a second, from 9.5 to 10 seconds for 100 yards, seems like such a little difference, but .5 seconds converted into yards is *five* yards, or the difference between the 5-yard line and a touchdown—which might just mean a difference of seven points.

The fast ends like Hayes (and Homer Jones at the Giants) are spoiled, and think they can simply outrace the defensive backs. They expect to get their famous "half step" and be gone. Hayes is so fast he actually hardly needs moves, because by only shifting speed he can throw defensive backs off stride and force them to play him loose. Ray Berry's job is to teach the moves and finesse to Hayes, to teach him to channel his speed and use it more effectively.

"Bob Hayes is developing into a fine receiver because he is always working at it," said Irv Cross gallantly, but Cross always compliments the end he will play against the following Sunday.

"I was more serious about things before this game than I've ever been," said Hayes before the second Cowboy-Packer championship cliff-hanger. "I love football, but I also love money and this sure was a money game"—a sure sign that Hayes was growing up. Bullet Bob is a rarity, one of just a handful of track stars who learned to play football.

Some fugitives from the Mexican Olympics—from shot-putters to speedsters—are trying to make their presence felt in football. One is the world's fastest Jimmy Hines, at the Miami Dolphins. Hines demoted Bob Hayes to second fastest when he won the 100-meter dash in 9.9 seconds in Mexico City.

"I've told Hines he's got to learn to catch the ball in a crowd," says Hayes. "There's always going to be people trying to tear his head off when he goes out for a pass. He has the natural ability. But all his speed won't help if he can't take the knocks and catch the ball too."

Some ends never really make star billing because they lose concentration at the very last second—for fear of getting hit by the defender—and they drop the ball. Such a phenomenon is called "hearing footsteps." Bob Hayes was bestowed with this rap after a sensational rookie season. Hayes' critics said defenders had caught on that he didn't like contact and knew how to contain him when they played against him "the second time around."

"Hayes would rather catch a deep pass than a medium pass, so most of us give him a lot of room," said Irv Cross. "Of course, if he gets one step on you, he's gone. I think he prefers the deep pass because he doesn't like to get hit."

"You don't think about the guy coming up," says Jack Snow, "because you're going to get hit either way, whether you catch it or miss it." Jack Snow was the Rams' first flowerchild. He wore a hair no-cut when the Rams lost to Green Bay in thirteen degrees below zero and had the only warm head on the field. "You have to concentrate and you can't ever take your eyes off the ball," added Snow, who has made some spectacular juggling catches that have to be seen to be believed.

Snow makes it a habit never to eat breakfast. His usual daily menu includes two midmorning sandwiches and two more before he goes to bed. The Saturday night before a game he eats dinner at home with his wife, Merry Carole, and then Jack doesn't eat again until they go out for dinner Monday night.

"I can't stand the sight of food," says Jack. "For eighteen hours before a game and eighteen hours after I'm too unstrung to eat."

Snow almost qualifies for the "new breed" of receiver who is the envy of all—a matter-over-mind kind of end—combining speed, height, and strength; Snow comes up a little short in the speed department. Kansas City's Otis Taylor is one of these super types who is as fast as the fastest flanker but also tough and strong enough for contact. Taylor can block with the best of them, if he wants to.

"It's always a great thrill to me to block for Curtis (McClinton)," says Otis. "I know blocking is one thing that puts me closer to clothes and a new car, and I love them." Taylor has the reputation of being miserably conceited. "Not really," says another Chief. "Just say he has lots of confidence."

"I always had a natural talent for maneuvering my body," says Otis, not blushing. He is telling the truth. Originally a quarterback Otis could throw the ball 80 yards. He could high-jump 6′ 6″. And he's so fast that when he missed the team plane for Super Bowl I, he caught another flight and beat the Chiefs to their camp. He was fined $500 anyway.

Taylor is a home-run hitter, a constant deep threat who gets extra dangerous around enemy end zones. Instead of spending the afternoon trying to grind out scores with sideline passes and tiring smashes into the line the Chiefs can just throw it to Otis and pick up an "instant" touchdown. Best of the new breed, besides Otis, are Dick Gordon at the Bears, Gary Collins, Al Denson at Denver, and Homer Jones. Beauty has a step or two on the beast in Homer.

"In high school I didn't play football," said Homer. "I played saxophone in the Pittsburgh marching band." That's Pittsburgh, *Texas*. "I was on my way to the clarinet but I wanted to go to college, and they didn't give scholarships to sax players. So I thought I'd go out for football. My friends laughed and said I'd never even played. I said I'd been saving it all up.

"My best friend was an end. I wanted to be the other end, but they had one. My cousin got hurt—he was the fullback—so I went to fullback and scored the first time I got the ball."

Miracles just seem to happen to Homer, who for the past few years has been turning New York on with his naïve airs. When there was a transit strike they asked him how he'd get to the stadium practices. "That won't bother me," he said, "because I come by subway."

Homer Jones eludes Saints' defender Ben Hart.

45
88

Homer is a sublime spirit. He has a sense of humor, flat feet, and a wide smile. He has huge hands, great speed, is hard as a rock yet loose and relaxed. He likes fishing and he likes football. Homer is tough enough for a tight end's blocking duties, but not quite heavy enough, at 220, to endure long seasons of punishment.

In 1968 Homer slumped, dropping almost as many passes as he caught. He complained that the quarterback (Fran Tarkenton) wasn't throwing to him enough. Some agreed with Homer, some didn't, saying Tarkenton shouldn't throw to Homer if he was going to drop the ball. But when he caught one, and held on, Homer's catches had the same magic as before. All he really has to do is stop daydreaming when he's roaming around at wide end for the Giants.

7 Running Backs

At the end of the season three years ago the Associated Press was counting up votes for its all-star team and discovered, in red-faced dismay, that they were missing a fullback—that a halfback (Leroy Kelly) had won the starting fullback honors. Which should tell us something about wire service polls and something about running backs. Neither knows who's who or who's where.

As is their wont, broadcasters didn't help to clarify matters. Instead they created more jargon, replacing halfback and fullback with terms like slot back, set back, and scat back. Everybody was confused.

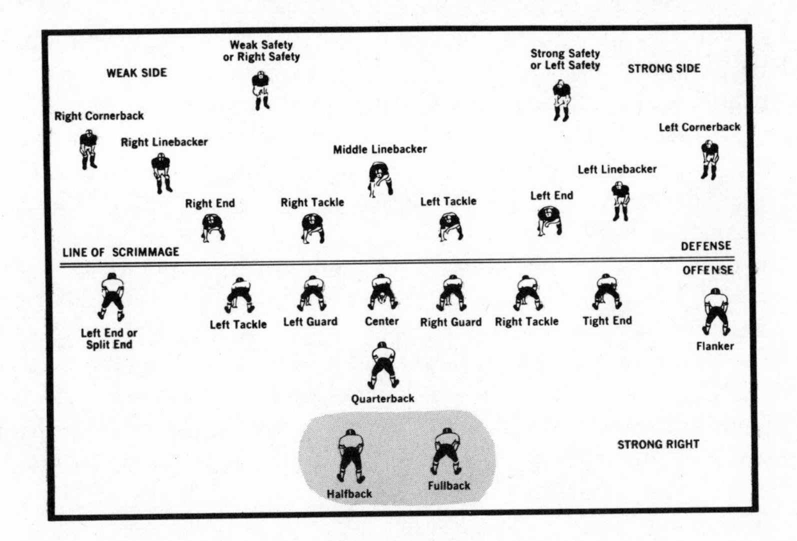

Traditionally there were two running backs, the halfback and the fullback. The halfback weighed 205 and had speed for ball-carrying and good hands for catching. The fullback weighed 220—at least that was the optimum—and had size and power for blocking and ball-carrying.

In those old days when fullbacks were synonymous with power, Jim Taylor was synonymous with fullback. Taylor, who moved to the New Orleans Saints before retiring, was once the man behind the Green Bay sweep. When coaches dream of power running plays they think of the Packer sweep. The sweep is still sweeping at Green Bay, but not as cleanly without Taylor.

The sweep play seems to flow, with rhythm and power. The eleven offensive players flood toward one sideline and try to "sweep" the fullback around end with enough room to run all the way to a touchdown, the way Taylor did.

You just don't run into Jim Taylors any more. He was one of the last head-down, nitty-gritty, power-through runners who ran blindly where he was supposed to. Old-fashioned fullbacks used their heads for ramming; new-fashioned ones use their heads to pick and choose where they will run. They have less power than the Jim Taylors did, and, except for Jim Nance at Boston and Larry Csonka at Miami, are smaller and quicker. The new breed thinks with his head and runs like a horse. Jim Taylor ran like a stampeding buffalo.

But what about poor Larry Csonka? Ten years ago he was typically suited for the pro game, at fullback. Today the heroes Csonka might have identified with are gray-haired and in easy chairs.

"I'm a short-yardage man," says Csonka. "I'm not a speedster. Third down is where I come in. I've patterned my play after Jim Taylor, who ran so hard and low."

Csonka's nickname at Syracuse was "Zonk," which he liked. "Zonk sounds like the kind of player I am," said Zonk. "Not exciting, not much of a swivel. It's not entertainment for the fans when I go four yards in a cloud of dust."

For much of his rookie season Csonka couldn't provoke a speck of dust without a vacuum cleaner. He missed several games with headaches and assorted concussions. The final insult is that there is always talk that Csonka, that cloud of hard-nosed dust, might be converted into an offensive lineman or linebacker.

What happened to the fullback was gridiron automation, the emphasis on passing. Passing did to the fullback what the airplane did to the railroad, replaced him with something faster. The new passing attack required a fullback to catch passes in addition to his other chores, and as a receiver he needed more speed. As a result football coaches stopped dreaming about old-fashioned fullbacks and began dreaming about Jim Brown, everyone's dream. He was the prototype of the new-fangled fullback.

Brown was one of the greatest athletes who ever ran. All-around ability gave him tremendous balance and strength, and he was almost never injured, because he was almost always under control. Raw unbridled speed is not enough. When a running back runs too fast he can't recover if he's hit, or change direction. Balance and control are more important.

Brown never fell awkwardly and was never hit hard. ("One of his secrets was taking only 25% as much pounding as everyone else," said one coach.) Brown was a unique combination—a strong power runner with speed and swivel-hipped agility. He had moves—a hip dip, a limber leg, a high knee, a straight arm—which he could make at top speed. Plus, he could catch.

In the summer of 1966, Jimmy was in London making a movie and the shooting schedule fell behind. He had to choose between the Browns and the movie, and with less class than he carried the ball, Brown retired at the tender age of twenty-nine.

Even at the peak of his career Jimmy carried a chip on his shoulder—a chip of bitterness as big as a telephone pole. He was a proud man and he did things loudly. A motel incident went into court (Brown was sued for assault and battery and paternity, and found not guilty), and into the headlines. A feud with Paul Brown, the founder, namesake, and head coach of the Cleveland Browns, ended up with the new owner, Art Modell, gaining majority control and firing Paul in favor of keeping Jimmy. (Jimmy turned around three years later and paid Modell back by retiring several years ahead of schedule.) After a half dozen movies Brown was making top dollar in Hollywood when he was arrested. His girl friend was found injured outside his apartment and it was unclear how she had fallen from his balcony. They later reconciled and Brown was given a choice—a $300 fine or 60 days in the clink. He paid.

Brown had such tremendous success on the field that it's tragic he found so little fulfillment in football. He was always frustrated and miserable and with more adulation came greater frustration. He was often criticized for not blocking, for not putting out on plays when he wasn't the ball carrier, but Brown rarely bothered to defend himself. His real problems stemmed from the fact that he was a Negro and didn't want to be. This trouble kept bugging him and, combined with the lure of the silver screen, caused him to retire so early. One of the first things he did was to push through his brainchild, the Negro Industrial and Economic Union, an organization which tries to help Negroes help themselves in the business world.

Brown's retirement came in the nick of time. Owners and coaches who had been trying to find another fullback like Brown were on the brink of suicide. Defensive game plans got goose bumps when Jimmy was Sunday's coming attraction. When he retired, defensive platoons to a man shouted, "Good riddance!" under their breaths and danced a jig.

Not coincidentally, it was less than six months after Brown retired that the Associated Press couldn't find a National League fullback for its all-star team. When the problem was resolved, it was simply a matter of an "adjustment" in the backfields. Halfbacks and fullbacks went the way of the steam engine, and in their stead were left two ball carriers who were called just plain running backs—left and right—with similar responsibilities, running, blocking, and catching. The NFL even went so far two years ago as to legislate "halfback" and "fullback" out of its official vocabulary, which is like baseball eliminating the terms "shortstop" and "basemen" in favor of four infielders.

As for the designation "running back," what a catchall that turned out to be. There were as many theories on what constituted the perfect running back as there were experts.

Running backs ranged from petite Mike Garrett (5′ 9″, 170) to a giant vintage fullback like Jim Nance (6′ 1″, 240). They were as quick on the trigger as Green Bay's Travis Williams (who is just a baby step slower than Bullet Bob Hayes) or as slow getting off the dime as the Giants' Ernie Koy. Nance is the giant economy size package, Gale Sayers is regular size, while Mike Garrett is one of the fashionable new minibacks, pocket-sized and perfect for traveling.

Oakland's Ben Davidson says, "Mike Garrett is the squirmy type of runner. If you make too quick a commitment, he has the speed to run right past you."

"There is room for the little man in this game," says Mike, "but the little man must work twice as hard as the big man to achieve success. Every time I carry the ball I feel I'm running for every small fella who ever wanted to play football."

"I guess there will always be a place for the small guy, but at flanker," disagreed Red Hickey, ex-coach of the 49ers, "where it's in close a little man can't live long these days."

"I only expect to play a total of five years," says Mike. "I don't think I can last much longer." The punishment given to Garrett by the giants just has to take its toll. The facts are cold. A big man can hit a little man just so hard so often. It's possible to look at football as a weight war. Hickey says, "I've seen the weights go up fifty or sixty pounds since I've been in the game. I don't think I'll live to see the day of the 400-pounder, but I think it's got to come."

The worst victim of the weight war is the running back, who must have acceleration. A running back with a slow start isn't a running back for very long. It's death on a simple hand-off; if a runner can't get started he'll be tackled behind the line of scrimmage.

"It's very difficult for a running back to go higher than 215 and keep the quickness necessary to get through that little hole in the line," says Dallas Coach Tom Landry.

In 1966 Ernie Koy, a running back with the New York Giants, gave the impression that he was counting his money as the quarterback finished calling signals. Driving a car, Ernie couldn't make it through an intersection without going through a red light. He was that slow a starter. Giant Coach Allie Sherman was about to give up on Koy. Allie even tried to trade him, but no one wanted a running back who needed the length of Utah's salt flats to get his speed up. Somehow in the last year or two Ernie learned to step on the gas.

At some teams there is very little difference between halfback and fullback. Duties vary from team to team depending on how the coach tailors his offense to the talents of his players. "The only real difference between the two positions is who blocks for who," declared Wendell Hayes, who played both positions for Denver. "I just want to play and do my best. I've moved back and forth from halfback to fullback about five times this year. It's no problem."

Not at Denver, perhaps, but at other teams where the fullback and halfback have different roles, changing jobs is dangerous. Accustomed to short runs up the middle, a fullback might run over his blockers on a wide run where he picks up speed for ten or fifteen yards before cutting downfield.

"You can only run a play as fast as your guards," says Baltimore's Tom Matte, whose all-purpose talents at running back earned him the nickname "garbage can runner" from Detroit's Alex Karras, the tackle-movie star. "I don't have such great speed, but it doesn't make that much difference most of the time."

Matte admires Gale Sayers and Leroy Kelly as superstars. Jim Nance's idol is Jim Brown. In the backfield, as it is everywhere else, the grass is always greener. The Zonks of the world would like to be a little flashier and the flashes wish they were bigger, to flash longer and harder. The littlest runner, Mike Garrett, is Jim Nance's biggest admirer and loves to watch him on television.

"He is everything that I'm not. He is so overpowering. I love to see the way he bruises men, the way he breaks through. Rather than hit Nance head-on, a cornerback will very carefully miss a tackle instead."

So Matte is slow, Jim Nance and Larry Csonka are big, Mike Garrett is little and Gale Sayers is fast, and they are all running backs. So much variety creates an identity problem. A running back doesn't know who to pattern himself after anymore.

Only a couple of winters ago at Miami's Racquet Club, Eva Gabor was held up. Her earrings were ripped off and she was relieved of $25,000. Eva ran out of her apartment, down the hall, and into Frank Gifford.

"Why don't you call a policeman, you halfwit," she screamed hysterically, and Gifford, suspecting a put-on, answered calmly, "I'm not a halfwit. I'm a halfback." Poor old Frank at least knew what he was.

Halfback

A halfback is happiest when he has running room. He would prefer to run to the outside, running around the defense, while the fullback tends to run straight ahead, through the defense, bursting up the middle.

"A back is supposed to go inside or outside," says Gale Sayers. "He isn't a running back if he can't."

By Sayers' standards many running backs who are currently employed shouldn't be.

Good ones have been scarce on the market. Every team tried to find a Jimmy Brown but came up with unreasonably slow facsimiles. Every team now tries to find a Gale Sayers, but the candidates are usually smaller and, again, slower. Sayers is today's greatest halfback. Fast, powerful, tough, Gale can bust a game wide open any time he has the ball, and most of the time he has it because the Bears' passing attack has been practicing non-aggression for years. Bears' fans describe their offense: "Sayers left, Sayers right, incomplete pass and on fourth down, punt."

If a halfback doesn't have power to go with his speed, he can't break tackles. The ballcarrier has momentum going for him, so he shouldn't be brought down by only one tackler. A runner avoids a would-be tackler in the open field in only two ways—by powering through him (fullback-style) or by faking around him (halfback-style).

Dick Bass at Los Angeles and Gale Sayers are the types that can avoid tacklers at top speed—with a head move one way, a shoulder move another, with a side step, a dragging leg, a split-second change-up—leaving fallen tacklers in their wakes. There have been very few runners who could cut and turn, slide and veer—at full speed—which is called broken field running.

Sayers is a master at "cutting." Halfbacks who can't cut get cut, quickly. Sayers can make perpendicular cuts. Most important, he makes them without slowing down. Sayers will be running in a slanting direction to the right and all of a sudden he straightens his right leg, drives into the ground, and pushes off. In one instant he is now running in a slanting direction to the left—a 90° cut.

Hugh McElhenny was the best broken field runner by reputation, but Sayers is as good. Until he tore up his right knee in 1968, Sayers, like Jimmy Brown, hadn't suffered a serious injury. Excellent balance is the reason. According to Gale, "The secret is in not getting hit too solidly. If you can roll with the tackle like a fighter does with a punch you're going to last longer."

Runners with a low center of gravity usually have exceptional balance. Mike Garrett is only 5′ 9″ short, but he has a 17½-inch neck and shoulders

Floyd Little.

to match. At Houston Hoyle Granger is much bigger and stronger at 225 and, according to Hoyle, much of his power comes from his legs, sturdy driving pistons with huge 22″ calves. Floyd Little at Denver is famous for his bowed legs, which may help his balance and surely help his faking, making it easier for him to hide shifts of weight and direction. It was so very natural for Floyd to take up horseback riding when he joined the Broncos, and his wife Joyce soon followed in his hoofsteps.

At Syracuse, Floyd came toward the end of a winning streak of great runners which began with Jim Brown and went through Ernie Davis (who died of leukemia before he could play for Cleveland), John Mackey (Baltimore's excellent tight end), Jim Nance, Floyd, and Larry Csonka. For his size and speed Jim Brown had the best balance.

"Brown was so big," says Mike Garrett, "that he didn't even have to wear hip pads, because he ran into the tackler and wasn't hit so often from the side. I have to run away from the tackler, and I wear every piece of equipment I can get my hands on."

When Garrett arrived at Kansas City, he was accussed of a duck-footed waddle à la Charlie Chaplin. The duck image stuck because, for some reason—surely Mike didn't receive extensive practice in the rain at Southern Cal—there is something about Garrett's style, his sturdy legs and low center of gravity, that makes him extra dangerous on a muddy field. When it rains he pours it on even harder.

Oddly, Gale Sayers is another super "mudder," most unusual for a breakaway type of runner. The dazzlers in the open field are usually the first to slip, losing their footing on a slick field.

"I cut on my heels," says Gale. "That's what helps me keep my footing in the mud. Most backs cut on the balls of their feet." Gale grew up in Speed, Kansas, which he describes as "right down the road from Nicodemus," for those uninformed people who can't exactly pinpoint the whereabouts of Speed any better than tacklers can pinpoint Gale.

"Gale Sayers is the greatest of them all," says Mike. "He has very quick feet and blinding speed. I have to weave to get past the defense, try to keep them off-balance. If a linebacker comes at me too quickly his weight is forward and I can move to the right or left, fool him, go around him. If he waits, then I have to run away, laterally. My forte is great lateral movement. But Sayers—give him a tiny opening and he explodes."

Compared to Mike Garrett and O. J. Simpson, who came out of Southern Cal with the Heisman Trophy, Ben Wilson was a lesser luminary. (The University of Southern California is, like Syracuse, another running back factory.) A few seasons back Wilson arrived at Green Bay a has-been, a 250-pound straight-ahead steamboat, but Vince Lombardi took the slow-starting Wilson, set him to jumping rope for better footwork and agility, put him on a diet, and sent him to the eye doctor.

"The doctor said he was surprised I ever caught a football with these eyes of mine. Come to think of it, the football did look pretty small."

Wilson became a matinee idol during Super Bowl II when he spent the fourth quarter of the game in front of a national television audience of 70,000,000, crawling on his hands and knees about the sideline. Ben had lost the contact lens from his right eye when a doctor had mistakenly swabbed it onto the ground. "That thing cost $43.50 to replace," said Wilson, who collected $15,000 for showing up that afternoon.

The latest and bluest chip back of all, of course, is O. J. Simpson, class of 1969. No college runner in a decade created such a furor as Simpson. Not even Gale Sayers.

"O. J.'s electrifying the way he can break open a game. He runs over, around, and through people. I can't," says Garrett. "I don't have his size, strength, or speed. I just hope to run them ragged."

"When Gale Sayers plays, I watch him," says Simpson, who runs with a fast, fluid style, not high-stepping, but with his feet close to the ground. "No man in football can compare. When I watch a game I naturally watch the backs, to see if I can do what they do, and I usually think I can, but I don't know if I can do some of the things I see Sayers do. He's the greatest breakaway runner ever."

Gale leapt on the O. J. bandwagon with reservations. "He's a fine back but he doesn't impress me as having outside speed. He sees holes and hits them and gets out fast, but he'll find a different game in the pros.

He'll run less. He's used to grabbing the ball and running fifty times a game, but in the pros they throw on second-and-eight and third-and-five. He'll be asked to do different things, to learn to block, to analyze different defenses, and he'll have to pick up audibles at the line of scrimmage."

It's this mutual admiration society of speed merchants like Sayers, Simpson, and Cleveland's Leroy Kelly that has set teams like Chicago and Green Bay to thinking and dreaming about making more out of their running potential. Before the invincible Lombardi moved to Washington, he said he'd like very much to have a backfield with three runners. It was in his plans for the Packers. Vincent was saying he wanted the best of two worlds, that he was ready to borrow from the past and start the offensive pendulum on its way down—from pass, pass, pass, to run, run, run.

A backfield with three runners only means that the flanker is a good runner—part halfback, part end. Lombardi announced his plans as if he were Moses on the mountain, but the idea of moving Donny Anderson wide to flanker was hardly new. The man Lombardi replaced as coach of the Redskins, Otto Graham, had experimented boldly three years ago by moving his super Halfback Charley Taylor out to flanker. Kyle Rote had made the same move a decade before.

As far as former Ram Cornerback Irv Cross was concerned, moving Taylor out to flanker was a brilliant move by Otto. When Cross sees Charley he gets nervous. "Charley Taylor is a dangerous runner when he gets the ball, even more so than Bob Hayes. The Redskins like to get the ball to Taylor quick—on quick slants and short cuts—because he can really go. That's how he makes most of his yardage." (Forward passes are measured from the line of scrimmage to the spot where the play ends, not where the pass is caught.)

This is exactly what Lombardi wants, as many really good runners as possible playing at the same time. With Elijah Pitts, Jim Grabowski, and Travis Williams all healthy, Donny Anderson was semi-expendable and could have been moved to flanker. Anderson was happy about the idea.

"In college I always thought I might go as a flanker in the pros. I'm a little taller at 6′ 3″ than most halfbacks and run the hundred in about ten seconds flat."

Flanker is a more appealing spot because receivers last a lot longer, take less hitting, and have easier blocking duties than halfbacks. "But I'd like another year or two at halfback," continued Anderson. "The experience will really help me in running with the ball after the catch."

It will be interesting to see what happens to Donny Anderson. His $600,000 bonus, just for signing with Green Bay, was the biggest ever, and surely doesn't lessen his status as Green Bay's most eligible bachelor. Donny is an overwhelming favorite to eclipse the original Packer Golden

Boy, Paul Hornung. Donny lives in Green Bay's biggest apartment house, but there are more apartments on Joe Namath's *floor* than in Donny's whole building. "If you want to have fun you go to Milwaukee," said one of Donny's friends.

While Lombardi was contemplating Anderson at flanker, the Bears were trying a similar experiment with Gale Sayers. By putting him out at flanker, Coach Jim Dooley would have Sayers over the line of scrimmage and out in the open that much qiucker. Nailing Sayers in the open field is a tremendous chore and one that would put great pressure on opposing defenses.

Unfortunately, the experiments aborted. Sayers tore three knee ligaments, and Vince Lombardi demoted himself from coach-and-general-manager to just general manager. Unaccountably, one of the first things that Vince talked about changing when he went to Washington was Charley Taylor—back to running back.

"Moving from running back to flanker isn't that easy a transition," says Houston's Ode Burrell, who made the switch. "You know a ballplayer is supposed to do everything automatically, but I'd go into the huddle and automatically I'd think what the halfback does, instead of what the flanker does."

Burrell finally learned flanker with the help of the Houston cornerbacks. Practicing against them he learned he was giving away his post pattern by leaning inside. "A flanker has to run all his patterns straight. They told me always to concentrate on lining up the exact same way, so that the defense wouldn't know whether it was a pass play coming up or a run."

Ode Burrell, Charley Taylor, and Kyle Rote, all flankers, wore jersey numbers in the 40s, a good clue that the flanker was once a running back.

Sometimes when you see Charley Taylor it's hard to tell what he was or where he was going. He arrived at the Boston airport for a game and a confused Washington football writer, Dave Brady, thought he was in London, on Carnaby Street. Taylor was wearing a dark blue shirt with gold flecks, white collar and white cuffs. His tie was blue-on-yellow and he wore dark blue pants with bold chalk stripes and a two-inch-wide bell. "Taylor's slacks were slack only at the ankles," said Brady.

When he saw Taylor's groovy outfit, Sonny Jurgensen was aghast. "I wonder what my wife would say if I came home wearing something like that."

Running backs are thrown to so often they need good hands for catching and holding on to the ball after they've caught it. If you're going to last long as a ball carrier, you can't fumble the ball when you're tackled.

The Travis Williams caper belongs in a textbook on how to hold on to the ball.

Travis was an unknown junior college runner in California, the first to run the 100-yard dash in 9.3 (Bob Hayes later pushed the record to 9.1). When Williams later went to Arizona State he had a wife and two children and was too busy earning money to go out for both football and track. He skipped track, was a mediocre halfback ("I just didn't do anything") and was way down (93) on the list of college prospects chosen by the pros.

"I had a tendency to overrun holes in college and not pick up blockers. And as a pass-receiver, I was running before the ball even got to me." This is as sure a method for fumbling as has ever been discovered.

Lombardi prescribed a football for Travis's fumbleitis. "Every time I see you I want to see you holding it the way you should. Everyplace. Carry it in the chow line. Take it to the drugstore. Take it to bed with you. If I see you without it, it'll cost you."

Quarterback Zeke Bratkowski made Travis a football with a pair of handles taped on and Tackle Henry Jordan told him, "Around here we don't think of it as a football. We think of it as a loaf of bread worth thirty thousand dollars a man."

"I guess I didn't help matters by fumbling," said Travis, "but I didn't know if I would be there from one day to the next. Every time you looked around another rookie was packing his bag." Travis, of course, was still packing the ball around.

"Everybody'd try to take it away from me, but I carried that thing everywhere, even to see the *St. Valentine's Day Massacre* movie. You never knew where you might run across *him*." Him being Lombardi, whose remedy worked. Travis regularly returned kickoffs and regularly went all the way to a touchdown.

During the Lombardi era it was always an asset if a Packer rookie could sing. It was Vincent's habit to call upon Elijah Pitts for a song or two, to entertain at supper, and, at Vincent's going away party—Lombardi Day, 1968—Travis Williams belted out his own version of "That's Life," to thunderous applause.

Travis Williams suffered a severe sophomore slump, but the whole team slumped with him, and Travis's fans were quick to rally to his defense, saying that opposing teams were doubling their defenses against him. Time will tell, of course, but Travis appears to have a rare instinct for carrying the ball. All the good ones have it. Their styles vary—Emerson Boozer has bounce to the ounce, Leroy Kelly runs smooth as silk, Gale Sayers veers and glides wide open—but never is that special instinct more apparent than on kickoff returns, when coaches are willing to risk their super stars to the hazards of such suicidal duty.

"I just look for a hole and let instinct get me loose," says Sayers, who is infuriated when opposing kickers aim away from him and complains at loud length. He can't get enough of that dirtiest work.

Leroy Kelly blocking for his quarterback, Frank Ryan.

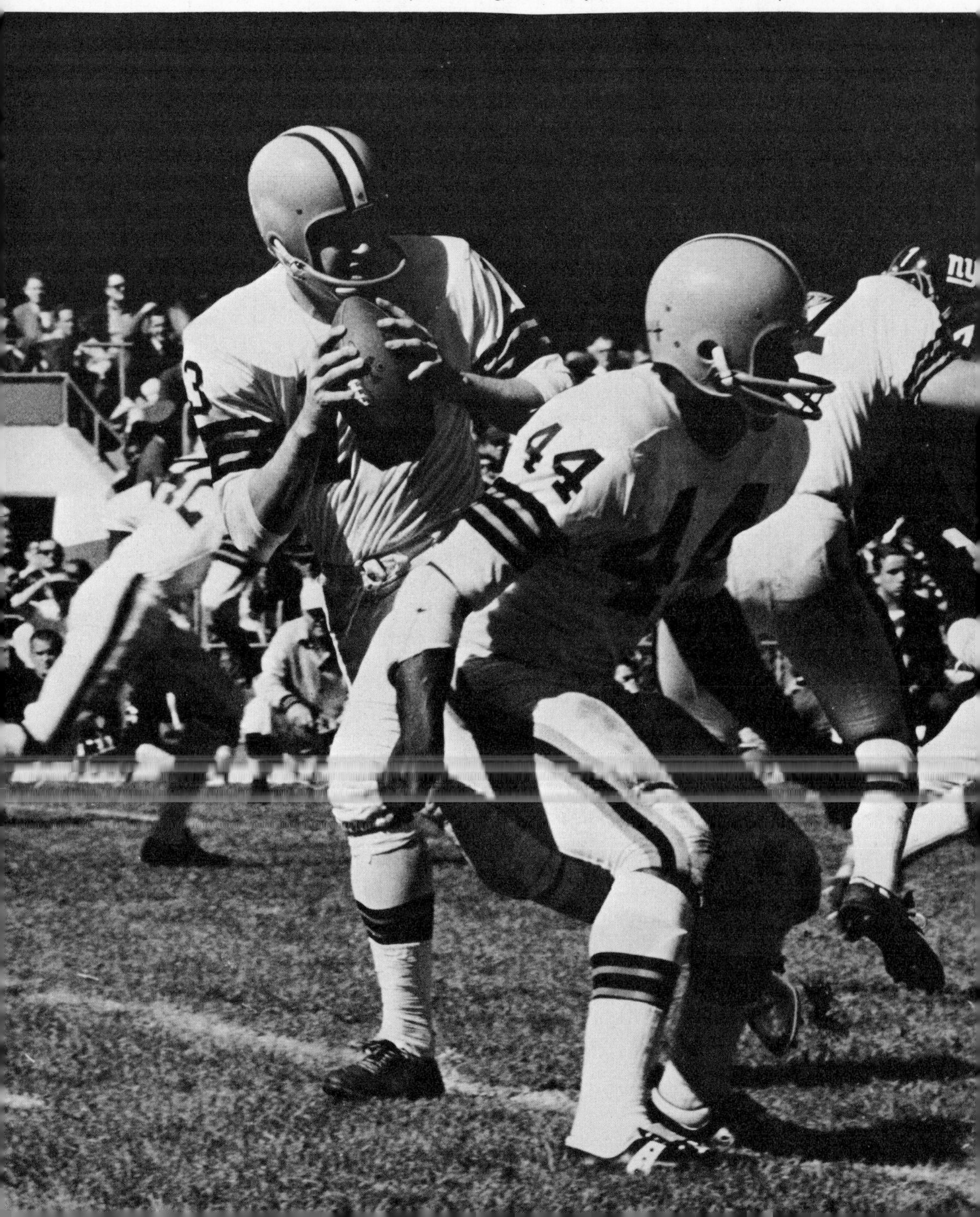

At Cleveland Leroy Kelly, who ran along after Jimmy Brown, was first discovered running back kicks. He did it so well he was chosen to perform in *The Fortune Cookie*, a Billy Wilder movie with Jack Lemmon, and ran back kicks for hours of shooting. Kelly is now such a celebrity that the Browns use inferior but less valuable players to return kickoffs, unless in the direst of circumstances, like a championship game.

Leroy has the perfect hands for cliché-lovers who like to mutter about "a good pair of hands." He is an excellent receiver and would be the perfect instructor for fumbling Travis Williams. Kelly almost never fumbles. He has a baseball background, at shortstop, which naturally helped to develop his catching ability.

Leroy's high school baseball coach, Pete Lorenc, said he could have been a major-leaguer. "He could do it all, throw, field, hit with power, and run. In fact, Leroy was the best base runner I ever saw."

With the Browns, Leroy is one of the best broken-field runners in football, not as powerful as Gale Sayers but a little faster. He has such a fast start that officials are always alert to make sure that he doesn't start too soon (an offsides penalty). He's also a fast man with a buck—that is, a coin.

"My most valuable coin is a French nickle dated 1802," says Kelly, the collector. "It's worth about a hundred dollars."

Kelly is a swinger. A bachelor, he has a penthouse apartment in Cleveland with a leopard sofa, a closet full of golf clubs and fishing tackle, a huge stack of records (many are Motown sound), and a few other closets full of tailor-made English-cut suits—the longer the jacket the better.

"Not many people know where I live, but the paperboy tells his friends, 'yeah, I know Leroy Kelly' and brings his friends up to meet me and get an autograph."

When Leroy is described as a "slashing runner" he laughs. He also laughs at the "Kelly hurdle." ("I only hurdle when I have to. It's an instinctive move, but I don't do it that much.")

Kelly is such a fast man with a buck that in 1967 he played out the option year of his contract at a 10% salary cut. Originally, Kelly had been at somewhat of a bargaining disadvantage, coming to the pros an unknown and chosen only by the National League. Playing out his option was a big gamble. If Leroy had broken his leg and couldn't play again he'd have been sunk without a contract. Then, the following spring, he came to terms with the Browns and signed for $60,000.

Kelly's shortstop background surely contributed to his super reflexes, which may be the quickest of the running backs'. Ten years ago, reflexes, especially the mental ones, weren't as necessary as today when a superior running game requires split-second time on hand-offs and blocking assignments. When Jimmy Brown came to the Browns, it was the day of the quick opener, and the blockers were supposed to open a hole for the back to run through. When Leroy Kelly came to Cleveland, the blocking assignments were more flexible, and often Kelly is given a choice between holes or is even told to find his own. It isn't the runner's role that has changed as much as it is the blockers'.

The old way, the offensive lineman was on the attack with a specific duty to block a specific defensive lineman out of the way in a specific direction. The new way, the offensive lineman can wait, forcing the defensive lineman to make the first move, which puts the defender on the attack. As the defense moves, of course, a hole (daylight) is left somewhere and the halfback runs for it. Both the blockers and the runner are *reacting* to the moves of the defensive linemen.

"You just let the blocker take the defender where he wants to go," explains Kelly. "When I see what direction they're going in, then I just cut away from the traffic."

Vince Lombardi calls this his "daylight theory"—giving the runner his choice under one basic commandment: to run to daylight, wherever it happens to show up.

"In college I either hit the hole the play called for or was thrown for a loss if it wasn't there," said Detroit Halfback Mel Farr, brother of Houston's Cornerback Miller Farr and Rookie of the Year in 1967. "I didn't do any option running, finding the hole and running for daylight wherever it was. So, in the pros, I first have to find the hole the play called for with my head, and then have to be able to turn it on with my feet."

Rookie runners have the most difficulty with blocking—their own and other players'. They're used to running out on their own and it's hard to get used to following an escort, who might be a guard, a tight end, or the other running back, or a combination of same.

"I made mistakes like breaking away from my blockers when I could have gone all the way if I'd stuck behind them," said Farr after his rookie year. "I can't blame anybody but myself."

Farr was also critical of his own blocking. "Pass-blocking is one of the hardest things to learn. In the pros the running backs have to do a lot of it and it's not that easy. Anybody can learn to block a man coming in, but sometimes a safety and a linebacker will come in together and you have to learn which one to pick up. In college I wasn't taught to pick up a linebacker. I had to learn to pick up the inside man. If I got the outside man, the inside one could get to the quarterback." Mel was explaining perfectly why Weeb Ewbank kept Emerson Boozer benchbound for most of his rookie year.

When Boozer first came to the Jets, he moved into a bachelor apartment and had trouble with his cooking and his blocking—which wasn't unusual, but Ewbank would be about as ready to let an incompetent blocker play halfback in front of his $400,000 quarterback as he would be to wear his hair shoulder length.

What was unusual about Boozer was his feet. He had bad bunion trouble. He still has.

"I have a bunion on the side of each foot off the big toe, and that's the part of the foot that you get most of your balance from. I'm afraid if I had those bunions taken off I would lose my balance, like Billy Joe did."

After Billy Joe was Rookie of the Year he had his bunions removed. According to Boozer, "After the operation he seemed to topple over quicker, lose some of his balance. I don't want that to happen to me. Balance lets you twist and turn like I do." Boozer and Billy Joe give the Jets a bunion backfield.

Emerson kept his bunions and got new shoes that weigh four pounds each. "I'm wearing size EE shoes and my feet swim in them, but I've got them lined with foam rubber and extra soles to brace my bunions so they never even touch the bottom of my shoes." Still, Boozer runs in constant pain and sometimes after a game he'll have to soak his feet for an hour before the pain goes away. "He's really got tremendous courage," says Weeb Ewbank, his coach and number one fan.

Emerson's blocking talents are long established, but in 1967 he suffered a serious leg injury, much like Gale Sayers', and he never regained top form during the Jets' 1968 Super Bowl season. It's urgent that he recover. Besides having one of football's most fascinating last names and a brand-new double breasted wardrobe (1970-look "threads") Emerson's running is vital to the Jets' plans.

"I've never seen a more punishing runner," said Boozer's Lucey Laney High School coach David Dupree. Boozer, the graduate/hero, returns to Augusta, Ga. frequently to speak to Lucey Laney students.

"My high school coach made us hit the tackling dummy and then spin off," explains Boozer. "That's what I still do. I'll hit the primary hole, but under control, in case it's not open. If it's not open I go outside and look for another hole, spinning off into the open area. Tacklers don't expect that extra spin. They don't expect you to come right in on them and then bounce off. It gives the runner a surprise edge."

Gale Sayers started off at the Bears just like Boozer, on the bench because of questionable blocking ability. George Halas kept Gale off the field except for returning kicks for the first three games of the season, three games which the Bears lost. In desperation, Sayers was allowed to play and the Bears won all but two of their remaining games.

"I told him right at first about the way McAfee used to hit 'em, just below the knees," said Halas. "I told Gale if you hit 'em right there, you can knock down an elephant."

"I stick my helmet in people's stomachs," says Gale, who is the only halfback to be consistently compared to George McAfee. Comparing a runner to McAfee is, like comparing a blonde starlet to Marilyn Monroe, the supreme compliment.

The ideal way to block is to hit the tackler low, natural for a short runner. The ideal way for a tackler to hit is around the numbers, much easier for a tall defender going after a short runner. Minnesota's Coach Bud Grant took great pains to teach his Defensive Tackle Alan Page to tackle high. "If you tackle a man low, around the legs, he still might be able to run over you for a few extra yards or even get away. Some players take years to learn it and others never learn."

"The legs are what move when a man is running—not his trunk," said Page. "The numbers make a better target." Page was very successful as a rookie. In one game when the Lions set an anti-record—fumbling eleven times—Page caused three of the fumbles himself. It's lucky for Alan, who is 6′ 5″, that his orders are to tackle high. He would have quite a time trying to tackle one of the minirunners low, around the knees.

As in the other jungle, nature happily provides the little football player with some pluses of his own. Some have been as wide as they were tall—Tom (The Bomb) Tracy and Charley Tolar resembled mobile fireplugs. Tolar was almost 5′ 6″ and weighed in at 200. "Tackling Tolar," said one 6′ 5″ AFL tackler, "is like trying to grab a manhole cover."

When Tolar was running with the ball the linebackers couldn't see him. A hole would close up and he'd shift along laterally, looking for another hole, and the linebackers would lose sight of him behind some big lineman. When Charley was blocking it was another story. Running along crouched over, he was like a big cannonball that kept gathering momentum until plop! Charley would hit his man low and prove all over again that the bigger they are the harder they fall.

Which brings us to Dick Bass, one of the best blocking backs of all, though he doesn't look it. Bass is one of the "new look" halfbacks, except that he has been around playing fullback for nine years. When they vote for a "petite All-Pro" team, Bass will be on it, along with such midgets as Dick Post and Mike Garrett. Garrett is a great Dick Bass fan. "I think we run quite a bit alike," says Mike, who is earning as hardnosed a reputation for blocking as Bass has. The minibacks are good blockers, but they need a knack, like Charley Tolar's cannonball.

"I try to overcome the bigger linebackers by technique," says Bass, who needs guts to pick up a 240-pound linebacker with a 10-yard running start. "I try to get the backer before he can get his steam up. If I do I can block him from an upright position. If he's coming in at full speed I have to hit him low, cut him off at the legs. A man's legs are his weak spot. If you can upset him you've got him."

Dick Bass as Hobbs of British Intelligence.

Bass also has a knack when he's running. "When I'm tackled in the line, usually the tackler relaxes for just one second. He figures he has me. That's when I drive forward. Sometimes I can break the tackle by spinning or lunging. Even if I can't get loose, I usually can fall forward for another couple of yards."

Dick Bass has been a wearer of many hats—a sports announcer, a disc jockey and a bail bondsman, but these were professions which absorbed the inner man. Outwardly, as suits a man of so many talents, Bass looks at life as a mad, mad costume party, and he appears au go go (green hiphuggers, Mexican sandals, no socks), as Jungle James (pith helmet, bermuda shorts, and lots of buttons on the jacket), as Engineer Bill (pin-stripe overalls, oil-resistant brogues, red bandanna) or, and this is Dick's long-time favorite, as Hobbs of British Intelligence. Hobbs is Bass's most celebrated other self. "That's my traveling outfit, especially when I go East. For a Sunday I might wear gray accessories—Homburg, English-cut suit, vest, double-breasted overcoat, high-button shoes, umbrella-cane, and attaché case."

Bass says he's a natural-born dresser, with four closetsful of clothes. One is only for shoes and one just for slacks. "I was wearing psychedelic things long ago. I like to wear something different. I like to dress according to climate. If the sun is out I dress happy. I feel I look best in whatever I like, whatever suits my fancy. It doesn't make any difference how loud or quiet your clothes are, it's how they're cut and how you wear them."

Dick isn't the only chic Ram. "Claude Crabb dresses well and Deacon Jones, for a big man. He wears stripes and the polka dots, the clashing colors. Good taste. When Gale Sayers was out here for the Pro Bowl I took him to some shops where I buy my stuff. He said he wouldn't touch 'em, that he couldn't wear them in Chicago. Heck, what makes me different is that I'm the only one with nerve enough to wear my array of things."

Dick somehow managed to gain 5,000 yards during an era when, if Mike Garrett had shown up at a training camp the coach would have called for a flyswatter. As a 195-pound fullback in 1960, Bass was as ahead of his time on the gridiron as he is in his closet.

"Everything goes in circles," said Dick. "We've gone back to the double-breasted look. I've always been fond of that. The next trend is going to be the Roaring '20s—wide ties, wide lapels, big hats. I can't wait."

He won't have to. Dick is already in. The biggest spotlights today are saved for the littlest running backs, the smaller the better. They are the rage.

Except for the offensive linemen football, like fashion, runs in cycles. In the beginning the glamorpusses were the scorers, the quarterbacks and halfbacks. Then in the Fifties the New York Giants' defensive line was the first "front four" to come into style, and since then the latest fads, in order, have been linebackers (Sam Huff's "violent world"), blitzing safeties, track stars playing wide end, scrambling quarterbacks, soccer-style placekickers, and now no team is chic or in vogue without a miniback.

Fullback

San Diego Coach Sid Gilman can't say enough about his 5' 10", 195-pound runner Dick Post. "He's really something. He opens up our offense." Post is a sprinter who ricochets off tacklers and lands in motion going in another direction. In spite of his size, tiny Dick doesn't mind blocking and picks up a blitzing linebacker with the best.

Jim Nance sometimes ricochets too, but whoever he uses for a wall won't laugh. Nance has 800 more ounces of bounce than Dick Post.

"He likes to hit the line and then bounce off to the outside," says Jet Defensive End Gerry Philbin, reciting his ode to Jim Nance. "I have to make sure he doesn't get around me, so against him I play a little farther outside than usual.

"We try to gang-tackle him every time, with everybody. You give him an inch and he goes, so you've got to get him before he gets up momentum, behind the line of scrimmage. After that his momentum is unbelieveable."

Jim is the only old-fashioned B-I-G superback in pro football today. He's a 240-pound battering ram who can catch, block, and run over people—the perfect fullback. Jimmy Brown and he are often compared, more often because they went to the same college. Nance is less sophisticated but more powerful than Brown. His success has come much slower.

Unfortunately, Jim Nance's favorite treats are lobster, pecan pie and chocolate cake, all of which contributed to the fat, out-of-shape self that Jim presented to Boston in his rookie year. Because of his jelly belly the Patriots began calling him the "Jelly Soldier," and Jim decorated the bench for most of the season. At one point, before Thanksgiving 1965, Nance ballooned to 260 pounds and was told off royally by the Boston coach. The next week he crash dieted, lost 14 pounds and gained 66 yards against Kansas City. Unfortunately that wasn't the happy ending to Nance's story. His weight still goes up and down like a roller coaster.

Jim Nance was one of ten children who came from a mining family in Western Pennsylvania. "My father set the caps on the dynamite that blows the coal loose," said Jim, "and he thinks it's safer than what I do."

What a fullback should do is bull his way through the crowded middle where the traffic is, maneuvering like a motorcycle.

"Some days I run more outside than usual, to see what I can do. It really doesn't make that much difference, but when I go up the middle I take a little turn here, a little turn there, and I'm off." He hopes . . . especially in crucial situations. When his team needs to scratch for an extra yard, when it's fourth-and-one late in a game, the fullback is the man.

Although running to daylight gives so many alternatives to both backs that their roles are more and more similar, the lighter backs still prefer to find daylight out wide where it's less painful, and Jim Nance still feels more at home inside, where it hurts.

"With our system of options there are so many things I can do when I go up the middle," says Nance. "If there's a hole where it's supposed to be, I take it. If it's not, I find my own. But it's a split second thing, and I can't delay my decision."

Nance says the decisions don't come easily until at least the third year. As a sophomore he learned some blocking techniques, like who to look for on blitzes, but it wasn't until a year later that decisions were automatic.

"The third year you start adding everything up," said Jim, whose best year was his second, when he ran wild for 1,500 yards. "You get to a point where you know when your quarterback is going to check off before he actually does. You can see when the other team is going to blitz, and you don't think of who you're going to block, but how."

Fullbacks might block any defender from a little 185-pound blitzing safety all the way through blitzing linebackers and up to the 280-pound defensive ends. Both the fullback and the halfback also block for each other on running plays. Two of the best: Don Perkins at Dallas, who blocked for his halfback Dan Reeves, and Curtis McClinton, Kansas City's erudite bachelor fullback, who spends much of his time blocking for Mike Garrett. Garrett has these famous outside moves, often thanks to his co-worker McClinton.

"The first block is from the leading running back, and that's me," explained Curtis. "From that point of attack everything is built up, so you can see how important it is. On a running play I'm the traffic cop. I set up a traffic flow by hitting the linebacker or defensive end. The pulling guard comes on by, convoying the running back."

In this situation McClinton is blocking like a lineman. "I block as much as the guards. Why don't you call me a third guard, who also runs and catches passes?"

Jim Nance enjoys catching passes because the more he catches the more the defenses will have to worry about Nance the Receiver, which might take a little pressure off Nance the Ballcarrier. And there's another reason too. "On pass receiving I like being one on one with somebody so I can try to run over my man," says Nance, who is nicknamed "Big Bo" after his high school singing group, the Beaumarx. "And I don't think it hurts my running either. In fact I think running a pass pattern outside every so often helps my running inside."

It's important that a back doesn't lose his balance when he's blocking, and stays on his feet so that he can run out afterward to catch a pass. The safety-valve receiver fullback is exemplified by Hewritt Dixon of Oakland.

Hewritt came to Oakland from Denver as a tight end, but Al Davis immediately moved him to fullback. A combination of reasons at the Raiders—brand-new, learning quarterback; not the fastest receivers; and Halfback Clem Daniels' sitting out the second half of 1967 with a broken ankle—pushed Hewritt to the top of Oakland's list of receivers, which is one way Hewritt helped to push his team into Super Bowl II.

Clem Daniels is one of the game's great running backs, and blockers. He's now a senior citizen with the 49ers, but in his heyday at Oakland, Daniels, who could play both halfback and fullback, was devastating. Some backs don't make good receivers because they can't get wide open. They advertise to the linebackers the fact that they are intended receivers. Daniels did the opposite. He advertised that he was just a blocker.

"I would check back like a blocker, then streak off downfield," says Clem. "If I can catch the middle linebacker asleep, the lane is clear and I'm wide open for the pass."

One linebacker spy tells how the Jets' Matt Snell used to give himself away and tip off the defense.

"When Snell is blocking he doesn't need to keep an eye on the ball. He looks ahead, watching for a lineman or a blitzing linebacker. But I can tell when he's going to be a receiver, because he switches his eyes and keeps looking at the ball."

There are hundreds of ways for the defense to guess what's coming next.

"I gave it away in San Diego once," said Jim Nance, "and we saw it afterward in game films. I tipped San Diego by my stance that I was going to drop back and block—so they knew to expect a pass."

Jim Nance is full of idiosyncracies. He doesn't eat anything before a game because he feels he's quicker on an empty stomach. And meaner.

"When I wake up the day of the game I want to hear my stomach growling. I want to feel mean. If I don't think I have something wrong with me, then I'm inclined to become complacent."

He showers before *and* after a game, which has always been duly noted by the Fourth Estate as superstitious. "Wrong," says Jim. "The dressing room is so noisy and crowded that I figure taking a shower is a great escape. I like to get up for the game when it's quiet and easier to concentrate."

Jim is strong and likes to carry the ball twenty or more times per game. If you watch him you will see he gets up very slowly after a play, which leads people to think he is injured, or is pretending to be. (The colloquialism for pretending is "dogging it.")

"I get up slow to rest," says Jim. "There's no point in jumping up and rushing back to the huddle. I try to conserve energy."

Clem Daniels was always quick to say that the key to any offense is the line blocking. "The timing between me and the fullback in coordination with the guards on running plays," said Clem, "that's the whole thing."

At Boston, Center Jon Morris is unusually talented. He can lead runners like a guard. The runner he usually blocks for is Nance, who gives Jon a little extra incentive.

"If you miss your block Jim will run right into you and it really hurts," said Jon, who runs the risk of becoming instant pavement himself when he leads the way for Nance.

Jim has an 18½ inch neck and won ninety-one out of ninety-two matches as a collegiate wrestling champion—not necessarily because he was crazy about wrestling. "When I was a freshman at Syracuse," he explained, "the football varsity was going to the Liberty Bowl. After the last regular game they needed our freshman team for guinea pigs—to scrimmage with the varsity and keep them sharp for the Bowl—so I went out for wrestling." The one match Jim lost he says was a mistake and in his senior year he was undefeated. He keeps toying with the idea of taking off-season professional wrestling seriously and Kansas City's Tackle Ernie Ladd is always throwing out a challenge.

One of the linebackers Jim occasionally had to block was Wahoo McDaniel. Wahoo is gone now—his exit was rather hasty—but he's not forgotten.

Wahoo first became famous with the Jets in New York—he was the first famous Jet—but went to the Miami Dolphins in 1966. A Choctaw Indian, Wahoo came from Oklahoma and wrestled on the pro tour in the off-season using a nom de theatre, Chief Wahoo. Far from being a clown, Wahoo was a serious sort, stocky and headstrong. He felt strongly about the plight of the American Indians and worked hard in their behalf along with leaders like Marlon Brando, a long-time and loud fighter for the Indian cause. Wahoo would often turn bitter in the middle of a conversation and begin enumerating the problems of the poverty stricken reservation Indians, especially those in his home state, Oklahoma. In his prime Wahoo once came to New York to wrestle in Madison Square Garden. The crowd was a sellout, and in the front row among the rabid wrestling mob sat Mr. and Mrs. Sonny Werblin, cheering for their linebacker.

Wahoo's wrestling style was pure "television traditional." He wore white boots with fringe on top, full headdress and war paint. A year or so ago Wahoo added a new gimmick to his wrestle. He wore a patch of adhesive tape on his forehead, just below his jeweled headband, and along about the middle of a match after some contact with his co-star, blood would come spurting from a "cut" on Wahoo's forehead. In seconds his face would look like a slaughterhouse floor, but Wahoo never flinched, never even accepted a towel no matter how the blood coursed forth. It would be unkind to question such a brave warrior, but Wahoo's chronic "cut" stopped bleeding like clockwork, and hinted that a capsule of catsup might lie concealed beneath the adhesive.

Before Miami played Boston, Wahoo always sent a wild message to the ex-wrestler playing Patriot fullback.

"Tell that Nance I'll give him a rolling leg lock and break his foot off," Wahoo would warn, putting his best footlock into his mouth.

Wahoo warned each year that he planned momentary retirement from the gridiron, but such plans are always subject to immediate change. (For example, half a dozen of the "retirees" after the close of the 1963 season were still playing at the end of the 1968 season. Charley Bradshaw, a tackle at Detroit, staged an annual farewell every winter but reinstated himself as regularly as the spring thaw.) Then, one night in Denver, a small scuffle at a bar landed Wahoo in jail long enough to miss the Dolphins' curfew. Simultaneously Wahoo retired and was fired.

"It was a raw deal," he said. "They wanted to get rid of me, I knew that. But they're never going to win until they straighten out a few people about how to run a football team. I know, I've been talking to a lot of the players. We're all still good friends. But they're all unhappy. I'm glad I'm out."

The following January Wahoo retired again, this time from the wrestling tour in front of 5,000 screaming Miami Beach fans. It was probably the easiest thing he'd ever done. The next morning he flew to Hawaii to a new tour. In Hawaii the money is four times what it is in the States because wrestling is king.

So it was on to Honolulu for Wahoo—Honolulu where the golfing is easy, where wrestlers work only two nights a week, not seven and where, a few days before Wahoo's departure, the top wrestling attraction in the islands had dropped dead.

At Wahoo's last hurrah, stateside, it was advertised he would wrestle a one-shot "Texas Death-Match"—a fight to the finish.

"It's a good thing Wahoo never thought of that before," said Larry Granthan, who played linebacker next to Wahoo for several seasons. "He'd have been dead every night of the year."

PART IV

8 Defense

"The biggest thing I resented was guys going after my face—fingers under my mask, after my eyes," said Jimmy Brown.

A great rash of recent writing has made it fashionable to search for self-understanding against an animal-world background—to chat about our human behavior and neuroses in terms of bowerbirds, sticklebacks and primates. But authors like Robert Ardrey, Konrad Lorenz, and Desmond Morris are missing a bet. Using gridiron territory for behavior research would be fascinating.

"Strenuous competition brings about a speed-up in the evolutionary process," wrote Robert Ardrey in *Territorial Imperative*. It could as easily be glib Bernie Casey describing his life as a Ram: "I think there is a speeding up of one's life in athletics. In eight years your life is intensified; it's a microcosm, but only in athletics."

In his bestseller, *The Naked Ape*, Desmond Morris describes how an animal's sympathetic nervous system prepares his body for the violent activity of the arena and makes him hostile: "When strong aggression is aroused adrenalin pours into the blood . . . the heart beats faster . . . there is an increase in blood pressure . . . salivation is restrained . . . the blood is flooded with sugar . . . breathing becomes quicker and deeper . . . and the hair stands on end and there is profuse sweating." Morris should see Ben Davidson's moustache bristling and glistening at the Raider sidelines during the *Star-Spangled Banner*, or an unsympathetic player like Boston's Larry Eisenhauer psyching himself up.

"I've calmed down a little lately," said Eisenhauer, "but I really used to get psyched before a game. I'd try to tear anything apart—walls, doors, lockers—my teammates sometimes. They stay away from me now." Eisenhauer, before a game in Buffalo, once got up a head of steam and "got this partition" with his helmet. His head was inside.

There are all kinds of ways to win a football game, and, after all the laughs, words and bruises, winning is the only thing and underlies every anecdote, torn hamstring, training torture and game plan. There's so little difference between top and bottom teams that every Sunday is a hard fight. As an additional equalizing factor bottom teams always get more up for top teams than top teams do for them, which makes good games and the commissioner's favorite old refrain, "On any given Sunday any team can beat any other." Most upsets happen when the underdog hits harder.

Talk about naked apes, Eisenhauer once led his team onto the field at Kansas City shouting, "Go get 'em!" He was wearing a helmet and nothing else.

In *African Genesis* Robert Ardrey wrote: "If I am a baboon then I leap to the defense of my social partner not at the sight of his danger but in response to my troop's special cry." Ardrey should hear the Detroit Lion linebackers shouting "Jumbo! Jumbo! Jumbo!"—the defensive troop's special cry to indicate a red dog (blitz). (A baboon playing lineman better not leap too soon when he hears the quarterback's signals or he'll be called for an offsides penalty for sure.)

On the gridiron as well as in the jungle the fundamental form of aggression concerns establishing rights over a particular piece of ground. When Robert Ardrey writes that in all territorial species without exception possession of a territory lends enhanced energy to the proprietor, he's furnishing us with an interesting scientific explanation of such clichés in reportage as "momentum," "turning point" (Weeb Ewbank always says "*one* of the turning points"), or when teams *lose* ground, energy waning, the statement that they "roll over and play dead." After the Giants beat Dallas 27–21 in one of the biggest upsets of 1968, the Cowboys were complaining that they couldn't get moving, while the Giants were hot as a pistol.

It's ironic that, after all the hours of coaching and conditioning, nothing causes more games to be won or lost than such an intangible as momentum. Defenses are better able to sustain momentum than offenses. "It's much harder," says Ram Coach George Allen, "for offensive players to get up for a game than it is for defensive players." Surely the reason is that playing defense is more uninhibited and natural than playing offense. The offensive players, forbidden to grasp with their hands, are civilized, constricted fellows who use guile and deception, their heads instead of their paws. The defensive players are doin' what comes naturally, aggressive and hostile, fighting to defend their territorial rights. They use brute force—

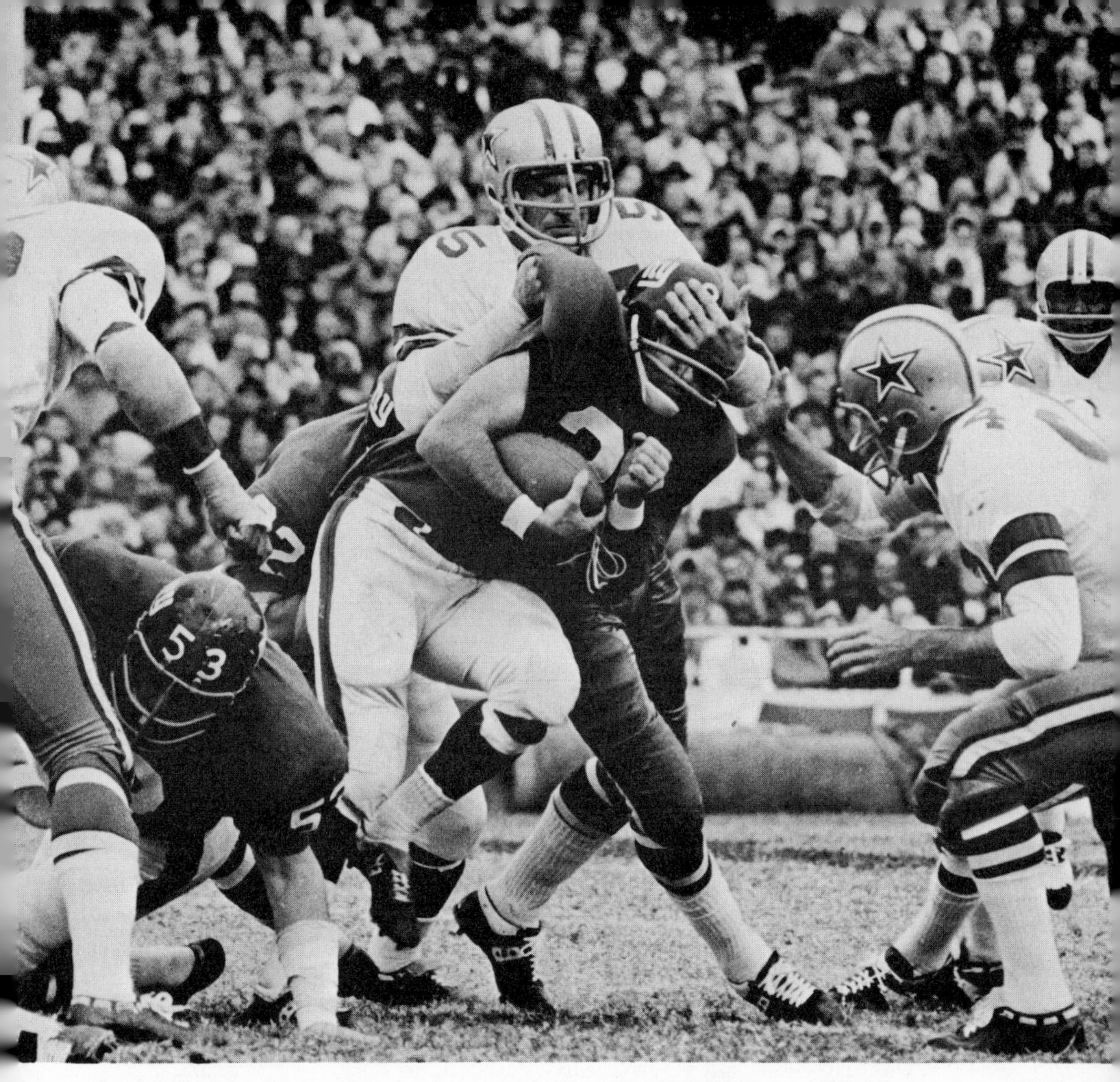

Cowboy Linebacker Lee Roy Jordan manhandling Giants' ballcarrier Ernie Koy.

unsophisticated and instinctive. On the football field the most aggressive, least naked apes play defense.

One of the defensive lineman's favorite tricks is to drive the heel of his hand into or under the offensive player's face mask because the natural reaction is to blink and drop your head—for self-preservation. In that one instant he's around the blocker, on his way to the quarterback.

"The teeth are used to bite, slash and stab, the head and horns to butt and spear, the body to ram, bump, and push, the legs to claw, kick, and swipe, the hands to grasp and squeeze," writes Desmond Morris, noting that other primates' teeth are the most important weapon, but for us, the naked apes, it is the hands.

Morris is not quite correct. The uniformed apes of the gridiron are closer to primates in their behavior! They claw, kick, spear and *bite*.

"One time I remember a Philadelphia Eagles defense man jamming his hand up under my mask and clawing for my eyes and I got my teeth in that hand," said Jimmy Brown. "Man, I tried to eat it up!"

The noted Austrian naturalist Konrad Lorenz believes that the beginning of all sport was highly ritualized but serious hostile fighting. He emphasizes that in sport there is always a certain pride in doing well, and that the most important function of ritualized fighting is to determine which rival is stronger without hurting the weaker. "We have a healthy Christian regard for each other," says Ram Tackle Merlin Olsen. "The violence is built in and accepted, but if you were in a game and played like an animal you wouldn't last in the game very long."

"Sport contains aggressive motivation," says Konrad Lorenz in *On Aggression*, "and its main function today lies in the cathartic discharge of aggressive urge."

Man has inherited this aggressive drive from his prehistoric progenitors, says Lorenz, but there is no way to release aggressions in our society. Sport provides a healthy safety valve. Bill Koman, who used to lineback for St. Louis, couldn't agree more. Koman's solution was violence every Sunday.

"All week long my construction business drives me crazy, having to watch guys who don't put out," said Koman, who was once one of the annually honored "Football Fathers." "I want to annihilate them but instead I have to be nice to them. On Sunday I don't have to be nice to anyone and I get rid of all my hostilities in the game."

"I was an orphan when I was fourteen and I took it out on all the kids in the neighborhood," said Packer Linebacker Ray Nitschke. "What I like about this game is the contact, the getting it out of my system." Although the author of *The Naked Ape* says football is only a harmless symbolic substitute for war, Ray Nitschke plays the game like a madman.

Although each team has stronger and weaker members, there is no peck order, the so-called ranking system of the barnyard, because a younger, stronger player, a tackle or a linebacker, can't overthrow the quarterback or the coach the way a young monkey or ape might; he can only overthrow another tackle or another linebacker. Norman Mailer pointed this out when he put linemen and backs into an unhappy class relation with no hope of mobility.

The unhappiest class relation is on offense, between the backs and jealous linemen who open the holes and get the backs bigger paychecks and headlines, which is why linemen prefer to play defense. Defensive linemen have the attitude that while opposing backs may have "artistry" which will earn them glory, the linemen have "toughness" which will ultimately make the backs pay for that glory.

We could actually tell there was no peck order on a football team just by looking. According to Desmond Morris the dominant male is "invariably the sleekest, best groomed and sexiest monkey in the community," and one look would tell you that that fellow comes at various positions and is not so often quarterback or coach. I mean, like Vince Lombardi—sleek and sexy???

"You're always in the game when you have a defense," says George Allen, who means that a good solid aggressive defense not only stops the other team but helps its own offense, by periodically getting them the ball. After a successful goal-line stand, before a punt, after a recovered fumble or an interception, television announcers always sigh, "Defense is the name of the game."

It's a big moment, a grandstand play, when a defensive player can hand the ball magnanimously over to his offense. Sometimes he is even able to score himself. When 300-pound defensive Tackle Jim Dunaway blocked a Jet kick and ran 72 yards for a touchdown he said, "Everything I've ever done in football is nothing compared to this."

"Pro football is half offense and half defense," said George Allen, "but if you don't have defense you can't win. If you have a good defense you can even win on an off day. Nothing builds confidence on a team like a defense that won't budge."

In football today defenses are much more imaginative than offenses and the best coaches—Lombardi, George Allen, Wally Lemm, Don Shula—make their marks defensively. It's much more creative than the boring three-end offense. Defensive coaches take their eleven defensive players and mix them up and move them around in all kinds of crazy setups. Someone's defensive brain has dreamed up a different defense for every situation because there are not just so many things you can do with eleven players. Mathematically there are around forty million variations, but that doesn't count the "special situations," such as against kickoff and punt returns, or the last two minutes of each half.

"It's more challenging," said Allen, "and it's more difficult to teach. The offense calls the play, the formation, and the snap count. The defense doesn't know any of these things, doesn't even know if the offense is going to throw the football or run. That phase of it intrigues me."

"Defense is three things," said Packer End Willie Davis, "the quick rush, strong linebackers and a good secondary. We have all three."

Until the last couple of years the eleven defensive players were lined up in three rows. Each row took care of one of Willie's "three things"

Linemen—four in front, on the line of scrimmage, to rush the passer
Linebackers—three in the middle row
Defensive Backs—four in back, two cornerbacks to the outside and two safeties toward the middle; all four are called collectively, "the secondary."

One refers to this setup as the "standard 4–3" defense, named after the two front rows. Nicknamers probably assumed the four defensive backs would stay where they belonged, but of course they didn't.

Pretty soon one of them, the right (free) safety, crept up a few yards and hovered behind the linemen, and, on occasion, he *blitzed* the quarterback as if he were a linebacker. This safety blitz was called "shooting the safety" and turned the "standard 4–3" closer to a 4–4–3. The safety most often shot was the Cardinals' Larry Wilson.

The Cardinal defense rarely lines up the same way twice, and they are as likely to use an eight-man line at midfield on first down (an eight-man line is usually used when defense is backed up near its own goal line, and only in the most crucial third and fourth down situations) as they are to use a three-man line in a short yardage situation (a three-man line is expected on an obvious passing down). Just before the center snaps the ball, Cardinal linemen are shifting and scuttling about, and their linebackers too, hoping that all the movement will camouflage their actual plan. The Cardinals pretend they will blitz so often that it's almost expected, and when they don't the element of surprise works in reverse, keeping the enemy guessing and off guard. The Cardinal defense and Oakland's are crazy-quilt types, and all the motion and moving around just before the center's snap is called *stunting*.

Defensive strategy is creative, of course, because defensive lineups are not bound by rules as offensive lineups are. The defensive players may move around and change position after the offensive players are set, and while the offense must have at least seven men in front, on the line, the defense can have any number of linemen they please; they can have none, or they can have eleven. You sometimes see all eleven on the goal line making a stand, but you never see a defense with fewer than three linemen. Even when everyone at home in front of the boob tube and everyone in the stands knows a pass is coming, there are still three defensive pass rushers on the line.

Recent fashionable defensive "twists" include Kansas City's "stack defense," which was devised, like the Cardinals' crazy-quilt motion, to cause confusion.

"Everyone was using a 4–3 setup of linemen and linebackers and we came up with the idea of going 3–4, with four linebackers," said Hank Stram, coach of the Kansas City Chiefs. "This puts our big man Buck Buchanan (6′ 7″, 300) right opposite their center [smallest offensive lineman] and puts one of our linebackers right behind three of our front men. This makes all kinds of spacings and shifts possible and we can change into a seven-man line in a second. Every time he leaves the huddle the quarterback sees something different, a 'new look.' "

The basic reason for inventing different defenses is to confuse the quarterback and to avoid being stereotyped. If a quarterback knew that by lining his men up in a specific way the defense would automatically go into a certain formation, well, such a defense could easily be had. The defense must hide its plans.

Houston Coach Wally Lemm was head coach at the St. Louis Cardinals when Larry Wilson was perfecting his safety blitz. Lemm falls into that catchall, "A Keen Student of the Game," but he has a sense of humor too, and his coaching methods include a stipulation that any defensive backfield prospects must be able to run faster than their coach.

"When you plan a defense you try to make the opposing quarterback believe he's seeing something he's not," says Lemm. "You want him to think you're going to use a certain type of defense when you're actually going to do something else."

A rather complicated new defensive formation used by Oakland and the Vikings is designed to improve their pass rush, to break down a passing pocket and cream the quarterback more quickly.

"If one defensive man can occupy two offensive guys at once, by confusing one of the offensive guys and rushing at the other, that leaves an extra defensive man free, to smash the quarterback," explained Baltimore's Right Guard Dan Sullivan. According to Baltimore's general manager Harry Hulmes, Dan Sullivan has been called underrated for too long, but it might also be said that Sullivan has been called underrated so long and so often that he's the most overrated offensive lineman in the NFL.

"Suppose you have two offensive linemen playing opposite two defensive linemen, the old-fashioned way," said Dan, who needed a pencil and paper to explain the Vikings' new defensive variation.

"The defensive tackle, instead of charging straight ahead, at the opposite guard, charges at an angle, at the tackle next to the guard."

If the guard continues as planned and blocks the defensive tackle, one defensive tackle has occupied *two* offensive linemen, which releases the defensive end from his regular assignment and leaves him free to rush at the quarterback. Dan Sullivan is the guard the defensive tackle is trying to sucker with this scheme, which can be varied to aim at either guard or offensive tackle.

Oakland has another variation for a better pass rush, moving a linebacker up to the line and moving left Defensive Tackle Dan Birdwell wide, putting him outside the defensive end, the better to barrel in at the passer.

These variations only emphasize what can be done with the same four linemen, three linebackers, and four defensive backs. By moving them around, adding something here and subtracting something there, the coaches change what used to be strictly man vs. man (one-on-one) into the "blitz," "stack," or odd-man lines and make football more like a chess game than ever.

Each defensive change requires a period of adjustment by the offense which is exactly why defenses change. Game films shorten this period of adjustment, but the "new" and more imaginative defensive concepts have changed football's most fundamental theorem; offense acts, defense reacts doesn't hold quite as true as ten years ago.

Any defense that can stop a runner behind the line of scrimmage and flatten the quarterback before he passes needn't try new concepts or look for gimmicks. Short of such perfection the surest way to have a strong defense is with big, fast, powerful linemen. The pass rush comes from the front four, and, theoretically, if the front four does its job the seven other defenders could stay on the bench. One school of thought says the secondary is the most important part of defense, that good defensive backs, especially cornerbacks, separate the winners from the also-rans, but such schools of thought aren't thinking quite straight. The best defensive back can't keep his receiver covered for many more than five seconds, and if his front foursome hasn't gotten to the quarterback by that time they're in the wrong line.

One of the new breed of linemen, the Vikings' Carl Eller, says that thinking is the most important part of playing modern football.

"Our defensive backs and linebackers give us extra freedom," says Eller, "but you can't rush blindly at the passer. My idea of the pass rush is that I'm going to either get to the quarterback myself or put so much pressure on him that he is required to do something unnatural or get out of his rhythm. If I can get him to break his rhythm or hurry his throw, it brings about a lot of results. There might be a blocked pass or an interception. Pressure is the important thing."

Super Bowl III is an excellent example of pressure applied with perfection. The Jets never once got to Colt Quarterback Earl Morrall, but the Jets must have rattled him. Morrall, the NFL's leading passer, threw three interceptions and went 6-for-17, for only 71 yards.

Eller practices what he preaches. In 1968 Minnesota beat Green Bay twice. In the second game it was really Eller beating Bart Starr. Eller flattened Starr so many times he had to leave the game. Bart still can't remember the second half. If he could he would remember that Eller also blocked a field goal and caused a fumble which the Vikings turned into a touchdown.

Good coaches learn to adapt their theories to what Norman Mailer calls "the talent in the room"—which is why Los Angeles emphasizes its defensive line, the Chicago Bears emphasize their defensive backs, and the Giants are building their attack around a running quarterback. When George Allen thought he had five huge starters in his defensive line, he said he hoped to have all five of his big rushmen on the field at one time in a special defense. Allen would replace the middle linebacker with the fifth man (Rosy Grier) for a 5–2–4 alignment, which would lengthen his defensive line by roughly three yards and virtually eliminate any wide running. If he had introduced the 5-man line, Allen would have forced an offense to react to something "new," but of course in football nothing is ever new. Greasy Neale had a 5–2–4 at the Eagles twenty years ago.

"Heck, when I was at Cleveland [1950–56] we used oldtime switch blocking and ran the 5-man line out of business," said Abe Gibron, who coaches the Chicago Bears' defense.

"I'm not surprised by their 5-man line," said Bear Middle Linebacker Dick Butkus. "When George Allen coached our defense he always took me out when it was third-and-long [yardage]."

The Bears' story was quite different from the Rams'. Chicago found itself with a wealth of defensive backs three years ago, and often, in obvious passing situations, the Bears employ the "Dooley shift," named for coach/inventor Jim Dooley. Dooley puts a defensive back in place of the weakside linebacker for more speed and agility on pass coverage (when the linebacker's size and strength are less necessary)—a 4–2–5 alignment.

The easiest way to look at defensive formations is in terms of three rows, with the middle row of linebackers flexible, a variable almost like a pendulum swinging back and forth. When the defense expects a run, the linebackers will play toward the front; when the defense expects a pass the linebackers will play pass defense and help the defensive backs (unless they blitz).

Near the goal, inside the 10-yard line, the situation is different for both the offense and the defense. The wide ends are no longer a deep threat because the bomb per cent of the offense is eliminated. The defensive backs, therefore, move up closer to the line and think more about stopping a run.

An obvious running situation (linebackers move up):

Third-down-and-only-inches-to-go, or a goal line stand, are obvious running situations . . . and a nine-man line is the normal defense for stopping the short-ground gain.

An obvious passing situation (linebackers move back):

Second-and-10 or third-and-long-yardage are passing situations. When a team is losing in the fourth quarter and it's third down and 15 yards to go, everyone—from the players to the fans in the stands to the TV viewers (even the TV announcers)—everyone knows the quarterback will pass.

The defensive alignment is a 3-man rush line with eight linebackers and defensive backs (3–3–5 or 3–4–4) spread farther back than usual, the better to break up attempted passes.

Prevent Defense

The prevent defense is used in the last two minutes of either half when time running out makes a losing quarterback a man in a hurry. Teams practice a "two-minute" offense during the week so that they can run off a series of plays at the end of a game without huddling in between, to save time. A smart two-minute quarterback sends all his ends, backs, and whatever else he can find out for a pass, hoping for a quick-scoring strike.

A prevent defense works, or doesn't work, on the principle that with time running out the defense can afford to give up the short gains but must prevent a bomb at all cost. Sometimes prevents can backfire. They don't work if a field goal will provide the winning margin, and they don't work against a series of short sideline passes, which can score a touchdown in very little time. Otto Graham had some dramatic misfortunes with the prevent defense at Washington. The Redskins' prevent didn't prevent anything. Many prevent defenses don't.

9 Defensive Line

The Compleat Front Four

Though a bit elderly, the front four with the most prestige belongs to the Los Angeles Rams. "They're Dempsey, Firpo, Ruth, and Gehrig," said Norm Van Brocklin, before the "Dempsey" of the Rams' front four, Rosy Grier, was injured and a replacement, Roger Brown, was traded for—which was when George Allen began contemplating the possibility of a front five. Unfortunately, Rosy Grier never fully recovered.

During the week before Super Bowl II, the Miami Touchdown Club put on a giant banquet where over a thousand men fans, some with sons, gathered for cocktails, dinner, entertainment, and two honored speakers,

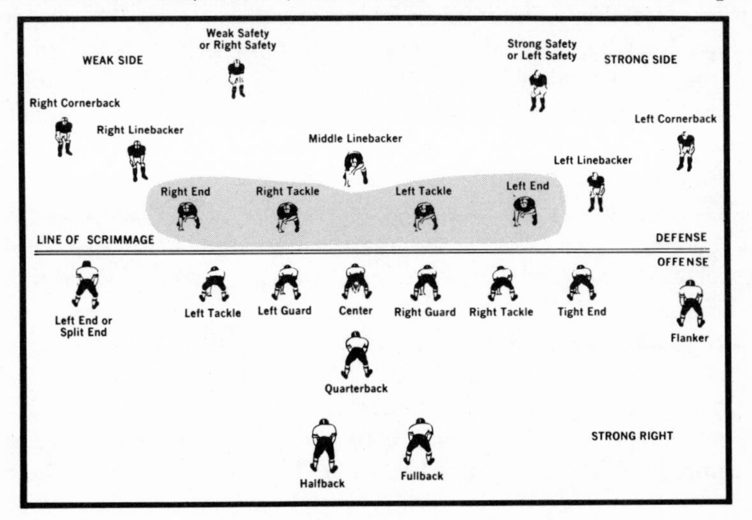

The Original Fearsome Foursome.

John Unitas and Pete Rozelle, football commissioner of the world. Part of the entertainment featured two dancers whose routine à go go was accomplished with arms folded across their chests. Lo and behold, as the act's grand finale the dancing duo flung their hitherto folded arms akimbo and revealed bare bosoms. The number was named *The Front Four*. Heaven only knows what would have happened to the show if George Allen's "front five" had become the standard defensive formation.

The Rams' front four began to develop during Harland Svare's interim at Los Angeles (which has had as wild and topsy-turvy a succession of leaders as one might find anywhere, from Greenwich Village to the Latin American governments). From left to right they were David ("Deacon," as he led pregame prayers in college) Jones, Merlin Olsen, Roosevelt Grier and Lamar Lundy, who has been with the Rams longer than any other player in the club's history. Lundy began as a tight end, Jones as an offensive tackle.

It was in August 1967 that tragedy broke up the front four. At the age of 35 Rosy Grier, a man mountain who smiles a lot and looks like a bespectacled chocolate Easter angel, tore his Achilles' tendon in an exhibition game.

When he was young, Rosy sang gospels and spirituals and later, playing tackle and guitar at the New York Giants, Kyle Rote introduced him to some people who helped him get started on his folksinging way. He sang before a sellout crowd in Carnegie Hall and one off-season he toured with TV's *Shindig* and introduced a bestseller, *It's Not Unusual*. When Rosy was traded from New York to Los Angeles, he organized the front four into a group, which was spectacular size-wise if not music-wise, and while he was recuperating from his torn tendon Rosy entertained at halftime in a Ram-Eagle game singing *Spanish Harlem* in front of 58,000 fans plus the television audience. Rosy is one of several ex-Giants to name a son Kyle, after halfback-turned-sportscaster Rote.

Not all football players grow big fast. Rosy Grier did. He weighed 225 when he went to Penn State. Merlin Olsen is the opposite, a late-grower. Olsen weighed 180 in high school, graduated at 230, and called it quits at 284. Grier, like Olsen, could and should have kept his enlargement to fifty pounds. Instead, in his last season with New York, he arrived at the Giant camp in July at 329. Rosy really tipped the scales.

"I got there the only way you can, by eating and drinking," said Rosy, who signs his autographs "Rosy" though his name usually appears in print either Rosey or Rosie. When Los Angeles lost him, they lost the most musical member of the front four's quartet and a fearsome 285 pounds of pass rush. The Rams, however, in no longer than it takes Barbara Hutton to find a new mate, came up with a replacement for Rosy. They lost musical talent, perhaps, but when Roger Brown's 31-year old, 300-pound self was installed at right tackle, next to Merlin Olsen, the Rams' front four gained fifteen pounds in a fell swoop.

Roger Brown used to cut up at Detroit where he acted ornery and rode a motorcycle—that is, he overlapped a motorcycle. Jimmy Brown said he always imagined Roger hopping up in the air, springing from his massive thighs like some huge frog.

When Roger was traded to Los Angeles, he was recovering from a leg operation and had reported to the Detroit training camp weighing 322. He left for the Rams at 293 and Coach George Allen said he finished the season with "consistently good games."

"Brown came to us a little heavy," said Allen, "but he got his weight down to 285." Allen is always saying his fat players are "down to 285." One of the coaches most skilled at psychological warfare, George Allen keeps Roger Brown's weight strictly classified.

Next to Brown, Merlin Olsen is one of a dozen tackles who came to the pros from Utah State. Merlin wrote his masters' thesis on "The World Sugar Crisis," kept an A average through college and was once quoted at length in *The Wall Street Journal*. At 6′ 5″, 276 Merlin is the largest football-playing financier in the world. He explains his game easily.

"Defensive football players are trained to reaction," says Merlin. "Even more than that, it's a preconditioned response . . . like the Pavlovian thing, there's no opportunity for thought on a defensive team.

"We're always conscious of the pass. As defensive players we are playing the pass almost before we play the run. Our responsibilities are so keyed to the passing attack because we feel we have to stop the passing attack in order to control an offense."

The poor quarterback is, by the same token, always conscious of the Ram defensive line. If for no other reason, their height makes it difficult for the quarterback and his receivers to see each other. The Rams are equally effective against a running attack. "Fortunately we have people who can react to the run," said Olsen, "and we do a good job playing against it."

"Once the snap begins, everything is a matter of reaction," says Merlin. "We have practiced these reactions for months—many of us for years and years. They have been honed to a point where we sit there like computers. Across our minds are going all these different possibilities of things the offense can do to us, and after the ball is snapped we fix on what is happening in front of us and that calls for a response. If we're right we stop the play, but if we're not, if we're a little bit slow and the offense is stronger on that particular play, then they make the play go."

It should no longer surprise anyone that the front four is so famous.

Merlin was a small-town boy and never left Logan, Utah, until he joined the Rams. The Olsen family lives in a house with a big yard and lots of grass and trees. "I have to have those three things or it's not home. I've got to get out and dig around the flowers and watch the grass grow."

Olsen says he hates all quarterbacks. Roger Brown's approach is to hate everybody ("I'm gonna hurt them first"). But Deacon Jones says he can't hate a guy one minute and like him the next. "I can't turn it off and on," says Jones.

Deacon Jones (6′ 5″, 260) is the fastest defensive end in the league. "He is so strong, so quick, and so tricky that after watching films of him I didn't know what I'd do," said Washington Redskin Tackle Jim Snowden several days before the Redskins played the Rams. Jones is from a town of 857, Eatonville (near Orlando), Fla., and went to South Carolina State. On January 27, 1967, Orlando celebrated Deacon Jones Day with a parade and the trimmings. Jones went by Miami on his way to Orlando. "One thing I'm not is a dog or horse fan," said Deacon ruefully after a costly week; "I couldn't pick any winners and I got carried away at the dog track."

Jones and Green Bay's Willie Davis are reputed to be the best two defensive ends in the business, but it wasn't always thus. After the 1963 season Lamar Lundy was the big name of the Ram line, but Deacon worked hard before the next season, studying the methods of Baltimore's great end, Gino Marchetti. Deacon makes his first move, like Marchetti did, with his hands, instead of his feet or his head.

"It's hard to explain the difference between Jones and Willie Davis," said the Bears' Bob Wetoska, who played tackle against both of them. "Jones has blinding *speed,* and pursuit. I mean, he can race *around* to get to the quarterback. Willie is so *quick*. He can make such short, sudden lateral moves . . . a few steps one way and all of a sudden he's going the other way . . . They're both tough."

"People just don't realize what an athlete's made of," says Deacon. "Why, I'd play a game against the Packers for nothin'." Once, after Jones had tackled Cleveland Quarterback Gary Lane so hard Lane fumbled, Deacon announced, rhetorically, "I play defense. Blind side, full steam. A tackle like that means just as much to me as a touchdown would mean to somebody on offense. I got just as much fun out of it as if I had never hit anybody before. Yes, and I want to do it every play every week. After I hit 'em like that they're supposed to get up slowly . . . or not at all."

Deacon sells beer in the offseason, and when he arrived at training camp one summer, looking extra trim, he joked, "It's my beer diet"—which was blown up in the sports pages. Deacon was furious, fretting about damage to his image, but philosophical.

"You learn to live with publicity," he says. "Ink means money. Don't quit pouring."

Lamar Lundy (6′ 7″, 260) is the chattiest of the front four, especially if there is a newspaperman within earshot. Lamar once played a man-eating tree in a science-fiction show on television and in the *In Cold Blood* movie he offers a ride to the two murderers. A team captain, he has been talking about retirement for four years, but with the Rams winning, at last, Lundy will probably be around for several more.

Defensive Tackle

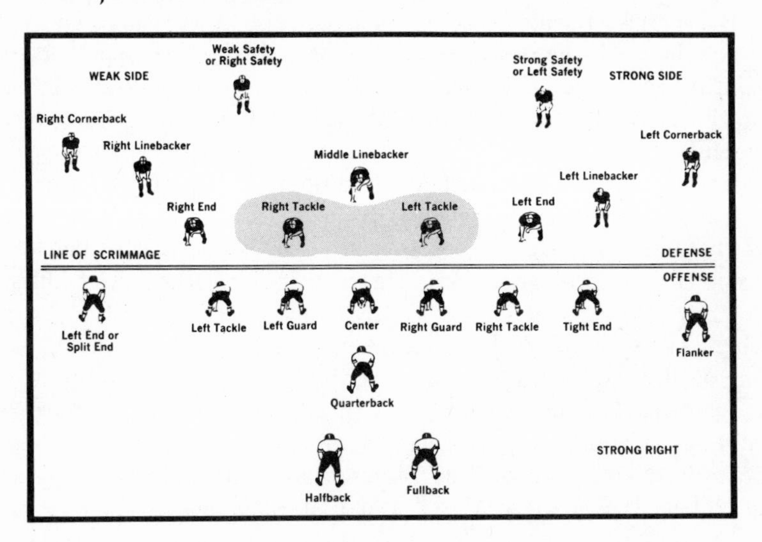

This is the heart and soul of a defensive club. It's where it all happens . . . the tackle is faced with the quick, hard-hitting guards, and flanked by the center and offensive tackles.

He is vulnerable, to say the least, and needs exceptional strength to fight off blocks coming down by the tackle or out by the center.

On short yardage when the offense attempts straight ahead wedge blocking for the score, or first down, he [defensive tackle] alone is responsible for piling it up and back. This he does with sheer strength.

If there is one position I always lacked any incentive to play, it has to be defensive tackle.

—Frank Gifford
NFL CBS Football Guide 1967

It would be a mistake to judge Frank Gifford on the basis of the cool, aloof, "pretty boy" image he projects via video, because Gifford played football with courage-plus. Rather than being conceited, as his critics are wont to judge him, Gifford is instead rather shy and conservative, and it is typically wise of him to single out defensive tackle as the spot he'd least like to play. If there were a peck order in football, the defensive tackles would be at the bottom. At least they would have been until a couple of years ago. Now even the bottom of the gridiron hierarchy is supposed to be able to think.

"Strength isn't enough," says Kansas City's Buck Buchanan, one of football's biggest tackles. "I have to learn new moves all the time, and try to think with them. Learning means getting to be more agile, better able to use your hands, learning to maintain your momentum. A defensive tackle has to keep moving forward, toward the passer, wherever he goes. Where you get in trouble is hitting and stopping." Boston Center Jon Morris gives Buck credit for being the best and toughest tackle he faces ("those tricky moves keep me off balance"). Many times the tackle doesn't get the credit he deserves. On a pass rush the first man (probably the tackle) doesn't get the quarterback, but just forces him the other way for the second man (the end) to pick him up. And the fans clap for the end.

The defensive tackles are football's "immovable objects." Half a dozen good ones, like Buchanan, weigh 300 pounds. Defensive ends are usually quicker, because they are farther from the quarterback; the tackles are closer, slower and stronger. Taken as a pair, some of the best tackles belong to Los Angeles, Oakland, Dallas, and Green Bay. Only Green Bay, which has won most often, hasn't given its defense a special name. It seems as if other teams, as soon as their defense has gotten to the enemy quarterback three times, decide to give their unsung heroes some glory and recognition, and so defenses are being nicknamed as readily as boats. New York writer Paul Zimmerman once called the Raiders' defense "The Eleven Angry Men," and that title flew in Oakland headlines from that moment. Dallas nicknamed their trenchermen the "Doomsday Defense" and the Rams' front four has long been called "The Fearsome Foursome."

Perhaps the most important member of the Doomsday Defense is Tackle Bob Lilly. Lilly is so strong that in college at Texas Christian he parked cars from the outside . . . picking up a Volkswagen by the bumper and moving it. "But I only did that once," he said.

"Bob Lilly is so quick," admired his coach Tom Landry. "He reacts fast and is so strong."

Lilly began his career at defensive end, but moved to tackle in 1963 and was soon All-NFL. It was always hard to distinguish between Lilly, Alex Karras, and Henry Jordan when it came time to pick the NFL All-Pro tackles, but the voters usually snubbed Alex Karras, not because of ability, but because of his record (a one-year suspension for gambling). The NFL Establishment has the forgetfulness of elephants. With Karras on the outs and Jordan older and slower, Lilly and Merlin Olsen are now the premier pair.

Tackle is different from end. At tackle you have people coming at you from both sides.

"More is happening at tackle," says Lilly. "You still have defensive assignments, but a little more is left up to your own judgement. On the pass rush you don't have as far to go from tackle, and when you expect a pass you can time your rush better from inside. You don't have to be bothered watching for sweeps, like the defensive end does." Lilly plays next to Dallas's right end, George Andrie. Lilly and Andrie sound like hairdressers.

The last man in America who needs a hairdresser is Green Bay's Henry Jordan, who combs his hair with a towel. Jordan plays tackle next to Ron Kostelnik, and they are perfect complements. "Kostelnik comes at you strong, punishes you, tries to overpower you," says Oakland's Jim Otto. "Henry Jordan plays softer. He uses his hands a lot, stunts a lot. He gives you the soft shoulder and uses a lot of spinouts."

"Jordan is quick and doesn't give you a lot to hit," said Gene Upshaw, who is the guard next to Otto. "He uses his hands to keep you off him, away from his body. If you get to his body he's whipped." Which sounds sane of Jordan, a wit, who is approaching 35 and has a drawl from his days at the University of Virginia. Jordan's wife says he's a worrywart; Henry admits he's a hypochondriac, and Jerry Kramer says Jordan turns pale just driving by a hospital.

"The only time I was ever in a hospital except to have my tonsils out," said Jordan, "was last year, when they found some blood in my urine, which every football player has. They were going to put a tube in me and that scared me. So do needles. I just don't like things like that." Jordan is always talking about retiring or about his ex-coach. The best

Lombardi stories come from Jordan and that other Packer ex, Fuzzy Thurston. Rumor has it Jordan steals most of his lines from Thurston.

As Gifford pointed out, the defensive tackle's peculiar problem is not only the man opposite, the guard, but also the center from the inside and/or the tackle from the outside. It's entirely possible that the offensive tackle might block the defensive end first and then slide off and in, hitting the defensive tackle from the outside while the guard is firing into him from the inside. Such two-on-one situations are called "double-team blocking." Painfully, the double-teamed tackle can always look at the sunny side, that the offense is paying him a compliment by using two men against him.

The Henry Jordan of the American League is at Oakland, Tom Keating, whose agility in Super Bowl II, even with a swollen right ankle, was nothing short of fantastic. Keating is small for a defensive tackle (6′ 2″, 245) but tough and quick, in the wit department, too. He is Oakland's leader. "Keating sets the club's attitude," said Al Davis, who runs everything at Oakland, down to the temperature of the water cooler. Davis spoke highly of Keating when Tom was a big factor behind the Raiders' appearance in the second Super Bowl. But in 1968, when Keating's injury forced him to sit out the entire season, Davis told Keating he was garbage and tried to cut his salary in half. Keating threatened a suit and they settled out of court. Though Davis acts like a cheap pirate, he's a brain, especially in football matters. In people matters he leaves much to be desired.

Before the second Super Bowl the Raiders spent almost a week in Florida cooped up in a motel between practice and film sessions.

"Some of the guys are tense, but most of us are loose and confident," said Keating, a bachelor. "The only thing that bothers me around here is there's nothing to do. The youngest girl I've met in Florida was 35, and she was in a wheelchair. All I do is watch TV and play cards and think about the game." Keating is an excellent cook—handy with spices and seasonings, particularly chili powder. Keating and his roommate, Halfback Pete Banaszak, live like *The Odd Couple* all over again, with a Bayview apartment and what you could call conglomerate housekeeping. Keating cooks, Banaszak cleans up.

If you like the quiet type, Linebacker Gus Otto is a handsome Raider bachelor. So is Quarterback Daryle Lamonica. "Tom Keating is our most eligible bachelor," said Ben Davidson. But didn't Keating grow a mustache? "Sure," said Ben, "but he looked so ugly we made him shave it off."

"Ben and I like to clown around before practice," said Tom. "He puts flowers on his helmet. I don't think (ex-coach) Rauch cares for that."

Keating plays tackle between End Ben Davidson and Tackle Dan Birdwell. At the other end is Isaac ("Big T" after his middle initial)

Lassiter, the least known but perhaps the best all-around defensive lineman at Oakland. Lassiter is strong and quick, but he's a quiet man and his three co-linemen aren't.

"Dan Birdwell is amazing," said Tom Keating. "I've never seen anything like him. After we won our title over Houston he kissed me and I almost got sick. Anybody would, with that big, drooling, foaming face coming at you. But he's got a heart of gold. He'd give you the shirt off his back, but who'd want it?"

"Birdwell looks like Clark Gable," said one of his Raider pals, "because he looks like a taxi going down the street with its doors open."

Birdwell is clumsy and has, besides big ears, huge hands. "He's got size seventeen fingers," says Keating. "You can put a quarter through his wedding band."

Birdwell is a wild, ornery Texan who wears a cowboy costume, but it's not a costume. His usual outfit includes boots, string tie, silver belt buckle, 10-gallon hat, and a cowboy-style dress suit. Once, the Raiders were playing an exhibition game in a jumping-off spot in Nebraska (they were all made honorary admirals in the Nebraska navy), and Defensive Back Kent McCloughan, who is from nearby Broken Bow, described his smallest of hometowns, "Danny Birdwell will like it."

"When Danny came to Oakland he was just a big strong bull," said ex-Raider Bob Mischak, "but he's just great now."

There is no end to Birdwell stories. Once, in a game against Houston, Birdwell couldn't get through the Houston's quarterback protection so he jerked the towel out of the Oiler center's belt and threw it at the quarterback, who at that time was George Blanda. (Blanda is now the Raiders' No. 2 quarterback.) The pass fell incomplete.

No one gets himself psychologically higher for a game than Birdwell. After Super Bowl II he was the last to leave the dressing room, disgusted with Oakland's defeat. "Jerry Kramer [Birdwell's assignment most of the afternoon] threw one good block at me all day," he said. "I told him when he did it. I was beating him by a yard and a half. Most of the time Kramer'd whip his leg at me as I went by and that's a last-resort thing. I told one guy who did that I'd have to hurt him. I club guys alongside the head when they make me mad. I can hurt anybody."

"He keeps elbowing me in the head," said Joe Namath after Birdwell spent a game twisting Namath's shaggy neck at every opportunity.

The thing about Birdwell's face is that he doesn't have any lips. His face is like a skin farm. A person shopping for skin would go to Birdwell's face for light and to Sherman Plunkett's neck to buy dark. His teammates nicknamed Birdwell after Herman Munster, TV's monster, but given a choice for companions on a space trip a person could do a whole lot worse than the Oakland front four. Perhaps by the time the entourage was nearing the moon Ike Lassiter might get a word in edgewise.

The best defense—smash the quarterback and everything takes care of itself—sounds crude, and it is. Still, defensive linemen have technique and style, and the smaller ones like Keating and Jordan have to make up all kinds of subtle tricks to make up for their lack of size.

The other type of tackle, the giant economy-size, might try some subtle moves and spice up his action with a little guile, but he really doesn't *have* to. At Kansas City, next to Buck Buchanan is 6′ 9″, 300-plus pounds of Ernie Ladd. Ladd's style is as positive as Norman Vincent Peale's. He swings his arms like a scythe at the blocking guard, slams him flat, and moves on to the quarterback. Ladd is so big and strong that the guard must come at him twice, or three times—if he hasn't been transformed by the Ladd Scythe into a topless lineman, spectating sheepishly, head in hand.

Some defensive tackles are so big in the chest and shoulders that they're really too topheavy for tackle. The smaller guard can hit the giant low and knock the feet out from under him. "Try and get one of those big guys high and he'll run right over you," says Matt Snell, the Jets' 219-pound fullback and one of the best—if not *the* best—blocking backs in football. "If I can time it right and hit him low, I can get a pretty good shot."

Bubba Smith almost quit pro football after his rookie season. "I'm too tall to play tackle," said Bubba who is 6′ 8″. "Too much height, and all that traffic, and you get hurt."

Ernie Ladd is built for tackle. Ernie has a massive top half (handy for his off-season wrestling career) but he also has a hefty bottom half with 22″ calves.

Ernie has had this weight problem, and weighed as much as Sherman Plunkett (330) on occasion. They still talk about his appetite at Chicago's All-Star Game headquarters.

"Ladd has the record," said the trainer. "For dinner he'd ask for, and eat, six steaks. He ate like a horse, and so did his pal Earl Faison. We had a poem for them: Ate together and late together."

One summer Ladd reported to the Houston training camp very overweight, and in his first day's workout, he lost eighteen pounds. Even on a percentage basis, eighteen pounds is a lot of pounds. They might have originated in pancakes. Ernie once lost a pancake-eating contest to a man-and-wife *team,* 137 to 124.

"I want to set that record straight," said Ernie, whose hair has an orange tint. "I got there thirty minutes late and I was already fifty-three pancakes behind."

The American Football League once published a "Gridiron Gourmet" which included Ernie's favorite recipe:

"BIG CAT SPECIAL"

Late at night, and especially after a tough ball game, I need something to give a little "body" to my body—so, I just fix up: a pound of okra, a frozen pack of corn, a pound of shrimp, a can of tomatoes, one small onion, a touch of garlic, salt and pepper. Cook okra and onions together until brown. Boil the shrimp for 3 minutes and add to okra along with tomatoes. Let simmer for 20 minutes. Then, dig in!

Ladd digs cooking. He digs money. He wrestles. Once, before the end of the football season, Ernie became engaged in an unscheduled match of name-calling, shouting and scuffling at a Houston arena with one Fritz Von Erick. Coincidentally Fritz was Ernie's first post-season match. Ladd's coach fined him $2000 for unbecoming conduct.

Ladd's obstreperous nature hasn't made him a favorite of his various coaches. They love him when he plays well, but Ernie isn't always in the mood and seems to need a special incentive to put himself out. He always plays well against his first coach, whom he doesn't much care for —Sid Gillman at San Diego—and in New York, which is media central.

When Ladd is in New York he's got money on his mind, even more than usual. Two years ago Ladd was traded from Houston to Kansas City and he didn't like it. He threatened retirement to the wrestling ring. But about that time there was a rumor that he might be traded again, to the Jets. Would he like that? "I'm ready," said Ernie. But what about wrestling and retirement and all that? "I'm ready to go to New York tonight," pleaded Ladd. The deal never materialized.

A day or two after he arrived at Kansas City Ladd sent a telegram back to his Houston teammates saying goodbye-and-be-good in a very honest and touching way—too honest for a high-paid wrestler.

Dear Oilers,
It has been very enjoyable and I'll miss you . . . and look forward to seeing you win the division . . . Dear Caveness [linebacker Ron] please don't whup your grandfather again. Haw! I have only this to say, *unity is the key to success.*
"The Big Cat"

Ladd has been less than a roaring success at Kansas City. He arrived in the middle of the 1967 season when the ex-champion Chiefs were losing. The inside story supposed that the team was being torn asunder because of an extra-large proportion of Negro players. Certainly the number of Negroes at Kansas City wouldn't have bothered Ernie, because Houston has as many, but coming to a new team in the middle of a season is never easy for "the new boy," no matter how old or how big. And the Oilers, in an ironic twist, unexpectedly won their division as Ernie's letter predicted. Houston was an overnight success while Kansas City was almost an overnight failure.

Ernie missed Houston because he didn't like Kansas City. It is possible he missed Houston even more because he missed his uncle, Garland Boyette, who linebacks for the Oilers.

Boyette is 29, 6′ 1″, 240, and one of the best linebackers in business. He has run 100 meters in 10.5, broad jumped more than 22 feet, put the shot 58 feet plus. He has high jumped 6′ 3″, raced 400 meters in 50 seconds and covered the 110-meter hurdles in 14.6. And that's not all. Garland has thrown the discus 165′ and the javelin 230′. He won the decathlon in the 1959 Panhellenic games at Sydney, Australia, and in the 1960 Olympic trials he beat the champ, Rafer Johnson, in several events.

Boyette is important, not just because of his track prowess or his famous nephew. He is an excellent linebacker. It is a frequent topic in idle conversations that Negro players can't make it at linebacker, especially middle linebacker, just as they can't make it at quarterback. With Boyette in the middle and George Webster on the strong side, Houston would have had three starting Negro linebackers if Pete Barnes had beaten out Olen Underwood on the right side. It is a new look, but other faces which are linebackers' and black are the Eagles' Ike Kelly, the Giants' Henry Davis, the Steelers' Ray May and the Chiefs' Willie Lanier.

How Boyette, a year younger than Ernie Ladd, happens to be Ladd's uncle is relatively unimportant, football-wise, but imagine Ladd, assigned to wipe some guard out of the way of a blitzing Boyette, missing his man . . . and then turning around: "Gee, I'm sorry about that, Uncle Garland."

Ernie has an unusual hobby for a big old larcenous country boy. Whenever he is on a wrestling tour and hits a new town he tries to find the town's best chess player, to challenge him ("except in New York; that's too tough!"). Ernie loves to play chess. He doesn't love poetry, although he once wrote an endorsement on the flyleaf of a book of war poems ("I don't often dig poetry but a man can enjoy these"). Ernie loves endorsements.

If Ernie should ever retire to the wrestling ring (the other wrestlers don't like him much because he's serious about their racket), you can be sure financial considerations were the basis of his decision. If there's one thing Ernie loves more than food it's money. And his philosophy of life is simple. "I'm for Ernie Ladd first."

The Ernie Stautner Finishing School for Young Tackles

Ernie Ladd is not the inventor of the head hammer. To give credit where credit is due one must go back to the Steeler Tackle Ernie Stautner, who now coaches the Dallas Cowboy defense. If Ernie Ladd is crude oil, Ernie Stautner was strictly slick. You would never see Stautner pitting strength against strength, belly-to-belly and nose-to-nose over the line —that would have been much too uncivilized.

Instead, Ernie developed the sophisticated head hammer technique, which proved most successful. He would slap the blocker's helmet to get him going in one direction while Ernie went another. Gutter-fighting tactics like these can give a guy a five-day headache, because a Stautner slap could turn a guard's brain waves into Silly Putty . . . and no 50-pound cast was necessary on Stautner's forearm; on the guard's head, maybe.

"A forearm blow isn't an upward blow with an elbow; it's more a blow from the wrist," explained Stautner. "You get more striking power with the lower part of your arm, not with your elbow. Elbows are college."

One of Stautner's first pupils was a Pittsburgh Steeler end, Ben McGee. McGee's first game as a rookie was against the New York Giants, against Mr. Roosevelt Brown, an eleven-year veteran. Ben and Rosey were thrown out of the game.

"That guy McGee hit me in the head with his forearm," said Brown after the game. "I took that stuff from Stautner for ten years but I'll be darned if I'll take it from a rookie."

Ernie played offense for one season (his first) and believes the experience was valuable. He has been successful as a tackle teacher and will probably be a head coach after the next big coaching turnover.

"He tells you like it is," says young Cowboy Larry Cole, a dead ringer for Joe Palooka. "You know Stautner knows what he's talking about because he's a veteran, he's been there. He doesn't just tell you to do something. He tells you why."

Here are some of Ernie's theories:

"The defensive tackle should key on the head of the man he's playing against. I teach them that where the man's head goes, his body is sure to follow. He can't fake with his head. If I can get a defensive man to control the offensive man's head, to make his first shot at the head, I'm happy.

"I played the right tackle so I brought my left hand up first and tried to drive it straight at his head. Straight into his face mask is best. It's no penalty if you don't grab the mask, or hold on too long. *The best is to drive the heel of my left hand straight at his nose,* and many's the time my hand was cut and the heel of my palm black and blue after a game. I started wearing a piece of knee padding on my hand.

"Right after I hit him a good shot with my left hand I gave his helmet a good hand slap with my right hand. You should put a helmet on sometime and see how it feels if it's hit. The reverberations are really something, and your head gets a heckuva jounce. I'll tell you who's really a good head hitter, Deacon Jones. Your head really *hurts* after a game against him. Of course, there are some linemen who don't hit helmets at all." One gets the idea that Ernie held the non-hitters in rather low esteem.

There is more to teaching tackle than meets the eye. In college it is unusual for more than three linemen to rush the quarterback. The pros rush four, and they also pose the constant threat of blitzing linebackers. Rookie defensive linemen are surprised by the concentration on the quarterback. Even the practice drills aim at the passer, over and over.

"I don't feel a defensive lineman reaches his peak until the sixth year," says Stautner. "You get so excited in a game that you can't think something and then do it. You have to do it without thinking, and that requires experience. After six years you can plan how to attack your man during the week before the game, and then in the game you just do it. No thinking."

One of Stautner's pupils at Dallas is Bob Lilly, who has played eight years. Lilly is crazy about photography and looks like Huckleberry Finn with red hair and freckles, but he combines an un-Huckleberry, Stautner-style infighting with his own, almost unlimited, physical ability. Opposing offenses are always dreaming up creative new two-and-three-man blocking concoctions, designed to counter Dallas' one-man flower-power, and Lilly enjoys the challenge. He is extremely quick, agile, strong, with great balance—plus, he's very bright and easy to coach.

"Bob Lilly keeps notes on every opponent," says his coach. "By now he can tell how they are going to block by how they lean. After a while Lilly's notes can even tell him how the opponent is disguising what he plans to do. But it doesn't matter if he hasn't played against his particular man before. We attack *types* of blocks, not particular plays nor particular players."

Lilly has the perfect temperament for playing tackle in the Dallas system. The Cowboy front four charges the passer scientifically. The tackles, who are closest to the quarterback, try to force him out of the pocket for the ends to sew him up from the outside. They have specific areas of responsibility, they contain and charge.

Says Stautner: "The defensive tackle covers his area first. That's first responsibility. Then he reacts, after the first hit, but that's second."

On Lilly's first hit on every play he grabs the guard's shoulders and, when he feels the first move—outside or inside, he pushes the guard off balance, in that same direction.

Says Lilly: "When we charge we must protect our lanes. If I took off outside, the quarterback might escape through my area." This is a different concept entirely from the Rams', where the front four blow and go. "But otherwise we've got freedom. I like to have at least four good moves in mind when I line up for a play," says Lilly. "Regardless of whether one works or fails I will always fake it through and do something new next time."

The lineman opposite Lilly has a few tricks too, and is watching Lilly as carefully as Lilly is watching him. In fact, Lilly and his foe opposite are engaged in a mental outguessing game similar to the one between the quarterback and the linebacker who calls defensive signals.

The cat-and-mouse mental gymnastics going on between opposing linemen might go like this: Bob Lilly is watching the opposite guard. He looks at his knuckles. If they are turning white from pressure Lilly smells run (thinking that the guard is going to fire ahead with a block right at him). If the guard goes light on his hand Lilly figures pass (thinking that the tackle's weight is back because he's going to move back to protect the passer). *The smartest guards will frequently have white knuckles on a passing play and go light with their weight before a run.*

A Steeler guard who played him head-to-head said Lilly was the quietest, most even-tempered guy in the league. "You hold him, trip him, he never says a word—just plays his game." At TCU they called him "Purple Cloud" because he was everywhere, and so quick. "Lilly anticipates the signal count, and hogs the line of scrimmage so close you couldn't put a hair between his helmet and an offside penalty," said Cowboy Center Mike Connelly. "He slithers *around* blockers."

Lilly once appeared in a hair tonic commercial. He sided with the prosecution, against "Greasy Kid Stuff." The camera zooms in on Lilly, who growls: "I just had my damn hair done. Wanna make something outta it?"

If someone were game enough to want to make something out of something against Lilly, the rest of the Dallas Doomsday Defense is always around to help him. Next to Lilly at left tackle is Jethro Pugh, a candidate for some season's "Harlon Hill" award (players who come from the most obscure colleges are always given the epithet "this year's Harlon Hill" after the great Bear end who came to Chicago as an unknown from Florence State College in Alabama). Pugh's alma mater is Elizabeth City State College in North Carolina.

When Ernie Stautner came to Dallas he worried about Jethro, who didn't have the proper gay abandon for playing defensive tackle. Jethro was afraid to make a mistake and so was slow to commit himself. He worried about being embarrassed so much that he got ulcers. Under Stautner, Pugh is coming along.

"In the beginning they kept talking to me about experience," said Jethro. "I never believed it would make that much difference. You either beat a guy or you didn't. At least that's what I thought. But now I can tell what the play is so much quicker. I've learned a lot about what my blocker is trying to do to me."

Next to Jethro is another Stautner pupil, Willie "Babycakes" Townes. Townes came on like a potential Ernie Ladd in the beginning with a waistline problem and a happy-go-lucky air. Stautner discovered from some personality tests that Townes was covering up, that he was full of doubts and rookie insecurities.

Babycakes is getting over them and he has even stopped eating in between meals, after several $500 contributions which Townes felt were unfair.

"I bought some scales and weighed at home," said Willie. "My weight was okay. All I can tell you is that these are what we call heavy scales.

"And there's something else. The sea level's different here. It makes you five pounds heavier."

Ernie Stautner has come a long way, from a human head hammer to a combination of teacher, psychologist, nurse, and mother to the front line of the Doomsday Defense. As a player, of course, Ernie had enormous experience with hammerheads, and unique personalities. For a number of years he was Bobby Layne's constant companion and bodyguard at the Pittsburgh Steelers. The only hammering in Bobby Layne's head hammered the morning after.

Defensive Ends

Defensive ends are usually taller, lighter and faster than defensive tackles. The defensive end and offensive tackle are almost nose-to-nose over the line of scrimmage, the tackle a little to the inside. The first one

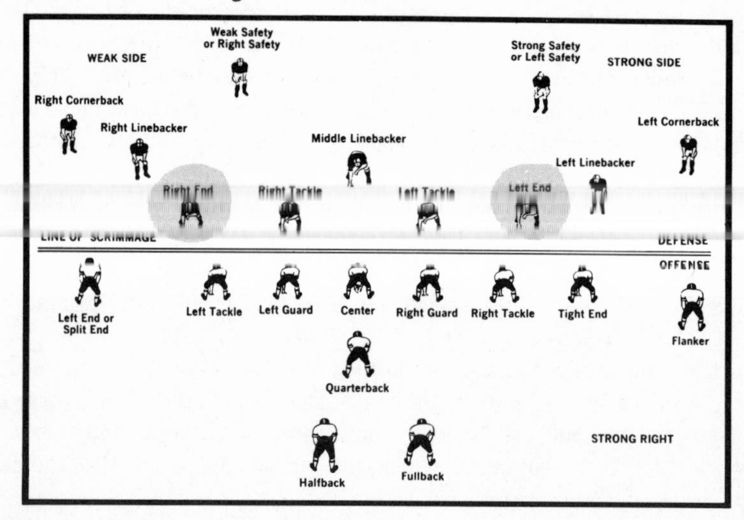

to move, after the snap, has a big advantage—the no-hands tackle wants forward momentum and the end-with-hands wants to use them, to straighten his man up, break his momentum and take away his power. The end can often catapult by the tackle by using leverage—pushing down with one hand on one shoulder and pulling him out of position with the other hand.

"Larry Eisenhauer is the best end I have to play against," says Houston's Walt Suggs. "He's the hardest to block head on, because he really comes at you. There's no time to get up steam. Some of the others wait and look around, but Eisenhauer's tough, like a wild man. He's a real test."

According to Buffalo Quarterback Jack Kemp, Eisenhauer hits harder. Kemp is sore for three days after Ike takes a shot. Once, after he had left Kemp badly shaken up, Eisenhauer said, "I knew I had him. How could I tell? Well, do you know what it feels like when somebody lets the air out of a tire?"

Eisenhauer has a reputation for slobbering and biting, but others swear he's a long-haired intellectual. In his senior year of college, the night before the big game, Larry went on a wild night on the town. The following Friday at lunch he was called upon and everyone expected him to apologize to his Boston College teammates. "I got stoned last Friday and I'll probably do it again tonight," said Larry, "but this time I'll know better and I'll take half the team with me, particularly the sophomores."

Eisenhauer legends need annual supplements. In 1968 Larry and a friend, Boston Linebacker Doug Satcher, went out and got a bit tipsy. Satcher was arrested and charged with being drunk and disorderly. Eisenhauer naturally tried to help, and came to Doug's rescue. There was something about knocking a door down at the police station and Eisenhauer was arrested for trying to free a prisoner, Satcher. Eisenhauer is living proof—the defensive end-with-hands wants to use them.

Defensive ends don't try to overpower the offensive tackles. It takes too long. They try to get *around* the tackle, which is why they would rather be quick than strong. Ram Tackle Charley Cowan says Packer Willie Davis is the quickest.

"I more or less try to meet him short," says Cowan, "so I try to cut down the ground between us, to take his start away from him. Davis is the quickest, most versatile end I face. He has all the techniques. He gets you leaning one way and then he grabs you. Or he'll step back, and then try to breeze past you."

One's sympathies lean toward the offense. Imagine trying to keep Willie Davis (6′ 3″, 250) off your quarterback. "Never believe it's easy," said Viking Coach John Michels. "Take Davis, give him free use of his hands, and try to stop him, without using your hands. It's murder."

As he rushes in toward the quarterback, a defensive lineman tries to recognize the play. It's hard to spot a pass immediately because the blocking has been set up to fool the defense. For example, blocking is the same for an end sweep as it is for a roll-out pass. Blocking for a draw play, or a trap, begins like pass blocking, in which case if the defensive linemen rush blindly at the quarterback they will be suckered. For that reason a defensive end cannot key exclusively off the offensive tackle; he keeps one eye on the tackle, one eye on the ball, and another eye on the running back, to see if he is blocking, running, or *pretending* to block en route to catching a screen pass.

Defensive linemen are also suckered if the offensive linemen only pretend to be blocking for a runner. The quarterback fakes a hand off to a running back, the defense reacts to a run, and before the pass defenders come up the quarterback throws a pass over their heads—a play action pass.

"Play action always means I have to fire out at my key a little higher than usual, in order to keep my body in control after the initial contact," said Jim Cadile, a Bear blocker. "It's much harder to recover if you fire out low. With play action the main thing is to keep the defensive lineman's hands down until the ball is thrown. I'd have to hit his stomach with my head on my second charge, because contact with the lower anatomy causes a man to fold forward. At least it should."

Play action, traps and draws surprise lots of defenses and illustrate why defensive linemen need speed and agility—to recover quickly if they've been fooled and to pursue the ball. No one knows what will happen next in any football game. Which is why defensive players, even if they aren't immediately involved in the play—if it's to the other side of the field, for example, are still expected to pursue the ball. The offense may fumble, there may be an interception, a number of things just might happen to create a situation where the rest of the defensive players would be needed. If they are standing off to one side speculating, they won't be in the middle of the action ready to help. Pursuit is as important in football as it is in romance, and means the same thing—to get back in the game after you've been shot down.

"The best plan is for the whole front four to meet at the quarterback," says Viking Jim Marshall, "but that's sort of hard with Fran Tarkenton. You never know where he's going to be."

Marshall, Tarkenton's ex-Minnesota teammate, is better qualified than any other defensive end to meet Tarkenton as he scrambles out of a U-turn, because Marshall watched him from the sideline and practiced against Tarkenton for years. Jim knows that if he runs in the opposite direction and just waits, that Fran will soon come scrambling back. Marshall even went so far as to practice running in the opposite direction. He once scooped up a fumble against the 49ers and ran 66 yards to the end zone—*the wrong end zone*. Jim sensed something was amiss when the 49ers started congratulating him.

Fran Tarkenton was the first to reach him. "Jim!" shouted Fran. "You ran the wrong way, *the wrong way*."

Marshall is the end. He surfs, skis (both water and snow) and dives (both scuba and sky). About his first water-skiing experience:

"I was going great, cutting back behind that boat," said Jim. "I jumped a wave, just like the good guys do. Then the ski tip caught the water. As I went sailing through the air I kept thinking, 'Big Jim, there's something you forgot to do, man.' I forgot to let go of the rope."

When Marshall went sky-diving he had no rope to worry about. "I've had ninety-six free falls," he said. "What a fantastic feeling of freedom—detached, suspended, like a bird. *There's no sensation of falling*." When Marshall retires he wants to dive into the stadium for his last game.

Running the wrong way prompted Larry Merchant to comment on Marshall's sky diving: "When Marshall goes after Tarkenton he'd like to fall on him from 15,000 feet. But Jim Marshall just might fall up.

Giants' defensive tackles rushing St. Louis passer Jim Hart.

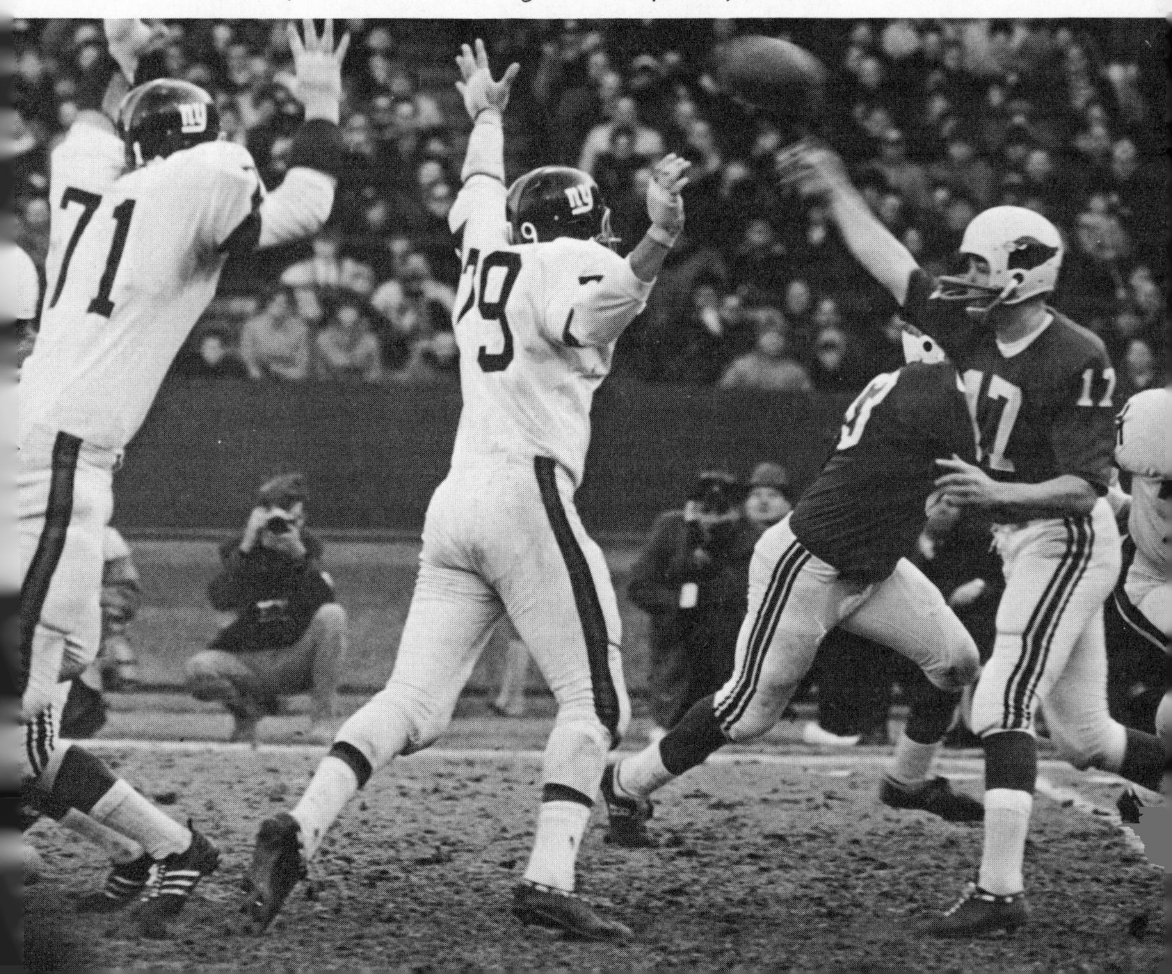

If he were Marshall, Leif Ericson, The Original Viking, would have discovered China."

Marshall carries this reverse thing a little far. Several years ago he was unloading his .38 revolver and accidentally shot himself in the left side and ended up in the hospital.

"Since I was a kid I wanted to fly and do things like that," said Jim. "I've always wanted to do adventurous things.

"I don't sky-dive just for kicks," says Jim. "There are problems you set up—loops and turns and trying to land on target. I'm usually on target." Which sounds like good practice for his regular job, when Marshall flies in at a two-legged target.

At 6′ 3″, 235, Marshall is small for defensive end, but he's very fast. Speed is useful for skittering around blockers and picking their pocket. Height is handy when the end flails his arms like a windmill and tries to bat down a pass.

"Don't forget," said 6′ 7″ Ben Davidson, "on a quick look in [pass] the quarterback throws so fast he really doesn't need a pocket. The only thing the quarterback has to worry about is if the defensive linemen can knock the ball down by reaching high. So the offensive linemen fire out low, and hit the defensive linemen in the legs. The natural thing to do is bring your hands down to protect yourself. It's just instinctive.

At Kansas City, Chuck Hurston has the height. At 6′ 6″, Chuck (who calls himself Charles) is three inches taller than Jim Marshall, but he weighs less—which is rather slight for playing defensive end. (When you consider that Ben Davidson at 6′ 7″, 270 is considered rangy, Hurston 6′ 6″, 230 is absolutely skinny.)

"On about every play I hit my man as hard as I can. Then I try to get to the ball as fast as I can," explained Chuck. "But playing on the weak side with Buck Buchanan next to me is something. He's always threatening, daring . . . just begging the split end to run our way. Me, I'm just the opposite—I beg 'em to go the other way." Chuck's another of the new breed, wise beyond his years. "Being the smallest, I tend to worry, but playing next to Buchanan (6′ 7″, 280) makes all the difference. He says, 'Chuck, you take outsides and I got everything else.' He's really something."

Chuck regularly eats four meals a day, trying to keep his weight up. One of football's best-kept secret "injuries," of which there are many, was before the first Super Bowl when no one knew that Hurston was down to 205.

"I was hit by stomach trouble around Thanksgiving," he explained. "I lost thirty pounds in two weeks. They thought I had an ulcer. I even tried baby food for a week, but I couldn't handle any kind of food. Weight was a big factor in that game. I just didn't have the power to fight through—the straight-ahead stuff—especially on the pass rush." Chuck is back up to 235 (he says), but that's still too light for a defensive end. They are busy converting him into an average-sized linebacker.

Ben Is for Benevolent

"You can't play football if you haven't got a gimmick," says Ben Davidson, Oakland's defensive right end. Davidson was referring to his long blond handlebar mustache, which from grip-tip to grip-tip measures eight inches.

"It is a bother," admits Ben. "I have to wax it and sometimes it looks crooked, so I have to keep straightening it out. And after practice it drops into my mouth."

But it's worth the trouble. Without his hairy lip Ben would be just another tall end. Big Ben would be a London clock. "The mustache has been good to me for four years," said Ben. "I just made the All-AFL team again. If the mustache made me All-AFL, well that shows I'm that much smarter."

Ben's mustache gives him publicity and, there isn't, and will never be, a player's pocketbook that isn't fattened by ink. Ben rejoiced after the Jets won the Super Bowl III.

"I think the Jets' victory means a top dollar reward for all of us in the AFL," said Ben. "There will be more and more engagements and endorsements from now on."

Ben didn't exactly rejoice when he heard about one of Joe Namath's endorsements. Namath was paid $10,000 to shave off his "Fu Manchu" for a television commercial.

"He got $10,000, huh?" asked Davidson. "Well, he's no idiot, that's for sure. But I'd probably have to double that before I'd shave. After all, I've had mine considerably longer, and it would take too long to grow back again. I spent two thousand dollars for the big sign on top of my bar (outside Oakland) and the big thing about the sign is a mustache. Shaving would be a bad move."

Ben's mustache gives him something to do when he's talking with newspapermen or other people he doesn't quite trust. Some people who are constantly putting people on have nervous eyes, or they blush. Davidson pulls at his mustache, tugging at it and fiddling with it and patting it like a girl fussing with a miniskirt. Ben looks like a singing waiter and a walrus, and he talks soft, like his boss Al Davis, with the difference that Big Ben succeeds in fooling all of the people almost all of the time with a slyly mischievous sense of humor. Big Al doesn't always fool anyone.

Big Ben has a headhunter reputation. Each year, several days before the Oakland-New York game, Joe Namath calls Ben a dirty player to the newspapermen. Namath entertains his favorite writers to the tune of Bad Ben Davidson stories and thus the annual headline: Namath Calls Davidson Dirty.

"He just does that because it's New York and he knows it will be big publicity," says Ben. "I'm no cheap-shot artist. I read what he says, and I figure the Jets must not be sold out. It sounds like a ticket push. What the hell, a little publicity never hurt anybody."

"Oakland is the dirtiest team in the league," says Namath, "especially Davidson and Birdwell."

Because they are good friends and room together on the road, and because Big Ben is the blithest of spirits while Birdwell is rugged and down-to-earth, they are like Don Quixote and Sancho Panza. They sally forth from the line, in full armor for the tournament; they joust with the blockers and pursue (according to Namath) errant paths, and after the game long tales are spun about their deeds. Davidson actually has real qualifications, besides a woeful countenance, for a contemporary Quixote. He has a steed (a Triumph 500 motorcycle), a Spanish nickname "El Grandote" ("you could translate that loosely as 'Big Guy' "), and has been taking off on assorted expeditions through Mexico at the drop of a sombrero.

"I love the Mexican people. They're the greatest, and they love football," said Ben. "They want me to come and coach at their university, in Mexico City. It's the Latin approach, always wanting to fire the coach."

Ben grew up in the same Los Angeles melting pot as Mike Garrett, and it was a potfull of Mexicans. Several years ago he took off on his motorcycle and traveled down through Baja, California for a thousand miles, then took a ferry to the mainland and spent a month motorcycling over the unbeaten paths of Mexico.

"No, it wasn't that comfortable," said Ben about his cycle, "with the rough roads. The seat was hard, but I got to know the people and ate with them and slept along the way. They're great. The small Mexicans can't get over anyone being so big, and they're very jealous of my mustache. They love it. You know, Mexicans all have long mustaches and they try for years but they just can't seem to get theirs to grow as long as mine." Ben's motorcycle tour added up to 3,400 miles.

One fall the Davidsons bought a motor home camper, a Clark-Cortez, and Ben's wife Kathy and his brother drove it from Oakland to Miami to meet him after the Super Bowl.

"A camper would be great," I said. "You could sit in the back for part of the time and eat, or drink or sleep."

"I wouldn't like that," said Ben. "I'd like to be up front and drive."

"He's the kind of driver who sees a dirt road and wonders where it goes," says Kathy, "and he finds out."

The Davidsons used to travel by Volkswagen bus. Ben would pile his family inside and they would take off. Two summers ago in their new camper they took a typical trip, which includes visiting friends, digging around obscurer parts of Mexico, collecting occasional objets d'art, practicing Spanish, and forgetting football. When they make a travelogue of Ben's life, Steve McQueen will play the lead. In fact, he's already practicing. McQueen races motorbikes, and takes summer trips with his wife and kids in a Cortez camper.

"Most people think you should save up all your money for when you're old," said Ben. "I think it should be just the other way around."

Ben was a hurdler and a basketball player in high school, and even in college he didn't throw any scouts into a tizzy with his football. He was drafted by New York but the Giants traded him to Green Bay soon after the All-Star Game. They threw him into the final minutes of that game, in the offensive line. He played opposite one of the best and most ferocious middle linebackers who ever emerged from Pennsylvania, Chuck Bednarik.

"He kept punching me in the face," Davidson said. "Why did he do that? I didn't do anything to him." Although he spent most of his Packer year on the bench, Ben picked up his first championship check when the Packers beat the Giants for the NFL title ($5,195 for winning in 1961; for losing Super Bowl II, six years later, each Raider collected $7,500).

Ben was traded to Washington, where he spent two lackluster seasons, was dropped, and ended up at Oakland. Ben gives all credit for his regeneration to Al Davis, who was the Raider coach when he arrived. Ben is still improving, partly because, physically, he is a late blossomer who grew too big too fast, and because he isn't a natural football player and has to work harder than most of the others.

The Packers remember Ben.

"I remember when Ben bought one of his first cars," said Jerry Kramer. "I think it was a Porsche. It was beautiful to see him unfolding himself from that little automobile."

"Davidson used to wear Bermuda shorts on Green Bay's streets in December," said Packer Tackle Bob Skoronski. "If I had legs like his I'd show them off too, all the time."

Ben remembers his time with the Redskins.

"When I was at Washington we shared dressing rooms with baseball's Senators," said Ben. "Only a thin wall was between. First time I was there we all wanted to look at look at their famous new player Jim Piersall. We climbed the wall and peeked through the cracks but couldn't see anything. Then we opened the door and saw *all the Senators peeking through their crack at us.*"

"We all wanted to see the big animals," said Piersall afterward.

"I'm kind of a Piersall myself," says Ben.

At Oakland, Davidson is a legend. "Before my third year I grew a beard during an off-season construction job, and when I got to camp Coach Davis asked me to shave it off. But I liked the mustache so I kept it."

Oakland fans adore Ben, who until not too long ago kept his telephone number listed; there were finally just too many calls. In the beginning fans would telephone and ask him to come over to dinner.

"Fine," Ben would say. "What time?"

Before Super Bowl II there was some doubt about Davidson's talent, particularly against running plays, but he acquitted himself well, as did the Raider defense. (It was Oakland's offense that was lacking in the loss to the Packers.)

"Wait a minute," said Jerry Kramer, "the mustache did better than I expected. He gave us a little pass rush. He was in there two, three times, and I didn't expect to see him in there at all."

"I heard my name announced over the loudspeaker a couple of times," said Ben, "so I figure I must have been doing something." Ben had a speech prepared about how the press had mistreated the Raiders during the week before the Super Bowl, but when Oakland lost he didn't want to look like a bad loser. "If we had won," he said, "I would have conducted a forum."

Davidson's primary opponent was the tackle next to Jerry Kramer, Bob Skoronski. "We didn't talk," said Bob. "He grunted and was breathing hard but we didn't talk. As far as I'm concerned he's a good clean player. Several times he had chances to hit Bart [quarterback Starr] after the pass but he didn't take any cheap shots."

"Is it true you talk a lot during a game?" Ben was asked before a game against New York. "You know, name-calling, the whole bit, to get the other guy upset?"

"Never," said Ben. "It wastes energy, and I'm always trying to conserve my strength. When we play the Jets for the first time, and I haven't seen Winston Hill since last year, before the game I'll say something like 'How are you, Winston? How've you been?' "

Their game against the Jets in New York was the only game the Raiders lost in 1967. It was a Saturday night game. Most players prefer to play in the afternoon because there are fewer hours of pregame tension and, playing earlier, they have more energy. The Raiders were resting during the afternoon, and Davidson was telling how rarely he is called for penalties and how he couldn't imagine how Namath could be calling him dirty. In typical pregame fashion, Davidson was complimenting his enemy, and listening to him, gentle Ben, you wouldn't think they would need any officials that night.

The Jets weren't as chivalrous.

"That Eleven Angry Men stuff, that's all wrong," said one Jet. "Actu-

Ben Davidson flattening Joe Namath.

ally only ten are angry. One's nuts." Namath began talking too, launching his own psyching campaign. Four days before kickoff Joe cried foul.

Namath, as always, was using his head. Joe knows that, by crying wolf in loud black ink, he is alerting the game officials to watch Davidson more closely, with special attention, and that in the case of a close judgment call, Davidson might lose the benefit of the doubt and be given a penalty. There is also the chance that the headlines might cause Ben to shift part of his concentration during the game from playing end to worrying about penalties—a small added advantage to Joe and his Jets in this game where concentration is everything.

It's only fair to mention that the Jet offensive linemen are guilty of more holding than most teams. Sherman Plunkett was a whiz at holding. So is Winston Hill.

Winston Hill is a cagey tackle with a good reputation among his peers. An eccentric, unlikely sort of athlete, Hill looks like he couldn't move fast to save his life. He was a tennis champion in college, still plays in the off-season, and wears spectacles. Hill was a slow starter and took several years in the pros to mature. At times he still sounds rather ingenuous. After the Jets beat the Colts in Super Bowl III, Hill acted amazed: "One time we ran for five yards around Ordell Braase's side and he stepped on my hand. I asked him why. Then the next time I blocked him he started cursing me. I didn't know what was going on."

The heck he didn't. Winston played a good game against Braase, and finally admitted it. "They choked early," he gloated.

Hill went deep sea fishing for the first time a few days before the game and caught a seven foot shark. After the game, in the midst of the celebrations, when most of the Jets were planning how to spend their $15,000, Hill was worrying about finding a way to get his shark mounted and where he'd hang it.

Winston "launched" his younger sister, Sharon, socially at a party given by Sonny Werblin at Toots Shors'. Jet Punter Curley Johnson was M.C.—Johnson is very funny, popular and the team wit—and he told some raunchy jokes that brought down the house. Mrs. Werblin, who sang and acted as Leah Raye before marrying Werblin, sang several songs, and Sharon Hill sang "Trees." Winston introduced Sharon around to the Jet bachelors and everyone had such a smashing time that the party, an annual affair, was never repeated. Sharon is now singing on the Playboy Club circuit.

It is in non-social circles that Winston has made the most news.

"Hill blocks low," described Ben Davidson, "especially on the run. I have to get down lower than usual, and fire into him trying to stop his charge. If you're any good you have to be quick—fight off the block and recover quickly. Hill is a good pass blocker."

The Jets hold more because they pass more. It is hard on an offensive lineman when the defense expects a pass, and with fragile-kneed Namath at quarterback the defense expects a pass more often. The blockers figure it's better to risk a holding penalty than to let a rusher flatten Joe, and if they didn't figure this way they wouldn't be working for Weeb.

"I may waste part of a second looking for a run, but on every play I rush the passer. Period," said Ben. "That's the easiest part of the job. If it's third-and-ten I know he has to pass and wants to wait as long as he can, to give his receivers a chance to run out at least ten yards. I'm only trying to go seven yards, to get to the passer, although Namath throws from a deeper pocket, say about nine yards deep. Of course, I have Winston Hill in my way."

Ben is an expert on the subject of offensive tackles. "They aren't supposed to hold, but in tight they grab your shirt with both hands," said Ben, "and that's when you should let them have it over the ear, to discourage them. If other offensive guys around the league see in the game movies that I'm being held and don't do anything about it, they will all pick on me and pretty soon I'll be unemployed. The trouble with doing something about it is you have to resort to illegal tactics, which you hate to do because then you're lowering yourself—down to his level."

As it happened, in that game in New York, Davidson got to Namath only once, with an obviously clean shot, and Ben went out of his way to avoid official wrath. Once he even helped to pick Namath up, playing Mr. Clean after Dan Birdwell had flattened Joe.

It was a different story when the Jets played in Oakland two months later, in December. On one play Ben fought past Hill and smashed into Namath's head. His forearm came up under Joe's double-bar face mask, sent his helmet flying off his head, and fractured Joe's cheekbone into smithereens. The officials called it a late shot—that Ben hit after the ball had been thrown—and gave Oakland a 15-yard roughing the passer penalty.

"No, it wasn't a cheap shot," said Ben. "I saw the movies. But after all the publicity I got lots of crank letters. One was from a wrestler, Bobo Brazil. He came on pretty strong and used a lot of racial stuff, calling me 'Whitey.' I don't know what color he thinks Namath is."

"Davidson's in a class by himself," said Winston Hill. "He is the number one cheap-shot artist in the league. It's all after the whistle with him. If they change the rules and allow kicking in the groin after the whistle, fine, we'll play it that way. But this stuff isn't football." Hill had no choice but to yell because it was past him that Davidson had taken his shot. Hill was not to blame, actually (Namath moved from behind Hill), but to escape public censure Winston yelled loudly to aim the spotlight elsewhere. Elsewhere was Davidson.

"I want to take back what I said about Hill," said Davidson. "You know, about being a good pass-blocker. Like I said before, the Jets are the ones who started all the talk. They may think I'm dirty, but other clubs don't necessarily agree (notably Green Bay). I've got no hard feelings toward Joe. Actually, players say he's a great guy. I'd like to meet him some day, have a few beers."

"I saw him at an All-Star game, but I didn't talk to him," said Namath. "I have no relationship with him. When I was a rookie I was on the ground and Davidson twisted my knee. That's something else. I like Oakland less than any other team. After they broke my cheekbone I had an extra bar put on my face mask. Every team has a couple of cheap-shot artists like him."

10 Cheap-Shot Art

By definition, a cheap-shot artist is a player who hits late, after the whistle, or out-of-bounds. Actually there aren't many cheap-shot artists around anymore, mostly for fear of retaliation and because of sharp-eyed officiating. The addition of the sixth official means twelve eyes are now watching for transgressions and errors of judgment. Ten years ago only four officials worked a game.

In the old days of the famous headhunters like Bucko Kilroy (now a Ram scout), Don Paul (now a restaurant owner), and the bad Bear linebackers—Joe Fortunato, Bill George and Larry Morris—rhubarbs and personal feuds were an every-game occurrence. Don Paul, ex-TV announcer, gives current TV announcer George Connor credit for an educated foot. "His elbow wasn't as good as mine," said Paul, "but he was the slickest tripper in the league." Public opinion always held that Don Paul, one of the last linebackers to play without a face mask, was the dirtiest player in football.

"When I was playing, it was common before a game to get up a pool of two bucks a person and designate an opposing player who had to go," said Paul. "It was winner-take-all. In order to collect, you had to knock the target out of the game without getting caught by an official. If you drew a penalty, you blew the pot, and it carried over until next week."

It's a mistake to allow the Don Pauls into the same conversation with the cheap-shot artists of today, who are tame by old-school standards. It would be like comparing Murph the Surf with Dillinger.

There was a fleeting revival of cheap-shot art a year or two ago at Kansas City, where Defensive Back Fred Williamson used to throw his forearm ("The Hammer") late, if he made the tackle at all, where Mike

Garrett had been known to instigate a debate (but by the time both benches are going at it, the slight, smart Garrett is safe, probably behind Fred Arbanas) and where the last almost-old-school artist still around, Jon Gilliam, departed as tradition dictates, feet first. Gilliam, a center, missed thirteen games during the season that Kansas City went to the Super Bowl. He was only *onlooking*, standing at the sideline watching an *exhibition* game when The Incident occurred. The Chiefs were returning a punt in Gilliam's direction and, instead of getting out of the way, Jon chose not to budge, hoping for a chance to take a shot. Gilliam was carried out on a stretcher.

The Eagles' fullback, Tom Woodeshick, was kicked out of a game against Dallas for fighting, which wasn't easy. Like Gilliam, Woodeshick was on the sideline. Woodeshick rarely misses any action. The more he plays the better he likes it, and if the field is muddy and the weather is cold, that's fine with Tom, who says that bad conditions are invigorating. Woodeshick missed three quarters of that Dallas game and felt the whole episode was a disaster, and unfair besides.

"It was an ultra-emotional thing," cried Tom, who had flown to the aid of a teammate. "I can't give a reason why I did it. But I don't understand why I was ejected. I don't think players should be ejected for fighting. It's foolish, because the only one you hurt is yourself. You break your knuckles on a helmet or something."

A fracas like this happens once in so great a while as to be almost curious. Also on the wane are the famous hardnosed feuds, like the one between Joe Fortunato and Monty Stickles. Stickles, the Saints' lantern-jawed tight end, was suspended for a week in 1968 for physically abusing an official. Stickles would just as soon belt you as look at you, and says so.

"I'm aggressive because when you hit somebody real hard you upset their way of thinking," says Stickles. "You take their mind off what they are trying to do. If I get their minds off what they are doing, they are going to be playing the way I want them to. When a guy is worrying about getting hit he loses his concentration."

Today's so-called dirty players fall into three categories. They are either loudmouths, like Johnny Sample (before he "reformed") or Fred Williamson (now retired); they have trouble controlling their tempers like Greg Larson at the Giants; they are extemely hardnosed like Ed O'Bradovich at the Bears, John Baker at the Lions (Baker does social work at a women's prison in the offseason and must have a soft heart to go along with his hard nose), or Jerry Sturm at the New Orleans Saints. *Saints* is a misnomer, what with Stickles and Sturm in the fold. Sturm, in a game against Green Bay, grabbed Willie Wood by the face mask, yanked off his helmet and punched him. Wood finally retaliated, by biting Sturm's thumb, hard.

But none of these really comes close to the classic hardnoses of some years ago. Most of today's cheap-shot art is created by inferior players. The good ones are on time. They don't have to hit late.

More than any other position, linebackers are labeled cheap-shot artists. They have more ground to cover, make the scene a little late and end up the second man on the tackle. Immediately the fans of the offensive team yell "Dirty!" at the late-tackling linebacker, who could care less.

"We hit each other as hard as we can," says Sam Huff, Vince Lombardi's middle linebacker and assistant coach at Washington. "We try to hurt everybody. This is a man's game."

"We don't necessarily try to hurt a quarterback," says Packer Linebacker Lee Roy Caffey, who is so tough he once broke the Golden Boy's (Paul Hornung's) nose in *practice*. "But when he's running with the ball, he's live meat."

The meanest linebacker by reputation is Ray Nitschke, who was Vince Lombardi's middle linebacker at Green Bay. Stories about his toughness build an image of Nitschke sitting in his hard chair thinking ugly.

"People sympathize with us because we have to play in cold weather," said Nitschke, "but that's part of football. They call off baseball games because of rain. Basketball is played inside. But football is played in cold, rain, heat, or what have you, and that's the way it should be.

"That's why this game is great, because there's a cerain amount of privation that goes with it. When you have to make sacrifices it shows a little in your character. Football is an emotional game, and I prefer to start preparing early in the week, as early as possible. By Sunday my concentration is complete."

The higher up you get the harder it is to deflate when it's all over. After the second Super Bowl, Nitschke and Caffey were men berserk in the Packer dressing room. Television caught Caffey running in search of his teeth while Ray Nitschke was showering his teammates with blood-caked kisses. A week before, an announcer had introduced Nitschke on television as a madman. Many have called him a madman in the past, so it was nothing new, but Nitschke deeply resented this nationally televised, in-person namecalling. The incident developed into a rhubarb.

"Dogs get mad," he said. "People do not. I have a family to think about and a career." His family and friends gathered at the Nitschke house one Christmas Eve and his wife Jackie surprised him with a present. She pulled back the curtains and there on the lawn was a Lincoln Continental. "When I was a kid," he said, "I rode in a Lincoln once, and I dreamed that I might own one when I grew up." Very few offensive players would be moved by a glimpse at this soft side of Nitschke. Few would believe he had one.

The Jekyll and Hyde aspect of football causes some funny scenes. Bob Dee, a defensive end at Boston, tells a story about a championship game against San Diego. Between plays, Ron Mix congratulated Bob on his new son, asking for Mrs. Dee. Bob was thinking what a nice guy Ron was, how thoughtful, when on the next play he found himself flat on the ground thinking he'd been hit by a streetcar. It was Mix.

What's most incongruous about pro football, if indeed it's not a paradox, is the merciless brutality of the most religious players. One would expect a tremendous conflict between the piety of Sunday morning and the mayhem of Sunday afternoon; instead hostility and holiness are surprisingly compatible. It would not be so astounding if a player outside the violence, a placekicker perhaps, turned out to be a preacher. But Jerry Stovall, Maxie Baughan and Bill Glass, who recently retired to devote his time to evangelism, were three of the hardest hitters, notorious for playing aggressive defense. Glass particularly had been singled out for vicious, even dirty play. Yet all three are leaders in the Fellowship of Christian Athletes, the very ones who lead their respective teams in pregame prayer.

"I play as legally as I can," said Glass. "It wouldn't be right if I played illegally. Because football is very aggressive, if not violent, if I didn't play rough I'd be second-rate, and that would be un-Christian, not to realize my potential. Christianity is a live and vital way of life. Pro football is live and vital, too. They have something in common."

The Jets' Defensive End Gerry Philbin has a philosophy about violence in football that approaches sadism. "I want to get at the quarterback so bad I can taste it," says Philbin, whose habit is to stoke up anger and a kind of hate before a game, "but I've got to get the offensive tackle first. I've got to be prepared to hate him and hurt him and, if necessary, to put him out of the game. It's me or him. My reward is not just to get by the tackle, it's to really hurt the quarterback. You've got to want to hurt him."

Emotions like Philbin's are what make football a unique sport. Every good football player must like—make that *love*—to hit, which is another way of saying to inflict pain, and possibly even to inflict pain on a good friend. Every good football player also has to *take* hitting, which means a high tolerance for pain is imperative. A good hitter—a hardnose—reaches an emotional peak every time he hits. A hit with no emotion behind it doesn't hurt.

More players fail because they can't hit, can't be hit, or both, than because they lack size or speed. A number of small defensive backs, Pat Fischer and Bruce Maher for example, stick around for ten years by making up with hard hitting what they lack in physical equipment. George Webster is thirty pounds light for his linebacker job at Houston, yet George was a Rookie of the Year.

"It's hit or be hit," said Webster at the end of his first season. "I get very tense before the kickoff but I don't hate anybody. At least, not to start with. But they're all out to get you. Somebody may stick me good, and then I'll get mad and look for somebody to hurt. Things like that make you strong."

Depending upon the amount of hitting required, different positions have their own particular psychology. Linemen work in a constricted, heavy-traffic area where the hitting is constant. Offensive linemen are inhibited, mucking out holes for the more attractive, richer runners. They have to sustain the hit for several seconds. Defensive linemen just hit and run, charging the quarterback. There's no opportunity for thought at the line.

"Let me try to explain what's happening on that line of scrimmage," said Merlin Olsen. "It's a very intense time at the beginning of every play. There's a tremendous amount of nervous energy being burned up on both sides of that line of scrimmage in preparation for the snap of the ball. Once that ball is snapped there's an explosion of activity. You're sitting there coiled and almost shaking, ready to move, and when you're finally allowed to know what's happening, then you explode into your responsibility. This is true all across the defensive line and even into the backfield."

The linemen and the backfield don't explode alike. The linemen could never hit on every play with the same emotional intensity as, say, a cornerback who might have to hit hard only five times in a game. If we assume that the players' energy reservoirs are 100 per cent full at the beginning of a game, the linemen, on perhaps fifty plays, might spend that energy 2% at a time, while the defensive backs might spend theirs 20% at a time—five smashing open-field tackles.

Farther away from the line there are individual performances, less hitting and more thinking. Quarterbacks are always calculating and cool. The free safety, ten yards deep, is a troubleshooter who roams far afield.

(The kicker, of course, never hits. He may make two tackles in his whole career. Kicking requires dedication and concentration, and since he's often called into a pressure situation, the kicker's efforts are more mental than physical.)

In between the line and the far backs, the running backs and the linebackers romp. The hitting isn't constant but it's frequent and fierce. Jobs in the middle are the most demanding. Middle linebacker is the most brutal. The middle linebacker may have to make a tackle on any play, with no warning, so he stays emotionally peaked, ready for total hitting and total pain, throughout the game. He may make a dozen devastating tackles by himself and assist on a dozen more. He usually plays man-to-man against the fullback, but the middle linebacker's job is tougher, more emotionally draining, because he also calls defensive signals. Keep in mind that the fullback knows the upcoming play ahead of time and the linebacker doesn't. His signals are guesswork, and he reacts to the fullback's first move.

The smallest middle linebacker in football is 215-pound Lee Roy Jordan at the Cowboys. Jordan is typical of a certain type of linebacker that comes out of the Southeastern Conference (SEC). He is small, smart, quick and mean, and the meanness makes up for the smallness. The Jets' Larry Grantham, and Maxie Baughan, are like Jordan—small, southern, and hostile, hard hitters who like to knock heads off. If they didn't like the head knocking they'd just be lousy little linebackers.

One of the most publicized linebacker vs. fullback duels starred Sam Huff and Jim Taylor. When he was at Green Bay, Taylor was the all-time hardnose, a totally peaked performer for every minute of every game, because he simply loved hitting. During a normal midweek practice in sweat clothes, Taylor would come up to Lombardi and ask: "Say, coach, can't we put on some pads and do some hitting?" Lombardi loved him.

At Green Bay, Taylor's "man" in practice was Ray Nitschke. Practicing against a tough tomato like Nitschke was a good way for Taylor to get himself up for the likes of Huff.

"The nature of the game is to take the ball carrier and hang him up there and let everyone take his shot," said Sam Huff. "That's gang tackling. That's how a defensive player gets his kicks.

"When we used to play against Green Bay it was my job to stop Taylor. Taylor is rough. He brings out the defensive ballplayer in you. He'll crawl and scratch to make yardage."

The roughest meeting between Huff and Taylor was the 1962 championship game.

"That was about the roughest game I was ever in," said Taylor. "Right at the beginning I was hit in the mouth, my tongue was cut, bleeding a lot. I got the misery all through the game."

Green Bay won; that is, Taylor beat Huff 16–7, and Taylor was voted the game's most outstanding player.

The Taylor-Huff and Nitschke ilk support the theory that the hardest noses play either linebacker or fullback. It's hardly coincidence—rather it's additional evidence—that Ray Nitschke averaged 6.5 yards playing fullback in college at Illinois. Other fullbacks turned linebacker are Joe Fortunato (who recently retired to coach linebackers at Chicago), the Giants' Ken Avery (who hits so hard that on one tackle he broke three front teeth, pinched a nerve in his neck and broke a bone in his hand—and learned about it after the game), and Mike Curtis at Baltimore.

Mike was a fullback at Stanford. He's good looking—angelic-looking—and a quiet, unassuming bachelor who plays with such enthusiasm that he frequently breaks his nose and other assorted bones belonging to him and others.

"I'm a gentleman off the field but on the field I'm an animal," says Mike who is such a wild man that he often ends up fighting with his teammates in mid-week practices. In one session before a Ram game,

Mike got so ornery that Don Shula had to send him to stand on the sideline for one hour as punishment. Mike is 25.

Jimmy Orr's locker adjoins Mike's. "I get dressed fast," said Jimmy. "Since he's been next to me, I'm the first one out."

From the beginning it was obvious which path Curtis's career would take—the bumpy one. During his second season the Colts beat Atlanta, which wasn't surprising. It was the Falcons' first year in the league, and they lost almost every game. Mike was discussing an incident after the victory. "I didn't swing at anyone," he said. "I tackled him, maybe a little over-zealously, but if he can't take it he should get off the field. He cracked me with his elbow while we were on the ground, so I gave his head a little twist."

Both Mike and the erring Falcon were thrown out of the game. "That's a record," said an Atlanta announcer. "That's the first time anybody got mad enough to take a swing at us."

11 Linebackers

"They hit like tackles and they run like halfbacks," said John Unitas, "and they're agile as monkeys."

If a linebacker isn't versatile, he either gets fired or converted into another position. Linebackers are like a pendulum swinging between two extremes—run and pass. They act like small tackles when they run up to plug holes left by the charging front four; they are fast, with quick reactions, for spinning into reverse like defensive backs; they are smart like a quarterback for diagnosing plays, especially the middle linebacker who usually calls defensive signals; and if they're a little loco it comes in

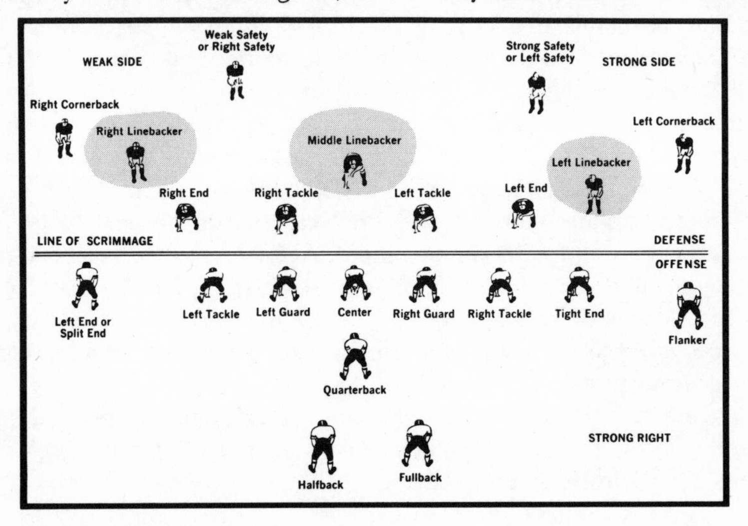

handy on a blitz. Blitzers act like a band of renegade outlaws, swarming out of the hills and attacking the stagecoach, the quarterback.

Like a pendulum, the linebackers do their thing best when they can swing freely. An unbalanced offense, built around a superstar, inhibits them. Facing a great passing offense, the linebackers have to play farther back than usual. Playing against an offense with a superrunner, the linebackers have to play up closer to the line. A superstar is like an anchor hanging from the defensive pendulum; it just can't swing free when a Gale Sayers is just across the line. A superstar gives a linebacker complexes. Linebackers would much prefer slamming heads around. NBC's chatty color man, Al DeRogatis, says the free-wheeling fun part of the game is played around the linebackers. At least, it should be.

Linebackers actually first came into vogue in New York with Sam Huff. The cold facts might show that Huff wasn't better than any other linebacker, but New York is the easiest place in America to start a fad, and Huff was the darling of his day. In 1965 he was traded to Washington, where he spent three unspectacular years and retired at the end of 1967. In the typical pro fashion Sam said he was through unless he could be persuaded. He moved his family near his job, back to New York. It wasn't a unanimous vote. "Mary and I decided not to talk about it over Christmas," said Sam. "Then we said we would not talk about it on weekends. Then we ruled out the middle of the week. My kids just hated to leave Washington. But I'm still not going to be persuaded to come back to the Redskins."

Then that mindbender, Vince Lombardi, arrived on the Washington scene and Huff, who had suffered through a year lay off as miserably as Lombardi had, quickly unretired. Huff wasn't the first retired 35-year-old to change his mind. Many Giant fans have never forgiven Coach Allie Sherman for trading Sam. He was a household word not only in New York but nationally, thanks to a TV special, *The Violent World of Sam Huff*. Coincidentally, the Giants' defense, or lack of same, hasn't been worth talking about since Sam's departure.

There is a slim chance that the Giants may have a new hero lying undiscovered in the midst of their miscellaneous linebackers who will soon bloom and blossom. His name is Ken Avery and if they ever make a TV special about Avery's world, the background music will be Tchaikovsky and the script will be non-violent. Avery is a ballet dancer. Granted, he is built more along the curves of Babar than Bambi, but Ken has been in and out of ballet school all of his life and he recommends it as ideal football training. For one thing, the stretching exercises prevent those gridiron pests, muscle pulls.

"Dancers need much more endurance than football players," Avery declares. "Why a football game is no more than eight minutes of full exertion. That's nothing to a dancer."

At 6′, 225, Avery is small for a linebacker. "Short," he corrected. "I have strength. I can knock those big guys on their cans." A ballerina friend of Ken's was amazed at how easily he held her over his head with one arm in a dance maneuver. "Boys who've studied ballet for ten years can't do that," she said. "They're not strong enough."

Ken's parents operate a dance school in Miami. Ken started to take lessons at age five—tap dance, modern dance, and ballet—and in college at Southern Mississippi in Hattiesburg, he took modern dance and folk dancing.

"If football players were properly introduced to ballet, it would improve their agility extension, and maybe their motivation, too," said Avery Sr. "A lethargic student's mind quickens as his body quickens, you know."

"High school and college is the time to begin," said Ken, "not at the pros. When you get here they expect you to have all the equipment. Coaching is in constant evolution; right now isometrics and weight lifting are big, but coaches used to frown on both. All coaches are looking for quickness though, and ballet teaches agility and speed. Ballet helps me with twisting and spinning, too. I know where my body is at all times so I'm not tripping over my feet." If Ken ever makes it big and a testimonial is given in his honor, they can have a dinner dance and call it the Game Ball.

"I was the littlest and slowest on my high school team," he said, "but when I graduated I had my dash down to 10.5. In college my coaches didn't believe in weights, so I tried gymnastics to develop my upper body, and ballet to develop my legs." It worked. Now no one kicks sand on Ken at the beach.

"I didn't do the hand movements or anything like that, and I didn't wear any leotards either," said Ken, "but did you ever see a ballerina's legs? Real development. A dancer can do anything a football player can do involving leg movements, and a whole lot more."

Dancers can practically fly. If only Edgar Degas could be on hand to capture Avery blitzing through the air and striking down a quarterback with a deftly pointed toe.

"On pass defense the first thing I do is set my right leg firmly and shift my weight, to open my stance," explains Ken, "which is just the second position in ballet, the *plié*."

Avery was classified 1-A in the draft but flunked the physical because of such mundane ailments as an arthritic wrist, surgical knee and a cracked vertebra. It's a wonder he can execute a graceful pirouette at all.

Wouldn't it be a crowd pleaser, though, if the Royal Ballet ever came to New York in the fall and for one series of downs they put Rudolf Nureyev at corner linebacker for the Giants, and Ken Avery into the grand pas de deux in the last act of *The Nutcracker Suite*?

Avery may be the first, but he isn't the only dance devotee in pro football. Paul Gibson, Atlanta's big back who studied drama and wants to be the first Negro Tarzan, says he pulled a muscle every time he turned around until he began taking dance.

"I was a mess before I discovered ballet," swears Paul. "It really straightened me out. Running backs are graceful, like good dancers." That old Tarzan was pretty graceful, too.

The Blitz

Kansas City Coach Hank Stram says a linebacker's face lights up like a Christmas tree when he hears the word blitz, because that means he has only one thing to think about; on other defensive plays he might have several.

On every play the front four rushes the quarterback. When any or all of the linebackers (or a safety) rush the quarterback, it is called *blitzing;* a defensive lineman rushes the passer, a linebacker blitzes him. In either case, pity the quarterback. Linebackers often have a hard time learning to rush the passer. They've heard hands high so often that they rush in, arms up, leaving their rib cages exposed—which gives the blockers a big target to aim for.

The blitz is a gamble. The point of a blitz is to send one more man at the quarterback than there are blockers protecting him. The defensive team transfers one player from pass defense to pass rush and gambles that the blitz will get the quarterback before the quarterback exploits the empty spot in the pass defense.

Pro football defenses can be described in terms of blitzing. Hip defenses blitz, square defenses don't. Green Bay doesn't and neither does Kansas City, or Los Angeles. The Rams never have to blitz because their Fearsome Foursome is so tall, and so successful at nailing the passer, that the Ram linebackers are excused from blitzing chores and allowed to drop back and help the defensive backs. Thanks to the Fearsomes, Ram linebackers were able to intercept thirteen passes in 1967; when the Fearsomes had an off-season in 1968, the linebackers' interceptions fell off to six, though two by Jack Pardee went all the way to touchdowns.

Dallas and New York blitz occasionally, about 15% of the time. Cleveland blitzes about one third of the time, but conservatively; the Browns never go all out and blitz three linebackers. Heaven forbid.

Washington, Chicago, Boston, Philadelphia, and Pittsburgh are frequent blitzers, but the best, wildest, and most flamboyant blitz belongs to St. Louis. The Cardinals are the biggest gamblers. There are really only four potential blitzers—the linebackers and the free safety—but the Cardinals are so avant-garde they once blitzed a cornerback! That shook up the oval world of pigskin. The Cardinals are so likely to blitz anything they can get their hands on that it's dangerous to walk by their bench during a game.

Blitzing makes the quarterback throw faster, hopefully for fewer completions—and an occasional interception. The offense reacts to blitzing either by keeping a pass receiver in to block or by shortening the receivers' patterns (so the quarterback can throw sooner). Blitzing comes and goes, in and out of style. At first, conservatives like Weeb Ewbank said the blitz was a sign of weakness, but after running a blitz or two up the flagpole even the conservatives decided to salute, and in one game Weeb's Jets almost surprised the Bills out of Buffalo by blitzing 50% of the time.

"The blitz is the way to get the ball," says Weeb, hinting that the way to stop those boring, grind-it-out, ball-control offenses, like his, is to shake 'em up with a blitz.

When Weeb's Jets surprised the Colts out of Super Bowl III, linebackers were the key to the game. The Jets sacrificed their linebackers, letting them help out against passing, and the Baltimore runners couldn't take advantage. The Colt linebackers also planned to help out their cornerbacks, but Joe Namath solved the Baltimore defense and read the Colt blitz out of sight.

"Our idea was to invite them to blitz," said George Sauer, who caught eight Namath passes. "When they blitzed we could get man-to-man coverage, and that's what we wanted."

The quarterback doesn't always recognize a blitz as easily as Namath did. Defenses are becoming ultra sophisticated at disguising themselves. One blitzing formation might have six variations, all depending (keying) on where and how the left running back lines up. Imagine if the quarterback had told his left running back to key off the right linebacker, who is waiting for the running back who is waiting for the linebacker . . . Everyone is acting, and reacting, and reacting again—with options on options. One should make it a rule to stop after third-guessing.

"We have seven basic defenses," says one of Hank Stram's linebackers, Bud Abell. "With the variations, we have to know at least fifty formations."

Collectively, Kansas City linebackers have always been a three-ring circus. The most versatile linebacker in football is Bobby Bell, who began his career at defensive end. According to Chuch Hurston, who replaced Bell at end, there is no defensive end fast enough to rush the quarterback without hitting a blocker first. It's just not possible to get around the offensive lineman without touching.

"Except Bobby Bell," said Chuck. "He's so fast he could do it. I saw him."

"I'd rather block anyone rather than block Bell," says Matt Snell. "You never know what he's going to do. He'll come right to you and then slide, in either direction."

"I never saw anyone love to play football like Bobby, at any position," says Stram. "He gets such a kick out of it."

Bell is tall, strong, with broad shoulders and a small waist. A marvelous athlete, Bobby can do anything, from basketball to horseshoe pitching. He dives, skis, and makes miraculous moves on a bongo board. He is a nut about antique cars, loves to refurbish them, and drives a 1928 Olds with his giant St. Bernard sitting next to him.

The Chief linebackers have always been relatively small but very fast, and noisy. The opposite side from Bell used to be home for the voluble E. J. Holub ("E. J. doesn't stand for anything; that's my name"). Holub lives on the lonesome prairie in West Texas. His ranch is 125 miles from Odessa. "Out there we get mail deliveries twice a week and it's ten miles to the mail box," says Holub. The family homestead had its first telephone installed in 1966 and is still without television. E. J. plans to raise cattle when he retires from football.

"I'm going to name it 'Bar 5 5' after my jersey number," he said. After Kansas City lost in the first Super Bowl ("I didn't do worth a darn. I was overanxious and went wrong."), Holub retired to his ranch and built a new house. He reported to the Chiefs the following summer in terrific shape, but later in the season he tore several leg muscles. One was torn loose all the way from the top of his thigh and Len Dawson said it was the worst looking leg he'd ever seen. Holub had seven knee operations before this latest injury, but he always came back strong. Several times during his career Holub played both ways, at center and at linebacker (which is fifty-five minutes of work per game). A year ago, the Chiefs found themselves with a wealth of linebackers and no center, and so Holub is at center. Center is easier on knees than linebacking.

Though it seems inconsistent with his ranching life, Holub is the Chiefs' holler guy. His trademark is chewing tobacco. He wears a cowboy hat, size 13E boots, and jeans . . . but in the city he wears a bowler and a pin-striped suit. E. J. begins to sound like the Danny Birdwell of the Midwest until you look next to him at middle linebacker where you find a Birdwell by the name of Sherrill Headrick—that is, you *would have found* Headrick, before he left Kansas City for Cincinnati in the expansion draft. Headrick is a nut.

"He's a wild man!" "He's crazy!" say opposing players, because "that dumb Headrick," as Joe Namath refers to him, is way outside the gridiron pale.

Headrick refuses to wear some of the usual protective equipment, thigh pads, for example. Thigh pads are designed to prevent extensive bruising, and so Sherrill is always beaten, and bruised. During a timeout Headrick once asked the trainer to fix his thumb, which was torn loose from his hand and was just dangling with broken bones breaking through the skin. Headrick told the trainer to grab it and then he sort of fell backward

E. J. Holub at home.

jerking the thumb roughly into place. The trainer put a splint on it, cleaned off the blood, and Headrick went back into the game. The trainer almost fainted.

"Headrick plays as if he's blind drunk," said one Chief. "He just doesn't feel pain, and he's never too injured to play." Headrick comes to the dressing room as high as the sky. It's his habit to throw up before every game.

Sherrill is further distinguished by a wife with the same sounding name, Cheryl, and umpteen master points won at the bridge table. The day he left for Cincinnati was a sad one for Kansas City fans. When leagues expand every team makes available a certain number of veterans, and the new team chooses three or four players from each old team. Headrick was quickly chosen by the Bengals, who no doubt had little idea what a package they had picked.

Right Linebacker (Weakside Linebacker)

The right linebacker is a fan's best friend. In these days of defense only the offensive players' mothers and girl friends, and the broadcasters, are still watching the offense and rooting for the quarterback. When an old-timer sitting next to you gives free advice, "Watch the guards," just smile—and watch the right linebacker, because his job is to go to the ball.

The right, or weakside, linebacker plays a waiting game. Because he is on the weak side, there is no tight end to bug him. He has a flexible

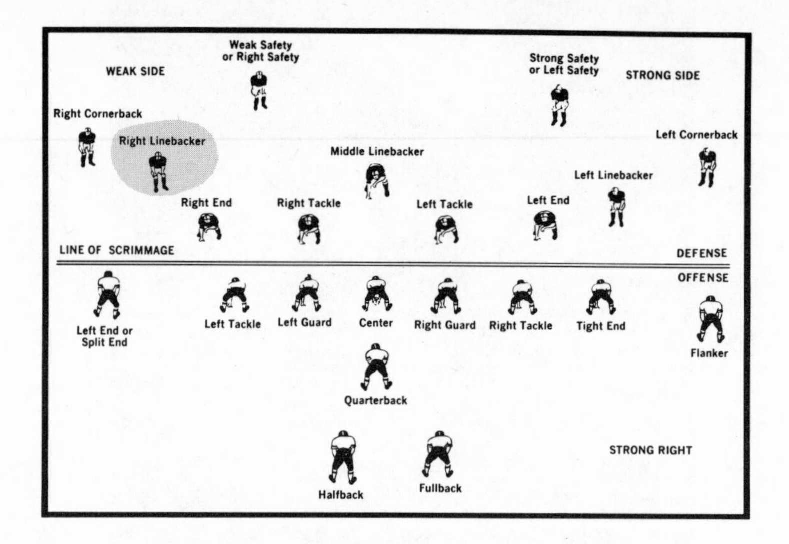

assignment and is a freer spirit. In general, he moves up on runs and back on passes, but he should finally rendezvous with the ball; if he doesn't, he has probably been knocked down or made a mistake. Too many mistakes and you won't have to worry about watching him anymore. About the only time the right linebacker doesn't play the ball is on a blitz, when all assumptions go out the window. A blitz is a blitz, to the quarterback's dismay.

A spectator who is keying on the weakside linebacker will be watching such notables as Ken Avery, the ballet dancer; Chris Hanburger (Washington's good young linebacker with an easy name to remember); Wayne Walker at Detroit, who admits, grinning with narcissism, that he can't wait to get up in the morning to see himself in the mirror; and Maxie Baughan at Los Angeles. (Each of these players wears No. 55 except for Avery, who pirouettes under No. 54.)

While a fan is keying on him, Baughan also has a key.

"We've got two hundred different defenses, and I've got different keys for each one," says Maxie, who is an oddity in that he is a right linebacker who calls defensive signals. This job usually belongs to the middle linebacker because he has a better vantage point. "You watch two or three people at one time really. Sometimes one's in the way of the other, so you watch your key through the quarterback, or the quarterback through your key, or something like that.

"But you always have to watch your key. If he takes a step one way, then I have to go another way. If he does something, then I have to do something.

"I'm watching the quarterback, too, to see if I can pick up an audible by the tone of his voice changing, by a movement of his head, or hands—something I might notice from watching him in games, or in films."

While the offense is in a huddle the defense has a quick, informal minihuddle where the defensive captain gives his side verbal signals. Sometimes the signals are given by using fingers so as not to be overheard, and the captain will hold up the proper number of fingers of each hand to indicate a 4–3, or a 4–4, or whatever. In the case of an 11-man goal line stand, one assumes he gives his orders verbally.

During a game, certain tendencies are established which the defensive captain takes into account. After he sees the offensive formation, he may want to change his defense at the line of scrimmage. He may be tipped off to something, which is why you often see him shouting his head off just before the ball is snapped. Maxie Baughan does this shouting at Los Angeles, and his last-second calls have been so uniformly excellent that the Ram defense hardly holds even a minihuddle any more. They just wait for Maxie's audibles.

"Suppose we're playing the Bears," says Baughan. "Suppose they show us a 'Brown' formation. Now, if they've been throwing to Sayers off of the Brown we might audible into a zone, or a man-to-man defense or a combination, but it would be according to what they've been doing in the game, and what would be their favorite patterns from this formation."

A few years ago Maxie learned that San Francisco Quarterback John Brodie didn't call signals with the usual "hut-huts," but used "set-sets" instead. Accordingly, Maxie called defensive signals using "set-sets," jammed Brodie's signals, and all hell broke loose. San Francisco demanded retribution. Baughan, of course, had absolutely no idea of what the ruckus was all about, but consider it evidence that Ram Coach George Allen was at the time only one season removed from the Chicago Bear School for bad eggs taught by the 20th Century Fagin George Halas. Halas's Bears have been jamming signals since before George Allen was born.

The current crop of middle linebackers is a rather taciturn lot. Two young ones, Tommy Nobis at Atlanta and Dick Butkus at Chicago, let their actions speak for them. Nobis had such potential after his senior year at Texas that an Oiler fan, hoping Tommy would go with Houston instead of Atlanta, sent a message urging him to sign with the Oilers. Which was not so extraordinary, except that the Oiler fan was Major Frank Borman, who sent the message from outer space while he was orbiting the earth.

When Nobis received the Outland trophy, which goes to the country's top collegiate lineman, he said, "I hit'em right in the goozle—high and hard. That way they don't go anywhere but down."

His coach at Texas, Darrell Royal, was asked to describe his star. "He ain't exactly eat up with a case of the stupid," said Royal, and so along came Nobis to Atlanta, with his bowed legs, freckles, lantern jaw, and short red crew cut. And his neck. How big?

"I'd rather not say," Tommy has said, blushing. "It's like asking a girl what size bra she wears."

Middle Linebacker

Many linebackers have played center, and vice versa. Because offensive linemen are about fifteen pounds heavier than linebackers, ex-centers make big linebackers. E. J. Holub (who really does have a whole name—Emil Joseph Holub), Jon Morris and Bill Curry are three centers who have played linebacker. Both Mr. Curry and his Mrs. wish Bill were still linebacking.

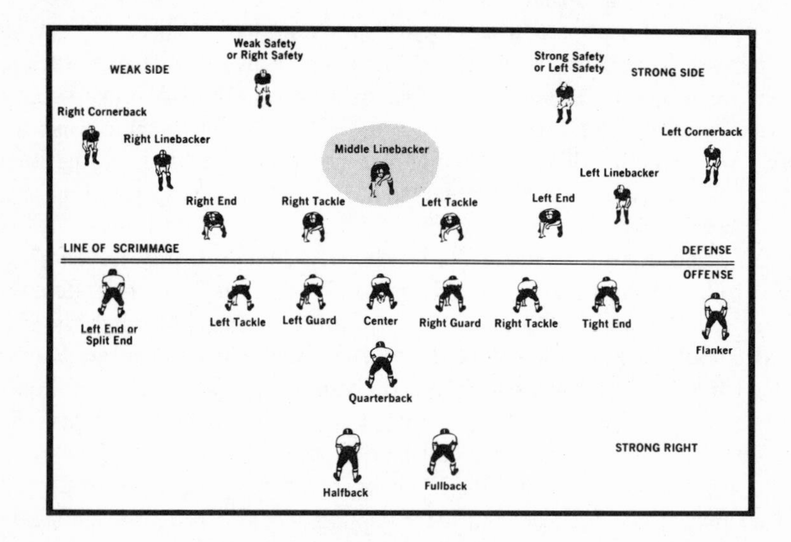

"I like defense," says Caroline Curry. "It's a lot more exciting at middle linebacker. There's more action there, and more territory to cover, and Bill gets to do different things—make tackles and hit. That's football."

Linebacker isn't an entirely new job to a center because centers and middle linebackers play opposite each other and know each other's tricks first fist. "I already knew a little about linebacking," said Caroline, "and it's more interesting to watch. Middle linebackers drop back to cover the pass, but on the running plays they do something different every time. Bill likes it better than center because defense is his real love. The center just gets down and blocks, blocks, blocks. It's important to protect the quarterback, but it's monotonous. He may make different moves and step differently, but essentially he's just getting down in an abnormal position. It's more natural to stand in an upright position and run."

"The middle linebacker's number one duty is against the run up the middle," explained Bill Curry. "I try to see the center and the quarterback, and then get the blocker as he comes through the hole. But that's on a run. On a pass, I run back, looking at the quarterback, in case he throws a short look-in pass to a back or right end. The problem then, besides running backward, is not to be fooled by a draw play. In case of a draw I have to get back up to the line and go after the runner."

The new breed halfbacks, who are tremendous receivers besides being so fast, create a problem for linebackers, who have to act like defensive backs when they cover them. When you hear that newly clichéd offensive wrinkle—isolating a halfback against a linebacker—you are hearing about an offense which is trying to pick on a linebacker like Bill Curry with a superback like Gale Sayers. The first "isolated" halfback was Timmy Brown at Philadelphia. Using Timmy as an end, when there wasn't an extra defensive back to cover him, meant a bigger, slower linebacker, like Curry, had to try to do the job.

"Look at the advantages the halfback has," said Bill. "He only runs in one general direction, he knows ahead what he's planning to do, when he plans to cut, if he's going to change pace, and whether the quarterback intends to throw to him at all (he may only be a decoy), and where and when—plus he's certainly got much more speed and agility than I have.

"Now look at my disadvantages," continued Bill. "When I see the halfback come out of the backfield, I don't know the play. I have to guess; I have to start running when he does but *BACKWARD*—so I can watch where he's going—and when he runs by I have to waste time and speed turning around, so I can run along beside trying to keep up and perhaps prevent a catch."

The halfback, of course, runs a different way almost every time because the offense has to keep changing. So does the defense. A stereotyped team loses. A winning team spices up its game with a variety of techniques, because the best weapon of all is surprise.

"If the offense came out strong right every time, and I always dropped into the right end's zone, there would be no such thing as a hook pass," said Bill Curry. "I could stop it every time. But that's an extreme example. If I did the same thing on every play I'd get fired. Every play is different and I have to do something different every time. I guess in the back of my mind I worry about a run first, but it depends on the situation and the score. When a team gets behind they have no choice. They have to pass."

If the linebackers know a pass is coming, they are half on vacation. They just play pass defense, which for the middle linebacker means he doesn't even have to bother checking for a draw play, and can blitz as much as he feels like.

"Second down and long yardage, like more than seven or eight yards to go, I might know that they are going to pass the ball every time, like 94% of the time," said Curry. "We have those statistics before every game by watching their films.

"Or I might know that in a certain situation they run the ball half the time, and throw it the other half. That will just pop into my head when I line up there. But most quarterbacks are too smart for you to get any tips. If they gave tips they wouldn't be playing. You just have to outguess him.

"In normal situations we have about six or eight different pass coverages," said Bill, "but actually there isn't such a thing as a normal situation."

When he was Green Bay's rookie center, Bill had ample opportunity to observe some great middle linebackers. Against the Bears he was responsible for picking up the Bears' blitzing Dick Butkus, also a rookie. Butkus was the best young linebacker in football from the day he arrived. "That Bear game was a close one," said Curry. "We won, 13–6. Butkus ran by me twice and moved Bart Starr right out of the pocket. Coach Lombardi didn't like it at all."

Against Detroit, Curry had to face the best old linebacker in football, Joe Schmidt, who retired to coach the Lions after starring at middle linebacker for thirteen seasons. Schmidt's No. 56 was a household number in Detroit.

"A rookie playing against Schmidt was in for trouble," said Bill. "The first time I played against him I was snapping the ball for a punt when he hit me. Then I got hit twice again. Well, I started swinging and all at once I saw No. 56 looming there and I had a moment of horror. I cringed, but by then it was too late to back off, and there were these two huge black shadows approaching, which turned out to be Alex Karras and Roger Brown.

"Well, I was still going at them—I had to—when Lionel Aldridge (Packer defensive end) tackled me, to save me. I was never so glad about anything in my life," said Bill. "I didn't act glad, of course. To look brave I acted as if I were really furious at Lionel for pulling me off." Curry, one of the most active members of the Fellowship of Christian Athletes, should be added to the list of holy hostiles.

Left Linebacker (Strongside Linebacker)

The left linebacker lines up opposite the tight end and is responsible for him for the first part of every play.

"People assume it would be easier to play on the weak side because you wouldn't have the tight end to worry about," said John Campbell,

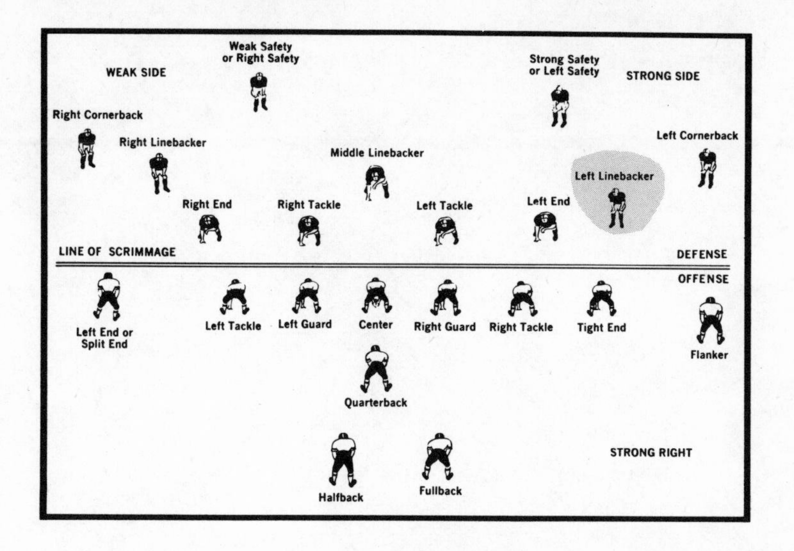

the Steelers' left linebacker who was traded from Minnesota. "But I like to know exactly where he is so I don't have to wonder about him."

The tight end is as big as a linebacker, and sometimes even bigger. Before he does anything else the linebacker hits the tight end a hard blow with his forearm. This gives him the first shot if the tight end is blocking. If the tight end is going out for a pass, the blow slows him up for a stride or two.

"You try to damage him as he goes by," says Campbell who was the M.C., script writer, lyricist and orchestra for his rookie show at the Vikings. "You want to keep him pinned to the line of scrimmage." If he can just hold the tight end up long enough—two seconds is more than enough—the pattern is delayed and the timing of the play is thrown out of whack.

Weeb Ewbank tells his strongside linebacker, Ralph Baker, always to keep his inside eye on the tight end and try to steer him toward the outside. "It's up the middle where the tight end is toughest," said Weeb.

The strongside linebacker is only responsible for popping the tight end at the beginning of each play. After the pop (if he blitzes, the popping is left to a defensive someone else) the tight end is covered by the tight safety, leaving the linebacker free to cover his new worry, a running back.

"Keying on the near[est] back," says Campbell, "if he's standing up and going to block, I back up figuring a screen or some other delay pass. If he comes straight at me and I commit myself and come up to him, I'm taken care of, but so is he unless one of us blows the play. If he comes out on a pattern I have to go with him. What's awful is if he lures me deep and the flanker catches a pass in the spot I left.

"Reading keys is the hardest. Norm Van Brocklin used to say, 'By the time you learn what you need to know it's too late.' "

One of the lightest (6′ 4″, 210) but bluest-chip strongside linebackers is George Webster at the Oilers. George is quiet, with a baby face and a toothpaste-ad smile. From the beginning he was a super linebacker for Houston.

In college at Michigan State, George Webster never missed a game, was All-America, and his number, 90, was retired when he graduated. In George's senior year the most important game of the season was against Notre Dame, a game that will long be remembered because Notre Dame Coach Ara Parsegian shocked the nation by playing for a tie instead of going for victory. The final score was 10–10.

"The night before the Notre Dame game, I dreamed we finished in a 14–14 tie," said George. "I usually don't dream, and never before a game. It didn't really surprise me but it was eerie to see the tie on the scoreboard."

The story was written and rewritten often enough to make George into sort of a gridiron guru. "I'm tired of reading about it and I'm tired of having other people read it," he said.

Webster was the Frank Sinatra of Michigan State football, the leader of a rat pack which was the most coveted group of college players in the country. After that season, when pro teams chose from among the college talent in their annual draft, four players from Webster's rat pack were among the first eight selected, out of 445 college players.

Webster's best friend and soul brother was Bubba Smith—like Webster, a vintage defender at a tender age. At Michigan State they lived together, blitzed quarterbacks together, and enjoyed life. Off the field they listened to Bill Cosby records.

"Something would happen during a game and we'd think of something Cosby had said, and we'd break up," said George. Oddly, he was referring to himself and Bubba. One shudders at the fate of the broken-up opponents.

Imagine a scene with Bubba and George flattening a Notre Dame quarterback and then giggling over Bill Cosby jokes on their way back to the huddle.

"We enjoyed ourselves," said Webster.

At Houston, George is enjoying himself less. He seems nervous and is the best customer of the Oiler training room, with so many assorted ailments he's approaching hypochondria. But George never worries about injuries in a game and only hurts off the field. Trainer Bobby Brown calls him "Mr. Aches" but more often Webster's slinky build and spaghetti legs earn him the nickname "Olive Oyl."

"He's tall and rangy," says Brown, "very skinny for football. He has a tiny waist. George plays so hard that he gets bone bruises, because he hasn't any padding. He had already flattened out the tops of his shoulder pads after six games."

George Webster tackles a blocking back.

Brown, the rogue trainer, is obviously a Webster fan.

"When he was a rookie and came to training camp he was always the first one in the tub," said Brown. "George is my star boarder, but he goes on the field and knocks heads off. He makes those big plays that win games for us. The way he played his first year no one could believe he was a rookie."

For years people called Green Bay's great defense a machine. The Packer linebackers made it go by helping out their cornerbacks. Packer linebackers think nothing of dropping back thirty yards, which helps destroy the composure of opposing passers. Sometimes, watching George Webster play, you can't believe your eyes. There will be a long pass to the split end, and as the ball arrives you see the end, the cornerback who is covering him, and there, right behind the cornerback, is Webster, waiting—just in case. No one knows how he gets downfield so fast. George averages ten tackles a game. When you consider that an offense averages sixty plays per game, George is the man behind one sixth of the opposing quarterback's frustration.

12 Defensive Backs

The defensive backs are four and called, collectively, the secondary. From left to right they are the left cornerback, tight safety, free safety and right cornerback. They protect their goal against the pass.

The left safety is called the tight safety because he plays against the tight end. He may also be called the strongside safety (or strong safety), in which case the right safety is called the weakside safety (or weak safety), instead of the free safety. The homo saps in the stadia have been laying them in the aisles for seasons and seasons with their puns and jokes about the weak safety who isn't and the alcoholic safety at the left. Ugh.

There are two types of pass coverage—man-to-man and zone. In man-to-man the defensive man covers an individual. In the zone he covers an area. Green Bay never uses a zone defense.

In general, man-to-man is more successful and used more often, but when the quarterback is in a desperate plight and probably going to throw long to his best receiver, the defense might decide to go into a zone, especially at midfield where there is plenty of wide-open space to worry about.

"I hated zone teams," said Y. A. Tittle, who was almost as famous for his head, which was bald, as for his arm, which was strong. Ben Davidson has more hair in his mustache than Tittle had on his head.

"The zone shackles a good quarterback and takes away his deep threat," explained YAT. "When you know a team is in a zone you can't eat it up. You have to nibble it to death."

A quarterback nibbles at a zone with short passes. Tittle was a famous drop-back passer at San Francisco and New York, and naturally wanted to show off as a bomber, not a nibbler. Even though short passes can beat the zone, when time is running out a quarterback has no choice. He needs his bomb, his spécialité de pocket.

The defense divides the open space into six zones. The three linebackers take three zones from the line of scrimmage to 10-or-12 yards back. The cornerbacks and a safety take three zones from 10-to-12 yards farther back.

The key to ruining a zone defense is hitting a receiver on one of the borderlines, or seams, of the zone. There is a good chance there will be no defensive man there, or there will be two. Either way, the receiver is in good shape. In the latter case the receiver can get lucky if both defenders collide on the edge of their zones. The receiver then scores.

Man-to-man defense matches:

The left cornerback vs. the flanker
The right cornerback vs. the split end
The left safety vs. the right end *after* he gets past the left linebacker
The free safety is free, to rove and help out wherever help is needed.

Cornerbacks

The right cornerback stands about seven yards behind the line, opposite the split end. The left cornerback stands seven yards opposite the flanker. Because the defense can do as it pleases *before* the quarterback releases the ball, there are a few seconds (never more than four or five unless the quarterback is scrambling) when the cornerback can use imagination and "fool around."

"Most flankers are as fast or faster than me," explained Kent McCloughan, an Oakland Raider. "I bump them as they come off the line, to interrupt their start, then run with them. But I don't do it the same all the time. You don't want to establish trends."

McCloughan is the most silent cornerback extant, so silent and unnoticed that in the second Super Bowl, before 70,000 live and 70,000,000 bored-at-TV fans, McCloughan's pants were removed beside the Oakland bench, his needs attended to, and to this day no one has ever asked him why.

"He lines up so close to you you think he's offside," said Buffalo's retired Flanker Elbert Dubenion. "I didn't think he had the speed to stay with me playing me that close, but he does."

"In the AFL they like to bump and run," says Bobby Boyd, who retired from cornerback to cornerback coach at Baltimore after Super Bowl III.

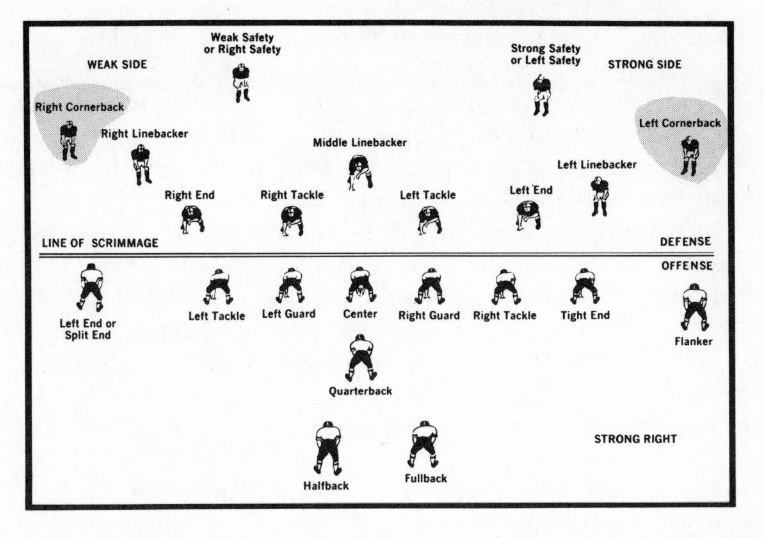

"They like to line up on a guy's nose and jam him before he gets out. I can see how you could do that backed up against a goal, but otherwise I'd rather sit back and read the receiver and the quarterback."

Pat Fischer, at Washington, is slow like Boyd, short like Boyd, and tough like Boyd. They both say that position is everything—being in exactly the right place at the right time. But Fischer prefers McCloughan's bump-and-run approach. "The big thing I have going for me is making contact first," says Pat, the midget of the cornermen at 5′ 9″, stretching. "The other guy is concentrating on the ball and I get him." Fischer says he's never been beaten by a receiver because the receiver was taller and Pat was shorter.

Concentration is so important that a thought keeps recurring. Why don't the defensive backs wear jingle bells on their feet? Bells would make it hard for the receivers to concentrate, and we would be forever rid of the dreary phrase, "hearing footsteps." (Every time a receiver drops a pass his critics say he hears footsteps, a polite way of calling him chicken.)

Johnny Sample calls all the receivers he covers chicken. Concentration is why Sample talks. His cornerbacking theory is simple: If my talking can get any of my man's attention, he's taking that attention away from making the catch. "I want him to concentrate less," says Sample, "so I talk." Like Pat Fischer, Sample believes in contact. He hits with his mouth full.

"He talks and talks and talks," says Chris Burford, a lawyer who used to catch for Kansas City. "If Sample could play as well as he talks he would be fantastic."

"Sample's fun," said Willie Richardson, the Baltimore flanker, before Super Bowl III. "He tries to get you upset but he won't bother me. The best way to shut a guy up is to score on him."

"Talk is my business," says Sample, who is always at a loss for silence. He bugged Richardson constantly in the Super Bowl.

"I talk as much as he talks," said Willie. "He got me, though, so I tried to break his head off." Willie had a frustrating afternoon. When Sample intercepted a pass intended for Richardson near the Jet goal, he stuck the ball right in Willie's face.

"Is this what you're looking for?" asked Sample, who wore orange silk undershorts and shirt for his Orange Bowl appearance. Sample also was involved in a name-calling fracas with Tom Matte, a tough guy to tangle with. Matte had run wild for a 58-yard gain and Sample was in on the tackle. Very much so. Matte went after him.

"You're a dirty player," said Matte.

"You're a bush leaguer," said Sample.

Boys will be boys.

In summer, 1967, John Sample presented the flankers in his league with a new image, which lasted a season. He became almost as quiet as silent Kent McCloughan and was elected defensive captain by the Jets. Sample was surprised. He had been his own favorite cornerback—at Baltimore, Pittsburgh, and Washington—but for the Jets to agree?

"I couldn't believe it," he said. "I asked one guy who voted for me why he did it. He didn't know why."

After the election, Sample immediately turned into the quiet man. "I used to yell at everyone because I thought it helped me," he said. "It upset their concentration and made my job easier. But now I can't afford to get that emotional. I can't cuss the officials anymore."

The man who decides to take, or not to take, a penalty is the captain on the field. Sample, as captain, confers with the officials when the Jets have been fouled against. If Sample is kicked out of the game he will not be on the field. Simple. So John stopped being kicked out.

"I can't afford to have the officials mad at me," he said. "And the younger players look up to me, so I have to watch myself."

As the 1967 season progressed the other AFL teams couldn't believe Sample's new self. Flankers came up to Jet games prepared for a Sample of mean streak and abuse, and that deafening staccato delivery.

"They keep waiting for me to let 'em have it," said Johnny, stretching his holier-than-thou smile, "but I'd just say 'Nice play' or 'Too bad' or something. In one game Dubenion said he had four children and he needed his salary money. I told him we had children, too. He really looked at me funny. So did the coaches. I was as close as five yards to a number of coaches and I never said a word. I used to love to give it to coaches."

Sample's talking again.

The Packers' Herb Adderley is one of the best cornerbacks in football. He is Sample's good friend, and they are naming their Philadelphia

Lem Barney.

cocktail lounge *The Left Corner*. When the Packers play the Rams, Adderley is matched against an old rival, Pat Studstill, who flankered for the Lions for many years before he was traded to Los Angeles. Studstill and Adderley were a great matchup to watch, and to listen to.

"We're great friends off the field but enemies in the game," said Herb. "What we talk about is not for public consumption."

"We're like a couple of old women who share a room," said Studstill. "We're hollering and arguing all the time."

The Lions have a young defensive back, Lem Barney, who is so graceful that he looks as much like a ballet dancer as Ken Avery does not. Barney was a rookie sensation, leading the league with interceptions, and he got the sharpest needling because he was such an instant success. The bench jockeys tried to rattle him, shouting and talking from the sideline. It was particularly annoying because Barney's coach, Jim David, was shouting at him too, shouting instructions.

"I would tell him about the offense, the formations and things," said David. "You see, Lem is not going to be beat physically. He's fast, quick-reacting and strong. But he needed a reminder now and then that he won't need when he gets more experience."

"In the second game with Green Bay, they kept yelling 'Look out, rook, look out, rook—this one's coming right at you,'" said Barney. "Or they said 'C'mon, Barney, you know a rookie doesn't make it where you're playing.'"

Rookies don't usually make it at cornerback because it's such a crucial position and experience is extra important. The cornerback and receiver are all alone, and a mistake glares at the spectators and coaches. Too often one cornerback mistake equals one enemy touchdown.

When the ball comes right at you there isn't a moment to hesitate, or to think whether to go for the ball or the tackle. Some of the best cornerbacks make the fewest interceptions—and vice versa—because the best cornerbacks don't gamble and go for the ball; they play safe and make the tackle.

The faster the receiver the more dangerous it is to gamble. If a cornerback covering Bob Hayes hesitates an instant, Hayes will score a touchdown.

"You can run only so far with Hayes, and then he's past you," said Irv Cross, who got to cover Hayes when Dallas played Los Angeles. "So I bump him, try to knock him off his pattern, upset his timing with the quarterback. If he dodges past and gets away there's only one thing left. You pray."

Cleveland's Erich Barnes is a talker with a roughhouse image and a high-pitched giggle. "I've got one philosophy," said Erich (pronounced Ee-rich). "When the ball leaves the quarterback's hand it's mine. I'm the receiver and the receiver is on defense."

The reason behind this philosophy is in the rule book. All nudging and jostling must stop when the quarterback throws. *While the ball is in the air,* the receiver and the defensive back have equal rights to it. At this stage an ill-timed nudge by a cornerback is a pass interference penalty (the officials give a completion to the offense, which means a first down at the place where the foul occurred).

By pretending he is a receiver, Barnes would theoretically be concentrating so hard on the ball that he would be less apt to do any nudging. This is a fine theory. In practice it is often another story. "This is a contact game, so I like to play it rough," says Erich. "And clean," he almost forgot.

"If I'm playing man-to-man I don't want to get close enough to bop my man," says Barnes. "If I'm close enough to bump him, he's close enough to bump me. I don't want to let him knock me off stride. Playing cornerback is a tough spot."

Cornerbacks need every advantage they can muster. Making contact first . . . intimidation . . . distracting conversation . . . and, of course, the blitz. The quicker the quarterback is forced to throw, the easier for the cornerback.

"When there's a blitz on I can cover the receiver short and close," said Irv Cross, "because I know the quarterback has to get rid of the ball. One time against Dallas they held up our blitz for just an instant, but that's all Bob Hayes needs. I was playing him close and that was that."

When the quarterback has all the time in the world, there is no way a cornerback can keep on covering his receiver. It is impossible, because any defender can react just so many times. What Irv Cross said of Bob Hayes is true of any receiver-defender duel—finally he'll get past you. Blitzing shortens the time span of the duel. A blitz is a cornerback's best friend.

The linebacker can help the cornerback near the line of scrimmage when he's not blitzing, especially the weakside (right) linebacker; while the left linebacker is giving a hefty pop to the tight end, the right linebacker can do likewise to the split end. Dallas Coach Tom Landry was once a defensive halfback with the Giants (All-Pro in 1954), and he explained the facts of life to Bob Hayes before an important game against the Rams. During practice one day Landry took a go at linebacker.

"Bob," he said, "I'm going to play you just like Maxie Baughan's going to play you."

Hayes took off with the snap, about to fly, and Landry grabbed him, spun him around, and knocked him flat on the ground.

"It happened so quick—Zap!" said Hayes. "Everybody laughed."

"You can't go up to the line with Hayes," says Erich Barnes. "I don't really like to press any receiver. It doesn't do any good to chop him down at the line. If you miss you're on the ground. You sure can't help anybody from there."

A cornerback has the same problems on pass coverage as a linebacker, only more so. The flanker and end always know where they're going, what route they will take to get there, and when the quarterback plans to throw. The cornerback doesn't, and like the rest of the defense he is reacting. He is also doing a lot of running backward, and this is one of the hardest parts of playing defense—hard to learn and a terrible strain physically.

"Any good tennis player with fair size could become a good defensive back," says Kansas City's Johnny Robinson. "Tennis taught me to back pedal and move laterally, and I think it's the finest training a defensive back can get."

Cornerbacks run forward, too, on running plays. When he sees a running play develop, a cornerback moves up. He might have to tackle the runner himself. He probably hopes not. On a wide running play the cornerback is caught in the middle. As the play begins, the quarterback may fake one back toward the middle while the other back picks up his blockers to take the ball around end. The cornerback is supposed to read (realize) this instantly and be up in time to prevent the ballcarrier from making his turn downfield. If the linebackers tackle the blockers, the cornerback is left alone against the runner.

The Giants have an exceptional cornerback, Spider Lockhart, who likes to hit. Spider likes nothing better than to see a big fullback bounce around end and chug toward him. Ask a 225-pound fullback about Spider's 175-pound tackles, and it's guaranteed he won't smile. Cornerbacks like Lockhart are few and far between.

The receivers, of course, don't stand around watching a running play. They run out their patterns as usual, as decoys, hoping to lure the cornerbacks away from the action. But once the cornerbacks read *run* they move forward. A smart quarterback can draw them forward with an option play. The halfback runs wide with the ball. If the cornerback runs up to tackle him, the halfback throws a pass over the cornerback's head to the wide end he left behind. If the cornerback stays back, the halfback keeps the ball and runs.

When the cornerbacks are lured forward, the two wide ends are left all alone with a clear path to the end zone—which emphasizes the disadvantages of playing defensive back, instead of up front. If a lineman misses his tackle there is someone behind him to correct the mistake. If a cornerback makes a mistake it probably means seven points for the enemy.

"Our job is the toughest in football," said Don Doll, who made his living coaching defensive backs. "We have to react off someone else's action. Ninety percent of our work is done going backward. We are in the last line of defense and all our mistakes are made out in the open. It creates a problem. You get the feeling of always defending. It takes a toll on persons who can't accept it. It breaks many of them down." Only a good cornerback can get used to the knowledge that he *can* be beat, and live with it accordingly.

Old, retired cornerbacks are insecure, ulcer-ridden neurotics and TV's isolated camera deserves some of the blame. A cornerback who gets beaten on a long touchdown pass becomes a household word by the end of that afternoon. After a succession of replays—the cornerback gets burned once on the field, a second time as an instant replay, a third time by the isolated camera, a fourth time during first-half recaps—and after

Cleveland's Right Safety Mike Howell making a sure tackle on Giants' Homer Jones.

postgame shows, news programs, Game of the Week, luncheon huddles with movies, weekly highlight shows, wrap-ups, warm-ups and next Sunday's pre-pregame show—the poor cornerback has been made into a bum all over the country. America is shouting him to the bench and his next year's salary negotiations are going to be tougher—and if the game happened to end with his team beaten by one touchdown or less, heaven help him.

In Memoriam

One cornerback, gone but not forgotten, deserves special mention, not because he was particularly talented at football. He wasn't. Fred Williamson was talented in communication, promotion, publicity, and advertising, all of self. Williamson made Johnny Sample seem tongue-tied.

Williamson is an architect, pipe-smoker, ascot-wearer, and, of sorts, an inventor. He invented "The Hammer."

The Hammer was Williamson's right forearm, swung with his whole arm as stiff as a baseball bat. Williamson used a short karate stroke and he has a cheekbone (Howard Twilley's), a nose (Frank Jackson's) and a couple of concussions notched on his black belt.

"Karate has nothing to do with The Hammer," said Fred. "But karate taught me to concentrate all my power in my forearm." Williamson claims Detroit's legendary Night Train Lane was the only other Hammer user. Night Train called his "The Bone."

Williamson's father went to Harvard and became a civil engineer. His brother went to Yale and became a lawyer. Williamson studied architecture at Northwestern and became a Kansas City cornerback.

"I am the black sheep of the family, the lamb that went astray." Some lamb. Williamson wore white shoes, like Joe Namath, whom he admires. But Fred wore white shoes because when his powder blue ones got dirty he couldn't find any powder blue shoe polish. The white cleats cost $20, and he had five pairs. He would change shoes at half-time if they got dirty or scuffed-up.

"I am an individualist. I do what I want to do regardless of what people think. I am a loner," he said.

At Northwestern Williamson played flanker, not defense, and drove a white Cadillac convertible. There were only three other Negro students and none were female, so he dated white girls. "Why not?" Fred would ask. "I'm not prejudiced." He married a blonde and they built a ski lodge at Lake Tahoe, designed by Williamson.

"We've had no trouble," he said. "I made everyone aware of the situation right from the start. I told them I was controversial on and off the field."

Williamson designed the family homestead. It is outside of Oakland, modern, and redwood. For one so handy with a hammer he might have helped the builder.

"I don't aim The Hammer," he said, a habit that could be painful. "I just throw it. I don't play to hurt people. There isn't a back in the other league with the guts to throw The Hammer because it's an invitation to fight. It makes you a marked man. I am unmarked."

The lamb that went astray used The Hammer to lay the receiver out after he caught the ball. "It's perfectly legal," claimed Williamson, and it was or he would have long since been banished by officials. "It's just a device to make the receiver keep an eye on me. A receiver must sacrifice his body to catch the ball, that's all. If he catches he's gonna be punished." (The man, of course, shouldn't have been allowed to catch the ball in the first place.)

Fred was the one who was punished. He was the heavy in Super Bowl I, when the Packers laid the loudmouth out cold. A few months later the Chiefs, sick to death of all the noise and baloney Williamson spread over the sports pages, dropped him. Williamson wended his way to Canadian football, appeared on TV's *Dating Game* and went to Hollywood, to try to make it in the movies. His wife was the one who was fooled. She thought she was marrying an architect.

Tight Safety (Strongside Safety)

Joe Namath, quarterback: "The whole aim of pro football is to get the defensive back's feet going in the wrong direction."

Bobby Hunt, tight safety: "The secret of the game is to not let the quarterback get your feet moving in the wrong direction."

In a nutshell, the tight safety plays cornerback against the tight end. Emlen Tunnell played tight safety for New York and Green Bay and now coaches the Giants' defensive backs. He was the first Negro voted into pro football's Hall of Fame. Around New York City Emlen is a kind of football folk hero.

"One reason I was good," said Emlen, with becoming modesty, "was repetition. I lined up the same way, same stance and in the same spot on every single play, in games or at practice, day in and day out. No tight safety does that nowadays." Emlen, exasperated, was voting for discipline. He was echoing his offensive counterpart, Ray Berry, who ran complete, precise patterns every time.

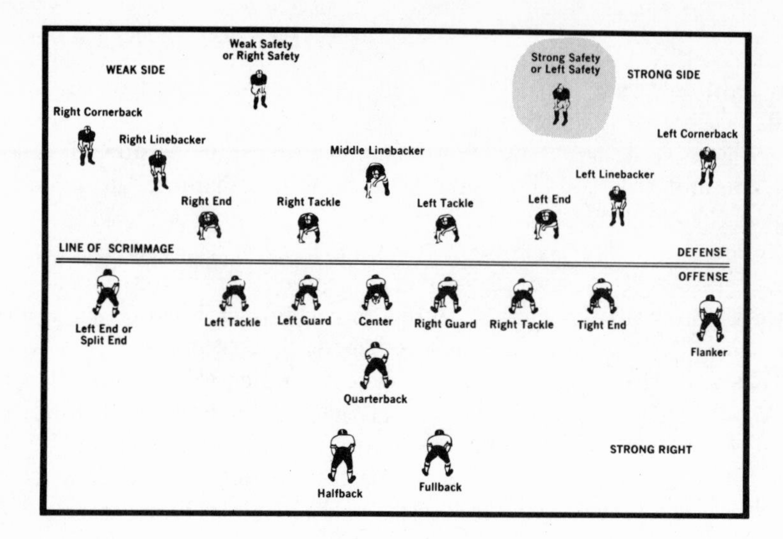

"If you're consistent your teammates can count on you," said Emlen. "They know where you are and what you're going to do. Young players today line up every which way. They're careless."

Tight safeties should be bigger than cornerbacks, ideally about 210; otherwise the tight end will be able to bully the safety, or, worse, ignore him and trample over him.

"The tight end always has a choice," explained Emlen. "He can veer inside or outside. I believe that the tight safety should *always* try to stay outside, and hold the tight end to the inside. That's what I used to do.

"You see, it's a proven fact that any right-handed person can run to the right quicker than to the left. If my man (the tight end) is to my outside I have to run to the left. He's running to his right and he gets the advantage. But," said Emlen, "if I can keep the tight end inside, to *my* right, I have the advantage while I'm going after him."

On a running play when the tight end is blocking, the tight safety's job is to force the runner inside, into the traffic. "One of the best against the run is Bruce Maher," says Emlen. "He never hesitates." Emlen had long admired Maher from afar, while he was playing at Detroit for eight years. Emlen finally talked the Giants into trading for him.

Maher is experienced, very tough and determined. "The key is determination," he says. "You stop the tight end from getting the ball any way you know how." Bruce means *any* way.

On location in Florida for filming the *Paper Lion* movie, the only untoward incident during any of the scrimmage scenes happened when Maher came up and flattened a rookie tight end, Gerry Zawadzkas, with a devastating tackle. Zawadzkas was laid out on his back for five minutes.

"Too bad," said another Lion, "but that's the only way the runt got to be a regular." Maher is pushing 5′ 10″.

"Size hasn't bothered me yet," says Bruce. "Aggressive football is the key. And speed."

"It's most important to be quick," says Emlen Tunnell. "You must get the jump on your man. Most of the best safeties aren't that fast when you look around—Jack Christiansen, Jim Patton, Scott Eaton—even at cornerback it's more important to be quick than fast.

"Look at Tom Landry. (The Dallas coach was a Giant cornerback when Emlen was at safety.) Heck, I was faster than he was. Why Landry's never even told me how good I was," needled Emlen, who in his lengthy career never got beat deep.

Free Safety (Weakside Safety)

As far as man-to-man coverage is concerned, the right safety is the eleventh man. On the offensive team the eleventh man is the quarterback. Because most quarterbacks would rather eat live spiders than run, the right safety has no specific man to worry about. He is a will-o'-the-wisp, all purpose remedy, roving about like a telephone company troubleshooter playing Superboy. The free safety arrives in the nick, stops the touchdown, and gets an interception instead of the girl.

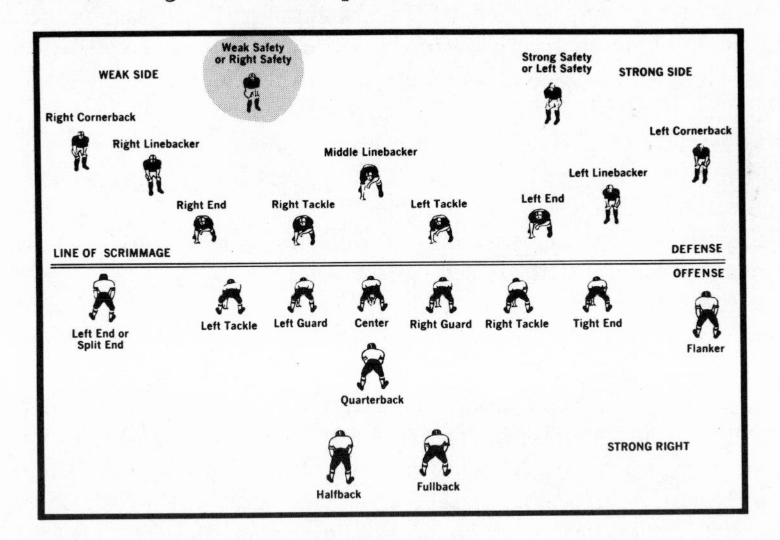

Terrific! But he does have to follow some specific plans. The safety thinks goal line. His basic assignment is to stop an offensive man from getting by him. He is his team's last outpost, the last man between the offense and a touchdown. The safety prevents accidents. Every defensive player, and coach, looks on a touchdown as an offensive accident.

When playing a team with an outstanding deep receiver, the free safety helps out the cornerback. Double coverage is the highest compliment the defense can pay. Charley Taylor, Washington's flanker, calls it stitching.

"One back comes up and plays me near the line," he said, "and the free safety picks me up downfield. I try to split them. Say the cornerback takes me ten yards and the safety picks me up at fifteen. Well, I go twelve yards and then cut in or out," which is like breaking open a zone defense by splitting the seam of the zones. Some speed demons, instead of trying to split up double coverage, might try to outrace them. When this happens the free safety is responsible for taking care of the speed ball deep, particularly toward the middle.

Receivers like Charley Taylor are usually taller than the safety. "A free safety has got to be able to jump," says Emlen Tunnell. "On a long pass he's got to knock the ball away. Look at Willie Wood. He's only 5′ 10″ but he could jump up and hook the crossbar of the goal post." Emlen is dating himself. Goal posts no longer have crossbars.

"These young receivers are so fast and so big everything is changed," says Paul Martha, Pittsburgh's free safety. "With all the new formations—my God—free safety is worse than being a cornerback."

Martha's first few years with the Steelers were catastrophic. They tried him everywhere but with little success. Here he was—a number one draft choice, in law school, married to the daughter of the President of U. S. Steel, but flunking on the field—too small to run, too slow to play end or flanker. He finally made it, at safety.

"Why do they call it free safety anymore?" asks Martha. "A free safety used to be able to play the ball and go anywhere, but now the offenses are putting him in man-to-man situations. There's nothing free about it. The position gets tougher and tougher."

Against a double wing (two ends at each side) there is no "free" safety. It's man-to-man, and the right safety is actually playing cornerback against the left end to the inside.

When the tight end lines up at the left it creates a dilemma for the safeties. Should they switch sides, or should the free safety take on the tight end and let the left safety roam free?

"It all depends on your personnel," says Emlen. "Some safeties just can't play man-to-man so you flip 'em, but the Packers don't. Theirs are tall and good on man-to-man; they can play either safety. We flip ours, but generally speaking, if you have two men who can play either safety spot it's better not to switch sides when the tight end goes to the left. It's better to always play on the side you're used to."

When the weakside linebacker blitzes, the free safety is anything but free; he must move up and play linebacker, against a big running back.

Sometimes the free safety blitzes himself, like St. Louis's famous shooting safety Larry Wilson.

Larry Wilson came from Rigby, Idaho. Several years ago Rigby had a Larry Wilson Day. "Our football field had so many rocks that Indians used to come at night to pray there," said his high school coach. "On the way into town," says Larry, "there's a sign—Warning to tourists: do not laugh at the natives."

When he came to the Cardinals, Larry, as is the custom, wanted to wear his college (Utah) number, 41. "But Jim Hill, another player, had forty-one and they gave me twelve," he said. "After the first practice quarterback John Roach walked over and handed me his jersey. 'Rookie,' said Roach, 'from now on you're eight and I'm twelve.' I've been eight ever since."

An odd number for a safety, No. 8 soon became famous shooting in at opposing quarterbacks. "In the beginning, when we were first trying the safety blitz, our coach, Chuck Drulis, used to tell me to jump up and run back to the defensive huddle as fast as I could—'They won't be able to tell who did the damage,' Drulis said. 'They'll think No. 8 looks like a number in the 80s, like a defensive end. They won't know it's you'."

"I line up about seven yards deep," says Wilson, explaining his blitz as if he were Alfredo giving away his fettucini recipe. "The middle linebacker takes the center out and I have seven yards to get going—get momentum—and I shoot between the center and the guard. The secret is to get your fanny low and move your feet—get them movin' real quick. Some guys kind of slide backward, but I think it's better to backpedal."

Wilson's safety blitz is based on the theory that since almost every team sends out three pass receivers, there are seven men left to block for the passer. In the safety blitzes eight men are rushing at seven blockers. Certainly a safety blitz is important psychologically, if only to unnerve the quarterback. With Wilson jumping around, the quarterback has to worry about him all the time, thinking, will he or won't he?

Larry Wilson is one of the few old-fashioned hero types left in our cool world. He is an inspirational leader, modest and unassuming, and plays injured as often as not, once with both broken hands in casts.

"That was a worse handicap at home than in a game," he said. "I couldn't eat, take a shower, get dressed, or do anything by myself. I couldn't even go to the bathroom." He didn't have much of a toothbrushing problem because most of his upper teeth are among the missing.

"If a man doesn't get hurt in the game," says Larry, "he hasn't been playing hard enough."

"Larry Wilson is so determined I believe he could do anything," says Emlen Tunnell.

But it wasn't always so. Wilson didn't believe he could do anything.

When he came to the Cardinals in 1960 Larry was so sure he wouldn't make it that he had his wife, Dee Ann, drive to the last exhibition game so they'd be able to drive home after he was cut. For the same reason, Dee Ann drove to the opening game in Los Angeles, but again nothing happened. And so for eight seasons Larry has been coming home from away games with the rest of the team, on an airplane. He still wears the same thigh pads he wore that day he arrived, in 1960.

"I'm superstitious," says Larry, who always tapes his big toes, for luck. "Everything has got to be the same. After three years they finally made me wear a new helmet."

13 Kicking

Except after a touchdown, which is a joyous occasion, kicking is negative, a sign of frustration. A team kicks off after losing the coin toss. A team attempts a field goal when it fails to make a touchdown. A team punts when it thinks it can't make a first down.

If a team could score every time it had the ball it would never have to punt, which is why Jet punter-comedian Curley Johnson says the perfect game is one he doesn't play in. "When I go in it means we're giving up the ball," said Curley. "If I'm on the bench it's okay."

On a fourth down play, unless the situation is last-minute desperate, the punter comes in to kick the ball deep into the other team's territory. (Even though some quarterbacks, like the Bears' Rudy Bukich, can throw as far as a punter can punt—60 yards—throwing on fourth down would be an incomplete pass and the offensive team would lose the ball at the line of scrimmage instead of sixty yards downfield. A bad idea.)

A fourth-down punt is automatic when a team hasn't passed the 50-yard line. From the other team's 40-yard line punting is debatable. If a team has a good, strong placekicker it's smarter to attempt a field goal from the 40, even from the 45-yard line. The theory is simple—everything to gain (3 points) and nothing to lose. From the 35-yard line and closer a fourth-down field goal attempt is expected.

A field goal is attempted from 7 yards behind the line of scrimmage, a punt from about 15 yards behind. The punter takes a couple of steps, drops the ball and kicks it, the higher the better. A high punt takes longer to reach the man who's waiting for it, which gives the punting team more time to get downfield to tackle the punt returner. Line drive punts go far but too fast. The tacklers don't have time to run downfield and the punt returner gets the jump and momentum. The best punts are a combination of height and distance, but if you had to choose one you would probably choose height.

Punts are measured from the line of scrimmage to the point of the catch, or, if not caught, where the ball touches the ground. A punter who averages 45 yards is really kicking 60 yards if he punts from 15 yards behind the line of scrimmage.

A punter isn't trying for record distance. His object is a return of zero yards. Punts are measured by smallest return yardage. When a punt is good and high the receiver is surrounded by members of the punting team when the ball arrives. Figuring he can't run it back, the receiver signals for a fair catch by raising one arm, which is the highest compliment you can pay a punter.

A man does not signal for a fair catch willy-nilly. Giving the signal is like signing a contract to make the catch. If the ball as much as brushes him, but he's unable to hold on to it, he's in trouble. The ball can be recovered by the punting team.

Punts and kickoffs are different. A kickoff is a free ball and can be captured by any player on the field. On a kickoff it is the receiving team's responsibility to obtain possession any way it wishes—catching it, falling on it, knocking it out of bounds, any way at all. On the other hand, a punt belongs to the receiving team and the only way they can lose the ball is by catching it and then fumbling.

Since the ball belongs to his team the punt receiver (called a *safety* but not to be confused with the 2-point safety, or the defensive back with the same name) doesn't have to try to catch the punt, and can watch the ball roll where it may. Wherever the ball stops becomes the line of scrimmage. The punter considers the perfect punt to be one which rolls dead or out of bounds on the 1-inch line. The 1-inch line then becomes the line of scrimmage and puts the offensive team in bad field position. Very bad field position.

"The punter is very instrumental in giving his team good field position," says Oakland's punter Mike Eischeid, an ex-schoolteacher. Mike has streaks where he excels at placing punts. In the 1967 AFL title game he put one on the 6 yard line and one on the 1.

"Trying to place the ball," says Mike, "I try to keep it inside the 20 but when we're on our own 40 I kick for the corner." He hopes the ball goes over the sideline, not into the end zone.

A teammate can help a punter when the ball is rolling dead by "downing" it close to the goal line and preventing the ball from going into the end zone (a touchback to the 20-yard line). Ideally, as a punt bounces toward the end zone, a teammate leaps at the last second and bats it back in bounds and dead right next to the goal line.

"We figure it takes our players five seconds to get down the field to cover a 40-yard punt," says Cincinnati Coach Jack Donaldson. "Curley Johnson's kicks average 4.6 seconds in the air."

At the St. Louis training camp in 1967 the Cardinals were looking for a punter (poor punting cost them two games in 1966) and held time trials for the candidates. Coach Charlie Winner was looking for punts that stayed in the air 4.5 seconds, and all the coaches were standing around with stopwatches as the sky was filled with pigskins (cowhides). No one was paying much attention to distance.

Tight End Jackie Smith had always been the Cardinals' punter but Smith had been injured. From one blow Winner had lost both his end and a punter. Conservative creatures that they are, coaches prefer kickers who only kick and ends who only catch. Two or even three jobs wasn't as unusual several years ago, but when teams lengthened their rosters, from thirty-four or thirty-six players, to forty, the luxury of one or two specialists was more easily afforded. The players really prefer to concentrate on one job too.

"I really don't miss punting," says Packer Flanker Boyd Dowler who used to punt for Green Bay. "It's a burden you don't have to carry. If you're not punting well, it's just another thing that can bother you."

Donny Anderson is punting for Green Bay now. He is unique, a three-way specialist. Donny punts, return punts, and plays running back. Anderson punts high and with his left foot, which happens to be a bonus. Punt returners are used to right-footed punts; the reverse spiral Donny gives the ball makes it a little harder to handle.

Anderson practiced kicking in high school by trying to kick over a small wire stretched across the school stadium. At Green Bay Lombardi always told his punter to forget distance, to just kick high enough to prevent returns.

"Nothing gives a team as much life as a long punt return," warned Lombardi.

Punting and place kicking are like playing golf. A good swing has a consistent groove. Trying to kill the ball is all wrong. The kicker should whip his leg through the ball, lower leg stiff—eye on ball—with a good follow-through.

"Like hitting a golf ball, strength is not the real factor," says Gary Collins, Cleveland's punter-flanker. "It's all timing and leverage."

Their running abilities make Gary Collins and Donny Anderson football's most qualified *fake punters* (punter goes back as if to punt but tries to pass or runs instead). Bob Scarpitto at Denver was another good faker.

Before one Browns-Eagles game Gary Collins figured the Eagles were sitting ducks for a fake punt. The Eagles had run three kicks back for three touchdowns the week before and were still flying high.

"I thought they'd still be thinking 'return'," said Collins, "and they were." In a fourth down punting situation Gary ran for the first down. Cleveland's Coach Blanton Collier admitted later he had suffered a traumatic shock when Collins ran. "He told me he wanted to shoot me when I started to run," said Gary. "When I finished he wanted to kiss me."

Collins is an offbeat discovery. Gary went to a small high school (120 kids) in Pennsylvania where he played fullback, defensive end, and pitched a couple of no-hitters. He was all set to sign a baseball contract with the Phillies when a scout happened by, on a tip from a Pottsville barber. The scout talked Collins into football, at University of Maryland.

Collins and other fake punters never disclose their intention to the rest of their team. "If you tell someone, they will give it away by the way they line up," said Gary.

"I have no idea when I go on the field if I'm going to run," says Bob Scarpitto, whose fake punt for the lowly AFL Broncos beat the fat-cat NFL Lions when Detroit first condescended to play an American League team. "I'm always looking for the right time but it's a spur-of-the-moment decision. As the ball is coming back from the center, I look for a rush up the middle. If they rush from there, I just kick it because I don't have time to look elsewhere.

"But if no one is coming up the middle, I look to the right and then to the left. If they have only a one-man rush from the side, I generally can do it. Detroit had only one man coming from the right, and I knew I could go."

"We didn't know anything about it; it was new to us," said dejected Lion Coach Joe Schmidt.

"It's quite a feeling," said Bob Scarpitto. "I got a lot of satisfaction out of it." Scarpitto's next try, against the Jets, proved Waterloo.

"I couldn't believe my eyes," said Denver's brand new coach, Lou Saban. Although Scarpitto's fake-punting record at Denver was still a so-successful seven-for-eight, Bob was only one-for-two under new Coach Saban.

"Whatever could have gotten into him?" said Lou. Scarpitto enters doghouse. The next season he's sent to Boston.

Kicker-punter Sam Baker of the Eagles, like Collins and Scarpitto, is a free soul. The Giants seem particularly susceptible. Two years in a row they fell for Baker's fakery.

"We put in all our special plays for the Giants," said Sam, whose IQ is 142. 141½ points are spent on humor. Sam couldn't believe it, a year later, when the Giants blocked *three* of the four extra points he tried. Baker couldn't remember when he had missed an extra point. "It was dastardly," he said.

Gary Collins spends his IQ on melodrama. No one believes him except the officials, which is sufficient. What a sympathetic audience they make for his special performance, "The Gary Collins Swan Dive," which, if successful, earns a roughing-the-kicker penalty. Anytime roughing the kicker is called it gives the offense new life and changes fourth-and desperate into first-and-10.

Collins goes back to punt and, as the defense rushes near, indeed he does punt, following through with his kicking leg and letting it linger there in the air, in much the same manner as a lady of the evening raises an eyebrow or lowers a lid.

After a defender grazes his leg, or shoe, Collins whirls backward so violently one would think he'd been struck by a karate chop. Arms akimbo, he collapses, often throwing in a writhe or two. As the official's hankie—roughing the kicker—floats earthward, Collins giggles from his fetal position.

"I'll do it anytime one of those nuts comes close to me," he says. "Hell, I'd be a nut if I didn't."

Many copycats have tried the Collins' "Swan Dive" but no cat has quite achieved the master's touch. In New York Ernie Koy is still trying and has almost perfected an all-in-one fluid motion so that his follow-through turns into a back flop and leaves Ernie so flat and maligned that officials are tempted to call a roughing-the-kicker penalty every time. In 1968 Koy's flops won two close games for the Giants, against Dallas 27–21 and against Philadelphia a week later 7–6.

The Dolphin punter, Larry Seiple, scored a grand coup when he was only a second-year man. Buffalo was penalized twice in one game for roughing Seiple.

"They ought to nominate me for an Oscar," said Seiple. "I thought I did a great acting job. The funny thing is that Paul Maguire knocked me down once and he should know better—he's Buffalo's punter and one of the best actors in the game."

Punters who are actors are an asset. The defense has to treat them with kid gloves, making sure not to give them occasion to dive. Punters who are fakers and like to run occasionally on fourth down also give the defense an extra worry. The defensive rush has to slow down an instant, on the lookout for a fake. Gary Collins, who both acts and fakes, slows a defense down two instants.

"Any extra threat you have really helps you punting," says Bob Scarpitto. "If I can just take a second longer to decide if I can run, that gives my men an extra second to get downfield."

"We've clocked it," said Curley Johnson. "I need 1.8 seconds to get the ball off. If it takes two seconds, the kick is blocked. It's a pretty narrow margin. The worst thing for a kicker is not getting the ball off at all. I don't give a damn if it only goes thirty yards as long as I get it away." Curley has had four punts blocked in his career, but three came when the regular Jet center was hurt. Curley can blame those three on bad snaps.

Blocking a punt is harder than blocking a placekick because a punter stands eight yards farther back. However, when the ball is inside the 5-yard line the punter must kick from closer than 15 yards. In his own end zone the punter is the fairest game and a lost fumble gives the other team a quick touchdown.

Placekicking

Kickers are a strange breed. They get paid more for doing less—though a kicker's "less" is most important. Otto Graham blamed Washington's second-place finish in 1967 on the absence of a kicker (Charlie Gogolak was injured that season), and in 1968 poor kicking cost Green Bay a Central Division title.

"They're a damn bunch of prima donnas," said one trainer. "They don't do anything but kick, so to make themselves feel more important they act like big shots."

"Kickers want to feel like they are a real part of the team," said Northwestern Trainer Tom Healion, who had a grand opportunity to watch a variety of good kickers as the trainer and taper of the annual array of College All-Stars. "It makes them feel more important if they can find something wrong. Charlie Gogolak is a good example. He only taped one ankle but did he ever tape it. We usually use fifteen yards of tape for two ankles but Gogolak used twenty yards for one. He even wanted to have our goal posts changed, just for practicing."

"What about Van Raaphorst?" reminded Healion's assistant, Jim Nice. Dick Van Raaphorst came out of Ohio State in 1963. "Van Raaphorst used to take the tape off and then put it on again—over and over. He taped his back, knee, groin—everywhere."

"All specialists have something wrong," said Browns' Trainer Leo Murphy. "Cockroft always has something bothering him. Today it was his knee." Don Cockroft was a high Cleveland draft pick—third round—in 1967.

It's no wonder field goal kickers are neurotic. They go into a game cold, without time to warm up. They're on the field for only a play or two at a time—kicking off, kicking extra points and field goals, perhaps punting. In one game where Eagle Kicker Sam Baker kicked off four times, made three extra points, and had one field goal blocked he was in the game for only eighty-three seconds—a long afternoon for a kicker, unless he plays a second position (Baker is a long-retired fullback).

Kickers apparently have a special need for feeling like a part of the team and want their teammates to accept the fact that, even though they play only one minute out of sixty, they are earning their pay.

The kicking job is isolated, more so than the cornerback's. When the kicker is working every eye in the house watches only him. Kicking looks so routine, and because he's a specialist it's taken for granted he won't miss, but when he misses everyone sees. In the final seconds the kicker often wins or loses a game with a stroke—or mis-stroke—of his foot. A week of practice and almost sixty minutes of combat go down the drain when the kicker comes trotting onto the field, three seconds left, his team trailing by a point. He misses. His team loses.

Such pressure in the limelight helps turn kickers into ex-kickers, or at least, into guilt-ridden erratics with burgeoning inferiority complexes. Most kickers lose their jobs not for reasons of the foot but of the head. They kick up a storm in practice but in a game—a close game—they're liable to do anything. Lack of a cool head has unemployed many a powerful leg, and even though a modern football player needs a brain a kicker might be better off without one.

"Kicking is a mechanical thing, not mental," protests Ram Kicker Bruce Gossett. "I just never worry or even think about the score or the situation. The score of the game has absolutely nothing to do with the mechanics of kicking, so why think about it?" A wonderful theory that Gossett is pushing, but the woods are full of coaches beating the bushes for a consistent kicker—a pressure kicker.

So many kickers are loners. They practice by themselves and go their own way. At Dallas Danny Villanueva, a swarthy-cheeked, sensitive little Mexican, took pills on pills on top of pills. It's amazing in itself that a volatile Latin type could kick with any success at all. Sam Baker, pushing forty, refuses to give interviews. At Philadelphia Sam was blessed with a coach who had an "over-33" club—a unique plan which allowed players over 33 to report up to three weeks late to training camp.

"When everything goes well, who gives a damn about the kicker?" asks Baker, who was once told by a psychiatrist that he should be selling stocks and bonds to elderly ladies. "It's only when a team is losing that people look for flaws. What it really amounts to is that if you have a good kicker no one notices it. They take him for granted."

The new soccer-style kickers are the loneliest of the loners because their plight is compounded—they are foreigners and they aren't even football players.

One of the early imports was Garo Yepremian, who fled from Cyprus in 1960 when Turks and Greeks began skirmishing. Garo went to London, spent five years hustling fabric in Carnaby Street and wound up kicking for the Lions where the incumbent, Wayne Walker, was kicking erratically. Garo did fairly well but couldn't kick the long ones (over 35 yards) so he and Walker shared the job. Walker also plays linebacker. Garo—a balding, left-footed midget, 5′ 6″, 160—is too little to play even fourth string and so he was an outcast, unable to get into the combat and violence.

"No one likes a kicker," says Garo. "I practice alone, live alone—why I've never even had a roommate here. I don't like standing on the sideline but what can I do? I think if I make some points for them when it counts I will become more a part of the team." When last seen Garo was apart from the Lions practicing basketball—shooting baskets soccer-style, with his head.

Garo's job at Detroit was especially difficult because Wayne Walker is a leader in the Lion den. He is vain, witty, particular about his clothes and his (lack of) hair, superstitious and nicknamed "The King." Garo, on the other hand, wears a beret and inherited his full share of whatever it is that makes Armenians such successful rug dealers. Whatever it is, it isn't traditional gridiron. What sells rugs didn't sell Garo to the Lions.

The kicker's niche, of course, is the least traditional and the most absurd. From anxious roots spring a weird assortment of kicking nuts, from barefooted kickers and sockfooted kickers to San Diego's Dennis Partee, who travels with fourteen pairs of football shoes—different shoes for placekicking, punting, kicking off—different shoes for different moods, and for different football fields. The Dallas Cowboys stage an annual Kicking Karavan, with several coaches flying around the country conducting a series of kicking tryouts. One tour tested fourteen hundred kickers which included a homosexual, a basketball coach, a fellow who missed every try, and a bus driver who was driving by, saw the mélée and parked his loaded bus while he tried out. So far nothing startling has emerged from the Karavans, but they are a wonderful example of how the kicking world is chock full of nuts.

One of the oddest is an explodable myth named Ben Agajanian. Old Ben, one of the world's most able chatters, belongs on the cliché All-America team—as the kicker, of course—for promoting himself as a traveling tutor of placekickers. Ben has placekicked for nine different teams, and in this day and age when the fear of conflict of interest sets most men to writhing, Ben Agajanian moves along, hiring himself out, from training camp to training camp, team to team, advising, correcting and trading placekickers.

Two years ago Old Ben dropped Mac Percival at Dallas, criticized Roger LeClerc at Chicago, and then arranged for Percival to join the Bears. The next summer, on his visit to the Bears' training camp, Ben tried to change Percival's technique.

"He told me to keep my left foot farther from the ball and not to lock my ankle," said Percival, "but it wasn't natural. I compromised and I have my ankle taped now so that it's locked in a kicking position."

Because of an accident in a bottling plant elevator which cost him some toes Agajanian played with a size ten shoe on his left foot and a size seven on his right (kicking) foot. Ben tutoring kickers seems rather like taking violin lessons from the one-armed villain on TV's *The Fugitive.*

"It finally got to where I'd either have to do it my way or saw off my toes," said Mac Percival after Agajanian's last tutoring session.

A year ago the promoter in Old Ben presented his unique pair of football shoes to the pro football Hall of Fame, almost certainly after an argument with the salesman in Old Ben, who would have auctioned them off to the highest bidder.

The Cowboys' Karavan unearthed the fact that the world is full of kicking candidates. The Dallas office averages forty calls and letters each week from potential placekickers who have good excuses why they haven't as yet been discovered, ranging from parental discipline ("My mother wouldn't let me play football in college") to a lack of football experience ("I couldn't finish high school because of brain damage," wrote one. "I couldn't read.")

The most famous kicker in recent memory was Cleveland's Lou Groza who retired at the age of forty-four. Groza was a power kicker, a natural slugger.

"The biggest thing I learned by watching Lou Groza practicing was that concentration is everything," said a young Brown. "It's not power but the way you hit the ball. Sometimes when you hit the ball right *without power* it goes further." Which sounds like a conversation with Gary Player or Mickey Mantle.

On a kickoff the ball is held on a tee and the kicker takes a running start. He wants distance so the ball will carry all the way through the end zone for a touchback, which eliminates the threat of a runback.

On a field goal attempt, when there is a human holder instead of a tee, accuracy counts most. The holder—a player with sure hands, often a quarterback—kneels seven yards behind the line. Seven yards is a compromise between how long it takes the kicker to kick and how long the blockers can hold off the defense, which is trying to block the kick. It doesn't matter whether the goal posts are two yards away or fifty, the holder is still seven yards back.

It would seem logical and safer on a short kick for the kicker to move a few yards back. "Wrong," says San Diego Coach Sid Gillman. "The closer to the line of scrimmage you kick, the more vulnerable to the outside rush. Seven yards is right."

At Green Bay Vince Lombardi once built a fishnet wall (it looked like an eight-foot badminton net) for his kicker, Don Chandler, to practice kicking over. But Vincent ordered Bart Starr to hold the ball 3½ yards back from the net instead of the usual 7. Most of Chandler's kicks cleared the net, which was supposed to simulate 6′ 8″ defensive linemen trying to leap up to block his kick.

"As big as they are today, when they make a two-yard penetration that's an awfully big target," said Chandler, discussing the human windmills. "You need height on your kick. It's really something to see how fast you get elevation. I don't think about the net. I never even see it."

Chandler may not see the net but it would be difficult for Don not to see the defenders hurtling at him. They have to be *quick*. Once the ball starts up it is usually gone, which is why tall basketball types jumping high for the ball usually miss it. Successful special teams drill through toward the kicker, charging from the inside in specific patterns. They are getting so sophisticated that the automatic kicks from inside the 30-yard line are about 20% less automatic than they were two years ago.

"To be a top kicker you have to completely forget the pressure," protests wishful-thinking Lou Michaels, who sometimes moonlights as one-fourth of the human badminton net at Baltimore. "You can't be thinking about the position of the ball on the field."

But sometimes you can't ignore it. When the ball is spotted to either side of the field—the hash marks are almost seven yards wide of center—the kicking angle is difficult, especially for shorter field goals. A field goal attempt from the 2-yard line puts the kicker on the 9-yard line but seven yards off center. The kicking angle is then so difficult that a team may skip the field goal and try for a touchdown, or the team might waste the third down to run the ball laterally to a better kicking position, right in front of the goal-posts.

There is another alternative. With the ball so close to a touchdown no coach wants to waste a down to get better kicking position so on fourth down he might try a fake field goal. Once when the ball was off to one side Weeb Ewbank called for a fake field goal on Buffalo's 3-yard line. Weeb didn't think his kicker could make it and figured the Jets had a better chance for a touchdown if the kicking formation fooled Buffalo. It didn't. A pass failed to score. "We've missed those angled field goal attempts from the 2-yard line before," said Weeb, who is normally so conservative that second-guessers were amazed at his stroke of imagination. "That was a very difficult angle."

Weeb's kicker, Jim Turner, has a special problem when the Jets are playing at home in Shea Stadium. Open spaces and various nearby bodies of water contribute to an ever-present wind which blows in seven directions at field level. "At least seven," says Turner. "Sometimes I think a kicker who doesn't practice here is better off than the kicker who does. I get so worried about wind direction and the angles that I make a bad kick."

Human badminton net in action against the Giants.

Practice doesn't always make a kicker perfect. They are cautious about overpractice. Sam Baker is careful to regulate his kicking to fifteen minutes before an Eagle practice session and fifteen minutes after ("And I don't participate in other drills"). Sam is painstaking in his efforts not to overtrain. Booth Lusteg, who kicked for many teams, believed that kicking footballs in practice took too much out of his leg. Lusteg used to maintain his swing, form, and timing by kicking paper cups, cartons of them.

To begin a field goal attempt the center passes the ball to the holder, aiming for his chest. The holder's chest makes a better target than his hands because he is kneeling at right angles to the goal-post on his right knee. The holder puts the ball in a vertical position with the laces facing the goalpost—all in one handy motion—and holds the ball daintily in place with his left index finger. (All is reversed if the kicker is left footed like Garo Yepremian or Lou Michaels.)

Most kickers selflessly give 50 per cent of the credit (or blame) for a placekick to their holders and almost 50 per cent to the center. Every effort is made between center, holder, and kicker to repeat the exact procedure on each kick. Timing and confidence in one's holder are as urgent for a kicker as for a trapeze artist. The exact prekick machinations used to be a secret. Roles were anonymous. But when record books and all-star teams reached the saturation point there was still plenty of glory left to be spread around. The anonymous faces aren't so anonymous anymore.

"Babe Parilli is the best holder in football," says Jim Turner. Why shouldn't Babe be best? He's been holding for sixteen years. "He reminds me to make sure I'm lined up right, or to check the wind, and he has the fastest hands."

"The snap from the center is the secret," says the Bears' placekick holder Richie Petitbon, who held for Mac Percival before being traded to the Rams. The third member of the trio was Center Mike Pyle. "As long as I feel the strings [laces] of the ball in my right hand as I catch it I can set it down with the strings in front."

Back at the Jets the precise Parilli was figuring out a way to insure the laces faced front every time. If the laces are to the side the ball's balance is destroyed!

"Babe moved up the spot where he puts the ball a couple inches less than seven yards," explained Jim Turner. "He figured out that those couple inches would make the snap come out with the laces facing the goal posts every time. This way he doesn't have to spin the laces around, and I don't have to worry about kicking the laces." Kicking the laces doesn't matter on short kicks, like extra points.

"I discovered that if I placed my hand a quarter-turn away from the laces," said Mike Pyle, "it would come out just right, as long as Richie was exactly seven yards away and I threw the ball with the same impetus every single time. If it was seven and a half yards we'd have to learn to do it all over. As for snapping the ball with the same amount of spin every time, that's just practice. After thirty snaps a day for five or six months each year it's a reflex action."

One of the first kickers to single out his servants for praise was the Rams' Kicker Bruce Gossett. "A kicker is only as good as his center and holder," says Gossett, "and I have the best. Ken [Iman, the center] has his snap timed so well that when Eddie [Meador, the holder] gets the ball the laces are almost always in exactly the right position. In fact, if Eddie has to spin the ball at all, he does it *before* he puts it on the ground, something a lot of holders can't do. I can start stepping into it when the ball hits his hands, instead of having to wait until the ball is placed on the ground—which saves time.

"If the lacing is on the side, on a long kick the ball will curve in that direction," says Gossett, "so for long kicks—over twenty yards—the laces should be facing the goal post, for greatest accuracy. And the ball is not as resilient at the laces; if you kick them the ball won't go so far." This doesn't matter for extra points, when the important thing is moving fast. "On short kicks Meador just smacks the ball down without checking the laces."

Kickers, like jockeys, seem to come with clocks in their heads. Mac Percival says he gets the kick away in 1.3 to 1.5 seconds. Gossett estimates it takes him, from the instant the ball is snapped until his foot touches the ball, just a shade over one second. ("Inside the twenty, no more than 1.115 seconds; longer ones need more time.")

"The soccer-style kicker seems to need a fraction of a second longer to get the kick away," says former Eagle Coach Joe Kuharich. "If the snap is perfect Sam Baker will get the ball in 1.1 or 1.2 seconds. I don't think soccer kickers do it that fast."

The new trend in pigskin booters—kicking soccer-style—is enough to make a conventional kicker's neuroses triple. The patriotic kicking fraternity rallied together like Detroit awaiting the first Volkswagen. There are as many opinions on the soccer situation as there are kicking experts.

"When you play soccer you want to kick the ball low for passing and shooting at the goal," says Dolphin Kicker Karl Kremser, whose family fled East Germany three days before the Wall closed. "This presents a problem in football where the most important thing is a good swing and getting the ball high." Kremser's brother was born in Poland, in a covered wagon. The family settled in Tennessee where Karl's father is a used car salesman and his son's kicking coach.

A boost for soccer-style comes from an unexpected quarter, the Eagles' Defensive Tackle Floyd Peters, whose job is to bat kicks down. "We've got to put even greater pressure on soccer-style kickers," says Peters. "They get quicker elevation, and two yards off his foot the ball is too high to reach."

"Beyond twenty-five yards a soccer kicker is at a big disadvantage because he doesn't get the distance of a straight-ahead man," said Gossett, who really knows how to hurt a guy. Bruce not only puts the knock on a soccer kicker's distance, but also his accuracy. "When you hit the ball with the side of your foot and the instep you tend to develop a hook. If you put more toe in it, the kick slices." Golfers readily grasp such a dilemma.

"I kick with the long arc of the leg," defends Charlie Gogolak. "I make contact with the instep and get more leg on the ball than a guy who kicks the ball with only his toe. This gives me more accuracy *and* distance."

Actually Bruce Gossett's opinions on the subject of soccer kicking are prejudiced. His father was one. Besides, Gossett can't see very well. He might not recognize a soccer kicker.

"In the daytime the goal posts are a blur at forty yards," says Bruce. "I gauge the distance and don't look at them again. Instead I look at a spot on the ball when I kick. I should make 'em all inside the twenty, eighty per cent up to forty yards out, and fifty per cent is very good out to the fifty. Beyond that you pray." The record is 56 yards.

The Rams got Bruce some contact lenses and the world became bright, but a little too close for comfort. Bruce claims he kicks better in the dark. "I kick better at night," says Bruce, "when the light goal posts stand out in the darkness."

The only other night-time kicker I ever heard of was Arthur Modell, Cleveland Brown owner, who at the time employed Lou Groza as his daytime kicker. Billy Wilder was using the Browns in his movie *The Fortune Cookie*, starring Jack Lemmon and Walter Matthau. One November night in Cleveland—actually it was a bit after midnight—Modell was inspired to demonstrate his do-it-yourself style of owning. He ordered the floodlights turned on in Municipal Stadium and proceeded to entertain Jack and Walter with a placekicking exhibition. All in the spirit of jolly good fun, Modell proved he deserved a Mr. Moonlight award. He and Jack Lemmon have been thicker than thieves ever since, but to this day it has never been disclosed whether Modell kicks conventionally or continentally, which is to say, soccer style.

The jury is still out on kicking soccer style, but even if it turns out to be only a fad, the soccer kickers have been fun. They have focused attention on the kicking side of the game. Alfred Hitchcock, a football fanatic, is always complaining that they've taken the foot out of football and that it should be renamed handball (armball?). Soccer kickers brought the foot back and put kickers into the newspapers.

Because they kick with their insteps instead of their toes, soccer-style kickers line up at an angle to the goal post. The angle is always the same although the ball varies from left to right of center.

"I address the ball at about a 75° angle to the left," says Peter Gogolak, Charlie's older brother and football's first soccer-style kicker. "I catch it low with the side of my arch and I like the ball teed to slant sharply toward me, laces on the far side." Who would guess that the laces on the football are such a cause célèbre? Why don't they abolish the laces? What good are they?

A couple of years ago every kickerless coach looked East, to soccerland. When Allie Sherman and his wife made an off-season European tour Allie kept one eye peeled when he drove by playgrounds and empty lots (he probably wrote the vacation off his income taxes as a prospecting trip). Hank Stram, Kansas City's head coach, held tryouts all over England, Scotland and Wales, hoping to find three rugby or soccer kickers who would come to Kansas City for $8,000 for the four-month season, as kicking insurance. Stram had a nice vacation too.

With so many new teams good kickers were scarcer than ever and coaches were ready to try anything. Dallas once came up with an Olympic high jumper from Australia for punting. Dolphin Kicker Karl Kremser is an All-America high jumper who jumped over 7′ at the University of Tennessee. The Tennessee Stadium has artificial turf.

"It was strange," said Karl. "The artificial grass is just different. I lean a little when I kick, and it took getting used to."

The Chargers discovered a kicker for a season practically on their front doorstep, a mailman from the San Diego post office. Denver tried a discus champion. One of the last to turn up was one of the wildest yet, a soccer-kicking skier from Montana State, Jan Stenerud.

When Jan—pronounced "Yon"—was three, his father, in Fetsund, Norway, set him to jumping off tables to strengthen his legs for ski jumping. The movie of Jan's life will switch from early Ingmar Bergman to prewar Hollywood. Jan is at Montana State University on a ski scholarship: One afternoon while jogging around the football field working out with the rest of Montana State's ski team, Jan picks up a stray football, kicks it through the goal posts a few times, effortlessly; the coach perks up his eyes, walks over to Jan . . . and so forth.

Of all the soccer kickers Jan Stenerud is the best bet to make a big success in football. The Gogolaks are second choice and the rest of soccer style is a distant third.

If only for reasons of quantity football's first family of soccer kicking is a name apart. The Gogolaks were threatening to become the biggest, most luscious Hungarian family under "G"—when both Pete and Charlie were injured. The Gabors were immediately reranked No. 1, but with the Gogolaks healthy they're contenders again.

A dozen years ago the Gogolaks escaped from Budapest during the revolution. "I was fourteen, Charlie was twelve," said Pete. "One night we walked into Austria, my parents and us. My mother was pregnant. Now young John is a soccer kicker too."

"We lost hope and left," said Charlie. "The border guards were so busy they left the gates partly open and out of nine million people almost two hundred thousand of us got out. The Russians had tanks and star shells which made it light as day. We walked and hid for seven hours until a Red Cross truck finally came." No one ever wrote a script as good for Zsa Zsa.

The Gogolaks settled in New York State. Peter went to Cornell, majored in innkeeping. For two seasons he kicked for Buffalo and set a 28 field goal record on a champion team while playing out his option, in 1965. Pete's divorce from Buffalo (AFL) and subsequent taking-up with the New York Giants (NFL) was the catalyst which brought about the 1966 merger of the warring leagues.

Pete Gogolak's biography has everything for dramatic movie-making—escape, war, fear, temporary happiness, financial problems, a split-up, new home, happiness, and tragedy. Less than a year after joining the Giants Pete was drafted and fell, during basic training, seriously aggravating an old back injury. Pete was given up, forever lost to football. He spent long, boring months in Walter Reed Hospital, and then, dramatically, rejoined the Giants in midseason 1967, commuting from whatever barracks. In 1968, as the Giants' regular kicker, Pete estimates he played a total of about three minutes, which puts his earning power in the $11,000 a minute bracket.

The movie of Pete's life should be in flashback, opening up in Ogdensburg, New York. At the first football practice at Ogdensburg High, Pete appears to try out for the team. He has non-credentials—a Hungarian soccer player. He joins a group practicing kicking. His turn comes. Pete lines up, almost perpendicular to the normal path of approach.

"Wait! Watch what you're doing!" they tell him.

"You'll kick it into the stands," says the snotty quarterback, a senior. "You're aimed wrong."

"Let me try," says Pete, angling in and kicking the ball with the inside of his foot.

"Look at the funny way he's kicking," says the skinny team manager, wearing glasses.

Ball sails through goal posts—once, twice.

"Cut," shouts the director, "and print."

Brother Charlie's sequel begins at Princeton, two years later.

Charlie was chosen on the first round of the college players' draft (no other Princeton Tiger can make that claim) by Washington. Kansas City wanted him too, but Charlie signed with the Redskins for a bonus, plus $50,000 per year. Redskin President Edward Bennett Williams, the famous trial lawyer, presented an argument which won Charlie away from Kansas City (where the Chiefs replaced the lost Gogolak with skier Stenerud). Williams immediately announced he would insure Charlie's kicking foot with Lloyd's of London (for half a million dollars) and enroll him in law school in Washington. Williams is so gung-ho football that Charlie is only one of half a dozen Redskins who have been promised a spot in Williams' law firm. Almost every young player who goes to Washington immediately decides his lifelong ambition has been law, and Vince Lombardi is stuck with a clubhouse full of lawyers. The Redskins, not Bobby Layne, will set an all-time record at the bar.

With good reason the rest of the Redskins call Charlie "The Little General." When he practices before an audience of 'Skins he acts like a pompous professor, lecturing. The prima donna is just bursting in him, trying to get out.

"This will be the only time I know what's going on," he says, "so I want to be in charge."

Charlie missed his second season at Washington. He had been married in June, had a headstart on conditioning and was rarin' to go.

"All during July we went over to St. Albans and I practiced kicking," said Charlie. "We'd been married a month or so and I needed someone to hold for me. Can you imagine, at first my wife looked the other way, and said to be careful of her nails, but she's OK now." But Charlie was hurt at training camp, a pulled thigh muscle which refused to heal.

It was only a few months before that Pete had fallen and injured his back. The Gogolaks' bad luck couldn't have happened to two worse-prepared guys. If they had stayed healthy the Gogos would already be reaping a rich, green windfall, capitalizing on their success. Instead, everything that was planned has been delayed.

Long ago, when Charlie was still at Princeton and Pete was playing out his option at Buffalo, they had already signed with an agent, Mark McCormack, who is making so much money for Arnold Palmer and Fran Tarkenton. A special soccer-style kicking shoe—the Gogolak Special—was in the works, only the first of a series of lucrative business deals. With all the endorsement and investment opportunities, ripe for the plucking, it was little wonder that Pete wanted to get out of Buffalo and into New York.

Such enterprises can be merchandised and promoted.

"There's one absolutely sure way to become an overnight sensation in New York," I told Pete just after he signed a contract with the Giants. "New York fans are Giant-crazy anyway, and if you can just make a tackle on a kickoff return, they'll flip for you. And after you make the tackle don't for heaven's sake, get right up. Fake it a little, and get up slowly. Shake off the fogwebs and pain. The sympathy of the fans will snowball. You'll *own* New York."

When a runner is getting away, returning a kickoff, the kicker is the last man with an opportunity to prevent a touchdown. Because kickers are the last men on earth you would choose for tackling, the fans go crazy when the kicker makes what might be the game-saving tackle. It's all the more dramatic if the tackling kicker is small (Garo or C. Gogolak) or ancient (George Blanda or Sam Baker).

Giant Safety Willie Williams was once in the clear returning a Baker punt when old Sam dipped his shoulder and bounced Willie out of bounds. Cool Old Sam clapped his hands with joy and ran (unusual in itself) across the field back to the Eagle bench.

Did he enjoy his intrusion into the violent world of the Nitschkes and Davidsons? "No," lied Sam. "There wasn't anyone else to stop him."

Charlie Gogolak made a tackle as a rookie. Li'l Charlie got Aaron Martin, an Eagle runner.

"I really blocked him," said Charlie. "I was the last man. But it's too dangerous."

It was also against the Eagles that Pete Gogolak finally got his chance to make his first tackle, in 1968, his third year with the Giants. In the first Giant-Eagle game, in September, Pete made a false start. Alvin Haymond grabbed a kickoff and raced behind his wedge, broke through, and Pete was the only man in the way. Alvin went 98 yards to a touchdown.

"I set myself to get him," said Pete, "got a good angle, but he just drove by me. I guess I just tickled him." Pete's coach, Allie Sherman, wasn't tickled. Sherman almost died, watching Gogolak, only eleven days removed from Army duty in Germany, risking all on the attempted tackle.

The second Eagle-Giant game was in November, in gray, rainy Yankee Stadium. On the opening kickoff Al Nelson raced 69 yards, running the ball back all the way to the Giants' 17-yard line where Gogolak brought him down. Unfortunately, Pete's tackle failed to bring down the house, probably because the game was such a bore. The weather was miserable, the Eagles had a perfect 0–9 record going into the game, they netted minus one yard in the second half, and the Giants played almost as badly. The final score was bizarre, 7–6. Even ten Gogolak tackles wouldn't have brightened that mess. Pete will have other opportunities.

Besides, he's becoming famous in the offseason at one of New York's most famous watering holes, the 21 Club. Pete, planning to open a Hungarian restaurant in New York, wanted to learn the business from the bottom up. What better school than "21," where Pete spent an offseason learning buying, accounting, greeting, potato peeling, wining, cooking ("Skinning asparagus tenderizes them") and spying ("Aristotle Onassis eats a lot of caviar").

Special Teams

> For those who think pro football is the greatest of spectacular sports I'd like to call attention to a game I call "Annihilation." It's not for sissies.
>
> Annihilation is like football, but without the dull parts. It's a game of kickoffs. Each team takes turns at kicking off and receiving—and may the better team survive.
>
> It's simple. The idea of the game is to gain more yards and points than the other team. The teams would operate just as they do now on kick-offs—the most exciting part of any pro football game.
>
> An attraction of Annihilation is that it is a wide-open game. There are none of those meaningless plunges into a mass of bodies in the center of a pile, where it is difficult to ascertain what is happening. Nor would lady fans have any trouble following the ball. Everything happens out in the open where naked truth prevails.
>
> —from *Out of Left Field*
> by Stan Isaacs, *Newsday*

"Any thing you do on the extra teams, which are a very important part of the game, gives you a lift," says Vince Lombardi. The extra teams play in kicking situations—kickoffs, punts, and field goals.

"The specialty teams are as important as the offense and defense," says Blanton Collier (Cleveland coach), who divides his special teams into coverage (defense) and return (offense) teams. (The team that kicks musts immediately turn to playing defense against the kick return.)

All coaches are quick to compliment the nameless muscles on their bomb squads, suicide teams, or whatever name is currently in vogue. ("They called us the 'meat wagon' in college," said Houston's Carel Stith, "but pro teams take pride in their special teams.") Coaches' best-laid plans work best at midfield, not in the hole backed up to their own goal line. At their 15-yard line offenses find themselves in the same situation as Napoleon's at the steppes—very poor field position. Losing coaches blame everything from a pass interception to the common cold on poor field position, but putting a team with an ordinary offense in a bad spot can completely take away what little effectiveness it has. It's the special teams that hand the ball over to their offenses at midfield, and it's the special teams that provide inspiration at unexpected moments, often turning the tide of a game with a recovered kick or a long runback. Their work can be very motivating, when it is part of the coach's job done for him.

The object of the receiving team is to return the ball as far as possible. When they run the kick back all the way to the kicking team's end zone —a touchdown—that is the ultimate in field position.

The object of the kicking team is good *defensive* field position, by making the tackle quickly, deep in the receiving team's territory, and preventing any return yardage. What makes a kicking team ecstatic is to hit the receiver so hard he fumbles; the kicking team then recovers the ball and might even score a touchdown. The kicker then has to kick off again, right away, but it's doubtful he would mind.

The kicking team's strategy is simple arithmetic. The team lines up on the 40-yard line with five players on each side of the kicker. They are spread over the 160-foot width of the field with the result that each man has an alley, roughly 15 feet wide, which is his responsibility to plug up. The toughest and fastest players are used as plugs.

The players start downfield in their alleys with the kick. The outside men start closing in on the kick returner when they reach his 25-yard line. They are farthest from the ball carrier so these outside men are the fastest pair on this specialty team. Their most important responsibility is not to allow the ball carrier to get *outside* of them, no matter what happens.

The inside men, nearer the kicker, are not as fast. If the outside men do their jobs the inside men can play a more waiting game and get the runner as he's forced into the middle and up someone's alley.

The basic rule is to never leave your alley until you reach the closing-in point (25-yard line).

"Ten of us go down (on kicks) and we all have certain lanes," said Eagles' Ron Medred. "The most important thing to do is avoid bunching up so there's not three of us in one ten-yard area and then a space of thirty yards where there are no guys. Of course the main thing is to make the tackle, drop the guy any way you can."

The man on each side of the kicker has an awfully dirty job. He's the human bowling ball who's supposed to sacrifice himself to split the other team's blocking wedge.

"Now let me explain the wedge," said Y. A. Tittle. "On a kickoff a four-man group is formed in front of the ball carrier. This wedge is made up of four 275-pounders, and it is the job of the first guys down on the kicking team to break up this wedge and get the ball carrier. It is a suicide mission."

A born-to-be-a-bomb-squadder can't wait to get going. "The action is fiercer on kickoffs and punt returns than at the line of scrimmage," says an ex-Eagle, now-Saint Coach Ed Khayat. "Any football player worth his salt should be proud to be selected for the bomb squad."

The bomb squad comes crashing downfield to meet and be met, head on, their bodies bouncing and crunching all over the field. Niagara Falls by barrel is smoother.

"I can't see any reason to spare myself," says Baltimore's Alex Hawkins. "When I don't play regularly I can really open the throttle when I'm in there. I'd rather be a good backup man than a bad first-team man. I know I'm not the worst player in the world, but I'm not good enough to win on a day-to-day diet. So when that wedge of enemy blockers comes steaming up the field I don't have to worry about missing the Pro Bowl game when I throw myself into the mob. I know I'm going to knock down a few of them and if I churn up enough bodies and get lucky I might drop the ballcarrier too."

"Everything is done with everybody building up momentum," said Khayat. "A runner has thirty yards of steam behind him and a tackler has forty yards to pick up speed."

Boom!

The Eagle bomb squads have always enjoyed considerable prestige. They won a key game in 1966 against Dallas. Timmy Brown ran back two kickoffs and Aaron Martin returned a punt—total three touchdowns. The final score was 21–14. Philadelphia's best Kamikaze pilots are Tom Woodeshick and Ike Kelley.

Giant runner Clarence Childs (48) behind his wedge.

"It's a tough way to make a living," says Woodeshick. "Nine times out of ten after we cover a kick I come out dazed. I don't know where I am and I'm sure most of the others come out the same way. But these kids love to hit. Ooh, how they love to hit." Woodeshick says bomb squad is more exciting than playing the whole game on offense.

"Almost every time you go down, you get hurt," said Tom. "You come out with a bad arm or whatever. But I love it. I hate to admit it, because somebody's liable to say I can do it for the rest of my life, but I love it."

A special handicap is rushing off the bench for one or two plays without a chance to get warmed up.

"Especially when it's cold, your muscles are tight," says Viking Dave Tobey. "I ache all over on Sunday night, as bruised as the regulars."

"It takes ability but it takes pure intestinal fortitude most of all," says Woodeshick. "Speed has to help you but guts is most essential. Speed is what makes Ike Kelley so tough. Even though he's so stocky, I'd hate to have to race him in a 100-yard dash."

Kelley has left his mark around the league. In one game against Cleveland, Ike was supposed to block the punter, Milt Morin. "He kept getting up and I kept trying to knock him down," said Kelley, whose real name is Dwight (thus "Ike"). "It's my job." Kelley had set a record with three consecutive blocks on the kicker, Milt Morin, who was helped off the field with a severely bruised right leg. Morin was out of action for several weeks.

Tom Woodeshick is captain of the Eagle bomb squads. The first special team captain ever named, Alex Hawkins, was introduced with the offensive and defensive captains at the pregame coin toss ceremony.

"And this is Captain Hawkins," said the referee. "Captain Who?" asked the visiting captain, and the name stuck. Now every team has a Captain Who or two.

"The coach gave us incentive when he started naming a captain for the bomb squad," said Woodeshick. "It was like he was recognizing we were there."

On a kickoff return the ball carrier looks for gaps between the alleys being patrolled by the defenders. The five forward men are the team's best blockers, who try either to make gaps or to enlarge the ones they find. The man farthest front stands on the 40-yard line and he blocks the first player he confronts after the kick. He is the point of a five-man V, with two other blockers on the 30-yard line and two more on the 20.

Behind the V, on the 15-yard line, is the front of the wedge—three big blockers who act like a great delta wing—a bulky human launching pad for the ball carrier behind.

At the 10-yard line behind the wedge is a blocking fullback, in case the kick is short. At Minnesota this blocking fullback is played by Jim

Lindsey, who also acts as wedge director. Lindsey tells the wedge when to fall back, when to get in place and when to start forward.

"The relationship between the wedge and the ballcarrier is important," says Lindsey. "If you start too soon someone will get the ballcarrier from the outside. If you start too late he'll be running into you from behind."

Behind the blocking fullback, beside the goal post, are the two kick return specialists. They are brave, with extra speed for splitting gaps in the advance line into daylight and, hopefully, touchdowns.

Both on kickoffs and punts most teams use two return specialists when one would seem to suffice. One puts his full concentration on making the catch while the other acts as cruise director, shouting what's happening—which way the defense is going—and giving advice like a traffic cop. "There's a lot more to it than strikes a person's eye," says Atlanta Flanker Bob Long. "You have to work with the other man. You have to watch the ball, and if your partner calls for it you have to judge whether he should call for a fair catch. If he does fair-catch it you have to be there in case of a fumble, or to block."

At the last minute the "short" safety, the one without the ball, can often throw a block which springs his friend well on the way to the enemy end zone. One of the shortest "short" safeties is the Cowboys' "Little O," red-haired, freckled Obert Logan.

"My main job is blocking," says Logan. "I feel that if I can cut down that first man downfield, my partner has a chance of getting some yardage. If I miss, then I don't figure the play has much of a chance. Then, too, I have to be on the watchout for those short kicks and the ones that get sloughed off."

Things don't always go according to plan. Once the Flea, Walter Roberts, was almost exterminated by the Eagle bomb squad's Captain Woodeshick, on a punt return.

"Leroy Kelly, my very good buddy, was supposed to give me the call," said Roberts, who left Cleveland for New Orleans during expansion. "He was also supposed to take the first man down, but something went wrong. I haven't had a chance to speak to him yet." After a crisis with Tom Woodeshick, Walter was lucky he could still talk.

The National League has Flea and the American League has its Super Gnat, Noland Smith at Kansas City, who was nicknamed by his boss, the owner of the Chiefs, Lamar Hunt. Hunt has a "super" complex. Commissioner Pete Rozelle rues the day that Hunt gave The Loot Game such an undignified and colloquial title as the Super Bowl and Noland Smith has identical emotions for identical reasons.

At 5′ 6″, 154, Smith is a singular specimen in the world of annihilation. He has thirteen brothers and sisters, and is one of two sets of twins in the Smith family. His twin brother Norland weighs 190 and at 5′ 11″

is a housefly in comparison to Super Gnat. "Anybody who sees us together thinks I'm his baby brother," said Noland. "They think he's the athlete, but he played in the band."

At Tennessee State Noland kept a cigar-box collection of insects for biology and played running back.

As a rookie he ran wild over the American League, returning kicks for almost enough yards to lead his league.

"I don't get hit too hard too often," said Noland, "because I got my moves and speed. Even when they're bearing down on me they don't get too good a shot at me because I can avoid all but a glancing blow."

Noland doesn't know that the tacklers can't hit him because they can't *find* him. If his success continues, opposing bomb squads will need to carry a microscope. Noland runs kicks back so well that most teams try to kick away from him, or to kick short bouncers (squibs), or they try onside kicks.

An onside kick is one of the rare opportunities when a kicker can be creative. There is a rule that on a kickoff the ball must go ten yards before the kicking team can recover it. An onside kick is a kickoff which is deliberately kicked to one side and forward just farther than ten yards. Most onside kicks are attempted toward the end of games when one team is desperate to keep possession of the ball for another chance to score.

"It's all a matter of timing," says Sam Baker. "In every game there's time for a reverse or some sort of unorthodox play. It's just that a lot of people don't have the courage to try them." Baker made this statement immediately after a successful onside kick.

Kick return specialists detest onside kicks because it robs them of a chance to do their thing. Similarly, punt return specialists only signal for a fair catch as a last resort.

A punt return is a different species from a kickoff return. Punt returners must be extra tricky and quick, to maneuver near the sidelines. Kickoffs are returned behind the wedge up the middle; punts are returned along the wall of blocking which attempts to clear a lane up the sideline.

One of the best punt returners is the Rams' Alvin Haymond. Alvin periodically rips loose for long runbacks and practically gets his head ripped off several times a game. For two years Haymond was the brightest light in the dreary Eagle offense and opposing teams were gunning for him, keeping their clothesline handy, hoping to hand Haymond his head. Four years ago on one play he lost four teeth. A bomb squader reached Alvin at the exact instant that Alvin reached for the punt.

"Usually the defensive man has to stand there and wait for me to catch the ball," says Haymond. "That's all I want—the right to catch it. Unless he times it perfectly, hitting me just as the ball comes, I can get around him."

Alvin wears green leather football shoes and enjoys his dangerous profession. "Playing on the special teams is fun," says Alvin, "especially if you like that kind of humor."

Alvin's counterpart at Washington is John Love. "I like to run back kicks," said John. "That's like pie."

Bomb squad vernacular is the best. Allie Sherman was once inspired to call upon his Captain Who, Mickey Walker, for a few chosen words, hoping to spread the fever of annihilation before an important game.

Walker rose in the tense dressing room to address his teammates. "All right, guys, kick tail."

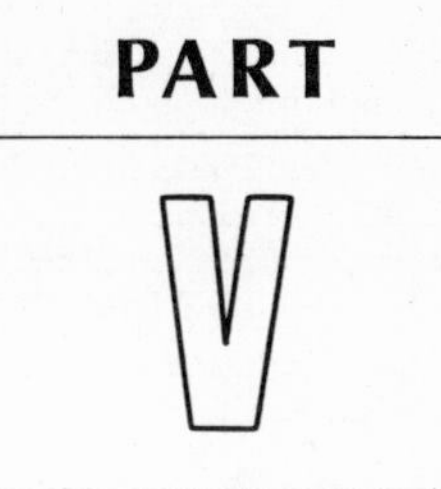

PART V

14 Background

Football players are just like people. They grow up just like other little boys, it's just that they grow up farther. Still, they come in assorted sizes. Kansas City's kick returner Noland Smith is only 5′ 6″, 154. At Cincinnati, Tackle Richard Sligh is 7′ tall and weighs 300. He wears 16½ EEEE shoes and has a forty-six inch waist. The other men in the Sligh family average 6′ 3″ but Richard's mother and two sisters are a foot shorter.

"Short women prefer me," says Richard, a bachelor, who cut his last molar only two years ago. "I never meet a tall girl."

Lots of football players grow up in big families, but some don't. Some are mama's boys, some papa's. Several years ago there was quite a to-do over a magazine article written by a Dr. Joyce Brothers prototype. The article suggested that football players became football players in rebellion, to "show Mom" that her son is grown up, strong, and independent. Rebel or not, many players send their laundry home to Mom, sometimes even married players send their laundry home to Mom, and Baltimore's Kicker Lou Michaels always had his paycheck mailed directly to his mother. Judging the book by its cover, one would never guess that Lou was close to his mother. He has to be kicked to wear a tie or coat, and for him to dress up requires a complex of circumstances like those required for a surfer's perfect wave—but Lou is a family type and when he came out of a kicking slump two years ago the first thing he said was, "My wife and mother never lost faith in me."

"The only thing that comes before football is a charming lady," said Joe Namath, "my mother."

Several summers ago Namath, who chain-smoked menthol cigarettes, made a $5,000 bet that both he and his mother could quit smoking. If either of them went back to smoking, Joe would pay the five grand. He said, later, he did it for his mother's sake, because she smoked too much for her own good.

In the locker room after the Jets won the Super Bowl, Namath was with his father and brother.

"My mother isn't here," said Joe. "She gets so nervous she swells up like a balloon. She just wants to stay home and pray the rosary."

Of football's many famous fathers the most famous have been the biggest braggers, who mostly seem to come from the Southwest, especially from Texas. Two Texas fathers, Joe Don Looney's and Ernie Koy's, were in professional sports themselves—Koy Sr. played baseball and Looney Sr. was an NFL official. Occasionally they have been called by their sons' coaches to ask for help . . . and insight into their boys' attitudes and how to handle them. Baltimore's big Tackle Bubba Smith receives a weekly morale boost and pep talk from his father, a high school coach in Beaumont, Tex. "He knows just how to give you a lift," says Bubba, "and he tells me to be patient." Bubba calls his mother before every Colt game, for inspiration.

"Why I talk to Mama Smith too," says Billy Ray, the other Smith who plays tackle next to Bubba.

No father-son duo in sports annals comes close to the drama of Ronnie Knox and his stepfather Harvey. Ronnie was the subject of such an enormous advertising campaign, conducted solely and loudly by his stepfather, that after three high schools and two colleges when Ronnie went to the Chicago Bears it was an arrival likened to the second coming.

"As I look back I realize it was all my fault," said Harvey. "I didn't try to get Ronnie Knox to do something he wanted, but something I wanted. You don't know what a great player that boy was until you understand the conditions he played under. He hated football. To him it was work. He hated work. He wanted to drift, and sleep, but I wouldn't let him."

Knox Sr. used to call up sportswriters and extol the virtues of his stepson, who fell far short, victim to his father's mouth. With each successive failure by Knox Jr., Knox Sr. felt called upon to make excuses, and noises of optimism, and his explanations of how Ronnie had been mishandled and misunderstood sounded like a diary of Tommy Manville.

After stints at three teams in Canada, Ronnie told Harvey to get lost. "I don't like you anymore," he said, and that was that.

The Cardinals' Jim Bakken is not an ordinary kicker. He holds the record for kicking seven field goals in one game, he is a bad golfer, a good skier, intelligent, not overly modest, uncommonly good-looking, and Bakken has a superfan father-in-law.

Several years ago the Cardinals were playing in Green Bay. Bakken's father-in-law, Herman Dahle, lived almost two hundred miles from Green Bay, in Madison. On Tuesday before the game Herman set out from Madison, by bike. He arrived in Green Bay Friday.

"All I did was fight mist, rain, fog, and tornado warnings," said Herman. "I had to walk a few hills and those country dogs were a problem—but I had a spray tube of dog repellent."

A similar sort of superfan-father is Larry Eisenhauer Sr., a good humored 275-pound ex-football player who travels with his son's team, the Boston Patriots. In San Diego the Patriots always stay at the Stardust, which is a motel/country club with swimming pools and a golf course and several cocktail lounges. One of the lounges is the Mermaid Lounge, where behind the bar are big windows which look into the middle depth of a swimming pool where girls undressed like mermaids perform three times a night.

"One afternoon my son went for a Turkish bath and massage and I wanted to go for a swim," said Mr. Eisenhauer. "By mistake I got in this mermaid pool. Of course the cocktail lounge was open, but when I got in the pool I couldn't see into the bar because the windows are one-way. So I'm in there and I'm swimming all around and everything and having a great time, not even knowing that all these people are watching. That night I really got the razzmatazz from the Patriots about my performance.

"Larry told me to go up there as that was the best place to swim. But I don't know if he was tricking me or not. A couple of days later they all threw me in the other pool with all my clothes on just for the heck of it. We have fun. It keeps us young," said Mr. Eisenhauer, who speaks gridiron jargon in the first person plural.

Football players come from big cities, like Mike Garrett, who grew up in a west Los Angeles melting pot, and small towns, like the Jets' Randy Rasmussen, who comes from Elba (pop. 184), a farming community in Nebraska. Randy often relates his cosmopolitan Jet life to life in Elba, comparing one of his father's "critters" to a juicy $8 New York sirloin at Gallagher's Steak House, and he reassures the city folks and sportswriters that in Elba he doesn't have to milk his own cow before breakfast. ("We go to the store just like everyone else.")

When Larry Csonka was drafted by the Dolphins he had never been to Miami before. On his first trip, to sign his contract, Csonka immediately decided to move his wife and young son to Miami.

"I've never lived where there was no heavy industry, smog, and smoke," said Csonka, originally from Ohio. "Anybody would be impressed with Miami."

Players come to the pros from religous colleges, Negro colleges, and, in rare cases, from no schools at all (some players are discovered on armed services' teams, on sandlots, or, sometimes, in jail). They come from big schools like UCLA and little schools, like Lester Josephson's alma mater, Augustana, in South Dakota, which has an enrollment rumored at about 1,000. Several years ago there was a joke going around about Green Bay's Halfback Elijah Pitts. Pitts became a sensation when he replaced the injured Paul Hornung, and people were asked if it was Elijah Pitts from Philander Smith or Philander Smith from Elijah Pitts. When Pitts was in college he had 600 schoolmates, but Philander Smith (in Little Rock) dropped football soon after Pitts left, for lack of participants.

If you had to pick the grads of any one particular institution to be shipwrecked with on a desert island you would think a long time about the all-around American boy types from the University of South Carolina (Dan Reeves, Craig Baynham, Alex Hawkins), who make versatile, thinking-man halfbacks, but you would finally decide to choose University of Arkansas alumni instead.

This colorful lot includes "Hawg" Hanner, a balding, blond, cubic coach at Green Bay; ex-Bear Fred Williams, who put his Arkansas drawl to good use as the gridiron's best all-time storyteller—"Funniest player we ever had," said Bear Official Rudy Custer. "I always thought that one of the reasons he wasn't the best lineman we ever had was because his sense of humor kept him from really being vicious enough." Also Billy Ray Smith, the Colts' quaint, crazy showman, and Lance Alworth, the "Bambi" of San Diego.

Arkansas Razorbacks make devoted alumni. "Lance gets blue in the face from yelling when he watches Arkansas play on television," said his roommate Keith Lincoln. "It's really somethin'. I always end up yelling for him."

One of the advantages of matriculating at Arkansas is the quick and easy method one graduate Razorback in a crowd can use to detect another —simply by shouting the Arkansas yell, "Sooey," or "Sooey, Pig!" It is said that many Razorbacks have issued their call in the middle of a metropolitan area, such as The Loop or Times Square, and received an answer. An old grad Razorback wouldn't just jazz up life on the desert island, he'd probably get you off sooner. As "Sooey, Pig" echoed across the waves any ships within ten miles would heave to.

There are a few generalizations about college players which seem to hold up. The fastest runners come from Negro colleges. The Big Ten rarely produces a good quarterback. Notre Dame players are the most overrated and much slower to mature than expected. Alabama boys are small but very quick, and they make good quarterbacks. Mississippi (Ole Miss) sends along highly publicized quarterbacks who don't make it. Utah State is a tackle factory.

It is much harder for a boy to make it in professional football when he has been prepared in a smaller school. At the larger universities like

Michigan State, Notre Dame, UCLA, and Southern California the coaching is superior, the competition is the toughest, and the style of play is similar to that of the pros, which means a player doesn't have to learn a brand-new system of play when he turns professional.

At the Houston Oilers, Coach Wally Lemm almost blew a superstar when his great fullback Hoyle Granger arrived, a rookie from Mississippi State. Hoyle spent the first half of his rookie season on the bench. Hoyle is the original Quiet Man, which was interpreted as dumb, not quiet. What was really the case, the Houston system was entirely new and different from the one at Mississippi State. "I don't believe our quarterback called more than one automatic in four years," explained Hoyle, who had a 7-yard rushing average soon after he began playing regularly.

Smaller schools tend to have inferior coaching and play against a lower grade of competition. The Ivy League schools (Vince Lombardi pronounces Yale with two syllables) play an almost all-Ivy schedule and their recruiting policies claim to put the emphasis on brains more than athletic ability, at least most of the time. Ivy League athletes are usually too small to play pro sports anyway, which gives some grounds for thinking the biggest brains come in the smallest frames.

The IQ department of the gridiron is bursting with mystifying anomalies. Boston's terror at tackle, Houston Antwine, originally came up with the Oilers asking their general manager, John Breen, if he could sign a verbal agreement. (Imagine the Houston Oilers letting anyone named Houston go to Boston?) And Minnesota's Punter Bobby Walden (now at Pittsburgh) asked a doctor who was treating his injured toe, "If you cut it off, how long would it take to grow back?"

The subject of football brains is a provocative topic. Senator Eugene McCarthy likens politics to coaching football: "You have to be smart enough to understand the game and dumb enough to think it's important." And Robert Ardrey, in *Territorial Imperative*, suggests that football players hardly need any brains. Ardrey proposes that the athlete is the single member of the species who is allowed to fulfill his aggressive instincts without the disapproval of society—"without, in many cases, benefit of a registerable IQ. The athlete, that respectable aggressor, sucks up like a vacuum cleaner the most minute particles of learning. . . . Whether the athlete has mental capacities to rattle about in the interior of a thimble or to strain the capacities of a ten-gallon hat, he will learn with equal facility complexities of plays, subtleties of movement, intricacies of rules and regulations to baffle an Einstein. Here is something to keep in mind when you hear about voting for such honors as Scholastic All-America teams or the various media lauding the intellectual achievements of the gridiron warriors. If all the players are so intelligent, why are the same two or three from each team interviewed over and over and over?

Unlike the Ivy Leaguers, the other and larger schools forget brains and go after the biggest frames they can buy with a vast array of alumni, area scouts, and coaches armed with gut courses and slush funds and recruiting policies reminiscent of Australian headhunting.

Many major football colleges include courses in basket weaving and physical education for their athletes, and one university inaugurated a new course in remedial reading this year in order to try and keep a highly desirable freshman player eligible for football. It wasn't long ago that the football players packed up the day after the last game and left school with out making any pretense at finishing their free education. Pro football offered a job and a way to make money. It still does, but now football players finish out their senior year, although many of them never graduate. Or they go back to several sessions of summer school to earn their diploma.

Michigan State was always considered the Schwab's drugstore of pro football until the Southwestern Conference won the title away. The Southwestern Conference is a football factory made up of small Southern Negro colleges with fascinating names like Grambling, Alcorn A & M, Prairie View, and Arkansas AM&N. (The more initials in a school name the better the chance that it is a state college for Negroes.) In 1968 Jackson State sent more players (eleven) to the pros than any other college or university in the country.

Michigan State gives plenty of attractive athletic scholarships and plays a big-name schedule, which means it's players go up against the toughest teams and get the best possible in-game experience. Michigan State's entrance requirements are low by Ivy League standards, but they are high by Southwestern Conference standards, through no fault of those colleges. Their fault is the state system.

A quick look at Grambling shows a small Louisiana school of about four thousand students with twice as many girls as boys. Grambling has one of the country's top marching bands (200 struttersteps per minute) and it is supposed to be harder to make the band than the football team. No girl student has even been able to make the band. Grambling is caught in the middle of Louisiana's system of segregated public education. As a state college, anyone who passes its entrance examinations gets in, as long as there's room. Families pray that their children will get in. (Grambling gives no athletic scholarships.) Clearly, Grambling takes the cream of the crop, but what an unfortunate crop. Students come to Grambling out of public high schools barely able to read, often with little more than an eighth-grade foundation, which forces the school to compromise its scholastic standards to a level between its brightest students and the less bright majority. It is a tragic situation.

At Grambling's 1967 homecoming weekend, in what proved to be an unnecessary precaution, the National Guard was called out in alarm over a student demonstration. Several hundred Grambling students (there were twice as many Guardsmen) marched and sang in orderly fashion to demonstrate against, of all things, overemphasis on athletics; they hoped for greater intellectual opportunities.

Louisiana is only one example of Southern states that try to afford two public school systems. Richer Northern states can't afford *one* integrated school system.

Oakland Raider Fullback Hewritt Dixon came from a town of 2,500. As soon as he could make the team Hewritt was allowed to play on the high school varsity. At the age of twelve, in the sixth grade, Hewritt beat his own 18-year-old uncle Rufus, a senior, out of the job at right tackle. Four years later the coach divided the team in two, into "city" boys from Alachua and the county boys.

"The city team didn't have any backs so I played fullback," said Hewritt, but whenever Alachua played a team with an outstanding offensive player Hewritt went to defensive tackle with instructions to flatten the enemy team's star.

There were eight children in Hewritt's family and his mother made sure all of them went to school, and to work afterward and on weekends—washing windows, raking, hoeing, and picking tobacco and string beans. They obeyed their mother, evidently. Mrs. Dixon is six feet tall herself. She had twelve brothers and the tiniest was 6′ 4″. After Super Bowl II Hewritt took his Super Money and built a home for his parents—the first one they ever owned.

Hewritt received scholarship offers from Michigan State, Wisconsin, and Northwestern, traveled to look them all over, but chose Florida A&M where his father had played. In college Hewritt played fullback where he was the slowest man in a backfield which included Bob Hayes. "The rest could run the hundred in at least 9.4," he said, "so they called me Freight Train. I could only go in 9.9." The fastest runners always seem to come from Florida A&M or a Southwestern Conference school.

Heaven forbid that one should confuse the Southwesterns with the all-white Southwest Conference (Baylor, Texas, Arkansas, Southern Methodist, etc.) or the Southeastern Conference (SEC) of Tennessee, Alabama, Georgia, and that ilk. These Southern teams say they are integrating but what they are doing is trying to recruit a few top Negro athletes under the flags and banners of integration. When a coach tries to sign a 6′ 9″ Negro basketball prospect or a 220-pound fullback with 9.8 speed, he's not necessarily trying to further civil rights. The idea, to the coaches. alumni, and other players, is that the colored boy doesn't smell so bad if he's scoring touchdowns.

Two years ago the University of Kentucky tried to integrate, admitting two Negroes on football scholarships (*two*, so that they could room together and have someone to talk to), but both dropped out, one soon after the other. A year ago the University of Florida football coach said the school would break the color barrier and recruit a high school fullback, Willie Jackson. Florida State University recently signed its first Negro to a football grant-in-aid, but such confederate bastions as Mississippi and Alabama are still holding the line in what is obviously a losing battle.

In the South, as in the North, "Winnin', suh, is the name o' the game," and the state of Alabama particularly worships at an altar made of gridiron. They name as many new highways, buildings, and schools for University of Alabama Coach Bear Bryant as the rest of the country does for John F. Kennedy.

But Southern schools like Alabama and Mississippi are often criticized for their easy schedules, which means playing each other and avoiding the tough teams, the integrated teams.

Alabama citizens annually name their team Number One in the nation, the nation not withstanding, but such proud Southern enthusiasm won't be able to stomach forever the little white string attached to their self-proclaimed supremacy, which leads one to assume that before too long football will be the catalyst toward at least token integration in the diehard Southern schools.

"You can play football without Negro boys," says Bill Yeomans, head coach at the University of Houston and a former assistant of Duffy Dougherty's at Michigan State, "but if you want to win you'd better have three or four."

Alabama's white power syndrome is carried out in black at Florida A&M, where Jake Gaither rules his "Rattlers" with the same iron authority as Bear Bryant. Florida A&M is the most famous of the Negro football factories, for having sent so many stars to the pros, for its famous marching band which is as good if not faster than Grambling's and because it plays host each December in the televised Orange Blossom Classic in Miami's Orange Bowl. Florida A&M chooses the guest team, usually from the Southwestern Conference, but Gaither only chooses an opponent he feels pretty confident about, which makes the A&M guest list as phony as Alabama's. It shouldn't need to be, because A&M gives twenty-five football scholarships and gets TV income from the Orange Blossom Classic; Southwestern College schools give no scholarships, and get no TV income, yet sometimes beat relatively bigtime A&M. (Really bigtime football teams like Michigan State and Alabama give forty or more football scholarships, and Alabama averages better than $150,000 annually from television.)

In the future there will be a slightly different look to the Rattlers, because in the 1969 Orange Bowl Classic Rufus Brown will be a sophomore on the team, and Rufus is white.

"Florida A&M offered me the most," said Rufus Brown, neglecting to mention that A&M's was the only offer he received, to the envy of his white high school classmates who received no offers at all and considered Rufus very lucky. "They are giving me a four-year grant-in-aid, all expenses paid for tuition, room and board, and laundry." Plus a free education.

Rufus Brown expected his lot would be as difficult as a Negro's trying to crack a white team. "It's going to be reversing itself," said Rufus, "and I want to see if I'm good enough to make it. I figure they'll accept me as long as I don't try to push my way around."

"I told him to go home and talk it over with his parents, teachers, coach, and friends," said Jake Gaither. "I think the whole situation can be solved by mutual respect. Times are changing down here."

Rufus, majoring in pre-dentistry, is one of seven children of a preacher. It took him a while to get used to campus life—he is one of six white students—particularly the attitudes and vocabulary. No doubt his acceptance came more easily because he was a football player. And he *was* accepted. An unknown art lover swiped his playmate-of-the-month gallery and he quickly earned two nick names, Blue-Eyed Soul and Rap. "I really felt I got accepted when they started calling me Rap," he said.

Rufus had been worried about his social life. "But there's a school, Florida State, right across the hill," he said. "I've got friends there, and I'm easy to get along with."

Integration is hardly an issue at Michigan State. Two seasons ago the most coveted football player in the country was Bubba Smith, who came to Michigan State all the way from Texas and became a campus hero. The cry from the grandstand, "Kill, Bubba, Kill" also made him a national legend, via video. Bubba drove around the campus in a white convertible with "Bubba" painted on the side and was a favorite of the sorority sisters.

"On most integrated teams there's always a little dissension," said Bubba, "but not at MSU. We're together, like a family."

Therein lies the genius of Duffy Daugherty, recruiter and coach. Year after year he comes up with extraordinary discoveries, big raw boys who under Daugherty's paternal hand turn into stars, ready for the pros. On prospecting forays Duffy's favorite gold mine is a section around Beaumont, Tex., where Bubba Smith's father is the high school football coach. While Bubba was playing for his father, Mel Farr was quarterbacking across town at Hebert High School, and other exports from the same high school league include Mel's brother Miller and Jerry Levias at Houston, Ernie Ladd (Kansas City), and Jim (Earthquake) Hunt (Boston). "What's the name of the league?" repeated Bubba. "I don't believe it had a name. It was just 'Our League.' " Our League just recently started playing an integrated schedule, against one team with white players.

Bubba Smith is a 280-pound illustration of why the Southern schools will integrate. They lose top talent like Bubba to the integrated Northern schools, which pay well in scholarships and convertibles and the like. To compound the loss, the Southern schools are then afraid to include schools like Penn State, Colorado, Southern California, and Michigan State in their schedules, for fear of losing both the game and face.

If you ever wondered how so many Texas boys stray up to such places as Michigan State, coaches like Bubba's papa with a hotline to Duffy Daugherty are the reason.

One gradute of Our League, Jerry Levias, didn't stray afar—only over over to Southern Methodist in Dallas. Levias is a jet-streamed midget, only 5′ 9″ short, but regardless of his packaging, football has always been his life and pro football his goal. Jerry has an extra incentive, the success of his cousins, the Farr brothers. Now that they have made good, and loudly, Jerry plans to die trying, with the Houston Oilers.

"Mel taught me how to swim and play football," said Jerry, who had polio for six months when he was twelve. Mel was two years ahead of him in school. Both Mel and Jerry played basketball, baseball, and track, but in that neck of the woods football is number one.

Mel went to UCLA, and two years later Jerry had more than a hundred scholarship offers. When he chose SMU Jerry was the first Negro to accept a football scholarship to a Southwest Conference school. Southern Methodist had once been a football power but was in dull decline for about fifteen years, ever since the heyday of Doak Walker and Kyle Rote. Interest in SMU football was revived, however, four years ago when a colorful addition named Levias made the scene. Jerry began exploding like a tiny bomb, bursting through defenses, breaking records and winning games and most-valuable awards. He did things with an exciting flair and obvious class.

Not everyone in the Southwest Conference was too overjoyed over events. When SMU played Texas in Jerry's sophomore year a li'l ole Longhorn halfback told Jerry, "Go on back to your nigger momma!" as he was on his way back to the huddle.

The week before SMU played TCU a man's voice had called the school and said "We're going to shoot that dirty nigger Levias on Saturday," and hung up. Policemen and plainclothesmen followed him for five days, and personally escorted him to and from the dressing room. His mother was surprised by a television broadcast which said that there had been an assassination attempt on Jerry. She didn't sleep for a month. Early in his career Jerry received filthy, threatening letters and telephone calls through the night.

"It was no fun—the stares and the remarks—but it made me a stronger man," said Levias. "If I backed down I don't think I could have lived with myself, and I'd never give those people the satisfaction of knowing they made me run away. I'd do it again, even if I knew what would happen, and, believe me, I'm no martyr."

Jerry Levias was popular with teammates and their leader, on and off the field. He roomed and socialized with a white boy. He may be too small to succeed at Houston but perhaps he can become the Mike Garrett or Noland Smith of the 1970s. A year ago Jerry came third in an affair naming the ten most eligible bachelors in Dallas. He accepted his award, a vision of pale green sartorial splendor. (Cowboy Flanker Lance Rentzel finished second.)

Not all Negro boys who choose to integrate a Southern stronghold emerge as popular as Levias. In Houston, as you would geographically expect, the university was always as white as the driven snow. But when Bill Yeomans came to Houston from Michigan State he began recruiting Negro players. One, Warren McVea, is with the Cincinnati Bengals.

As he integrated the Houston team, the Cougars, McVea's style was rather ruthless, and while he was grabbing the headlines he was also moody and smacked of the martyr when he wanted attention. Celebrity status went immediately to McVea's head, which swelled to the size of the Astrodome and earned him the nickname Super Rat.

When he was a senior at Houston, McVea signed up for both Shrine football games, conflicting postseason charity affairs, without telling either promoter that he had committed himself to the other. When the promoters found out what happened they thought about getting together and cutting him from both rosters, but they were afraid of trouble from civil rights groups. A white player who had been as high-handed would have been dropped immediately and that would have been that.

At Cincinnati McVea's coach is Paul Brown, of the sterner stuff school of coaching, and if McVea departs from the straight and narrow path under Brown he will depart from the Bengals. Brown had plenty of experience handling a similarly high-handed but considerably more talented sort, Jimmy Brown, and Paul learned the hard way.

Warren McVea's attitude at chic, big-time Houston was exactly opposite that of a star at segregated, little-time Grambling. At Grambling the most responsible student leaders are the athletes, who are taught good habits by their coach, Eddie Robinson. Robinson teaches them table manners, and churchgoing, and they wear coats and ties to away games. Most coaches at the Negro colleges try to teach pro-style football. They are dedicated to helping the players use football to escape the hopeless poverty of their youths.

"I can't remember when I wasn't big and I can't remember when I wasn't hungry," said Hewritt Dixon, who was 6′ 1″, 202, in the sixth grade, 215 in the tenth grade, and is 225 pounds now.

"Except for pro ball how else can these big old country boys earn so much money so fast?" asked one coach.

"I've got to make it," said Jet Rookie Bob Taylor, who graduated from Maryland State and had wanted to play pro football all his life. "That's why I went to school. I want to make the big dollar. It's my way of living." Taylor went to the same high school and college as Jet Halfback

Emerson Boozer, shared "a bad pad" near Shea Stadium with Boozer and signed a contract for $21,000. He failed.

Pro teams scout and recruit Negro players as enthusiastically as white boys, perhaps more so, but this is recent policy. It wasn't until 1946 that Kenny Washington graduated from UCLA and became the first Negro to play pro football, across town at the Los Angeles Rams. Two years later Tank Younger went from Grambling to the Rams and did something Washington didn't, became a star. Since Younger the parade to the pros from the Southwestern Conference has been long.

There are almost three hundred Negro players in the pros today, which amounts to about 30 per cent. The number increased sharply several years ago when more teams became more and more desperate for talent. The Washington Redskins was the last team to break the barrier and allow a black boy to play, in 1962. Most coaches try to keep the percentage of Negroes lower than one third, and indeed, until 1965 the Houston Oilers had a quota system that allowed no more than five Negroes on the team. Houston wasn't the only team with a quota and many teams made certain that they always ended up with an even number of colored players so that the roommate situation would always work out without anyone left over. It wasn't until 1968 that several teams adopted the policy of assigning roommates on some no-color basis, alphabetically or otherwise.

Because of coaches like Robinson at Grambling and because they have a line of interference made up of pioneers who have gone before, the big old country boys aren't as naïve as they used to be. They arrive at the pros with short-cropped college football haircuts, nervous and fearful, but by the time the regular season rolls around, if they are still there, they are identifying; they have adopted the natural haircuts of the Negro veterans, who in turn teach the rookie railroad the ropes—how to behave off the field, places to go and places not to go, what to wear and where to live. Still they have problems.

In Green Bay it's not that easy for a Negro to get a haircut and most of the Packers' colored players wait until they are in Milwaukee for their barbering.

When a boy has been attending a Negro college and playing against other Negro schools it is a jolt to all of a sudden find himself on an integrated team playing against white boys. He has twenty-one years of his own experience to overcome.

"Some of these boys haven't ever been with white people, spent any time with them," says Emlen Tunnell. "All of a sudden they're not only living and eating with white men but they're supposed to go out and TACKLE them, and they can't get used to it. Sometimes it takes years." Sometimes that's too long.

Where to get a haircut is a minor problem compared to the problem of finding a place to live. Almost ten years before Mike Garrett came along to Kansas City, Jimmy Brown was turned bluntly down by a Cleveland landlady: "We only take whites." Brown had wanted to live near the Browns' practice field, he said, for convenience.

"It wasn't integration I was after; I just was bitter about being segregated, you understand?"

When Mike Garrett returned to Kansas City before his second season he couldn't find an apartment and spent several depressing months living in and out of hotels and his car ("I cannot get keyed up. I don't have the rah-rah spirit."). Every apartment he wanted required a long lease and/or wouldn't rent to Negroes. Mike blamed his sophomore slump on a combination of things—reporting overweight, a chronic toe injury, and emotional problems largely stemming from his apartment hunt.

"I had a mental problem," he said. "It bothered me a lot. The thing that gets me is that people want to come and watch you play football, but when you're trying to find a place to live they don't want anything to do with you. It just doesn't seem right. If you have pride things like this can't help but get to you and what gets you most is that you can never get away from it."

The parallel between Jim Brown and Mike Garrett is striking. They came from poor families, their mothers worked as cleaning ladies; they are both sensitive souls, superbly balanced runners, and though much smaller than Brown, Mike Garrett carries almost as big a chip of bitterness on his shoulder.

Still Jimmy Brown, although bugged to death by his color, says he had no problem with anti-Negro feelings when he played. "It's not as bad in football as in other fields," said Brown, who has on occasion called all white men devils. "In sports they judge a man not on the color of his skin but on what he can do."

A white devil agrees.

"When you're on a football field it's all the same," said Rufus Brown when he was a Florida A&M freshman. "Actually I got accepted by the football team first, which made it easier all around."

"After twelve years in pro ball all problems and dissension are immediately forgotten when the players take the field for battle," said Jim Hill, a retired St. Louis cornerback who became sports editor of the St. Louis Sentinel, a Negro newspaper. "I don't believe racial prejudice was ever a factor in a team losing a championship or a game. The players have too much pride."

When you're on the field it's all the same but not at all the same positions. Probably because of inferior college coaching and because blocking is a more complex procedure there are more Negro defensive linemen than offensive linemen. There has never been a Negro center. When the civil rightists ask why there has never been a Negro pro quarterback they might also ask why there hasn't been a Negro center, a consistent Negro placekicker, or a great white cornerback.

In some quarters there is a feeling that a Negro is not intelligent enough to handle the quarterback's role. Indeed, there is a feeling in all professional sports that the Negro athlete is not quite as bright as the white athletes, that it counts more that he comes in large sizes and runs fast.

A report which was published in Russia in 1960 claimed that the Negro muscular structure is superior to the white man's, but Grambling coach Eddie Robinson thinks that's silly.

Still, Negroes make superior runners. It was unintentional that Donny Anderson is about the only non-Negro player mentioned in chapter seven —which is exactly what has thwarted aspiring Negro quarterbacks. They run too well. A coach hates to take a chance of waiting the usual four or five years to find out if he has a quarterback when he can have a flanker or defensive back immediately, with no risk. When good quarterbacks come along so infrequently anyway, why waste a good runner for four years? By the time a quarterback flunks he's almost too old to begin all over again at a new position.

Great things were expected from Sandy Stephens, a Rose Bowl hero who signed a $100,000 three-year no-cut contract with Montreal, but after four years' trial he was too fat, and he went to Toronto. It was generally believed that a Negro quarterback had a better chance in Canadian football where quarterbacks run more than they do in American football. But Stephens reported to Toronto a portly 225 and though they tried him at a number of positions, including running back, he never worked out. Stephens ended up at Kansas City where in one scrimmage he was wired for sound for a broadcast over a radio station. In the game at last, Stephens promptly forgot where he was and came out of the huddle yelling, "C'mon and get 'em, you ____________," and those thirteen letters spelled his swan song in pro football.

In the past no team wanted to risk developing a Negro quarterback for fear that the white players—especially the Southerners—would never take orders from a colored quarterback; after all, the quarterback should be the team leader.

"I think they are ready now to accept a Negro in a position of leadership, and I want to be the first one," says Eldredge Dickey, who comes from Tennessee A&I, the speed factory which fashioned Wilma Rudolph and the world's fastest half-time band. A fantastic athlete, Dickey could probably make it in the pros at either offensive or defensive halfback, or flanker, but he is getting a chance at quarterback at Oakland.

After his senior season Dickey played in the Christmas Day Shrine game and shared the quarterbacking for the South team. After the game the press took South Coach Jim Bridgers to task for not playing Dickey enough, saying his ten completions in seventeen was only a minimal opportunity, which shows how Oakland was asking for trouble by drafting him, a case of damned if you do and damned if you don't. If Dickey is switched from quarterback Negro sympathizers will say he was switched because he was black, not because he couldn't throw. Dickey is lucky to have a boss like Al Davis, who loves a fight and basks in controversy and word marathons with the press.

Fear of getting involved in a "situation" has held many pro teams back from signing certain Negro players. A Negro quarterback was untouchable enough, but a Negro quarterback with a white bride—that would have been a surefire knockout combination.

Jim Nance, Roger Brown, and Art Powell are among the good Negro football players who are married to white girls. Some Negro players with white wives have been given the cool treatment by teammates—both black and white. One boy came to the Giants a nervous wreck from the University of Nebraska. He didn't know if he would be able to bring his white wife to New York and, if he could, could they find a place to live. He worried all through training camp, his play suffered, and the problem almost disappeared when the boy just missed being cut from the team.

White women are the major cause of race problems between black and white players, according to Jimmy Brown. Brown felt that a situation involving women—particularly white players seeing a black player with a white woman—would end up just bursting with trouble.

"That's why black athletes don't try to socialize with white teammates," said Brown.

Perhaps that's why Brown didn't socialize with white teammates, but that's his hangup and not necessarily why other black players don't socialize with white teammates. Actually, isn't it naïve of Jimmy Brown to expect black and white athletes to socialize when black and white non-athletes don't?

Efforts at togetherness, like rooming blacks and whites together on the road, are being made. "I've encouraged Negroes and whites to mix socially," said San Diego Coach Sid Gillman, "but each seeks out his own and if that's what they want I'm not about to say 'OK, mix.' "

"I have observed segregated seating by choice in dining halls," said Bernie Casey. "Why am I sitting there at a black table? I suppose because I'm more comfortable there. I don't believe that because people are involved in an endeavor to better themselves financially—which is what professional athletics is all about—that the things one has been taught throughout his life can be easily dispelled."

"I don't believe in artificial separation, pairing people off by color to eat and sleep," said Ron Mix, a tackle at San Diego, who plans to run for office in San Diego in 1970. "Particularly in sports which theoretically embody all that is good in man. It's ridiculous."

Mix expounds on the "good in man" while Casey says sports are a business. Mix is white and a Jew. Casey is black, an artist and poet. Joe Namath is from Pennsylvania, but at the University of Alabama he changed his name and asked to be called Joe Willie, which just smacks of grits and pone. At the Jets Namath still prefers Joe Willie. The Jets always travel on two buses and one is predominantly Negro. That is the bus Joe Willie always rides in.

The spirit of the times causes athletes to speak out on the subject of racial prejudice. They evidently feel that their revelations are necessary. If so, it's because sports fans have an almost total misconception of the nature of the team. The biggest myth on the sports scene is the team syndrome—the idea that the "team" transcends the facts of life. It doesn't.

When you ask players why they go their own separate ways they mention the usual by-products of prejudice—suspicion, long-held attitudes and a lack of common meeting ground. Why not? In any other business group of forty individuals, an office or a garden club for example, people are pulled together by what they have in common and pushed apart by their differences. Among ballplayers there are differences of age and experience, color, ambition, geography, background, interests and finances. Why expect a rookie and a veteran to be closer than a mail-room employee and a vice president. Yet last year a rabid Jet fan couldn't believe it when, after the season, he found out that one young Jet had never met Joe Namath, had never talked to him.

According to Harry Edwards, the San Jose sociology professor who first proposed the Olympics' boycott, black athletes have long been used as symbols of a nonexistent democracy and brotherhood.

"They will block, shake hands, and embrace on the field," says Jimmy Hill. "Thousands of people see the blacks and whites back-patting and hand shaking and they're hoodwinked. Off the field it's a different story. That's where the gap is evident." This shouldn't surprise anybody. It should be expected.

Playing on the same team does create a sense of unity, but the unity of the locker room comes from isolation like a group of baboons. Isolated baboons are welded together by territorial defense. "The stranger must be hated," says Robert Ardrey in *African Genesis*. "One must feel at least rudimentary loyalty and devotion for the countryman." Until he walks out of the locker room.

"We once again become our own men and return to our own way of being," says Bernie Casey, whose own way is definitely very different from his teammates. Casey proposes that black and white players go their separate ways because they just don't care what the other fellow does when the game is over. Bernie doesn't care. He's an artist, a loner. He retired to paint and write poetry. The Rams thought he was too hippie, a beatnik.

It appears that some of the players themselves have fallen for all this team togetherness propaganda. Many players bask in the isolation of their locker rooms wearing the same uniform as the other forty and indulge in fantasies about life outside. They come to regard their football careers as the whole life process in miniature, come to expect the world to come to them and ask for product endorsements, political opinions, or a TV appearance. Then, when football is finished and every door isn't wide open, some players suffer tremendous traumas. They find out that the locker room did not reflect life in general and they can't handle the real world. The player, black or white, is no longer able to identify as a Jet or Ram and misses the spotlight.

Bernie Casey says discovering the real world can be particularly shocking for the Negro. The complacent fat-cat Negro is a sore thumb in today's tempo of boycotts, -ins, and revolts.

"For many years the black athlete suffered from delusions that he could just play the game and get his money and be a good nigger, but the Negro is aware now that he's got to have some kind of life when he takes that uniform off," said Casey. "The house nigger is dead."

The Draft

College players, in the middle of their senior year, are selected (drafted) by the pro teams. Once drafted, that's it, till death do part. The alternatives to signing up are Canadian football or early retirement.

"I've never been in Buffalo," said O. J. Simpson, soon after he'd been drafted. The Southern California All-America halfback's talents reached such dizzying heights that Norm Van Brocklin said he'd give up his pew in hell for him. "My image of Buffalo is cars stalled in a blizzard, with snow piled up to the roofs. Is it really that bad?"

The draft begins with the lowest teams in the previous season's standings drafting first, and continues through seventeen rounds of twenty-six players each until almost five hundred blooming youths have been chosen. Selections are based on elaborate scouting systems which employ a variety of methods from high-speed computers to group scouting pools to anonymous tips to eeny, meeny, miney, mo. The total cost is more than $4,000,000 a year. No cleated college pebble is left unturned.

Vince Lombardi's drafts at Green Bay were consistently among the most successful. "Our setup is simplicity itself," explained Vincent, smiling with becoming modesty. "We do it with a minimum of effort."

They also did it with maximum attention to detail. Lombardi's top draft choice for 1968 was an All-America linebacker, Fred Carr. "We rate all the college players in the country," explained Lombardi. "The ones we thought best were rated 1.0 to 1.9. Carr was rated tops, 1.0."

Carr weighed 240 but could run 40 yards in 4.6 seconds in full gear. In his heyday Jim Taylor could run 40 yards in 4.8 seconds, in shorts. "We don't draft fullbacks who aren't faster than Taylor," Lombardi was fond of saying.

Lombardi's genius at selecting good prospects was realizing their potential at different positions from the ones they played in college.

Everybody guessed that Fred Carr would play at linebacker. Lombardi, of course, was at that time bowing out at Green Bay and his coach tried Carr at tight end, where he flunked, before moving him back to defense at either linebacker or strong safety. They are still guessing about Carr.

The first-round draft choice has gone through a period of inflation during the last ten years. In 1959 when there were only twelve pro teams a top pick meant a sure shot at one of the top twelve players in the country and each team expected four rookies to make it. Ten years later with twenty-six teams drafting, teams are lucky if they come up with two decent rookies out of each draft.

Average non-superstars usually sign one-year contracts. A player contract includes an *option year* on the player's services (at a 10% salary cut) if he doesn't re-sign. Theoretically he is allowed to play out his option year (he can't *sit* it out) and become a free agent, but a free agent isn't really free at all. If a free agent goes shopping around for a new team, finds one, and signs up, the commissioner appropriates a player or two from the new team as indemnity for the old team. In cases where the players have played out their options and signed elsewhere, the commissioner has extracted a heavy indemnity, to discourage traffic.

In a great understatement Dallas general manager Texas E. Schramm said he felt this "forced trade" idea made it risky to fool with "free agents" and therefore might be regarded as a deterrent to the whole practice. "We [the NFL] are going to have to make a stand," said Schramm, Pete Rozelle's eye and ear west of the Mississippi. "You can't have great young players deciding where they're going to go." It should be noted that while a player may not switch teams of his own accord he can be traded at any time.

When Pete Rozelle, the Big Bopper of the gridiron, discusses the system he swears it prevents anarchy and tumult, and preserves competition. Without the system, Pete vows, all would be destroyed. The strong teams (strong teams are rich teams) would get stronger and the best players would flock to the rich, winningest teams or the warm-weather glamour teams. This warm-weather idea is a personal hangup of the Big Bopper with the year-round suntan. "There's not as much feeling as you'd think about players wanting to play in Los Angeles and New York," says Charley Bradshaw, a lawyer and a Lion who is a past president of the Player's

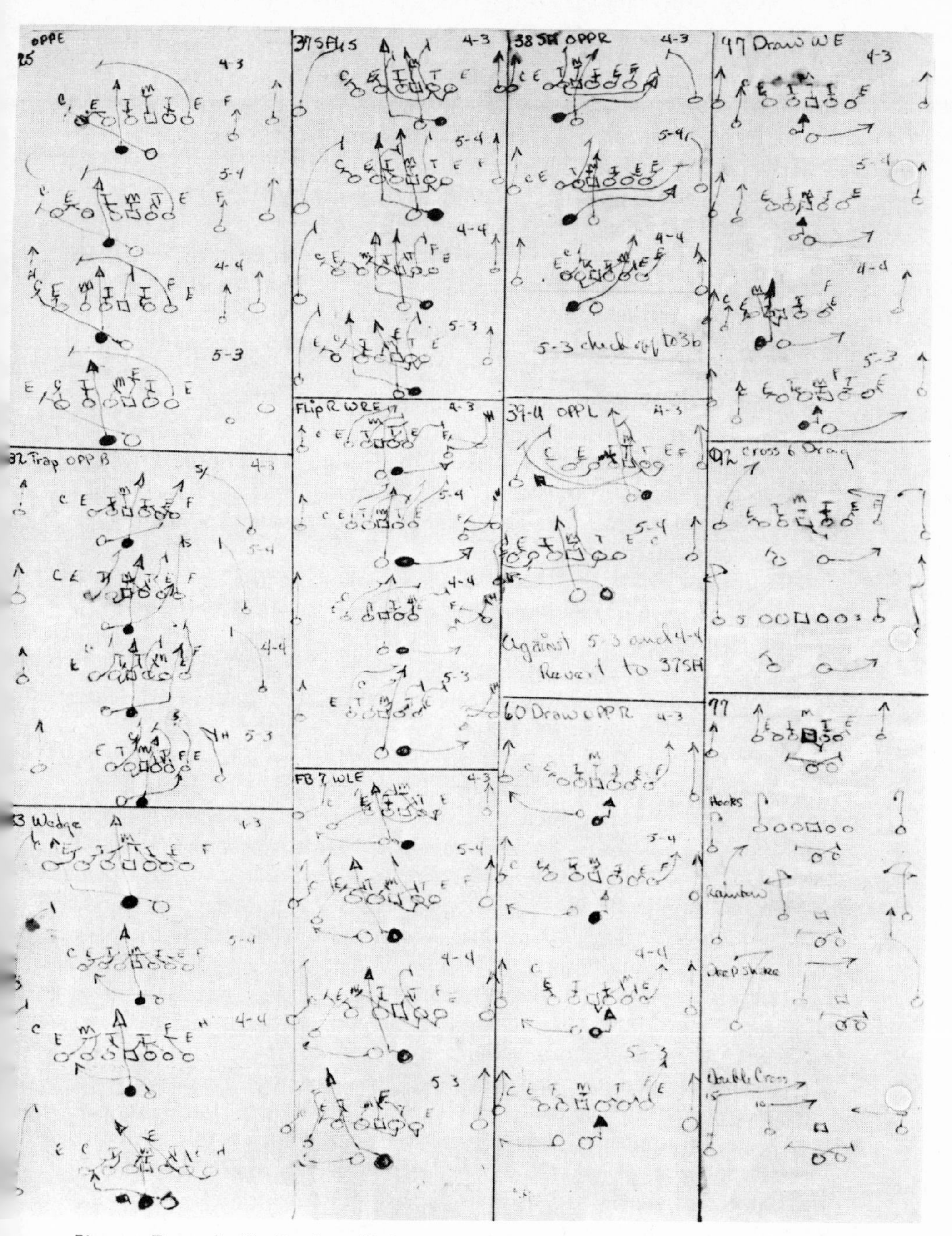

Jimmy Brown's "crib sheets" for one of Paul Brown's little weekly quizzes during Jimmy's rookie training camp.

Association. And there certainly is no great desire to play for Miami, whose management is notoriously slow with a buck.

Rozelle's arguments in 1966 won exemption for pro football from the federal antitrust laws. Pete convinced Congress that his game is unique and needs "certain unique survival measures," e.g., the draft. Indeed, no one has yet to come up with an alternative.

Pro football's situation, with competing teams dependent on each other, is special. Rozelle's important worry is keeping the competition balanced, because everybody knows what one bad apple can do to a barrelful. Rozelle argued in Washington that the draft helps to preserve healthy competition—which is bunk—that the draft is the great equalizer. It is and it isn't. When weak teams in desperation trade their top draft choices for experienced players, giving up future stars for mediocrity now, the weak get weaker and the strong stronger and the draft becomes a great unequalizer. If pro football really wanted to preserve maximum competition it would not allow draft choices to be traded. Pete Rozelle himself would probably like to abolish trading of draft choices. His owner bosses would slit their throats before they'd let him.

The basic problem with "the system" is a dramatic flaw in the player contract, the absence of any mutuality. If a player wants to go to another team and his owner wants to keep him, it's just too bad. And if the owner takes the case to court and wins, he actually loses. He's won a malcontent. Which is why the owners in the past have tried to make a deal in the first place, when it was obvious the player wanted to leave.

The players have very little at their disposal to fight the owners. The Players' Association has historically been a weak organization because the players prefer to negotiate their own salaries directly with team management. Who ever heard of a "union" where all the members were bargaining *individually* for their salaries but *collectively* for such items as a pension plan and fringe benefits (moving expenses when traded, severance pay, minimum wages). Most players were making more than the suggested $15,000 minimum wage anyway.

For many years the NFL owners didn't just refuse to negotiate, they ignored the Players' Association, which in the past had been run by "owner's players." It became more militant a few years ago and has now effected a generous pension plan which will be equal for players in both leagues in 1970. At the age of 65, players with five years on the books can collect $437 per month; ten-year players can collect $656.

The very mention of gold since May, 1966 is enough to send the players to their guru in hysteria. It was in 1959 that the American League came kicking and squawking into existence and began fighting the National League for players. The weapons were dollars and the fight continued for six years.

During the war each league conducted its own draft and the bidding for players reached astronomical proportions. Players were paid a bonus for signing, plus they were given healthy, long-term contracts. Bonuses took some strange forms. One player obtained a job for his brother so that the brother could win a parole. A Lincoln Continental (Joe Namath's was Jet green) proved to be a popular bauble for sweetening up a bonus. "What do I want with a Lincoln Continental?" asked Don Trull. "I only have one suit." Mike Garrett received more than $300,000 bonus money and Bubba Smith got $100,000. Garrett moved his family out of a $36-a-month housing project and treated his sister to contact lenses. Bubba bought his family a new house and gave his father a Cadillac El Dorado. Many players bought farms and ranches for the future.

The biggest bonuses were package deals, not cash. Cowboy Lineman Malcolm Walker was drafted on the second round of the last bonanza draft (1966) and received a car and $5,000 in cash. But he won a four-year, no-cut contract—starting salary $16,000—and a guaranteed annual raise ($1,000). $80,000 was invested for him in such a way that Walker couldn't touch the principal and begin to collect interest for ten years. When he's 40 Walker will be getting $800 a month from the money. When he's 65 his NFL pension will add either $437 (5-year man) or $656 (10-year man) to the pot. And Malcolm Walker is only an offensive lineman!

Some of the bonus babies didn't really have to worry much about football because of their long-term contracts. Such security kind of took "the edge" off their on-field hunger.

"They used to be more rah-rah," said the All-Star trainer Tom Healion. "With all the big bonuses they have so much less humility."

"They've been waited on all their lives," said Kelly Miller, the Redskins' equipment manager. "Sure, the spoiled ones hate to get cut. They hate to give up anything free."

"They don't know what football's all about," said Bill McPeak, an assistant coach at Detroit. "They don't know what it's like to put out, like the oldtimers who had to. If they didn't put out, they didn't eat." McPeak is a well-fed oldtimer.

The football war produced a novel tactic called "baby-sitting." Several days before a draft, players would be shanghaied by babysitters working for both leagues. The babysitter kept watch over his prospect, talked them into signing with his league, and then, immediately after they were finally drafted, signed them to contracts. Players were put on ice in motels, plied with wine, women, and cash, sent as far away as Las Vegas and Hawaii for safekeeping, and were often under lock and key. League agents tried to kidnap players right from under their babysitters' noses. There were chases through airports and stations, hotel maids and relatives were paid off, and one sitter even arranged a player's wedding and went along on the honeymoon. The college boys were chased with such energy and imagination, in an underground web of spies and counterspies, agents and double agents, that a full account would set Agent 007 to licking his chops.

Leaders emerge from every great war. Two of the best fighters in the football war were Al Davis and Don Klosterman. Davis spirited Harry Schuh away from his NFL babysitter, and sent Harry, his wife, and their baby to Las Vegas. But Harry had left some slips of paper behind with "Sahara" scribbled on them, which were found when the NFL forces broke into his apartment. When the forces showed up at Las Vegas, Harry's entourage was put on a plane for Hawaii.

"It was afterward that his parents, urged by the NFL, filed kidnapping charges," said Davis. "Imagine kidnapping a guy 6′ 2″ who weighed 260."

Don Klosterman traced Otis Taylor to an NFL hideout through one of Taylor's numerous girl friends. Klosterman's agent, Lloyd Wells, sports editor of a Negro newspaper in Houston, sleuthed and greased palms till he found Taylor in a Dallas motel. Wells finally talked the babysitters into letting him take a picture of Taylor for his paper. Wells barely had a chance to talk to Taylor before the babysitters caught on. Wells tried tipping a bellboy ten bucks to get into Taylor's room, but the NFL babysitters had already tipped the bellboy to tell them if Wells hung around.

Not much later, when the babysitters urged Taylor to sign with the Eagles, they refused to sign his friend, who had come along with Otis. So Taylor and friend crawled out a back window, sprinted through an alley and flew into the car of a waiting Wells. Klosterman signed *both* of them at the Fort Worth Airport. The friend has yet to make it in football.

The owners finally got tired of paying through the nose for the flower of gridiron graduates and in May, 1966, after months of surreptitious negotiating, they effected a peace treaty between the leagues. The merger was the hastiest sort of shotgun affair and actually only settled one thing: there would be a common draft. The players' monies were immediately cut down fantastically. In 1966 Donny Anderson signed a $600,000 package; a year later he would have been lucky to get $60,000 . . . and if he didn't sign, his "choice" was Canada. In 1966 his choice was Houston, which offered $750,000.

The players, of course, looked on the merger and common draft the way an automobile buyer would look on a merger of Chrysler, Ford and General Motors.

"This year we're telling the draftees what we think they're worth in the way of a bonus, and salary," said Joe Kuharich, ex-coach of the Eagles. "Times have changed, y'know."

The All-Star Game

The All-Star game is a fact of football life. It happens every summer in Chicago between the Super Bowl winner and a team of college stars who have been graduated only a little more than a month. The game is played in Soldier Field, which holds 100,000 fans, but only 18,000 seats are between the zero yard lines. The All-Stars almost always lose. They have won nine times since the annual insanity was started in 1934.

"Anytime the All-Stars win," said Willie Davis politely, "it's on individual excellence." He forgot to mention luck.

The All-Star game is like a familiar wart that's just fine as long as it doesn't hurt, but let a player get injured and the hollering gets loud. The majority of pro football people, including coaches, players and rookies, don't want it, not only because of the injury risk but because the game throws training camp schedules out of whack. Training camp for a rookie is like a six-week course in pro-style football. Theories are developed on the blackboard in the morning and practiced on the field in the afternoon. The All-Star rookies report to their prospective camps three weeks late and some never catch up.

"Oh, they gave us a few blocking drills," said Larry Gagner when he reported to Pittsburgh Steelers after the All-Star game, "but nothing like you get in a pro training camp. We didn't get any weakside plays at all and you use a lot of that stuff in pro ball."

At Dallas, Tom Landry puts in 75% of his offense in the first week of camp, and less than two weeks after the veterans report the offense is set and the offensive half of the playbooks are full of notes. It is at just about this juncture that the rookies arrive from the All-Star game.

"The game is a definite handicap to the new man," says Weeb Ewbank. Weeb is speaking from a wealth of experience. After the Jets paid a $250,000 bonus for Linebacker-Defensive Lineman Carl McAdams, McAdams broke his ankle several days before the All-Star game in a sidewalk scuffle, allegedly with some bad Bears. ("How would you like it if someone threw beer in your face?" asked McAdams. "Beer stings my eyes.") Two years later McAdams had still not fully recovered from the complicated ankle injury. Weeb Ewbank also blames the failure of Henry King, a defensive back, on the All-Star interim.

When a blue-chip rookie just misses making his team, the All-Star game proves to be an expensive few minutes of glory. No player has ever refused to report to the All-Stars, but many players and owners have thought about it and a player could probably get away with it—simply by refusing. What could happen to him?

In the last few years since the merger, rookies have reported to the All-

Star camp before they signed contracts with the teams that drafted them. Afraid they might be injured and their pro team would refuse to offer them a contract, Adrian Young (Eagles) and Mike Taylor (Steelers) staged sit-in strikes during All-Star scrimmages and refused to do any hitting until they signed pro contracts. An injury would have cost them mightily. "Sit there and rot," said Norm Van Brocklin, who was All-Star coach at the time. Nine Stars sat out the game in 1969.

But all All-Stars are anxious to get to their respective teams and Van Brocklin sympathized with their position. "They feel that being in camp is just delaying their start in a new job," said Van Brocklin. "I told them that it was an honor to be chosen among the top fifty in the country, that the proceeds go to charity and in part into their own pension funds, and that playing in the game was part of being a man."

And so the game goes on, because it's tradition . . . because it is played for the *Chicago Tribune* Charities . . . because George Halas and some of the older owners started it and worked very hard to make it a success. In those early years pro football was fighting for its life (college football was the big thing) and the All-Star game gave a much-needed shot in the arm to the pros in the way of national publicity. Halas isn't the type to turn around and kick an old dog when he's down and no longer needed, especially an old dog he fashioned himself.

The newer owners are the loudest All-Star antagonists and are frequently bitter. The game is no tradition to them. When he ran the Jets, Sonny Werblin was most outspoken against, and Joe Namath was the first dropout. Werblin just kept Joe home.

Other owners agree with Werblin's point of view although in quieter fashion. Art Modell complained about the cost of taking his Browns to Chicago to play. He expected a loss of $35,000 on the game which included a full game's pay (1/14th of their salary) for veterans. On the other hand Modell is carpetbagger enough to fall in love with the All-Star game if it were to benefit him, instead of the *Tribune* Charities.

"We'd pack 'em in at our stadium in August," said Arthur.

And so, when voting time comes around, the various political aspects and pressures seem to iron themselves out and the owners renew the contracts which guarantee they will supply both teams for the game.

One of the milestones in the life of an All-Star is a scrimmage several days before the big game, with the Chicago Bears, whose training camp is nearby. It's the first contact for the college kids against pros and it always ends up the scene of fistfights and sullenly-muttered profanity. It is always very hot, humid and buggy, but it is usually more exciting than the All-Star Game itself.

"The All-Stars aren't used to the pros," said a Bear. "Good clean blocks surprised the All-Stars, and so did all the holding. They couldn't fight back with any sophistication so they used their fists and caught penalties."

Bubba Smith set an all-time All-Star record for fighting.

"He got hit a little harder and more often than he did at Michigan State," said the big, bad Bear, laughing.

But banged up beginnings are de rigueur. Both Mel Farr and Floyd Little suffered broken noses in their pro debuts. ("They like to hit the college boys twice as hard," said Little after the All-Star game. "Sort of to give them their introduction to pro football. Ray Nitschke gave me a fine introduction.")

Mike Garrett's baptism came at the hands, that is *arms*, of Ernie Ladd's "clothesline," a killjoy if there ever was one. Garrett's nose has been mashed and broken often, the first time when he was very young and rode his bike into a car, but Mike was incensed at the new nickname, "Elmer Fudd," which was bestowed upon him soon after arriving at Kansas City. Nicknames are the mildest sort of hazing and the bluest-chip rookies, like Garrett, are the least bothered. The perfect illustration is supersprinter Bob Hayes' arrival at the Cowboys. There was another rookie, also trying out at flanker, Pete Gent (pronounced as in *Gent*leman) already in residence, but Gent was a free agent and Hayes was the World's Fastest Human.

"When you're a rookie, especially a basketball player, you have to take what they give you," said Gent. "I had just one tiny spot on the dressing room bench, crowded in between two others. I got up for a minute and when I came back someone had brought Hayes into the dressing room and he had my spot on the bench. I had to dress in the training room by myself."

By the time the All-Stars join their teams the weeding-out process is well under way and half the rookies and free agents are already gone. Veterans, knowing that their collective bread and butter depends to some extent on new young talent, mix some doses of help in with their haze. One often hears how the veterans, individually, help the rookies, help to teach them how the game is played. This is fiction.

"When I first reported to camp I was an outsider, a rookie threatening somebody's job," said Gene Upshaw, one of the blue chips of his year—a guard who was described as looking like a sleek 6′ 5″, 270 pound fullback, lean, mean and strong. "It's kind of a lonely world for a while."

Unless his retirement is impending and/or he plans, like Sam Huff or Ray Berry, to go into coaching, no veteran helps to teach his own job to a rookie unless the rookie has no chance of ousting the veteran from his regular spot. Veteran quarterbacks are often described as helpful to rookie quarterbacks, but a quarterback's job is least likely to be jeopardized by a rookie.

When he was writing *Paper Lion* George Plimpton asked a veteran

Lion linebacker if he would help one of the rookie linebackers mend the errors of his ways: "You must be kidding," said the veteran. "They're after our jobs, boy."

"Veterans don't love rookies," Joe Schmidt told Plimpton. "It's as simple as that. You always read in the paper that some young rookie coming up says he couldn't've done it if it hadn't been for some ol'pappy-guy veteran who took him aside and said, 'No, son, up here we do it this way,' and then showing him. Well, that's crap, you'd better believe it. A regular, particularly an oldtimer, will do almost anything to hold onto his position, short of murder."

Training Camp

Training camp isn't the beginning of the physical grind. "When Joe starts getting ready he jumps rope until I think the house will fall down," says Mrs. Dru Robb whose 32-year-old husband is a defensive end with the St. Louis Cardinals. "Then in June he starts running, and takes the dog and kids with him to the high school track."

At Kansas City Buck Buchanan goes through a two month off-season training program he invented himself.

"I play tennis, run a mile each day and do what I call the 3,500," explained Buck. "The 3,500 is all the running exercises added up. I'd do twenty 100-yard sprints and then I'd do five 100s backward, then five 50s, then five 50s backward. I'd close out with five more 100s. Running backward not only improves agility but it builds up the leg muscles both ways. It almost killed me at first."

A bad knee case starts working out even earlier. The knee is the most uncooperative part of a football player, his Achilles' heel.

"Football is a game the knee can't stand," said Bear Trainer Ed Rozy, who made a study among players and discovered the three major causes of knee accidents are accidents in a game, varying playing fields (taller grass, harder dirt, mud), and either under or over conditioning. Underconditioning is obvious. Overconditioning is best illustrated by the former Eagles' Tackle Bob Brown whose daily weight lifting may develop his strength and power to such an extent that his knees just can't hold up, just can't absorb the punishment that the rest of Brown can take.

A doctor tells of the injury suffered when a 260-pound bulk moving at high speed hits a knee from the side: "It's like snapping a dry twig over your leg, and don't forget the bulks are getting bigger and faster all the time." The worst injuries come when a knee is hit and can't give, as when a cleat is anchored in the turf. The most popular solutions to the knee

Learning to block.

problem are adjusting or eliminating some cleats, or playing on synthetic turf which doesn't catch them.

Dr. Daniel Levinthal, who describes himself as "the oldest man in football next to George Halas," has been an orthopedic consultant for the Giants and Rams for many years. Dr. Levinthal says that the cumulative effect of even minor sports injuries results in an increased vulnerability to injury of athletes over 30. Which explains why so many players can hardly walk by the time they are 45 and are afflicted with all types of arthritis and bursitis. It's estimated that one football player in three must have knee surgery and that many are repeaters.

A player coming back from a knee operation faces a grind so laborious that if he isn't totally motivated he hasn't a chance. Tucker Frederickson at the Giants has made three comebacks and almost couldn't bring himself to go through the third program of strain, pain and tedious monotony.

A bad-knee case starts working out as soon as he can, at the end of the season or whenever he gets out of the cast. Ten years ago a ligament injury meant a loss of at least twelve months but players now sometimes walk in a day or two and play again in six weeks. Serious ligament injuries require a lengthy comeback period. The player is all the while hoping that strength and flexibility will return. Even after successful surgery full recovery is never guaranteed.

Detroit Lion Quarterback Bill Munson went through terrible torture after a freak accident. Bill went back to pass and was hit twice. The second, most lethal hit was by a player who had been a college teammate of Munson's and had also gone to the pros, to San Francisco. The ligaments in Bill's right knee were torn, and after the operation his leg was put in a cast for six weeks. Then followed a period on crutches.

"The first couple of months I spent four or five hours a day, six days a week, trying to get the knee back in shape," said Bill. "I worked with a trainer who had all the equipment I needed. I'd start in the weight room at 10 in the morning and work on the leg machines, which operate with pulleys. I progressed from about 20 pounds to about 110. I also lifted weighted boots, using three or four different exercises. Then I'd run a mile and a half in the morning, or play basketball. I can't tell you how monotonous it got toward the end, especially with no one else around. But I knew I had to do it."

In the early days of training camp, early in July, when only the rookies and free agents are required to be on hand, is often the time when a handful of post-operative knees are given their pre-fire trial. The veterans arrive two weeks later, although some of the oldest players who feel they need extra conditioning come with the rookies. For the veterans training camp is the worst kind of agony.

Just suppose you are 35 years old, a college professor with four kids, a nice home, and you make $50,000 per year. You have two extra-dry martinis before dinner, and you have weekends to yourself. You keep in shape playing handball three times a week.

July 15 comes and you report to your team's training camp. You are one of the three oldest players living in a monastic college dormitory that is hot as hell with no air conditioning, one little window, and an iron bed. (Most school dormitories aren't air-conditioned because the schools are closed for the summer. Ninety percent of teams choose small colleges to set up summer training camp.)

"It's like something out of Camelot," said Fay Moore, the artist, after her first week of watching the training grind. "The self-imposed discipline and training—the acknowledged ambition, to be considered worthy to join a crusade—really, football camps are a perfect attempt at that Holy Grail business."

"It isn't so bad for me," said Tom Keating, "because I'm only 25 and single, but some of these guys are 30 or more with families, and they're locked up like little kids for two months. It's ridiculous. But I suppose some players are like little kids, so they have to be treated that way."

Training camp begins with sixty to one hundred aspiring crusaders, ranging in age from 20 to 40, ranging in size from 5′ 4″, 145, to 7′, 350, and definitely ranging in talent. Coaches always want fewer players for greater efficiency but always end up with more. It's the gold digger in them. "It's just like the Army, I suppose," said Norm Van Brocklin. "You never saw a general yet who had enough men."

Training camp traditionally begins on a note of optimism, but the dull routine sets in soon enough. There are two workouts a day for the first month, two two-hour periods of most dreaded torture. For one or both sessions the players are in full regalia under the broiling sun, the temperature is usually 90-plus, humid, bees are buzzing about in the clover, and afternoon thundershowers bring a cooling but temporary halt to activity (except in California camps where of course it doesn't rain and just stays hot). At some camps in California and the Dolphins' in Florida they practice later in the afternoon because the heat is so terrible, but it's terrible and almost unbearable in every camp. Even though they gobble salt pills the players suffer from heat exhaustion and everyone is bitten by bugs. A particularly grueling practice by the sixty-odd Packers, who have always had the most grueling practices, results in a titanic weight loss of five hundred pounds. In one exhibition game several years ago the Redskins lost from eight to twenty-two pounds each. Since Vince Lombardi arrived at Washington that sort of thing no longer comes like a bolt out of the blue.

The daily schedule is chock full of activities. Breakfast is at 8 A.M. Lunch is at 12:30 and dinner is at 5:45 or 6 P.M. The food is surprisingly excellent. To jolly up their meals the Lions have huge signs on the wall which spell out an assortment of platitudes: "Let's All Stick Together," "Why

Are You Here?" "Success Comes From Constant Achievements," and reminders like "Drive Dedication Determination" or "Personal Pride." Those in the "over 30" age group find these slogans particularly unmotivating. Film and skull sessions follow dinner, beginning at 7:00 or 7:30. Bedtime is 11:00, and it's not unheard of that players are so worn out they get there early.

The headwork begins along with the physical labor. The coaches begin installing their offense the first day, play by play. When a player rookie or veteran comes to camp he is given his playbook, which is like an arithmetic workbook, only four times thicker, full of notes, play diagrams, and charts. He is fined $500 if he loses his playbook.

Buffalo's Coach John Rauch has a slightly different method of teaching. At his training camp both offense and defense begin by learning the same things, because Rauch believes that the defensive team should learn offense first to better be able to defend against enemy offenses when the season begins.

"They start us defensive players out to learn offense," said Ike Lassiter, his pupil when Rauch was at Oakland. "That has taught me more about football than I ever knew."

"We want the defense to see what can happen to them," said Rauch, once a quarterback at Georgia. "We teach them everything we know

Learning to tackle.

about offensive variations and hope that a situation never arises that the defense can't recognize or define in some way.

"For the first two days when the players get to camp we don't even work out on the field. We just meet three times a day and go over everything we've even seen of offense, ours and the other teams'. The defense and the offense go over it together."

Training camp for many of the players, the non-starters, is as fierce emotionally as it is physically from the strain of the weekly paring down. Many rookies suffer from homesickness and every year or so a few escape and bolt for home. By the end of August the squad must be down to fifty players, to forty by the first game. A training camp which begins with eighty players means forty broken hearts, and borderline cases live all the while in fear and tension. They become nervous wrecks sleeplessly waiting for that step in the hall, the knock at the door—nicknamed "The Turk" in many camps—that will mean goodbye.

Training camp lasts for nine weeks, six days a week, and players often can't arrange to see their families until the regular season begins in September. Camps are usually stuck out in the middle of nowhere with no distractions, e.g., the Cleveland Brown camp in Hiram, Ohio.

"The only light on after 9:00 is in the phone booth," said Trainer Leo Murphy. "If the players want a beer they have to drive a couple of miles out to a lounge in a big shopping center."

Every camp has a watering hole where the players rush to squeeze a few beers in between afternoon practice and dinner, or between evening sessions and bedtime. At Detroit the Lions meet at a nearby bowling alley. At Carlisle, Pennsylvania, the Redskins who hang out anywhere hang out at Sharkey's Far Side Inn, and next to the Steelers' camp in Latrobe (at St. Vincent College) there is The 19th Hole in the New Mission Inn.

There are lighter moments to break the tension. As a sort of hazing rookies are made to stand on their chairs during dinner and sing, to entertain. The Eagles once had a 30-year-old rookie soccer kicker—a Czech machinist from the Bronx named Jan Benus. When his turn came Jan broke into the Toreador song from *Carmen* and walked around the dining room serenading each table. *Carmen* was so popular Jan was called upon every night until he was cut.

Training camps go through fads. Bubba Smith won the water pistol championship at the Colts as a rookie. Fright masks were featured in George Plimpton's *Paper Lion*.

"George was very surprised to find so much humor and horsing around in a serious place like a training camp," said Carl Brettschneider, the original fright mask. "He told me himself what a big surprise that was. He didn't expect there to be any fun at all."

Many camps have rookie shows, vaudevillian extravaganzas with a notable lack of three-, five-, six-, and seven-letter words. They reach a peak of refinement and sophistication at Detroit and Baltimore. Billy Ray Smith has produced and directed the Colt rookie show for many years, and his dramatis personae appear almost in the altogether. Some veterans get struck by show biz and perform along with the rookies summer after summer. Billy Ray is one of these perennials who went so far as to move his family permanently to Westminster, Maryland, where the Colt training camp is located, to return to the scene of his extravagant crimes.

"Training camp is the worst part of football," says Miami Coach George Wilson. "For two straight months you eat every meal with the same guys. Sometimes you feel like you're married to them. You'll do anything to break up the monotony." Which is why, when he coached the Lions, George Wilson let George Plimpton join the camp to write his bestseller.

Just when everyone is about to go up the walls the exhibition games begin, one week after the All-Star game. "Our fellows have been working hard and I think they're anxious to go up against another team," said Bud Grant during his first camp as Minnesota's head coach. "We've been beating up on each other and you can only take so much of that. It's tough to keep pounding on a fellow who rooms next door and sits beside you at the dinner table. It's time that we try it against a real opponent."

The last word on training camps should come from Joe Namath's back-up Quarterback Babe Parilli, who is rapidly approaching his fortieth birthday. The Jet stop is Parilli's sixth pro team, which makes Babe into a Duncan Hines of training camps.

"My college camp was the toughest of all," said Babe, whose college coach at Kentucky was Bear Bryant. Parilli left Kentucky for the Packers in 1952.

"Bear's idea of training and practice," said Babe, "began every morning early. We had to be on the field in uniform at 6:30 A.M. and the first thing we had to do was tackle someone head on . . . so when you hit the ground all the dew opened your eyes. We called it the Eye-opener.

"The toughest was at Oakland under Eddie Erdelatz," continued Babe. "He made us run two miles at top speed. Paul Brown's was the most mental (at Cleveland). We had six or seven hours of class per day and we had to take notes. We always had a weekly quiz.

"When I was at Green Bay I had two coaches. Lombardi always yelled a lot, was always shouting. He stressed fundamentals and contact. Before he came, the coach used a reward system—like he would give us a reward for running. We had sprints and he gave beer to the winner. Well, Tobin Rote (another elder) and I were the fastest quarterbacks, so we arranged a dead heat in every race."

Over the years the Bear, Packer, and Ram players have not enjoyed the reputation of their stoic training camps. The Rams reached an all-time peak of misery under Coach Harland Svare, who required them to run a clocked mile when they first reported in July. Svare wanted his backs to run it in less than five minutes and the linemen to come as close as possible. Rosy Grier's time was 9:28.

Svare's successor at the Rams, George Allen, learned the ways of training camps when he was at the Bears. Allen never played football himself, and when he drives his players hard many of them believe he doesn't know what he's doing, not having experienced such misery first-hand. They are kidding themselves. He knows.

George Allen's practice scene includes the closest thing to a Greek chorus this side of Thermopylae. Led by a beachy blond benchsitter, Claude Crabb, the substitutes chant cryptic two-liners in unison, commenting on the general happenings. When they think a Ram practice should end they shout, "Hey, Hey, how long today." "Papaya, Papaya" and "Ice cream, Ice cream" also mean it's time to go; they refer to George Allen's two favorite foods, which he eats to calm his ulcer. Allen works twenty hours a day and has a smooth, almost rah-rah approach to the game. No coach is as thorough.

Training camp practice sessions look more unorganized than regular season practices because there are so many more players. Often players are standing around idle; not at Vince Lombardi's camp; not at George Allen's. Allen has every detail planned. The players are directed from one stage of his schedule to another by a horn George blows, and he is in constant contact with his assistant coaches by walkie-talkie.

Vince Lombardi doesn't need a walkie-talkie. The Redskins could be spread all over their training camp and if Vince yelled they would hear him in the White House.

Leonard Shecter described Vince Lombardi drilling the Packers: "The crazy men run in place, double time, as hard as they can, while Lombardi shouts at them in his irritating, nasal, steel-wool-rubbing-over-grate voice. 'C'mon, lift those legs, lift 'em. Higher, higher.'

"Over and over, always that raucous voice, nagging, urging, demanding ever more from rebelling lungs and legs. 'Move those damn legs. . . . Faster. Move those legs. Dammit, what the hell's the matter with you guys? You got a lot of dog in you. You're dogs, I tell you.' "

One of Vince's ex-pupils was watching a Baltimore practice and said it was unmistakeably not a Lombardi production.

"You wouldn't have to know anything to tell the difference," he said. "Anyone could tell just by looking. At the beginning of practice you could see everyone watching for Lombardi, looking to see where he was. When he came close by everybody would start to do push-ups or jump around, just keep moving—trying to look busy so he wouldn't yell at them. No one can yell like Lombardi. He has just about perfect lungs.

"Then, later on, as each group began working, from all around the field came the sound of him yelling at somebody, chewing 'em out. Sometimes he gave encouragement—he had to—but his system works. People play for

him out of fear. I guess a few older veterans cut up once in a while—at Green Bay Willie Wood used to—even though they know he'll chew them out too.

"And you'd better not fall, or get hurt. Lombardi's players don't get hurt, or if they do they just keep playing and practice even harder. *You'd better not miss a second game.*"

Menu

The Miami Dolphin management has never been exactly what you'd call solvent, and at their first training camp it seemed as if they were cutting corners in the chow department. The first Dolphin training camp was a pretty chaotic place anyway, and the team even switched sites halfway through, which didn't help the new team get off to a roaring start. The only roar was their stomachs growling.

The players complained that there wasn't enough food. The kitchen put a quota on fruit punch consumption and a minor rebellion broke out after chow mein was served for the umpteenth time in umpteen days. There wasn't even a Chinese cook to blame for such a whimsical staff of life.

In comparison, the second annual Dolphin training camp was an epicurean delight. At least a pound of steak or a 12-ounce cut of roast beef was guaranteed for dinner, with shrimp a Friday alternate, or both. Miami sports writers had to go into training after they left the Dolphins' training camp.

"One player took a dozen jumbo shrimp and the beef," said a waitress. "In a couple of minutes he was back for another dozen shrimp."

A typical day's menu:

BREAKFAST—Half dozen eggs any style, sausage, bacon, juice, toast, donuts, sweet rolls, hot and cold cereals, coffee, milk.

LUNCH—Three eight-ounce portions of baked ham, vegetables, potato, bread, salad with dressing, cottage cheese, dessert, tea, milk, lemonade, coffee.

DINNER—Five seven-ounce center-cut pork chops, vegetables, salad with dressing, cottage cheese, a dozen biscuits with butter and syrup, dessert, tea, milk, lemonade, coffee.

The Detroit Lion Trainer Kent Falb says the Lions eat breakfast like champions—three or four eggs any style, hot cereal, French toast and pancakes. The Lions' office picks up a daily tab of almost fifteen dollars per player, for food. When Roger Brown was requested to diet he skipped sour cream on his baked potato and ate small portions. The rationing saved the Lions a sizeable chunk of their food budget because Roger's appetite is healthier than average, even healthier than an average lion's. When Brown went to the Rams he had company to starve with, Rosy Grier. Grier was a creative dieter, with a different diet for each season. He tried starvation, dehydration and a special mental approach one summer when he tried to fool his stomach with small portions. It didn't work.

"Where the average man will pour himself six ounces of lemonade or iced tea," said Rosy, "I'll drink a whole pitcher. And I'll do it a few times." When Rosy used to feel a need for pastry he would eat a whole German chocolate cake, his favorite.

Almost every team has a fining system for overweight. One coach may charge $10 per pound per day. Another may fine by the week. George Halas has been known to charge $50 per pound and his scale is accurate to a quarter of an ounce. Some coaches set up a desired weight by a specific-date plan.

Weeb Ewbank has faced some weighty problems, not the least of which was Sherman Plunkett. Weeb even tried to get to Sherman through his wife.

"I told her I'd give her a thousand dollars if she could get him under three hundred," said Weeb. "You'd think she'd starve him to death for a thousand dollars, but we couldn't do business. Anytime I would walk by Plunkett in the dining room he would always look like he wasn't eating anything, but I'm sure he ran out for hamburgers after dinner." That was a slip of the tongue. Sherman never *ran* if he could help it.

Everyone has a Plunkett story. Weeb used to tease him about having to screw his helmet on because his neck was so big it came in threads. Sherman's weight was a closely-kept secret for years, because the Jet scale stopped at 300. A new scale brought to light some cold facts.

"What's Sherm at now?" asked Larry Eisenhauer before one Boston-New York game. "About four hundred twenty-five? We're bringing a long pin down. We're going to take it on the field and stick it in Sherm. Then we'll all stand back for the explosion."

Weeb has another fattie, Verlon Biggs. Biggs comes in every year "around" 300 and Weeb wants him "around" 270. The weighing-in is high comedy. The first problem is to *find* Biggs.

"Biggs is in the shower," said an assistant coach. "He wants to wash the dirt off him before he weighs in."

After he weighs, Biggs begins slimming, until the weekend, when he will gain on soul food, candied yams particularly.

"The stupid ass," says Weeb. "He put on four pounds last weekend."

"Biggs gains five pounds when he looks at a piece of bread," said one of Verlon's partners in crimes of consumption. "I gain ten when I drink a glass of milk."

Biggs argues with Weeb about money more than pounds. He is always holding out, always the last Jet to sign his contract. He waited until May after the Jets' Super Bowl victory before he signed his previous year's contract. When he signed he promised to stay thin. In 1966 he was the terror of the league. In 1967 he was slow and fat and spent part of the season on the bench. In the Super Bowl he improved, but he wasn't the Biggs of old. Worrying about Verlon and what he's eating gives Weeb something to do in the off season.

For every Plunkett and Biggs wishing they were littler there are skinnies wishing they were bigger and trying an endless assortment of fattening projects. Football players are food faddists. At the opposite end of the Jet defensive line is Gerry Philbin, who works with weights 365 days each year and follows a super-high protein diet laced with health foods.

"I weighed only 190 in college," says Philbin, "and now I'm about 242. I put soy beans and wheat germ in milk shakes, to complement my meals."

It's the little guys trying to gain weight and put on muscle who do the big eating, not the big guys like people think. The biggest ones have to be the most careful. They avoid milk like the plague. Football is full of superstitions about food. Because weight is so important myths galore surround players' eating habits. Some believe in protein before a game and eat three steaks for breakfast. Others eat little, or take vitamins and tonics. Some eat extra carbohydrates.

"Some pros eat a lot of honey before a game and by halftime they will throw it up," says the Jets' Dr. James Nicholas.

"Someone told them once that carbohydrates before a game gives energy."

Old-fashioned coaches believed that eliminating water during practice sessions was the best way to get in shape, to sweat it out. Vince Lombardi allows about six *pints* of water for the whole team during a normal Packer training camp practice, and if he sees a player drinking water he shouts, "Whatddaya want to get, a bellyache?" The AMA says that Vince is inviting heatstroke.

"Not drinking water during a game is another superstition," said Dr. Nicholas. "We encourage the Jets to drink up to half a cup, and to sip ice."

The latest fad during games is Gatorade, which is a soft drink composed of glucose, salts, and flavoring and which gets into the bloodstream quicker than water. Many teams keep cans of Gatorade at the sideline and say it makes them better "fourth quarter" clubs.

Gymnasium gossip has always decreed that swimming is bad for football players and coaches often have ruled against any swimming during the season. In the last few years more teams are swimming.

"Medically it's a fallacy that it's bad for football players to swim," said Dr. Nicholas. "At our training camp we allow all our boys to swim." The Boston Patriots swim at Andover and the Detroit Lions swim at their Cranbrook training camp, which has a pond right in the middle. Boston Cornerback John Charles is a particularly fast runner and swimming is his favorite hobby. He swam every day during training camp and said it helped develop his arms and shoulders.

It seems the no-swimming myth goes back to the days when baseball teams were first integrating motels on road trips. The team shared sleeping accommodations in the hotels and motels but the swimming pools were not ready to be integrated, and so to avoid a jam the coaches decided to use the age-old fallacy that it was bad for players to swim.

Trades

"I know now," said Sam Huff who was traded from New York to Washington when he was probably the most popular player on the Giants, the darling of New York, "that for eight years I was just a piece of equipment."

"Timmy Brown of the Baltimore Colts," said Timmy Brown, rolling the strange syllables around as if he were Demosthenes with a mouthful of sour grapes. "That still sounds funny to me." Timmy was a Philadelphia Eagle only moments before. "It was spite work."

Timmy's reaction was typical. When a player is traded his feelings and pride are hurt and he is shocked. He resents the trade, becomes hostile to his ex-team's management, and probably announces he won't report to the new team. Many players announce their retirement five minutes after they're traded.

As far as players are concerned most trades are bad. Players only ask to be traded when they don't get along with the coach, when they are second-string on one team and believe they would be first-string at another team, or when personal problems cause extenuating circumstances (a family crisis, sick child, or a conflict between off-season and in-season employment). More money is not the major factor behind looking for a new job. Salaries are pretty much the same all over.

"When you stay with a club for a while you have roots and respect," says George Allen, a trader. Some coaches like Weeb Ewbank hate the bartering bit but George Allen acts like David Harum on LSD and will trade anything that isn't nailed down. "When you move you're a newcomer, with no standing. Another thing, boys with troubles may beat them on another team but every team has problems and the boys soon find they just have a new, different set of troubles in strange surroundings. And moving a family, that's a very big problem, to get a new home and kids in new schools."

Off the field, in the players' personal lives, a trade can have disastrous results. Players so often seem to be traded at the most inopportune times —when they are involved in starting a new business, when their wives are about to have a baby, when the player is over thirty and has only a season or two left to play. The longer a player has been with his ex-team, of course, with the various members of his family establishing assorted ties in whatever city, the harder the trade is to take. Buying a house seems to be an omen that a trade is in the wind. Joe Robb, Danny Villanueva and Zeke Bratkowski all happened to be traded while they were moving their families into new homes. Earl Morrall was traded to the Colts three days after renting a house in Connecticut for the season.

Trades are almost always unexpected. For some strange reason many players who are Players' Association representatives or team captains, and, as such, respected leaders, are often traded, which you can make of what you will. Whatever the case, it is always surprising to the fans when a team leader is traded, and much more surprising to the team leader.

On the field players have little trouble adapting to the new team. Ostensibly the "new boy" was brought in to help them win and so the new team tries to help, not hinder, his progress. When the "new boy" is a veteran he probably has some speaking acquaintances if not college pals or good friends on the new team, and they help to ease the pangs. Some of the pangs.

"I hear they retired No. 22 at Baltimore," said Timmy Brown, "because it was Buddy Young's (famous Colt runner) number. But it's mine too. I've had it for nine years and it's part of me, my identity, like my name. I'd feel funny with another number, just like I feel funny being a Colt instead of an Eagle. How would John Unitas feel if he couldn't wear his number?" Timmy was given No. 2.

Tommy McDonald has been traded a number of times. The first time, he found out while he was driving along minding his own business. He heard a siren.

"I was flagged down by a cop in Philly and I thought, ugh, a ticket," said Tommy. "But he just stopped to tell me that it was on the radio that I'd been traded to Dallas!"

At Dallas he didn't work out; next stop, Los Angeles. Two years later George Allen called Tommy into his office during training camp. Tommy expected that Allen wanted to pass the time of the day, as Allen's custom is to chat privately with all his players as often as possible.

"I was looking for a big season with the Rams," said McDonald, "and the trade was such a big shock. Allen always was calling me in to ask my opinion of defensive backs who were waived, and when he called me in that's what I thought he wanted. He said I was traded, and I said, 'Tell me another one.' "

Tommy went to Atlanta, an expansion team in its second season and thus guaranteed by football law to lose for at least five years.

A year later, when McDonald was thirty-four, Atlanta Coach Norb Hecker had told Tommy he was using the younger receivers a lot because he knew what Tommy could do. So toward the end of training camp Tommy wasn't sweating the last cut. Came the call, to the office.

"When they called me in on the Monday before the season I figured it was for a speaking engagement or something," said McDonald, the optimist who doesn't seem to learn from experience. "The general manager was there and told me he didn't know how to tell me, but . . . 'Tell me what?' I asked him. 'We've asked waivers [fired] on you,' he said. So I laughed and said, 'What's this, Candid Camera?' But he didn't laugh."

15 Family

Football players' wives are just like dentists' wives or fishermen's wives. Some are good and some are bad. Some are smart and fun. Some are boring, unattractive, and humorless. You can't generalize about football players' wives any more easily than you can generalize about football players, or fishermen.

Now, after disclaiming any sameness within a wife group other than the husbands' occupation, it's possible to make a few precarious observations. Football players marry young. Lance Alworth may hold the record. He married his wife Betty when he was seventeen. She was fifteen. Players often marry their childhood sweethearts.

"I met Randy after a football game when we were juniors in high school," said Ruth Beverly, whose husband cornerbacks for the Jets. "Everybody said how great he was but I thought he was the biggest creep I ever met. But we got married in our senior year. He was the first guy I ever dated and I was the first girl he took out. It sounds corny but it's true."

In high school the football team is glorified and the players are the school heroes. They are also the tallest members of their class. They start going with girls before the other boys do because girls are chasing them. It's so easy. They get spoiled.

Things go along about the same way in college except that football practices and studying take more time than they did in high school, and the team spends half the football weekends playing away, sometimes thousands of miles away, for two or three days in a week. The players don't have as much free time for socializing and fun.

Highlight of Baltimore Colts' training camp is the rookie show.

The best players, the ones who end up playing professionally, have therefore been sought after and paid accordingly for their physical prowess all through adolescence—in high school with great summer jobs, letter sweaters and travel opportunities to "look over" colleges, and in college they are paid with scholarships, expense money, even cars. This means that a player's chief concern is with his body, keeping it in top physical condition. His interests are different from the other male students'. Football is a tough game. The players have been men for years. In college when they have time off it's not the same big deal it is for the others, whose pursuits seem frivolous. Football players don't want to abuse their bodies—their livelihood—with booze and all night parties; pep rallies and proms are kid stuff; intellectual pursuits and the library are not for them; neither are demonstrations, rioting and pot. Football players are a world apart. The ones who plan to play pro football don't even have to worry about choosing a career. They have an immediate, well-paid job waiting for them a month after graduation. So there they are—with few financial problems, a job waiting, but preoccupied with athletics and tired and hungry after practices. There is a perfect solution. They get married.

"Their situation is like a medical student's, you know, like an intern's," said LeRoy Neiman. "They don't have time for a normal social life. Basically they're very selfish. They don't want to stay up late at night, they have to stay in top shape, and the whole dating thing is a lot of trouble. Having a steady girl or getting married is a time-saver, it's an economy thing—to conserve energy and strength. All that extraneous stuff that goes with young girls can be very—uhhh—tiring."

Football players who don't marry their childhood sweethearts naturally enough marry girls they meet in the course of pursuing the football—stewardesses or Playboy bunnies. Jon Morris met his wife when she was first basewoman on the bunny softball team.

"She asked me what I did for a living and I said I was with the Patriots," said Jon. "She asked me what they were. She's from South America and since Boston's so political she thought they were some kind of crazy right-wing organization. She couldn't believe I got paid for *playing* football."

Many wives are interested in sports themselves. Mrs. Dave Herman met Dave, the Jet guard, when she arrived at the Jet training camp dining room looking for Gerry Philbin, who had played for her father, coach at the University of Buffalo. Dave said he was Philbin and the romance began. Mrs. Earl Morrall met her husband at a pool where she was swimming instructor. Mrs. Larry Garron and Mrs. Alex Webster played semi-pro basketball and Mrs. Jack Concannon played on an amateur basketball team. Mr. and Mrs. King Hill are "frog-giggers" (people who hunt frogs with a pronged spear). Lots of wives were cheerleaders in college. Mrs. Fran Tarkenton was a drum majorette. Fran, who spent halftime in the locker room, never saw her perform.

It's amazing that most football players have never taken a girl to a game. If players go, they play in it.

"I never want to," said Chuck Hurston. "Even if I weren't playing I'd be keyed up, just watching the game. If I took a girl and she asked me questions—even intelligent questions—well, I'm afraid I'd just get right up and walk out of the game."

And when you get married?

"I'm afraid it'd be the same. I'd just have to leave my wife home."

Six months later Chuck married a stewardess.

Some wives are interested in the mental aspects of football. After the game Joe Robb and his wife Dru play the games over and sometimes they study his St. Louis playbook together. Some wives aren't as knowledgeable. Lou Slaby married a non-fan. "She invited me over for Sunday afternoon dinner after our first date."

"Wives' responses are real different and it's interesting," said Caroline Curry. "But they always know what their husband is supposed to do and they know well enough if he's doing it or not. I watch Bill to see if he's making his plays because later we talk about it, especially the plays he was involved in."

Wives can help. "After a terrible defeat we were afraid the fellows would fall apart after that game, and we wanted them to know we were behind them," said Dru Robb. "We got up a why-not-win party and had play money scattered all around, and pretended it was championship money. We all wore football jerseys and it was lots of fun. Maybe it helped. A team has to jell and know it can win."

The biggest problem for the wives is moving their families for the season when their home is in a different town from their team.

"From training camp till the end of the season, that's half of the year away from my family, and we know that that's not going to change," said Don Perkins, who, when he isn't running for Dallas runs a department of the New Mexico government and hopes to make politics his career. "Our home is in Albuquerque. I have three children in school, and it's not fair to my family to move them around the country, and it's not fair for them to expect me to be away half of the time." Perkins retired.

The worst kind of move is after a trade, and the worst kind of trade is the one that happens in September.

"We had rented a house in Darien three days before the trade," said Jane Morrall, after Earl was traded from New York to Baltimore just before the regular season started. "All we could get was a small apartment —really cramped quarters with four children."

Some wives, especially when they have several older children who can't keep changing schools, don't move at all, in which case they are separated from their husbands from July until Christmas.

"We kept our family apart one year," said Jane Morrall. "I was expecting our second baby, Earl had just been traded to Detroit, and I didn't know anybody there. I went back home, to Iowa, and Earl lived in a hotel. We decided never again."

"Moving twice a year is my biggest worry," said Elaine Tarkenton, "that and Fran doing a good job for the team." Elaine sounds just like Fran when she talks about the bright side. "It's a good life money-wise, especially for a quarterback because the money comes early."

Elaine doesn't worry about injuries to Fran ("It would be a terrible life if I did"), but his mother does. Some wives worry, some don't. Of course, much depends upon the player's past performance.

"I never worry," says Ginny Concannon. "Jack always gets up. It's expected."

"I don't worry," said Olive Jordon, "but of course when there's a pileup I make sure Henry gets up."

"Injuries are a part of the game," said Joan Ryan. "The wives accept this. At home we don't discuss injuries, except, once, when we were worried Frank's career might be over. After that we consider anything else to be minor."

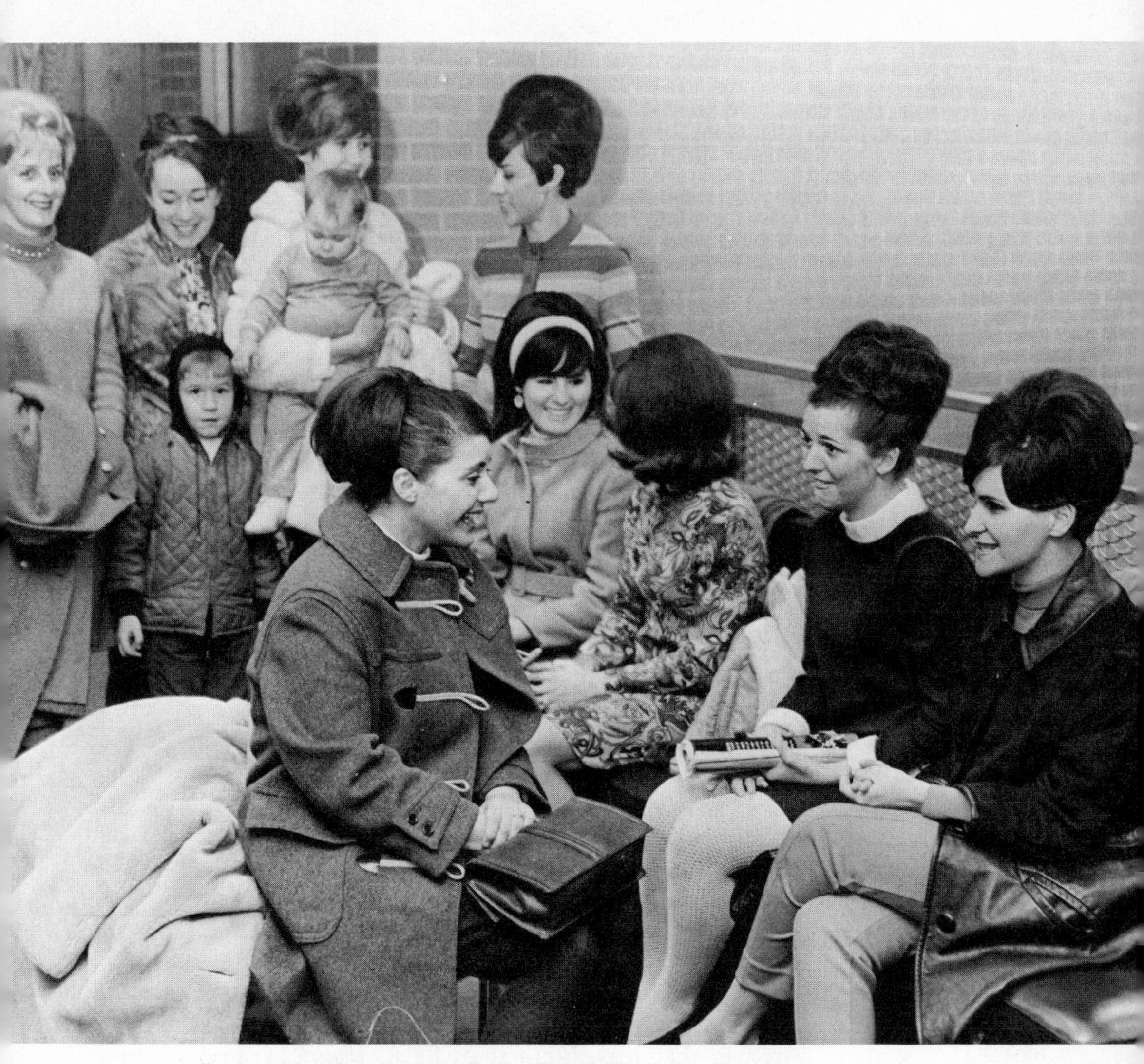

Packer "bouffant" circa Super Bowl II. (John Roemer)

"I always worry about Clancy getting hurt," said Andrea Williams. "He's been hurt so much."

"I hurt worse than he does," said Mrs. Don Perkins, whose husband is a minifullback and therefore susceptible to injury. "I don't understand why he has to get hurt more than anyone else? It's because of me that he's always talking about retirement, I think, but he's getting all broken up at an early age."

"I don't say that football is more hazardous than auto-race driving, but I know the physical and mental preparation is a strain," said Dru Robb. "We never go out the Friday or Saturday night before a game."

Which may be just as well, as Joe might not be the best company in the world. Anyway, half of the Saturday nights he's out of town for away games.

"Some of them," said a Viking wife, "get so cantankerous before their games their women are glad to get rid of them for the weekend."

Most players are moody and hard to live with during the season. "Before a game he's worked up like a couple of tanks," said Mrs. Bob Lilly. "When they lose he takes it like it's all his fault. It lasts five days."

"Randy is quiet now," said Ruth Beverly during the week before the Super Bowl, "but by Saturday and Sunday he'll be atrocious, a bear. If he gets any worse than he did before the Oakland title game I'll have to sleep by the ocean all night." Optimistically anticipating a trip to the Super Bowl in Miami, Ruth had taken swimming lessons in November.

"We were tough on our wives," said Dave Herman right after the Jet victory. "They were about to lock us in the basement and throw us raw meat once a day."

Mrs. Frank Ryan is most outspoken and for a couple of years wrote a column in the Cleveland *Plain Deal*er about life as the wife of the Cleveland quarterback. In one column she wrote that Dallas Quarterback Don Meredith was a loser and clearly implied that her husband agreed. The following Sunday when Cleveland played at Dallas a banner fluttered in the Cotton Bowl breeze: "Ryan is a Loser." The banner was correct, 26–14. Sillier things have motivated a winning effort. When Frank was Cleveland's No. 1 quarterback Mrs. Ryan said that much of what had been written about her husband's courage, playing with injuries, and pain, was overly dramatized. A year later when he was No. 2 she said he was at the peak of his performing ability and still first-string quarterback as far as she was concerned. Coaches often talk about the importance of a wife's contribution to a player's performance. Ryan's predecessor at Cleveland, Milt Plum, was always labeled a can't-take-charge quarterback, and there are those who feel that Mrs. Plum is partly to blame because she takes such complete charge of the Plums.

"The worst thing that can happen to a team is the wives becoming too close," said Larry Gardner, the Dallas trainer. "If they get too friendly they talk contract, and that can really destroy a team."

What Larry meant is that one wife will tell another wife that her husband makes so much money (more than he really makes). The other wife then tells her husband and asks why he isn't making as much as the other guy, or why isn't he making more. When the wives start talking this way everything gets all stirred up. The players rarely disclose their salaries to each other.

"One reason they never talk about salaries is because they're busy, and there isn't time," said Gardner. "The wives have plenty of time."

Many wives move in circles made up exclusively of players' wives. "Isn't that ridiculous," said Dorothy Unitas, who is surprisingly outspoken. Her husband John isn't. "They all go around together and they even go to the same beauty parlor." In scenes where the wives move in cliques the aura smacks hard of the eternal sorority sister.

It's a custom in Green Bay for the wives to gather in groups for TV parties to watch away games, and they always eat first because they're too keyed up to eat afterward. Everything about Green Bay is just a little bit different. The Packer wives know about football. The new wives often find the older ones to be intimidating. But after a few years' exposure the younger ones become football experts too.

Green Bay is the only pro football town with fewer than 100,000 residents, more taverns per capita than any city west of New York, and such a friendly atmosphere that children walk up to the Ken Bowman (Packers' center) household and ask Mrs. Bowman, "Can Kenny come out to play football?"

"I can't remember what I expected," said Caroline Curry after her and Bill's rookie season, "but I remember I was amazed it was such a little town. I came from Atlanta and even though I'd heard Green Bay was small I couldn't believe that such a small midwestern town could have such a big team. The people are wonderful, very proud of the team, and people in stores call all the wives by name. The team is the only thing."

The Packers expect to win. They buy their wives conditional Christmas presents that can be returned if they don't win the championship. After the second Super Bowl a Green Bay policeman said the celebrations were surprisingly moderate. "I guess people are kind of getting used to this winning stuff," he said.

Packer wives don't *hope*. They expect to win, and with all the trimmings. While Vince Lombardi was at Green Bay each Packer collected almost $100,000 in bonus money, over and above their regular season salary schedule, and the Packer wives were given championship presents which included mink stoles, color TV sets, dinner rings, and silver tea services. In the last few seasons, in October, the wives let it be known what they wanted for championship gifts. The tea service had to be lobbied through by the wife group that wanted it. All the wives thanked Vince for the mink stole.

The year 1961 was the year of the mink stole. "Those Packer wives knew what it was to win because they knew what it was to lose," wrote Vince. "I was overwhelmed with thanks."

In an article written for *Look*, for $30,000, Vincent said he believed that wives are very important to the success of a team. Then he practically called them a bunch of forty thieves, complaining that "peripheral passiveness" seemed to be invading his ball club, as indicated by the fact that thirty-seven Packer wives didn't thank him for their silver tea service.

Caroline Curry was one of the thirty-seven.

"When I read about that in *Look* Magazine I felt real bad," she said, "but we had already been traded (to Baltimore) and I didn't get it for about six months. The year before I remember I was getting a dinner ring (twenty thank-you notes, by Vincent's count), but there wasn't any card in it and I didn't know exactly who to thank. I remember I saw Coach Lombardi later at a gathering and I told him how I appreciated the gift but that, actually, I didn't really know who to thank, and he said, 'Why, you thank me.'"

Now that Vincent is gone the Green Bay pawn shop probably has a window full of identical rings and tea services.

16 Bachelors

Football players live up to their reputations, or live down them, in fine style. The best, most dramatic lore accumulates from tales of the road, dramas set in hotels and motels, or, perhaps, tales from training camps. Ernie Koy, the Giants' fullback, was voted one of six Bachelors of the Year in a contest put on by Hai Karate cologne. Ernie said that bachelors were glamorous because they have freedom. "Married men have to clear a whole lot of channels before they get to go out." Married football players' jobs take them all the way out of town.

Actually, with about half a dozen bon vivant exceptions, it isn't the players themselves who are the real stars of the road shows but the brilliant array of females they attract. An array of gaudy camp followers shows up at hotels, bars and restaurants where football players hang out. Like clockwork the barracudas show up, and they are expected.

"Some of them are great looking," said Trainer Bill Bates, who goes out of his way to extend Patriot hospitality to females who happen by, "and some of them are really tough. Basketball players call them stadium lizards but we call them barracudas. You can spot them a mile away." You don't always have to. Often the quarterback runs plays toward the infinite variety of spectators so the players can check things out for themselves from close up.

Football player collectors often get started collecting autographs. All visiting teams recognize familiar faces after a few years of playing in the same towns. One girl in New York is as expected a part of the scenery as the cemeteries on the road in from the airport. "She is everywhere," said Joe Pollack, the St. Louis drumbeater. "She is always around, outside the hotel, in the lobby, and outside the dressing room before and after the game. She must have some autograph collection."

Camp followers come and go at all hours, up and down elevators and hotel halls, and stories abound about the clever tactics and delicate nuances of espionage used by these avid fans. One owner's wife made a trip with the team and stayed in the same motel as the players. She went back to her room for something before dinner and was surprised to find two young ladies hiding under both bedcovers.

"Were they ever surprised," she said, "and disappointed."

The Los Angeles Rams' training camp was once at a school where a female on the faculty had a penchant for Rams. She had a montage on her wall of Ram pictures and autographs, and before the season began she would brag that she could tell which players would have the best seasons, basing her predictions on the relative aggressiveness of the various players. She once proclaimed she could predict which of three contenders would end up the starting quarterback. She did, and ahead of the coaches, too.

If the girls are ingenious about getting in—through kitchens, climbing in windows, bribing employees—the players are Einsteins about getting out. Weeb Ewbank is a stickler on curfews. When Weeb coached at Baltimore, one midnight Alex Hawkins left his window and started letting himself down from ledge to ledge like a human fly, with his nose pressed against the hotel. Just as he reached the ground there was Weeb.

"I'd just been traded from Pittsburgh," said Jimmy Orr, "and the Steelers' reputation was well known. I was very close to Bobby Layne and I guess Weeb was worried. We went on our first road trip, and I read the paper in the lobby, and Weeb was watching, so I said I was tired and went up to bed. Well, about an hour later I came down, real quiet, and very inobtrusively walked across the lobby and out the front door and there was Weeb. 'Where do you think you're going, Jim,' he asked, so I said I wanted some fresh air and thought I'd go for a walk. Weeb said, 'Good idea, I'll go with you,' and we walked and walked . . . until it was time we had to be in."

"Jimmy Orr was a sharp one," said Weeb. "Very tricky."

One player was sneaking back into the hotel at 7 A.M. and at the elevator he ran into two coaches and several players who were on their way to Mass. He got himself caught up with them and went along. Another time some coaches were alert to shenanigans and at 3 A.M. a player sneaked down a hotel fire escape only to find two coaches at the bottom. "I am on my way to meet my mother and father," he explained.

Coaches have to stay up nights to keep ahead of their players. Young coaches, just removed from playing themselves, are the toughest and know all the tricks. When Dick Nolan became coach at San Francisco his first move was to change training camp locations, from next to San Francisco to two hours away—just far enough to make temptation most inconvenient.

There was a night in Chicago when ex-Ram coach Joe Stydahar decided to intercept telephone calls for his players at the hotel switchboard. A young lady telephoned very late and didn't know she was talking to the coach. "What time are the Rams leaving town in the morning?" she asked. "I have one of the players here asleep on my couch and I want to make sure he gets to the airport on time."

Stydahar blew his top. "Tell me the name of the bum," he shouted, "and where to send the ambulance. He'll need one."

The San Diego situation is unique because every visiting team stays at the Stardust Motel and Country Club instead of spreading themselves around a variety of hostelries. The Stardust has an adjoining golf course and practice field, several cocktail lounges, and three swimming pools which makes it easy to keep the players playing without going out. The Stardust employees voted the Patriots their favorite team and said that the team from frugal old Boston had the best tippers.

After Detroit made its first and only visit the waitresses said the Lions were the wildest team ever to stop there. "Very fresh and rambunctious," they said. "The Lions made more smart remarks in the dining room than all the others put together." The Lions, on the other hand, grew fond of the Stardust, and let off steam by jumping off the roof into the pool when they weren't harrassing the waitresses.

From time to time there are beauty contests to name a "Miss" of such-and-such-a-team. What ranks as a supreme act of charity by one Miss was a hospital visit to an injured player. That same day the player was visited by three coaches. As the coaches stood around inquiring after the player's health, and chatting, suddenly there came a muffled cough and out from under the covers emerged "Miss——", who with head high walked into the bathroom, to fetch her clothes.

We Came To Play

A typical football bachelor goes up to his team's ticket manager the day before a home game and asks for a favor.

"Can you help me out?" he asks. "I need six tickets, scattered."

"My wife has some friends who want to be fixed up with football players," said Ben Davidson. "They want me to get them dates with Raiders, but we decided not to. Kathy tells them no. You know how football players are, and to fix them up with some girl—who might be kind of young and naïve—well, it just wouldn't work. It would be too much responsibility."

He sounded like an old square. "I don't care if I sound like an old square," said The Mustache.

"Listen, it's tough being a bachelor, with all the wives around," said Mike Pyle. "Anytime I take a date where there are any Bear wives around they just look the girl over—like up and down, the real treatment. Then later they say she wasn't pretty enough, or something like that.

"When you meet a girl, and she finds out you play pro football, it doesn't matter what you say, she won't believe you aren't married. I meet a girl someplace and ask her out and she says, 'All football players are married.' That's it. What could have ever led to such a situation?" Mike was a Bear bachelor for seven years before the bells tolled.

The trouble with most eligible bachelor lists is that they are subject to change without notice. A person would have to be touched in the head to attempt such a task. My dispensation must come from your realization that such a list is a day-to-day affair.

Donny Anderson: Packer halfback who wears black silk underwear and said, after Super Bowl II: "I like Florida. I just might not get home until next training camp."

Anderson is goodlooking and confident but he gets needled in the newspapers for his biggest bonus ever ($600,000) and his failure to turn into a new Paul Hornung overnight. Donny likes to sketch birds on his Texas ranch. Paul Hornung never sat still long enough to write his name.

"I'm sure people are wondering 'What's this guy like?' " says Anderson, hitting the nail smack on the head. "I like to swing, but I don't think it's anyone's business what I do with my own time."

All the Packers list their phone numbers, and Donny says he gets a number of calls from girls looking for a date but he doesn't go. "I doubt if any of them are goodlooking, and any broad who would do that has no class anyway."

Mike Curtis: Baltimore's left linebacker was seen last spring with the same girl for the second time, which set a record.

Pat Fischer: Washington cornerback on the subject of marriage, "I'd rather go through life wanting something I didn't have instead of having something I didn't want."

Marv Fleming: Green Bay's tight end is an ardent bowhunter who enjoys being called Marvelous Marv. "I would say that right now I'm the most eligible bachelor on the team," said Marv, "but I'm looking."

Tucker Frederickson: Giant halfback who lives in what used to be called, politically, New York's silk-stocking district. It's now called Stew Country after the jet age. Neighbors ring Tucker's bell and ask to borrow a cup of sugar. "I don't have much sugar but I don't run 'em off when they come," he said. "It's a good building with more than enough girls. You ought to go over there. It's hard to get to sleep." During the season Tucker doesn't go out much after Wednesday.

Tucker came to New York the same year as Namath. The Giants hoped that Frederickson publicity would capture part of Namath's limelight.

"I kind of snuck into New York," said Frederickson, who is a friend of Broadway Joe. "It seems like just about everybody was watching Namath."

(The sports world has an interesting theory to explain why New York teams seem to play better at home—whether in football or baseball or whatever sport. Simply, the New York players are used to the pace and excitement, take it in stride, and probably spend more nights before games at home. The visiting football teams come to New York at the most once each season, and have to see the sights, get around the town, and dig the whole scene in one afternoon and one curfewed night. While the visitors are rushing around, the home team players are casually settling down for bed. Theoretically this situation should be reflected in the morrow's score.)

Art Graham: Boston flanker who once planned to become a priest. "Boston girls are too possessive," he says. "Some girls have to keep their dates by their side every minute. I have to circulate at a party."

Paul Hornung: Green Bay's Original Golden Boy, now Chicago sportscaster, who was saying a decade ago, "I think I would rather score a touchdown on a particular day than make love to the prettiest girl in the United States."

John Love: Washington halfback, John is the best-named bachelor of all. He began his career by running the season's opening kickoff back 93 yards for a touchdown. John couldn't get over Washington ("Wait till I tell the fellows back in Texas about these glass elevators") and Washington couldn't get over him. A banner popped up in D.C. Stadium which read: "Pray For Love. You Can Get Sex Anytime."

"It's a lot, lot different here in Washington," said John, who is from a tiny town, Marlin. "Heck, 80% of the people live in apartments. I'll make my home in Texas and when I get married it'll be to a Texas girl. I can understand what she's saying."

Bill Malinchak: Detroit flanker, nicknamed Ballpark by teammates, after the hot dog. Bill is the team clothes horse and one of the few unmarried Lions. The *only* bachelor Lion to appear in *Paper Lion* movie in which Bill bared his bottom to the world in a dressing room scene. He is pro football's first technicolor nudie.

Bill and a friend, Wally Hilgenberg, once took a post-season tour through the midwest, just visiting. They loaded their car with two hundred souvenir Lion footballs (free) and two hundred Lion rugs ($600) and would lay one of each on the front seat of their car when they parked —in front of sorority houses, bars, or wherever.

"It's funny but every girl we met wanted a rug and a football," said Bill, "and if we acted like we were down to the last two they wanted them worse. Six hundred dollars is a big investment, but I'd say there was

Chuck Walker doesn't look so "eligible" in this pose.

a lot of return. The expense was definitely worth it." Wally later married a rug recipient.

Bill Mathis: Most Eligible Jet. The trouble with Joe Namath, romance-wise, he's a quarterback. A good quarterback cannot be a good bachelor. By definition good quarterbacks are hardnosed, the take-charge type; the best bachelors are softnosed and loveable, like Bill Mathis.

Bill comes from a small town in Georgia where he says they don't need zip codes.

"I thought all of New York was Times Square," said Mathis, when he first came to play in New York. "I was really frightened. I had been here once as an eighth-grader with my parents, but that was it. I wouldn't get in the subway alone and always had to ride with one of the other guys."

After ten years in New York things have changed. Bill sometimes shares Namath's Miami pad, he lives in an East Side building largely populated by airline stewardesses, works near Wall Street, rides in limousines, and would rather eat Steak Diane at El Morocco than football-style sirloin.

"Bill has sure come a long way from animal husbandry courses at Clemson," says Jimmy Orr, who stays with Mathis when he has business in New York.

Curtis McClinton: The Solid Citizen. "Everything I do is planned," says Curtis, kidding us not. He is the director of a bank, has an apartment construction project in the works, and does some radio and TV work around Kansas City. Curtis is sophisticated and substantial, like a good fullback should be.

Curt Merz: Kansas City guard and arm-wrestling champion. Merz understands German and translates during old World War II movies and would like to study German.

Buckey Pope: former Los Angeles flanker. "There are only fourteen games a year. I figure I can be ready that often, so after Wednesday I never date."

Chuck Walker: Quiet, religious, polite and blond defensive lineman at St. Louis. In his sophomore year in high school Chuck was marching with the band at halftime, blowing a horn. In his junior year he was spending halftime with his teammates in the locker room, and has been ever since. He still plays the trumpet and likes pop music "but in a classical style." Chuck is totally non-violent, except when tackling or driving a car. He hotrods his Pontiac around as if it were a quarterback.

"I don't know what the hell it is about Walker," said Larry Wilson, "but he knocks the quarterback flat and then he turns around and says he's sorry. He apologizes or says 'excuse me' or something like that."

In a game against Washington he got to Sonny Jurgensen several times. "God damn it," yelled Sonny after Chuck had smashed him several times, "will you quit apologizing. Knock me down but shut up about it."

"When I started to play for the Cardinals it made my mother a hero in her bridge club," said Chuck. "Last year my mother went to four games, and my grandmother went to her first ball game ever. She is eighty-six and was all huddled up and with a black scarf all tied around her."

Two Swingers

Philadelphia has been described by every writer from Ben Franklin to John O'Hara, but never more poetically than by baseball player Bo Belinsky: "Philly," said Bo, "is a town where you can see *Ramar* four times on the late show. Soon as I pop into the hotel I flip on the TV and catch the jungle scene. I say—Hey, Ramar, I'm back in town. The best thing about Philly is Sunday—you can go to New Jersey and swing."

Timmy Brown, the original stagestruck kid, started on the road to Philly, and the Eagles, from tiny Ball State College in Muncie, Ind. Legend has it Timmy entered Ball State from an orphan's home. "My mother chides me about that orphan bit," says Timmy. "She says, 'You're no orphan.' I say, 'Well, next time don't send me to a children's home.' "

Timmy is a handsome halfback, the greatest all-around offensive back in Eagle history. He has four sisters, one younger, and an older brother who is a successful businessman. His mother and all the rest of the relatives live in Los Angeles. Timmy went to Ball State on a basketball scholarship, straight from the children's home. His scholarship was only for tuition, and at college he worked at least six hours a day for dollars.

"I've only been in love once," said Timmy. "For three years in Muncie I went with a girl—a white girl—who was Miss Muncie and Miss Pepsi Cola. I still drink more Pepsi Cola than water, beer, milk—you name it."

Timmy made the move from Muncie to the Eagles without serious problems. Halfway through his Eagle career Timmy cut his first record. "Dionne Warwick and her sister did the background for me," he said. "They were unknown kids from New Jersey and I told them they ought to try hard and they'd make it."

Timmy began commuting to New York from Philadelphia on Mondays during the football season and took voice and speech (diction) lessons at the Herbert Berghoff School. He studied hard to get over beginner's shyness and stage fright.

"I'm so much more relaxed and better when I sing at home, in my own basement," said Timmy. His basement was the Philadelphia equivalent of Joe Namath's New York pad, with people of all sorts coming and going at all hours. "My basement is full of records, pop, drinks, TV and people, and when I sing I dance with the microphone. I'm best in my basement. If I could do as good in a nightclub, or on a record, as I do there it would be great. I like dancing more than singing, but doing both, with the mike, it gives a style—like Frank Sinatra or somebody."

Timmy went with Diana Ross, supreme Supreme, for almost a year. "She flew to see me in Philly, and after the Detroit game she visited me in the hospital," said Timmy. "I had about eight other chicks there and they all got friendly," he laughed, "real friendly."

Timmy had a long off-and-on romance with Dionne Warwick, who seemed to go for Timmy, but both said it was platonic and they were just good friends. His social life in Philadelphia was football-average.

"I never go out Friday or Saturday," he said. "And I don't like to go out for dinner much, on dates. I've eaten out so much. I'm a great cook, cake and steak.

Timmy is a perfect example of a football player on the road. In the first half hour after the Eagles arrive at their hotel Timmy gets several calls from strangers—female strangers.

"I try to set aside an hour when I take calls," grinned Timmy, who has a beautiful store smile. "I get more calls in Miami than most places. I ask them their measurements. If they say 38–26–40. I tell them to call back in an hour or so. Something better might come along in the meantime." The last time he was in Miami with the Eagles, Timmy invited the couple who run his alma mater, the Muncie children's home, down for a seaside vacation. He is The Graduate, and goes back occasionally to visit.

Timmy loved Philadelphia and the Eagles and planned to retire there. Instead he left under rather unpleasant circumstances and was traded to Baltimore. During his last two seasons at Philadelphia, Timmy was bothered with muscle pulls in his thigh. His coach didn't believe him.

"Walking or dancing isn't playing football," said Timmy. "People see me walking down the street and don't believe I'm really hurt. I could run straight ahead as fast as anyone on the team, but cutting and veering, that's something else. Hamstrings are the most annoying injury."

After he didn't play for several games the Brown Case became a cause célèbre. "The first thing people say is that my entertainment is involved. It doesn't make sense. If I went to a game dressed like this (sharp blazer, slacks, white silk turtleneck shirt) they'd yell 'Hey, Hollywood' and 'Pretty Boy' at me." The pressure became so intense that Timmy had to give up his weekly commute to New York City.

After the trade to Baltimore Timmy threatened to retire, and spent a month in Los Angeles trying to make it in a TV series. He's appeared in several segments of existing series and once was mentioned for Tarzan. As he made the rounds of filmdom he also worked in visits to the various California training camps, just to watch.

"But I got this feeling in the pit of my stomach that told me I missed the game more than I thought," he said, "so I decided to come back."

He came back to Baltimore and in a less than exciting season personally

Timmy Brown and Joe Namath with the Supremes.

he went all the way to the Super Bowl with the Colts. Timmy was slow getting into shape, and when he did he was bothered by several minor but nagging injuries. Financially he was well off.

"Baltimore is a blah city, not my bag," said Timmy who was living in a motel near the ghetto area, eating out, and importing chicks from New York or Philadelphia on the few occasions when he did go out. "Living here is kind of a weird nightmare. The only way to really make it in Baltimore is to wear a bib, coveralls and put a straw in my mouth."

Timmy doesn't make friends easily and never really got acquainted in Baltimore. He is sensitive, moody, rather shy, sentimental and a loner. Years ago, when the Dolphins were a brand-new team, their pretended Owner Danny Thomas offered Timmy a $50,000 bonus to quit the Eagles and become a Dolphin. Thomas also promised to boost his movie career but Timmy refused, feeling loyalty to the Eagles.

Timmy's big problem was choosing between his career and football. Things were beginning to break for him and he wanted to be in Los Angeles where he could do something about it. Instead he was on the bench, at Baltimore, and not enjoying it. "I'd give away my full share of this game," said Timmy before the Super Bowl (his full share would be either $15,000 for winning or $7,500 for losing), "if I were offered the chance to play the whole game in exchange for money."

That feeling in the pit of his stomach will probably become a chronic ailment every September.

The beginning and the end of football bachelors is Joe Namath, the Jets' star quarterback. The richest player in his league, Joe signed a new half-a-million dollar contract a year ago and he lives in places where it's happening. He spends autumn in New York, winter in Miami Beach, spring at the Kentucky Derby, and heaven knows where in summer. Namath cuts a meaner swath through feminine fandom than the Golden Boy from Green Bay ever dreamed, and he's a bigger spender ("It isn't that I think I have enough money," he said, "but I'll admit the way I spend it there probably isn't enough around to keep me going").

Joe Namath is the star. He has style. He lives like Jean Harlow. The décor of his New York pad is legendary—long, hairy white llama rug, marble this, fur that, a bar at one end, a wall with mirrors, a huge oval bed and green satin sheets. Definitely overrated, Joe's chic pad is a one-bedroom apartment and a legend of bad taste.

Namath came from Beaver Falls, Pa., a dull-looking steel town along the Pennsylvania Turnpike in northwest Pennsylvania. Beaver Falls is coal mines and Namath was Beaver Falls' star high school athlete—both football and basketball—and pool hall star as well. He won a scholarship to Alabama where he became Coach Bear Bryant's right arm and changed his name to Joe Willie.

At Alabama the football team has its own modern dormitory. The Bear had it built specially, with television and wall-to-wall carpeting. Bryant's philosophy is to tell his team they're the greatest, over and over, until they are, and for four years he told Namath he was the greatest quarterback in the country, until he was.

Number One in Beaver Falls, Number One in Tuscaloosa, Ala., Namath arrived in New York a shy, shaved, unsophisticated, cocky kid sporting a short college haircut. After four years he had accumulated a decorator, an

Irish setter named Faro (Joe calls him "my son"), three major knee operations, quantities of hair, a wild reputation, a closetful of garish velour and corduroy, and experience—off the field with "broads and booze" and on the field in the school of hard knocks ("Why don't they tell it like it is, tell kids that the real image of football is brutality?").

As a rookie Namath was naïve and green. "I don't know what love is, I don't guess," he said. "New York girls come across pretty phony. They've been through a lot and they aren't interested in you as a person. They stay prettier in the South because a lot of them don't have to work.

"I don't even have a steady girl friend. Too many pretty girls in this world. Why, I'd rather fight in Vietnam than get married."

Things immediately began changing. Namath became the Sinatra of the gridiron, the leader of his rat pack. One of the pack's girls was only too happy to keep his pad clean while Namath had to keep changing his unlisted phone number. Like other stars Joe doesn't have many normal public dates. Girls find him.

"I don't know anybody," he claimed. "I, like, run into people." Girls come over to his apartment. When Joe goes out it's with guys.

"Joe's nightlifing and playboying are so much overdone," said Sonny Werblin, the former owner of the Jets. "He's not even a drinker. He's affable, twenty-four, and likes a little fun. You can't blame him. He has a lot of nervous tension." At one time Mr. and Mrs. Werblin were promoting a romance for Joe with the daughter of a friend, but nothing happened.

Namath seems the most ill at ease when he is out in the public eye surrounded by wealthy, upper-crust society. He is most uncomfortable, as are other players, in Toots Shor and other sports restaurants where all the pseudo-jocks hang out to stargaze. Of course everywhere that Namath goes people stargaze. Sonny Werblin, who was responsible for signing Namath and negotiating his $400,000 contract, said it the day he brought Namath into New York: "He has the presence of a star. You know how a real star lights up a room when he comes in. Joe has that quality."

"Sure he likes girls," says Coach Ewbank. "I'd be worried about him if he didn't. Joe is comfortable with girls and he likes to stay up late, but he's not a wild kid. He's not a rounder, not a boozer.

"You take a kid who never had a dime and give him all that money and suddenly he's famous. Certain people are trying to exploit him, to use him. Everything is happening awfully fast and the kid is trying to keep his balance. I think he handled himself remarkably well."

Considering the events of Namath's twenty-five years he did handle himself well. There's no telling where he picked up what sanity he has, actually, because the conglomerate of influences that were exerted on him could as easily have resulted in a total emotional wreck. The product of a broken home, Namath is the youngest of five children. His mother, Rose Szolnoki, remarried, but Namath's three older brothers (John, 37, is a career Army officer; Frank, 31, sells insurance; Robert, 34, lives in Beaver Falls) brought him along and taught him to play ball well enough that he was offered fifty college scholarships plus a $50,000 bonus to sign with the Chicago Cubs baseball team. His father, John, a 61-year-old sport given to Joe-college straw hats and hail fellow-well-met handshakes, still works the graveyard shift as a roller on a hot mill for a Beaver Falls steel company.

Considering that he plunged from Beaver Falls into Bear Bryant's plush pasture at Alabama and then directly into glamorous New York, Namath hardly had an inkling of the postures and graces proper for what was to come when Sonny Werblin wore him around town at all the nicest, most expensive watering holes. His values were changing as fast as his girlfriends and there wasn't much direction—not from his family, not from Werblin, who at that time was completely involved with building his star, and certainly not from his coach, Weeb Ewbank. Except for his mother the person who has exerted the most influence on Joe is Bear Bryant, who once kicked him off the Alabama team for drinking. After the Bear is Sonny Werblin, who has remained close to Joe even though no longer connected with the Jets ("He's like a fourth son in our family," says Werblin).

Namath seems devoted to his family. He's always helping them and they're always calling on him. He gives money to his father and stepfather and bought a bar for a brother—who went broke. A brother has had an expensive illness. Namath and his mother are still extremely close and he is very considerate of her. He loves her Hungarian dishes ("stuffed cabbage, that's out of sight, man") and makes every effort to get home for regular visits. He wanted to keep the news of his second knee operation away from his mother until after Christmas, so as not to spoil her holiday, but word leaked out into headlines.

"I'm damn mad," said Joe. "I asked them not to say anything until after Christmas so my mother wouldn't worry."

After his second operation things started to look up. The previous season he had thrown 27 interceptions. His bad knees made him immobile and defenses, knowing he couldn't run, rushed him and he threw—for touchdowns *and* interceptions. He played every game in pain, sometimes almost unbearable. But after the second operation Namath's legs seemed stronger, he was moving around better and the Jets were winning more. Namath himself seemed to be growing up. Goodness knows how, or from where, but Joe was acquiring poise, a good-humored wit, and some class. Halfway through his third season he even fell into a new wardrobe.

"This is the new Namath, the Aubrey Beardsley fop," said LeRoy Neiman, who had been drawing Namath for several seasons. "He is changing, acquiring taste, finding himself. A lot more is going to happen to him. He's the first real playboy athlete of this generation. The pad, the clothes, the whole thing. Forget Paul Hornung."

Namath wasn't goodlooking when he arrived on The Scene. He is now. He's dark, intense, almost an El Córdobes. Knees or not, he is a magnificent athlete, powerfully built, and his bad, stoop-shouldered posture is identical to the high-fashion slouch. On television guest spots he sidles into a chair slumping in the best Greta Garbo tradition, the self-conscious hero. His new look is continental—vented jacket, turtleneck, narrow pants —a long way from Beaver Falls except that Joe *never* wears socks. Dressed up to receive an important award in New York there he was, splendid but sockless. Even when he plays golf he goes sockless. "If we win the Super Bowl," said Baltimore's Jimmy Orr, "the first thing I'm going to do is buy Namath some socks. We played in a golf tournament and he went into this deep trap with no socks on." Namath could be a good golfer if he worked at it.

Namath has remained surprisingly unspoiled, although his fame allows him extravagances—moods, surly attitudes, a loud mouth and dispensations from many rules. It's almost frightening to watch him walk into the bar at Miami's Palm Bay Club and hear people whisper a hushed "Namath!"—not *Joe* Namath, or Joe. Always just "Namath!" You can see him react, and feel called upon to do something consistent with their reaction. Lots of times he does something silly. But even with all the new post-Super Bowl adulation, a glint of modesty shows through the prodigal exterior. He is grateful when he receives presents from fans. Green undershorts embroidered with his name and number are a popular choice ("Man, I bet they spent hours on that," he grinned proudly). After the Super Bowl, of course, he made a trip to visit troops in the Far East, remarking that it would be worthwhile if they would enjoy meeting him. His father says Joe can do anything he sets his mind to. Sonny Werblin says he never met a man whose word meant more than Joe's. He is loyal to his friends and polite, more often than not, to his elders. For example, Joe was sitting in a bar one day in Florida when a message was brought in that some elderly women who knew his family in Beaver Falls were outside. Muttering about the "old dolls from home" Namath excused himself and went to chat for a few minutes with the women.

The nice side of Namath often gets lost in the shuffle and some of the times when he comes out looking like an impudent churl he isn't guilty. Witness Joe, sitting at a bar in a hotel, discovered by some fans and besieged by autograph hunters. He signs, and he signs, and after fifteen minutes the crowd is increasing. A friend calls him away. He apologizes to the fans but says he must leave. They don't budge. He spots some daylight and shoulders his way through. "Who the hell does he think he is," growls a voice at the end of the line. "He's got nuthin'." Namath has a definite dislike of being manhandled by crowds, which is most unfortunate because he's so often in crowds.

If one thing—many things actually—speaks well for Namath it's the thirty-nine other Jets. Unsung working stiffs, they bask in his shadow but are usually quick to spring to his defense. Never does a Jet knock Namath. Sometimes they marvel at him, his arm, his style, his courage, because they see him play in pain.

The Jet team admired Namath more in 1966 than they did in 1967 when, during training camp, Namath ran away and spent the night in New York, depressed and out drinking. He is such an untalented drinker. Joe became involved in a brawl with a writer, and it was on a night before an exhibition game. Several days later the Jets called a team-only meeting. "We talked things out," said team Captain Sam deLuca. "We told Joe we're behind him, but that the quarterback is the inspiration and the natural choice of team leader." Sam, the team leader at the time, was a teacher, thirty-one; Namath was twenty-four.

"I didn't want the responsibility of being the leader," said Joe. "On the field it's OK, but off the field I want to do what I want." He learned he couldn't, the hard way. He learned that if a sportswriter approached him with a handshake and conversation at three in the morning, when Namath and two friends were in the bar drinking and talking, that he couldn't slug him. Beaver Falls Joe could, but Broadway Joe belonged to the public and had to put up with ill-timed invasions of privacy.

Later that season it was reported that Joe was out drinking at three in the morning the night before a game. Especially in the case of a quarterback it's believed that preparation for a game requires a period of psyching, and that with only fourteen regular games in a season the least a player can do is be properly prepared. Namath was late arriving for the following day's game. He said he had been stuck in traffic and he played miserably, almost breaking his own interception record in the first half. The Jets were big favorites but they lost.

Although such elections are an in-joke among the players, Namath dropped from first to sixth when the Jets voted for their most valuable player at the end of that season. Perhaps it wasn't a case of cause and effect, but perhaps it was. One game can mean a whole season. Suppose the Jets lose one game because Namath is fooling around and at the end of the season they miss a title shot by one game, or half a game. Conceivably they would miss another Super Bowl win which, at $25,000 per Jet, adds up to a million dollars—pretty expensive for a night or two out on the town.

The big thing between Namath and greatness is maturity. Too often Joe puts Joe first. He created a furor before the Super Bowl by telling several Colts the Jets would kick the manure out of them, got in at 6 A.M. and missed a picture/press session ("I always sleep in the mornings; it's the thing to do. You've got to get your rest"). He makes it difficult for the coach, Weeb Ewbank, by taking advantage of his status. It poses a big problem for Ewbank, but how can he use the same yardstick for Namath as the other Jets when Namath isn't like the other Jets.

"I've had my disagreements with Weeb and I probably always will," says Joe. "I'm that kind. After we won the championship I told Weeb to break out the champagne in the clubhouse even though there's a league rule against it. I told him we were all over twenty-one and I'd pay the fine myself."

People tend to forget how young Namath is and they expect too much from him. But he has some growing up to do. He needs more self-discipline. It would be a tragic waste of natural ability if he doesn't grow up because when he's good, he's very, very good.

"Namath is going to have the impact of a Dempsey or Ruth, or a Sugar Ray, although the world wasn't ready for a Negro when Sugar Ray came along," said LeRoy Neiman. "I have a theory. If there was no Dempsey, the tough guy, there would be no Clark Gables or Jimmy Cagneys. I don't know how it's going to show up later on, but Namath is an original. He's in the Dempsey class."

Namath is the perfect litmus test for the generation gap. He has a compulsion to grow a mustache, beard or both and he grows his mustache and goatee so long that, with one white sheet, he would look like John the Baptist. The American League office chastised the Jets before the Super Bowl—too much hair.

"How can the league say it's wrong to have long hair?" asked Joe. "What's long hair got to do with being a football player? I understand they are going along with public opinion, with people saying it's a bad image for kids, but who's telling kids that mustaches are bad. The parents, that's who. It's their fault.

"The league rule is ridiculous and insulting. We're individuals. I like it. If I didn't like it I wouldn't have it. I like to give my face a different look."

Joe's steady girl friend, blond Suzy Storm, agrees. Suzy is a coed at a college in Tampa, Fla. Someone told her, before Joe had shaved off his Fu Manchu, that it was going. "Oh, no," she cried anxiously, "not his mustache, too?"

On the debit side of his image there is Joe's post-game "bit," which he performs on the wooden stool in front of his locker. He peels off his sweaty garments and then unharnesses his right knee brace, a complication of steel and rubber. He tries to give polite answers to the collection of newspapermen who ask unimaginative questions, often the same question more than once.

During this ordeal Joe proves his dexterity by picking the adhesive tape remains off his knee brace while talking, drinking from a can of orange

"I'd like to take this opportunity to thank all the single girls in America," said Broadway Joe.

soda, and, because of the snuff in his mouth, spitting into a glass or cup. Snuff so accelerates one's salivation.

"Snuff is masculine," said Neiman, who is rapidly becoming the Jets' historian. "Kids playing in sandlots who want to act grown up, like men, they always take snuff. So do cowboys."

Namath doesn't *take* snuff, he dips it. Maybe he will start a new vogue among football players. Baseball players always chew tobacco but football players don't, perhaps because they wear face masks.

Sitting in front of his locker, Joe opens his snuff box and puts some snuff between his lower lip and his teeth. So when he drinks orange soda, the snuff doesn't wash along on down to his belly.

The spit glass recalls one occasion before a Jet exhibition game on a Saturday night in Charlotte, N. C. Namath hadn't converted to his continental look yet, and his closets still were mod. He was one of only a handful of Jets who looked like a slob, coatless, when he got off the airplane on Friday afternoon. Before the evening practice (to take advantage of the cool) Joe was the special guest at a local football dinner and he was drinking Scotch and dipping snuff at the head table, before he spoke to the fans.

"It was a really wild scene," said one of the spectators. "We were all watching Namath's Scotch glass getting empty and his spit glass getting full, while he was getting tight. It seemed to be only a matter of time before he made a drastic, probably fatal, mistake."

The practice later on was a circus as Namath passes flew wildly about. Joe was hilarious and Charlotte will never forget. The Jets beat Houston the next night, with Joe completing eleven out of fourteen passes.

17 Gambling

The Highest Compliment

Gambling is our national pastime, no doubt inherited from our pioneering forefathers. American blood boils with the urge to gamble. Most fans at football games and those watching on television—in bars, clubs or at home—have some sort of bet on the game, with a friend, wife or bookie, for a beer, dollar or $10,000. Freud regarded gambling as a substitute for sex but the population of football fanatics is exploding so fast that the Freudian school might theorize anew about the football gambler. Modern theories tend to look at gambling as an escape and note that many compulsive gamblers were started on their way after a period of emotional stress (business failure, death). If so, it follows that a compulsive Giant fan and part-time gambler could become a compulsive gambler and part-time Giant fan by the end of a losing season full of horrendous Sunday disasters.

Gambling pervades all sports but is illegal except at racetracks and in Nevada. It would be great to walk into a stadium before a game, walk up to something, human or otherwise, and make a legal bet on the game. That will never happen. Even if the state laws were changed, an automatic betting facility would be too expensive to set up considering the potential return from betting on only one game on only seven home Sundays per year. Fans, of course, would want to bet on all thirteen games each Sunday. Still, setting up gambling parlors Nevada-style in all the stadiums isn't exactly feasible, though it would be fun.

The existing situation is enough to drive me to my corner bookmaker, but why not? Everyone else is there, and has been, for years. More money is bet illegally on football than any other sport—almost a half dozen billion dollars a year. During the season bookies handle almost two hundred million dollars worth of action each weekend. Gambling revenue is the lifeblood of organized crime.

To drum up business on football the national crime syndicate establishes a betting line which is distributed through a half dozen odds-making services around the country. Without the betting line here wouldn't be much gambling on football, because everyone would want to bet on the strongest team in each game, so the mob puts out a line—a point spread—to even up the chances of betting on both teams, which attracts many times more gambling money. All point spreads really do is rate the relative strengths of teams, establishing a favorite in each game by so many points. If a person wants to bet on the favorite he has to give points. If he wants to bet on the underdog he gets (or takes) points. *To a bettor it's not which team wins the game but how much it wins by.*

Bookmakers can only stay in business if their books balance, that is, if roughly the same amount of money has been bet on both teams. If too much money is bet on one team the bookmaker's books are unbalanced. If that team wins, the money bet on the other team isn't enough to cover paying off the winning bets. A bookmaker can get wiped out.

But the mob cherishes bookmakers, and protects them from wipeouts. If a bookie holds too much money on one team the mob arranges for him to balance things by laying off the excess. The bookie, in effect, just bets the excess himself with one of a half dozen syndicate layoff men around the country. Bookies charge their customers 20%, so the least that a bookie makes is 10%. Super Bowl III is a perfect example of a lopsided betting game. Everyone bet on the Colts, no one wanted to bet on the Jets, and the betting line went up almost as high as twenty points (if you wanted to bet Baltimore you had to give twenty points, meaning the Colts had to win by more than twenty points if you were to win your bet). Even the 20-point spread wasn't tempting enough Jet

Pro Grid Line

(Home Team in Caps)

SUNDAY

FAVORITE	pts.	UNDERDOG
Giants	3	REDSKINS
LIONS	4	49ers
STEELERS	1½	Eagles
BROWNS	13	Falcons
Rams	½	COLTS
Vikings	2½	BEARS
CARDS	8	Saints
JETS	11	Patriots
Oilers	4	BILLS
RAIDERS	20	Bengals
	MONDAY	
COWBOYS	7	Packers

* * *

money and the layoff men were full up to here with Baltimore money. Bookies stopped accepting any more bets on Baltimore a few days before the game, which turned into such a surprise, Jets 16–Colts 7.

For purposes of illustration, Baltimore was involved in another famous championship game which shook up gamblers pretty good. The Colts played the Giants in New York in 1958 and the game went into sudden death overtime. The Colts fought to the Giants' 20-yard line and an easy field goal would have won the game for Baltimore 20–17. Baltimore bettors had given 3½ points on the game and for them a field goal wasn't enough. For some wildly unexplainable reason Baltimore not only didn't kick, the Colts didn't run either. They passed, risking an interception. Unitas threw two passes to the 1-yard line and then his fullback scored a touchdown, winning by six and covering the point spread with 2½ points to spare. Weeb Ewbank, the world's most conservative coach, always goes for a field goal in unimportant games. How his quarterback Unitas ended up going for the touchdown is something for which each bettor has his own explanation. That game's splash is still rippling.

It is from organized crime that newspapers and wire services receive the betting line which some newspapers publish and some don't. The classy, or snobby, papers which deem point spreads beneath them cover up in stories by saying "Such-and-such a team, which is favored by a touchdown over . . ." or "______ is a slight underdog to ______" because these newspapers realize how much of a game's meaning is lost when there is no basis for comparing the two teams. Considering the contribution the line makes, Pete Rozelle should put out his own line for the benefit of fans in areas where the newspapers are too stuffy to carry the syndicate line; it's just a point rating of opponents. A Rozelle line would make his game more popular and that's exactly what he's paid for.

Most of the pro football writers who make selections in the newspapers pick games without taking the point spread into account. Nothing is more ridiculous. Suppose one team is favored over another by two touchdowns (14 points), the newspaperman picks the favorite, which wins by one point. The newspaperman gives himself a winner in the Monday paper but everyone who followed his selection had to give points and lost money.

One newspaperman, a Las Vegas sports analyst named Jimmy (The Greek) Snyder, does take the line into account when he makes his selections, which used to be very good when he picked only one or two games each week. When Snyder began picking all thirteen games his selections were no longer very good.

Snyder makes his own betting line, which usually approximates the syndicate's line, though it comes out a day or two later. Snyder's line is divined in such an imaginative way that it belongs in an anthology of fairy tales. He has this speed hangup, it seems, for every August he starts oohing and aahing that the Dallas Cowboys will be champions because they have more "team speed" than any other team. But team speed is an intangible, and no one has yet seen Snyder, stopwatch in hand, visiting each team trying to get a more tangible fix on speed.

Baltimore will long beware of The Greek bearing odds. He gave them a 17-point edge over the Jets in the Super Bowl based on such esoterica as, "Add three points for the NFL mystique and Don Shula's coaching." Snyder rated each third of the Colt defense—line, linebackers, secondary—four points better than the Jets, thereby breaking his own record ("That's the first time I ever gave more than three points to any defensive category"). Members of the mob love Snyder. As the self-styled little old national linemaker he is a distraction to the fuzz and takes a bit of the heat off the syndicate.

The opening line comes out on Monday and holds up so well that it often doesn't change at all during the week. The line acts as a mirror of national action. Fluctuations can be caused by a serious injury or by stories of dissension, rumors that someone saw so-and-so limping, or on the weekend by changes in weather conditions. Home-team betting can cause local fluctuations but even so the lines from the half dozen services rarely show a disparity of more than one point. The gangster's grapevine is the fastest in the country. When Gale Sayers sneezes in Chicago, syndicate men in 50 states say "Gesundheit" and five minutes later you can't get a bet down on the Bears in Tampa. Syndicate men somehow keep in constant contact with each team, even if it's only with a hireling watching a practice with binoculars "to see how, or if, so-and-so is running."

All the gambler is looking for is an edge. If he can find out something—an injury that isn't reflected in the point spread—it gives him an edge over the competition and he can bet accordingly. Any factor which is constant is of no importance to a gambler. He only cares about something different, perhaps a change in physical condition.

Immediately after a serious mid-week injury to a key player his Sunday game is taken off the betting board until the extent of the injury can be determined. Many times a game will be taken off the boards on a Tuesday and it isn't until Thursday or Friday that an explanation appears in a newspaper story. Newspapermen, of course, don't make as much money as mobsters, which perhaps explains the delay.

A large measure of football's popularity is due to the fact that it's honest. Many people have worked hard to insure that pro football maintains its highly respected image of utmost honesty and it goes without saying that football must not be allowed to have the slightest connection with gambling. The 1962 scandal, while it wasn't connected with any fix or bribe attempts, had serious implications. Paul Hornung was suspended for a season for betting on himself and giving information about games to gamblers. Alex Karras was suspended for associating with undesirable persons, also bettors. If players were allowed to gamble they would be consorting with criminals. If they happened to lose big they were risking blackmail. Even if they were only betting on their own team they could give information by omission, by not betting one week and betting another.

This presents an irony. It is an old axiom around the racetrack that information from the jockeys' room makes bettors go broke quickest. Information from inside football is just as expensive. During one pre-game warmup the Giant coaching staff looked at the lineup of Sunday games on the Yankee Stadium scoreboard, and made selections among themselves on the eight games "without any of that point-odds stuff." They picked two winners, neither of which was their own game.

Players' information is particularly irrelevant to a bettor, other than in matters of physical condition, because the players don't much care about games they aren't playing in and a player tends to look upon his own game in terms of himself and the man he plays against. Someone once asked Mike Holovak, when he was Boston's head coach, about a rumor he'd heard. "Those are only player rumors," said Mike. "You can't put any stock in what players say. They are probably the most misinformed bunch in pro football."

Almost every season there are rumors about brewing scandals. The best rumor sources are bartenders and cab drivers. Several years ago five Washington Redskins were subpoenaed by the Justice Department as part of an investigation into gambling in a Washington suburb. The players were interrogated, held blameless, and the rumors were squashed. In the summer of 1967 several Boston Patriots, particularly their quarterback at that time, Babe Parilli, received tremendous national publicity for doing business at a cut-rate store owned and frequented by known gangsters. It didn't help matters any that Parilli was throwing almost as many interceptions as completions about that same time, but the rumors gradually died away.

Pro football goes to considerable trouble and expense conducting its self-policing policy. The league employs several ex-FBI men to investigate rumors and to prevent trouble by stopping it before it begins. A league policeman visits each training camp each summer to lecture on the evils of gambling and consorting with undesirables. Local law enforcement people also talk to the players.

"Don't look for an overture to come from a guy in a trenchcoat who looks like Humphrey Bogart," the Miami district attorney, Dick Gerstein, told a meeting of Dolphins. "More likely it would come from somebody you know, under the guise of friendship."

The players are cautioned about certain restaurants. Teams have a rule prohibiting them from entering all places designated as undesirable by the commissioner's office or head coach. Some teams ask players not to hang out together at one bar, to make them less accessible to undesirables who want to make their acquaintance. The AFL forbade San Diego to make a working agreement with the Las Vegas Cowboy team. "It would be best if players did not make trips into Las Vegas," said AFL president Milt Woodward, "because of the gambling element and other possible influences."

It's hard to believe that there is a football player now alive that doesn't associate with gamblers. After Super Bowl III New York's Mayor Lindsay told of his admiration for Namath and that he'd won a bet on the game. A lot of newspapermen who cover pro football, who go into locker rooms before games after watching a team practice all week, bet on games and bet big. It was the greatest embarrassment of *Sports Illustrated's* NFL writer Tex Maule when a *Football News* column mentioned Maule's parlay on both games when he was covering Cleveland's annual exhibition doubleheader. One writer called the Super Bowl his "super annuity." Each year he bet $5,000 on the NFL team. Sportswriters' opinions are as valuable as players' and jockeys'.

Every sports restaurant is thick with gamblers and many bookies use restaurants for straightening up their accounts.

"If you never went anywhere with a gambler," said Kyle Rote, "you would have to eat every meal in your own kitchen, and that is just the beginning."

As far as fixing games is concerned, it is practically impossible. Gangsters have been successful trying to fix fights, and with only five men on a basketball team it would be relatively easy to "get to" a basketball player. A football "fixer" would have to reach the quarterback, or possibly the team's star end or runner, or kicker, in an attempt to shave points and manipulate within the point spread. Granted that this is possible, it is certainly risky. It's risky enough betting on a favorite anytime, but if a fix were on there are still two serious hazards: no matter how many points one team shaves, the other team might not be able to score. Additionally, there is no guarantee that if an end drops a few passes, or a runner misses a few blocks, or if the quarterback looks less than sensational, the coach won't simply remove the bungler from the game and let him review his mistakes from the bench.

"The bookies don't want the game tampered with," said an NFL investigator. "They're happy with the profit they make from the point spread."

The true measure of pro football's honesty is the amount of betting on it, and anyone who doesn't think that betting is what pro football is all about is Alice in Wonderland. If there were any possibility that pro football weren't on the up-and-up the fellows in organized crime would be the first to know. If the mob suspected hanky-panky it would immediately stop accepting big bets, which costs it money. If a gambler suspects hanky-panky he quits betting. People won't bet on something they don't trust. Either way the mob is unhappy.

Which puts organized crime and the pro football establishment in bed together. Both need to keep the game clean.

Pete Rozelle has found that his strange bedfellow performs many valuable services for him. As long as there's plenty of betting everything is quiet and pure as driven snow, but let a spot appear on football's Mr. Clean image and the mob announces it as loudly as a burglar alarm by taking the game off the boards. Rozelle's forces go on alert. By watching fluctuations in the point spread the establishment can even tell when considerable money is flowing in one direction and where.

Consider the strange case of the Kansas City Chiefs, who have always been erratic performers. In 1968 they were contending for the title in the AFL western division and for three weeks Kansas City was taken off the boards (which means there was no betting line on the Kansas City game). Immediately suspicious, Rozelle's investigators went to work and even went so far as to give lie detector tests to a number of key players. The results came up clean but for more than two seasons the syndicate has been wary of "unnatural money" showing up on Kansas City games.

Organized crime also aids the NFL-CBS AFL-NBC establishment by increasing the television audiences (more viewers mean higher ratings mean more advertising revenue mean more income from TV for football). Gambling, which gives fans a way to participate in a spectator sport, is the single most inspiring factor behind pro-football's growing television audience and it even keeps them at their TV sets longer. A big point spread can keep interest in a boring rout long after it becomes dull. One team can lead another at halftime by four touchdowns but if there was a 16-point spread, the bettors' interest is still alive and they won't turn to another channel.

It's ironic how gambling whets the football appetite. A person who is going to bet as much as a dollar of his money on a team has an active interest in that team. He wants to know more about it and the more he bets and the more often he bets the more he wants to know. Such snowballing effect explains in part the strange behavior of those homo saps who sit in windy below-zero weather, drive through blizzards, ignore frostbite, shout for three hours until their lips crack and bleed, and risk all sort of claustrophobic trauma to and from a tremendous traffic jam.

18 Sour Power

"It was probably in highly ritualized but still seriously hostile fighting that sport had its origin," wrote Professor Lorenz in *On Aggression*. "Sport is a specifically human form of non-hostile combat governed by the strictest of culturally developed rules." In *The Naked Ape* we see that a species can't survive unless aggression is inhibited and controlled, and so we have zoologically justified the necessity for six officials at each professional football game.

"Officials aren't cops," said Mark Duncan, head of all pro football officials. "They're not out there to call fouls. They don't get rewarded according to how many fouls they call. The job of an official is to make sure both teams play the same game. They should be the most anonymous men on the field. Without them there would be no game. That is, first you need players, and a ball, but the officials come third."

The officials are required to arrive twenty-four hours early, Saturday afternoon, and have a pregame conference an hour and a half before kickoff. They meet on Saturday night to go over the rules. On Sunday night they fly home. Officials are paid $250 per game for the first five years and $300 after that, plus expenses.

"They always fly first class," said Mel Hein, supervisor of AFL officials and a legendary center in his heyday with the Giants when, for one exhibition game in Canton, Ohio, each Giant received $2.50.

Officials begin running into shape in July, as they have to move pretty well in a game. "They get hot, wringing wet in a game," said Hein. "The two judges have to run backward with the defensive backs and there's some element of danger. Sometimes the umpire behind the defensive line has a hard time getting out of the way."

Officials also get cold. In the 1967 championship game at Green Bay the chill factor was minus thirty-seven and Referee Norm Schacter wore eight layers of garments. Still his nose and feet froze, the officials' whistles froze and were useless after the first play, and Schacter was sick for eight days afterward.

The Head Linesman is stationed on the line of scrimmage to one side. At the other is the Line Judge, the sixth official who was added several years ago when it was decided that football had become too sophisticated for only five mortals. No. 6 keeps time, watches the running backs for in-motion errors and keys on the passer, making sure a scrambling quarterback throws from behind the line of scrimmage. A running quarterback makes an extra problem for the Referee as well as the Line Judge.

"You have to give a running quarterback plenty of room so he can maneuver as he pleases," said NFL supervisor Art McNally, a Referee. "There's always the possibility that he will get up and go." The area behind the offensive line is really the Referee's zone of responsibility.

The Referee is the head official, in charge of the crew. The Umpire, the linebacker official, has the precarious position in the middle of the field right behind the defensive line. The Back Judge lurks about ten yards downfield and watches for interference on medium-range passes. Deepest back, about twenty yards from the line, is the Field Judge who covers the long bombs in man-to-man style and is anually voted the most unpopular by the most aggressive cornerbacks.

"The toughest call in football is pass interference," said Duncan, who watches films of every game, checking on his men. "There is only one question to ask—was the official in position? If he was then it's a judgment call and difficult to question."

There is no reason to expect that just because George Halas no longer coaches his Bears that he and Mark Duncan won't continue the lively relationship they have enjoyed in the past. Papa Bear has serious hip trouble but his lungs are in fine shape. "Blind" and "stupid" alternate when Halas converses about officials.

"They are prone to mistakes just like the players," said Halas, who has lambasted thousands of both. "They are human. But if an official hears no comment or caustic remarks he thinks he is doing all right, and may become complacent. In my own modest way, by telling them what I think, I'm really just raising the quality of officiating in the league. I don't question their integrity, only their judgment. The Bears can lose by themselves. They need no unwelcome help. Somebody even went so far as to suggest that officials be fined when they make errors, just like the players are. I concur."

Rozelle fined Halas $1,000 for these comments!

When Papa Bear retired he said he knew he had to stop coaching when he could no longer indulge in his favorite pastime, running up and down the sidelines berating the officials. The NFL has a rule that coaches must remain between the thirty yard lines during a game. Halas was exempt, of course, because as he crossed over the thirty he changed from a coach into an owner. There is no rule about where owners must watch games from, although it should be noted that Pete Rozelle discourages owners from watching games from the sidelines.

"I was chasing an official in our 1967 game against Atlanta," said Halas, "and I realized I wasn't gaining on him. I have always followed the ball and officials. The coach has to stay on top of the ball to make decisions. I cannot do this any more. My arthritic hip has made it so I can't move around quickly enough." Papa Bear retired one season short of his fiftieth.

By far the most frequent complaint about officials regards their eyesight, or lack of same. They are notorious for kicking the wrong man out of a game for fighting. As Kansas City's Fletcher Smith so poetically described, the second man to land a punch, who is only protecting himself, is usually the one who gets tossed out.

"I hit him with a forearm to the head," said Smith. "When he drew back his fist, to retaliate, the official saw him and said, 'You're out of the game.' When the official pointed I thought he meant me and was really scared, but he didn't. Luckily."

One of the extra weapons a veteran has over a rookie is how to use the officials. "On every play he would complain to the referee that I was holding," complained a rookie after a violent afternoon playing against a tricky old monster, "Mean John" Paluck. "But I wasn't. He did things all day that could irritate a person. Little things." The trickiest veterans make up for the step or two they've lost with a nice fat 15-yard penalty called against a hot rookie.

Since the coming of television some of the officials have turned into showboaters. When they know the camera is upon them they pose and carry on like method actors, or ballet dancers, embellishing their signals with bows, bends and flourishes. When an official turns starstruck he calls too many penalties, to get a chance to perform his routine. Even the officials who aren't showboaters call too many penalties, which interrupt the flow of the game. Actually, if they wanted to, the officials could call a penalty—probably a dozen penalties—on every play.

"Someone's holding all the time in pro football," according to Miami Coach George Wilson who, not incidentally, was one of the mighty Monsters of the Midway in Chicago, under Papa Bear. "It's up to the officials to catch it. Heck, that's how I made it with the Chicago Bears years ago. I learned how to hold."

"It's unbelievable how much holding there is," says Buffalo's Defensive End Tom Day. "If the officials called it every time someone held some teams would have more than three hundred yards of holding penalties in every game.

"To get them to stop you say 'Please don't hold me, Sir,' " added Day. "If they don't you may be forced to belt them."

Never Blow Your Nose on the Flag

When an official sees a foul he pulls a yellow (for TV) handkerchief out of his pocket and throws it at the spot where the infraction occurred. Then comes the whistle. Players are very conscious of flags and whistles. "On any run I'm never convinced I'm through until I hear the official's whistle," says Gale Sayers.

The most vigorous members of fandom want to anticipate the officials and are as whistle-conscious as Sayers. They are the ones who miss seeing a touchdown while looking for flags, so they can be the first to shout "Flag's down. Flag's down."

There are more flags on fluke plays. When Linebacker Tommy Nobis captured a deflected pass the first thing he didn't do was start running. "I was listening for a whistle. I wasn't going to run all that way for nothing," he said. When he didn't hear anything Tommy took off and scored a touchdown, his first.

Fumble recoveries and interception runbacks are frequent scenes of crimes. When his defensive tackle scored on a 92-yard return after a blocked kick, Buffalo Coach Joe Collier (now at Oakland) never saw the touchdown. "I was looking for flags," cried Collier. "I always look for flags on a breakaway." Lots of long punt returns and breakaways are whistled back because of clipping penalties, when a defensive player all of a sudden finds himself in the unfamiliar role of blocking for the ball carrier and clips instead of blocks. (Clipping is blocking *from behind* and is outlawed because it can easily cripple the victim's legs, which are unprepared and unprotected.)

The most absurd penalty happens even before the game starts. If a team is not ready to play it is penalized fifteen yards. In 1967 Notre Dame played Southern California in the game of the year. Both teams were undefeated and the officials were ready at mid-field, spectators screaming, television crews waiting, only one problem. The teams refused to come out on the field.

Psychological warfare, of course. Southern California's Coach John McKay didn't want to take his team on the Notre Dame field first. In a previous game against the Irish, McKay had taken the field first, but Notre Dame had kept his boys waiting in the rain for fifteen minutes. The Notre Dame team finally took the field and the game began six minutes late.

"That's never happened in our league," says Mark Duncan, something of a phrasemaker. "You come to play or no pay."

Understanding penalties becomes greatly simplified if you look at each play chronologically: Stage One, from the huddle until the center's snap; Stage Two, the time while the quarterback has the ball in his hands; Stage Three, until the ball is dead. The least serious penalties generally happen during the early part of each play; the most serious ones happen later, in Stage Three.

Stage One: After the referee spots the ball on the line of scrimmage, signifying time in, the team must huddle, line up and the center must snap the ball within 30 seconds. If there is too much chatting in the huddle it's DELAY OF GAME (5 yards). Before the snap no player may cross the line of scrimmage or he's OFF SIDE (5 yards). Offensive players must be stationary before the snap or it's ILLEGAL MOTION (5 yards) and no running back may move forward or he's called for BACKFIELD IN MOTION (5 yards). The single exception is a legal man-in-motion play where the back in motion may run horizontally in his own backfield before the snap, but must have no forward direction. Often the man-in-motion will, in fact, run slightly backward to make sure he won't be penalized.

Before the ball is snapped the defensive players are allowed to move as much as they like, trying to arrange themselves in the best way to counteract the offensive formation which they see before them. It is at this juncture that linebackers are hopping around like whirling dervishes trying to figure out the offense and, at the same time, confuse the quarterback.

"Officials," said Maxie Baughan, "think I'm trying to pull the other team off side, but I'm not. We've got all these audibles and we have to call 'em."

Stage Two: Before the quarterback hands off or passes, a defensive player may still do practically anything he likes. Anything goes. At this time the offensive players of course may not use their hands while blocking. If they do, and hold onto an opponent in order to keep him out of the play, HOLDING is called (15 yards). The older players especially have devious schemes for getting away with holding, trying to catch an enemy's jersey under their chins, or with their teeth if they have any.

When you see a flag in the middle of the backfield the chances are good it's a holding penalty, just as it's probably clipping when there's a flag on a long kick return.

Because the defense can do as it pleases (more or less) before the quarterback throws, the defensive backs take this opportunity to fool around, trying to break up the receivers' pass patterns. It is during Stage Two that the left linebacker gives the tight end his customary bop. The defensive player is allowed to push or pull his opponent out of the way on the line, or may contact him "above the shoulders with the palms of his hands during an initial charge" but a little too much nudge at a player away from the line of scrimmage is DEFENSIVE HOLDING and an automatic first down for the offense. Practically all contact fouls by the defense result in automatic first downs. Penalties are given according to the gravity of the foul. Fouls which interfere with a team's strategy are usually punished with 5-yard penalties. Fouls like offensive pass interference, offensive holding and clipping can cause injury and result in 15-yard penalties.

Stage Three: The most dangerous penalties (roughing the passer, defensive pass interference, piling on, and other defensive personal fouls like kneeing, kicking, biting, or grabbing a face mask) happen after the quarterback gets rid of the ball and are serious enough to draw both a 15-yard penalty and a first down. (As on a passing play, Stage Three of a kicking play begins when the ball is kicked.)

When the ball is in the air the receiver and the defensive back have equal rights to it, and there must be no contact except when the receiver is trying to make the catch and the defender is trying to intercept.

"I would say the burden is on the offensive team," said Mark Duncan, "because all during the play they know if it's going to be a pass. The defense doesn't."

When an official sees a foul he throws his flag. From that time until the referee signals the stands which team is to be penalized, and why, often seems interminable, especially when there is more than one flag on a play. It would help communications if the officials had two flags, one for the home team (yellow) and another for the visitor (striped or checked). The referee uses his own special shorthand to signal the transgressions from the field to the fans. The ritual is, to be charitable, quaint, and equal to a fast, sophisticated game of Simon Says. A brief vocabulary sampling from the referee's body language would have to include *a touchdown*—referee puts his hands up like in a holdup; *offside*—referee puts both hands daintily on his hips, hula-style; *holding*—referee grasps one wrist with the other hand, as in isometric exercising.

The officials measure off lesser penalties from the line of scrimmage, more serious ones from the spot of the foul. After a foul, the innocent team has the option of *refusing* (or declining) the penalty, refusing the gift of penalty yardage and letting the previous play stand as is. Or, it may *take* the penalty yardage, in which case the previous play does not count and is replayed. The innocent team chooses whichever alternative leaves them in the more advantageous position. The most surprising decisions usually come at the end of a half; time is running out and a defense will decline a penalty to rob the offense of the opportunity of another down.

"In penalty situations always think about the ball," says Weeb Ewbank. "You must think about the best way to get the ball quickest and in the best position. Anytime they have the ball they may score. You want the ball. You can always get yardage later."

Epilogue

Title 7

It seems I am always quoting Vince Lombardi. Vinnie says the future fun in pro football will come in 1970 when the owners wrangle about their realignment. Others insist the next major development will be pay-television. For myself, I have another idea.

In 1963 a piece of civil rights legislation was passed. One section of the bill, Title 7, forbids an employer from using sex to discriminate against a person. The law points out that just because an applicant at the unemployment agency happens to be born of the other gender, well, that is nothing to hold against her or him. She or he couldn't help it. Title 7 came just in the nick. It is pretty hard to tell these days, with flora-power replacing fauna-power, exactly which gender one is sitting-in next to with-a quick chromosome count.

Infiltration began subtly. Soon after Title 7 became reality, a sailor sued a maritime union for the right to become a yeowoman and a lady umpire asked pro baseball for the right to be herself, on third. After Kathy Kusner, an equestrienne, received a jockey's license to ride in Maryland, militant pastries in jodhpurs emerged from backstretches of racetracks everywhere. The Jockeys Guild Inc. greeted jockettes with open hostility and assured us that jockeys didn't fear women riders, they respected them and were concerned for them: "If racetrack heads want to see female blood flow on their tracks for profit . . . make a humiliating disgrace . . . then let them ride against each other."

Sportsmen have traditionally, and lamely, defended segregation between sexes by claiming the cost of separate but equal dressing rooms was prohibitive, but several thoughts give pause. One might note that a year ago at Texas Christian University one of the candidates for Homecoming Queen was blue-eyed with long wavy hair and measured 35–28–35. His name was Mason Dickson.

On November 22, 1968, the general manager of the Chicago Owls pro football team walked into the Soldier Field dressing room at halftime to deliver a few well chosen words to the team. The place blew apart. The general manager is a woman.

The epitome of infiltration was reached at a recent National Invitational Basketball Tournament (NIT) in New York's grand bastion of indoor sports, Madison Square Garden, when the St. Peter Peacocks came to play. Dr. Anne Robbins has been the Peacock team doctor for eight years.

"I tried to stay out of the locker room," said Dr. Robbins who is fifty and a chest surgeon. "I thought the kids would feel better, but it was impossible. They would send for me to patch them up."

At a game against Biscayne in Miami Beach Dr. Robbins went in to look at a boy who had broken his ankle. "As usual there was lots of gasping," she said, "a lot of shrieks from the shower. They always react with shock and stand in corners until they realize I'm not paying attention. Then they just get dressed. At first they giggled but the coach explained to them that I'm like any other doctor and now it doesn't bother them. When they use four-letter words I pretend I don't hear."

Before Super Bowl II, Miami News sports editor John Crittenden named three fans "the most exciting new figures in football: Miss Theresa (Bubbles) Cash, 19, 40–23–35, a freshman at Southern Methodist; Miss Terre Tale, 44–25–36, a delicate young exotic dancer from Houston who went onto the field during an Oiler-Dolphin game in a thigh-high red skirt, ostensibly to steal a football, but ended up kissing a surprised Oiler end, Don Floyd, instead; and Beverly Hutchinson, a cafe-keeper in Denver, who began this enthusiastic crusade, by swooping onto the Bronco field, swiping a ball from a gasping official, hiding it under her sweatshirt and racing off, hopping a fence en route.

Miss Cash achieved the least-fleeting fame and was almost immortalized in the Cotton Bowl when she wore a white satin mini-wedding dress down an aisle eating cotton candy. After classes at SMU "Bubbles" is a stripper in a Dallas lounge. "I'm not an exotic dancer," she told Blackie Sherrod. "And not exactly a stripper either. All I do is take my clothes off."

Bubbles came lately to the gridiron. Sally Rand was a fan in the 1930's, during the Albie Booth era at Yale where she was engaged to the Yale swimming captain. In football a Sally Rand is a naked reverse (running back carries ball in one direction as blockers go in another). "I'm not a strip teaser," says Sally Rand. "I don't strip and I don't tease."

In any event, at the risk of belaboring what must by now be most clear, the only fields in football still segregated are the playing fields. A thousand times why? Certainly a lack of physical equipment is not the answer. The lady track team from Tennessee A&I, the Tigerbelles, even in pads could outrace a number of currently employed flankers ("I'm skinny, and slow," says Rams' Jim Seymour). In the 1960 Olympics a frail, slim Tigerbelle named Wilma Rudolph won three gold medals and ran 100 meters in 11.2, only 1.2 seconds slower than the World's Fastest Human Bob Hayes.

If any coach is game enough to give a girl a break it will probably be Tom Landry at Dallas because Landry is famous for recruiting his Cowboys in strange places. Granted, Landry *will* have the dressing room problem, but the last time I saw Don Meredith, Lance Rentzel and Craig Morton their hair hung framing their faces in damp tendrils, their sideburns curled tuftily from beneath their helmets and, later on, they were a panorama of gray-on-gray with ruffles, medallions, velvet and patent leather highlights. A girl wouldn't stick out at Dallas, the way she would at a spot like Green Bay, for example.

When he does hire a female flanker, Landry will be faced with as unusual a dilemma as when Roger Maris broke Babe Ruth's home run record. Because Babe hit 60 homers in 154 games and Maris needed 162 games to hit 61, all Roger got was an * instead of a record. When Landry signs a girl he will become coach of the Dallas Cowboys*.

Not used to being on the defensive, one pictures a girl gridder playing offense. The feminine mystique would seem especially suited to the demanding quarterback position—calling audibles, a flair for faking, intuition. And psychiatrists are often quoted as believing women are better under pressure than men. Heaven knows, football is full of crises. Picture the little woman coming home loser and her husband chiding "Is that any way to run a passing pocket?"

It is not unthinkable that a female could make it in the offensive line, although the risk of an offside penalty is a clear and present danger. Britain's Olympic runners—female division—agreed that girls with big bosoms could have as much as a four-inch advantage over their less-endowed rivals. But while the risk of off side is great, the risk of holding is almost nil. What defensive tackle or linebacker is going to grab a lady linewoman with his wife watching on television or, worse, live.

After a track meet I once saw a sweat-suited lady, a Russian discus thrower/shot putter, packing up her gear. She put three shots (12 pounds each) into her Pan Am travel bag and tripped lightly off to catch her plane home. That Comrade carried her bag over her wrist so nonchalantly it might have been a beaded evening purse.

Her name was Tamara Press and she was a big girl—5′ 11″ and 217 or just a shade less lanky than the two Baltimore fullbacks. Tamara put the ladies' shot 61′ and the discus 194′.

What a Grand Experiment if the Jets would try Tamara in their line next to Dave Herman. With her power Miss Press just might be able to build a better mousetrap. (A *mousetrap* is a maneuver where a defensive lineman is allowed to come over the line en route to the quarterback instead of being blocked as usual. But before he can do any damage he is blocked from the side.) According to the Jet plan the enemy tackle (the rat) would rush at Joe Namath (the cheese) but BOOM! Tamara would just hit him from the side (the trap), thus saving Namath who, with a show of gratitude, would walk over, help her up, and ask her for a date that night. There would be a truly devastating scene, football's most memorable moment.

According to doctors, who claim that nature made women the hardy sex as an ally for childbearing, women are physically as well as emotionally suited for football. Certainly women live longer and one report made to a congress of surgeons singled out Catholic nuns as the healthiest group of women in the world. Still, logic and Title 7 notwithstanding, there seems little chance that football scouts will be paying more than usual attention to intramural athletics at Vassar, or hunting for talent in sorority houses or nunneries, or that in the future a pro player will come charging off the field after a game and change into a dress.

There is, however, a speck of silver lining gleaming from this gloomy segregated sanctum that is football. At least we won't ever have to hear a coach describing his All-Pro flanker: "She puts her pants suit on one leg at a time just like everybody else."